REVOLUTION

- SEX, GENDER AND SPIRITUALITY -
LOVE SET FREE

RICHARD BRUVOLL JR.

Balboa Press books may be ordered through booksellers or by contacting:

Balboa Press
A Division of Hay House
1663 Liberty Drive
Bloomington, IN 47403
www.balboapress.com
844-682-1282

Print information available on the last page.

ISBN: 979-8-7652-5012-9 (sc)
ISBN: 979-8-7652-5022-8 (e)

Balboa Press rev. date: 02/29/2024

The only sexual distinction of importance is the distinction between aggressive and non-aggressive sexual behavior. To express these tendencies in two categories, one can call the first *Egophilia* and the other *Anthropophilia.*

We are slaves of the past, we are slaves of both Abrahamic and Social Darwinian values and dogmas. And those two discourses are more connected than you would like to believe.

"Show me the stones that the builders rejected: Those are the keystones"

I am simply trying to do the same as Wilhelm Stekel, James W. Prescott, Niels Bohr, Michael S Kimmel, Jack Falao, Astrid Bastiansen, Barbara Engler, Suzanne Stiver Lee, Gunther Schmidt, Daryl and Sandra Bem, Thore Langfelt, Isa Abrahamson and many other pioneers.

My purpose is to add some forgotten, neglected and hidden keystones or missing links to the existing picture. Attepting to connect the "dots" anew. This book is my contribution.

Richard Bruvoll Jr.

CONTENTS

PART I: THE PREMODERN ERA – A SHORT JOURNEY INTO "HIS-STORY"

In the first part of the book I will discuss the beginning. Where do all these "truths" originally come from? When I'm on the road with my performance TRAX, I call this section "A Brief History of Sexuality."

Where did the normality come from and whatever happened to naturalness? This section is a short journey through the history of religions, cultures, genders and sexualities. Straight forward to our own recent, modern past and our own great-grandfathers and mothers.

An Introduction xv
- Central Concepts xix
- Credits xxv

About The Author xxix
Foreword: External Author xxxi
Prologue by Richard Bruvoll Jr xxxiii

Chapter 1: A Free Culture – The Written Language and the Wheel ... 1
Chapter 2: The Transformation of Dualism 12
Chapter 3: Most Atheists are Religious. They Just Don't Know It..... 19

PART II: THE MODERN ERA

In the second part of the book I address some of the great upheavals surrounding the birth of modern science. A birth where, among other things, the women lost their sexuality, or at least lost their right to, or belonging to their own sexuality. In addition masturbation became life-threatening. This marked the start of the painful birth of homosexuality as a category, eventually ending up as a diagnosis. And as an indirect consequence of the latter, modernism also became the beginning of the collective denial of bisexuals. Finally it got locked up into the darkest corner of the scientific "closet" as a result of this collective denial.

Bisexuality is probably one of the most "disobedient children" of modern science, both in terms of gender roles and sexual roles. The bisexual upsets. Maybe they even disrupt more than all the hetero-sexualities and the homo-sexualities together.

Chapter 4: The Transformation from Sin to Disease 31
Chapter 5: The Birth of Sexology 43
Chapter 6: The Old Order is being put Under Hard Pressure 49
Chapter 7: The Early Research on Homosexuality 56
Chapter 8: Identity – Heterosexuality and Homosexuality 60
  Part I: Who am I, and why am I 60
  Part II: Internalized and externalized homophobia 71
Chapter 9: A Child Welfare Educator's Considerations 79

PART III: THE POSTMODERN ERA – A NEW ORDER – THE WAY FORWARD

The third part is quite comprehensive, here I will discuss, among other things, the sciences' treatment of gender, gender roles and sexuality. I also take you from the modern birth of psychology right up to our postmodern days. Early psychology was perhaps the most outrageous "boy" in the social-science classroom. Yes, because it was a "boy" the early modern psychology actually was, or androcentric as it is psychologically called. But the epoch we are in the beginning of right now, is called postmodernism.

Although no one really knows, or totally agrees on what this really is means. The way I see it, it's a big mess right now. A chaos where most people mostly spin around, clinging on to old modernistic "truths". Truths that don't work very well anymore. Unfortunately, it is far from unusual to wrap old shit in new glossy paper and then present it as a novelty.

"The same old modernistic shit, in a new glossy postmodern wrapping." Perhaps it may turn out that "exponential development" is one of the phenomena that can describe the beginning of this much-talked about Postmodernism? And that chaos may not be such a bad place to start new beginnings from at all. Chaos-theory may be relevant to our new age. Biologist Bruce Bagemihl argues for the relevance of this, and several other theories in his monumental work "Biological Exuberance". Bagemihl and his research will be thoroughly presented towards the end of this book.

In the third part of this book, I will try to point out ways to new understandings, simply by using new perspectives on both existing knowledge and data, as well as all the new research that is falling in on us from all sides. We live in the middle of a major intersection, or a post-modernistic roundabout. At the same time, many of our old road maps are becoming more and less useless. If we are not to get back into the old tracks we need new road maps, not new terrain. We need a new reality picture. And as you will see in the last chapters of this book, I am not alone believing this.

Some would probably think I'm in over my head on this, but I'll take my chances. I do not fear water. In addition, deep dives have always appealed to me. Both to me and my inner oppositional child.

Introduction Part III 95
Chapter 10: Juno Enters the World. An Emotional Refugee 99
Chapter 11: Julian's Story 106
Chapter 12: Gender-Roles in a Developmental Psychological Perspective 123
Chapter 13: The Infectious Obsession of Gender Differences 134
Chapter 14: Gender Roles - Sexuality - Identity 146
Chapter 15: Classical Science and Meta-Theoretical Strait-Jackets.. 164
Chapter 16: Everything Revolves Around Sex – and Sex is Selling Everything.. 176
Chapter 17: When Sex Itself is the Product – The "Free" Market... 193
Part I: Sex, Lies & Phone-calls 193
Part II: Aggressive versus Non-Aggressive Sexualities 205
Chapter 18: Abrahamic Dogmas – A New Interpretation.............. 211
Chapter 19: From Sexual Straitjackets to Freesexual – A New Perspective.. 232
Part I: We need a new role-liberation.. 232
Part II: The liberation from the mono-sexualities.................... 250
Part III: How come so few have done research on scientists?.. 268
Chapter 20: NDE – A New Spiritual Paradigm 285
Part I: Juno's journey to freedom.. 285
Part II: The NDE Visions – A new and liberating worldview.... 297
Part III: No Fingerprints are "Normal" – They're All Natural 322
Epilogue.. 333

APPENDIX I

Excerpt from the Pilot Study 335
Excerpt from the Nova Report 1999 337
Excerpt from the 2013 Study 342

APPENDIX II

Risk and Resilience: A New Extended Interactional
Perspective on Personality, Development and Environment....... 349
The Integration of Transpersonal Experiences in a
Resilience - Psychological Perspective 358

APPENDIX III

Arsenokoités and Malakos: Meanings and Consequences
(To be added In a later edition) 365
"Sex, Lies & Phonecalls" (To be adden In a later edition).......... 375
The Internet: International Resources and Organizations 376

Bibliography 377

PART I

The Premodern Era – A Short Journey into "His-Story"

AN INTRODUCTION

"Did you know that religion, whether you're religious or not, is the single topic that has had the most profound impact on the species of human-beings?"

(David Fontana)

As you're reading this book, you will be reminded of the human madness and frequently evil attitudes and actions throughout recorded history. Much of it probably unknown to many of you. Our time's narratives have become cultural "truths", as so many times before in our history. This is often the result of posthypnotic injunctions, mass-suggestion or one might also call it collective mass-hypnosis. So how can you be so sure that our time's paradigms, the prevailing premodern and modern narratives, are the true stories.

The prevailing "religion" of the Social-Darwinian narrative is no exception, and it should probably been added to Dr. David Fontana's statement above. The original title of the "holy book" of the evolution-theory is: "On the Origin of species by Means of Natural Selection, or *the Preservation of Favored Races* in the Struggle for Life". Charles Darwin. (My italics).

Many people are also romanticizing old tribal pre-religious cultural worldviews, but every-thing wasn't necessarily better in those "good old tribal days". As a matter of fact many pre-religious cultures sacrificed children to their gods, even the Mayas did that.

Anyway, out of the Abrahamic and Darwinian narratives, emerged the mantra: Competition. Which is an underlying cause of anything from sexism, tribalism, racism to other human polarized behaviors in general. This has also led to history reflecting "his story", more than her story. However, recently "her story" has also been shed light upon. Luckily. But today these two versions of history is taking more and more the shape of a war between the genders. A meaningless polarization is often the outcome of that. A war with losers on both side of the big divide. I myself am more interested I *the* story behind his- or her story. You will read more about that in the second part of the book.

As you read along, you will notice the non-heterosexual thread throughout the book, often in connection with "Gender". Especially in Part II, but also in some of the chapters in Part III. This is partly because I consider the non-heterosexuals as the "litmus-test" on Human Rights. One important reason for that is that they are the only identities that still are forbidden in many jurisdictions on this planet. In some cultures they even risk death-penalties, simply for being who they are.

At the same time this is also the litmus-test on the freedom of expression, which also includes the expression of gender and love. In our polarized times the freedom of expression is too often interpreted as: "Freedom of speech for me, but not for thee." Well, who on earth would deny their own freedom of speech, freedom of thoughts or freedom of emotions and love (!) Anyone?

Some may perceive this book as an attack on the Abrahamic religions as well as an attack on the Social Darwinism (or religions and ideologies in general). It's not. If it is an attack at all, it's an attack on some authoritarians religious and ideological abuse of people. However, you will in the last part of the book learn about some of the good and important aspects of these religions and ideologies, including scriptures that were censored by powerful men throughout history, and therefore not known to the majority in most cultures. Before now.

In this same part of the book you will also learn a lot about the strong evidence which in fact do support a spiritual paradigm or world-view.

This includes findings in the scientific fields of quantum-mechanics, parapsychology and medicine.

One of these discoveries is NDE (Near Death Experiences). The NDE-Evidence, apart from being mind-blowing in itself, is as I see it the only serious and possible route towards a reconciling of this world's polarized religious, ideological and spiritual systems. In particular the dogmatic Abrahamic religious systems. But also atheistic ideological systems like Social-Darwinism.

Especially the NDE's "Life-review stage", or more precisely "The Life-relive stage", as the psychologist and researcher Kenneth Ring puts it. This stage resembles both Dante's inferno and the biblical purgatory, but with a very interesting twist to it. This stage is also the route to go in order to prevent aggressive behavior on all levels.

Another important feature regarding the NDE-research, is that the vast amount of case-studies shows that it's not associated nor connected to any particular religion at all. And they all receive the same spiritual "commandments". Therefor these findings may serve as a powerful moderator for all of us, for all religious, ideological and individual behavior.

I sometimes wonder if we are heading towards a postmodern dogmatic "religion" based on polarization and competition. The Social-Darwinian paradigm like the previous Abrahamic paradigms, are excluding paradigms. They judge and evaluate individuals as good or bad, simply for being who they are. This book is definitely not supporting worldviews that exclude the sacredness of every human being. The way I see it, we're experiencing a contemporary Spiritual-climate crisis.

"Modern science is based on this: Give us one free miracle, and we'll explain the rest"

This was Terence McKenna's comment on the Big Bang theory. Well, he certainly captured the arrogance of modern science in one sentence, and he's more right than wrong. Science is full of dogma, built on assumptions that never have been proven, and often have been dismissed later on.

I'll give you one example of the many dangers of "scientific" assumptions, namely the belief in superior races. This view was based on the Darwinian worldview, which as we all know was adopted by the Nazis among others. Thus, "Scientism" may have a built in danger of becoming a weapon of mass-destruction.

The general "scientific" view regarding the above mentioned, was that the white race was superior to Latinos and Afro-Americans. This was a scientific "truth" both in Europe and USA 100 years ago. One individual, an American psychologist named Floyd Allport, didn't find the IQ-"research" on this topic convincing at all. He noticed that when differences in IQ-scores between these races were not found, the researchers dismissed them as fault or frauds, because the results didn't fit into the general "scientific" paradigm. This phenomenon is also known as "The file-drawer problem".

Floyd posed a new hypothesis: Could it be that this "research" rather discloses the prejudice among American and European social-scientists? And his hypothesis eventually turned out to be right. Especially after WW2 this shift in focus gained momentum and became one of the main focuses of social-psychology. And this because Floyd didn't have a dogmatic view on his own profession's assumptions (or religious and cultural prejudice). Dr. Allport was brave enough to question "scientific absolutes".

You will find a lot of research on all of the above mentioned themes throughout the book, in addition to subjects that I have not touched upon in this introduction.

The book is divided into three main sections with underlying chapters. Some of them short, some of them long. I would recommend that you read about key conceptual explanations and models in Part I before embarking on the journey through this dramatic history of humanity.

Otherwise, I mostly refer to religions such as Judaism, Christianity and Islam with the collective term "Abrahamism" or "The Abrahamic religions". This because they all share the same basic dogmas, namely the Mosaic Laws. "The Abrahamic religions" is also a term used in the field of religious research and science.

Furthermore, I will mostly use "Non-heterosexual" as a collective term for anyone who is not exclusively heterosexual.

Disclaimer: This book is not recommended for people with high blood-pressure, especially if you are an extreme left-wing Darwinist or an extreme right-wing Abrahamist. You've hereby been warned. Have a good read and learning-experience!

Richard Bruvoll Jr
Blokus Denmark July 2020.

"If gender difference was so natural, then why does it have to be so methodically and continually forced on our children" (Michael S. Kimmel. Researcher and Professor of Sociology)

"Often sexual feelings are associated with shame and rejection. Condemning sexual feelings in children can, on a psychological level, contribute to a deep experience of not being as you should be, being wrong, or even evil ". (Elsa Almaas, clinical psychologist and professor of sexology.)

CENTRAL CONCEPTS

Anomalies - Deviations from the norm, the expected or the legal. An anomaly is an irregularity that is difficult to explain from existing theories.

Asexual – Being without a sense of sexual attraction.

Accentuation Effect - To emphasize something strong, pay special attention, often at the expense of what is left in the shade.

Anthropological Research - Is the science of human genealogy and society, all that is characteristic of human experience, from psychology and the evolutionary origins to the social and cultural organization of human societies

Assimilation - The term comes from the Swiss psychologist and biologist Jean Piaget's theory of children's cognitive development. This is done through an assimilation process where the child takes up new experiences and links them to past experiences. (Some call these early indoctrinated experiences cognitive forms.) I call it "maps."

Accommodation - (Also a term from Piaget): Is a developmental psychological process in which the child creates new, or adapts (expands) existing mental structures to new experiences. In other words: New "maps". (Or development as it is also called)

Attitude - When it comes to the term attitude, there are several different definitions of what this is. The following definition of the term "attitude" will be relevant to the context of this book.

This definition (Egidius's psychological lexicon) describes three aspects: 1, Cognitive; which applies to the perception of a phenomenon. 2, Emotional; which applies to the emotional reaction to it. 3, A conative aspect; that applies to endeavor or action.

These three aspects are also the "foundation wall" in several cognitive therapies.

Biphilia comes from the Greek word bi meaning bilateral, and philos meaning friend. The counterparts to biphilia or bisexuality are monosexual, which means attracted to one sex, and asexual, which means without any sense of sexual attraction to any of the genders.

Bisexual: The capacity to feel erotic attraction towards or engage in sexual interaction with both men and women (Allgeier & Allgeier)

Cooley's Looking Glass Self - Self-monitoring, Cooley believed that it consists of three basic elements: Our notion of our appearance in the eyes of others. The notion of "the other's" assessment of our appearance. And finally the self-esteem as a result of this. In short: 1) The imagination of our appearance to the other person 2) The imagination of his or her judgment of that appearance 3) Some sort of self-feeling such as pride or humiliation.

He also pointed out that our social monitoring of ourselves is constantly ongoing process. Even when we are alone. And social self-monitoring in the end always involves an evaluation of ourselves, which in turn will lead to one of the two social self-feelings: Pride or shame.

Empathy - Being sensitive to other people's feelings, how other people feel.

Apathy (apathy) - Indifference

Psychopath - Personality behavior which is expressed, among other things, by striking egocentric thinking, manipulative behavior, superficial emotional life, lack of empathy and sense of responsibility for other people.

Epiphany - Revelation, aha experience, "eureka experience".

Epi-genetics - Above genetics - The study of changes in organisms caused by modification of gene expression.

Etiology - The doctrine of causes. The term is used, among other things, in philosophy, physics and biology. The etiology studies why phenomena occur and the reasons why they develop as they do.

Ethnographic research - The study of peoples' way of life, cultural forms, social forms, religion and economics and more.

Epidemic - Infection that spreads quickly between people. If the infection spreads over large parts of the world, it is called a pandemic.

File Drawer Problem - The tendency to selectively present research data that supports one's own research interest (what one wishes to be true), in addition to avoiding data that does not support one's own research subject. Sometimes also a conscious deliberate fraud. This is a problem that is constantly emerging, especially in commercial medical research and other commercial research projects involving man.

Freesexual: A person who is capable of fantasizing and feeling erotic attraction to others regardless of gender, and who refrains from being placed in a general category such as heterosexual, gay or bisexual. A freesexual person is free from prejudice and aversion with regard to any consenting loving sexual interaction.

Cognition: Means perception and thinking, including, among others: Attention, perception and memory, problem solving, reasoning, language and communication.

Cognitive dissonance - Often defined as a state of tension that can occur when two cognitive elements conflict. For example, conflict between knowledge or a belief a human being may have about him- or herself, which is challenged, confronted or provoked by new knowledge.

This can either lead to the denial of the new knowledge (and thus only relate to the old "safe" knowledge), or to a new expanded perspective where the new knowledge is integrated. The latter is often called development (New "maps"). Not unlike Piaget's Assimilation and Accomodation.

Comparative studies - Comparative studies, either in contemporary or different historical eras.

Gender - Several people explain *gender* as a psychological gender. Gender Role Behavior is the term I use most frequently in this book.

The originator of the term *gender* is John Money, a New Zealand/ American physician sexologist and endocrinologist.

John Money's definition of *gender*: One's personal, social and legal status as a man or a woman. He further claims that *gender* consists of a combination of genetic, hormonal and social coding of a person's characteristics. He also emphasizes the distinction between *gender identity* and *gender role*, where he describes *gender identity* as the personal experience of the *gender role*, and the *gender role* as a performance or manifestation of *gender- identity*.

Gender Identity - Is the term for the individual's innermost, private experience of their gender. On the person's own sense of being male or female respectively. Most women, both heterosexual and non-heterosexual, have a distinctly female gender identity. The same goes for most men. (Bell, Weinberg, Hammersmith)

Gender Roles - Is the term for the set of norms and expectations that society sets to us depending on gender. (Bell, Weinberg, Hammersmith)

Homophobia - The fear of homosexuals or of homosexuality.

Meta-analysis - Using statistical methods to aggregate the results of a series of independent studies of the same issue.

Metatheory - Means a description of reality, based on basic assumptions, eg in relation to human view, ontology, scientific view, etc. (Flint-2003 / Eckhoff-98). Such a basic assumption need not necessarily be conscious either. Here it is important to note that an assumption is basically never a proven truth. It is always a belief.

Monosexual - Attracted by one gender

Monotheism - Belief in an omnipotent god

Nocebo effect - When a negative expectation of a phenomenon causes it to have a more negative effect than it otherwise would have. In medicine, the nocebo effect is explained as a feeling of illness brought about by an ineffective treatment which the patient himself thinks is harmful. The opposite of the nocebo effect is called the placebo effect. See below.

Pandemic - Human infection spreading across large parts of the world, unlike epidemic that is local or regional human infection.

Penile Plethysmography (PPG) - Fallometri in Norwegian - Measurement of blood flow in the external genitals to measure the degree of sexual arousal, erection or rigid clitoris (in other words, physically measured degree of horniness)

Placebo effect - Is a measurable improvement in association with an illness without the patient receiving real medical treatment or medications. In scientific studies, one group of patients is often given the drug to be tested, while another group receive fake pills, usually a sugar pill.

Projection - Is the transmission of unpleasant thoughts, feelings and events onto other people. This phenomenon occurs when one's own ideas and feelings about one's self become too heavy to bear, and thereby this (shame or guilt) is attributed to others. One example is projected homophobia, which means that when one's own gay or bisexual feelings and tendencies lead to self-contempt, this contempt will very often be directed at other gay or bisexual people, or people one assumes or categorizes as such.

Example: The most used curse word in Norway in 2018 is: "Fucking gay" or "faggott".

Pygmalion effect - Also called the Rosenthal effect (or expectation effect). The phenomenon was first systematically explored by American psychologist Robert Rosenthal. In a classic study at a school, Rosenthal and Jacobson (1968) showed that, educating teachers that some randomly selected students in a class was particularly promising, created an expectation that over time produced the expected effect. The effect was measured in an improvement in IQ. Further analyzes showed that these positive expectations were accompanied by a systematic difference in treatment of the "promising" pupils by, among other things, receiving more positive attention.

CREDITS

I owe a great thanks to Thore Langfeldt for, and not at least for his research and resulting book: "Eroticism and Fundamentalism, from Mesopotamia to the Women's Front, 2005". (Nowegian title: "Erotikk og Fundamentalisme, Fra Mesopotamia til Kvinnefronten" Thore Langfeldt was also one of my lecturers as a student of sexology. Why I owe him a big thank you I will explain more about below.

I am also indebted to my main teachers of sexology at UiA, Espen Esther Pirelli Benestad and Elsa Almås. Elsa and Espen Esther have taught me a lot about systemic-thinking. They also taught me that no approach to the human species can be based on only a narrow discipline of research, but that one must put all the microscopic "truths" into a bigger picture. And that one must also include the individual's subjective experience in the same big picture. Only then can we approach an understanding of both others and ourselves as unique individuals in a dynamic and ever-changing reality.

Not unlike what Niels Bohr claimed had to be a consequence of quantum physics' discovery nearly ninety years ago. He already said at the time that the revelations of modern physics should be important, not least for the social sciences. Bohr argued that complementarity was essential to understanding the human being, physics and the universe.

About Thore Langfeldt and his above mentioned book, it was precisely this book that I and five others of my fellow students chose to base our group assignment on in the first semester of sexology at UiA (The University of Agder). Langfeldt's research, insight and knowledge is an important inspiration and contribution to this book. This has both inspired and triggered my own journey beyond the assumed cultural "truths".

I also owe a big thank you to my Master of Social Psychology at UiO (The University of Oslo), Astrid Bastiansen, as well as my teacher in Minority Psychology, Hilde Nafstad and Suzanne Stiver Lee. The latter one was my teacher in the subject Gender and education at UiO. She awakened my great interest for "The gender role prisons", and introduced me to Michael S. Kimmel and his research. For this I owe her eternal thanks.

Christian Graugaard must also be mentioned. He was the first lecturer I had in sexology. His burning interest in the subject is, to put it mildly, epidemic, perhaps even pandemic.

I have met other mentors through the research literature I have read since the beginning of this millennium. You will learn their names as they are quoted along the way. One of them I still want to mention here is James William Prescott. I "met" him in a sentence in another book. A book that was neither a syllabus in my psychology or sexology education.

The neuropsychologist Prescott's research is groundbreaking, but possibly not popular. It may look like he's been scholarly "crucified". You get to meet him both in chapters 17, 18 and 19.

Perhaps it is the anonymous mentors who, by the end of the day, have meant the most to me personally, but also to the creation of this book. Regardless: All of these people have been "inseminators" that have led to the birth of this book you now are reading. But I am the one who gave birth to it.

I would also like to thank many of my friends on social media who, without knowing it, have made me aware of my own "hidden" cultural prejudices. They have thus contributed to an expansion of my own perspective. They have done so through countless conversations, which have almost unequivocally revealed how similar we humans really are.

We are more equal than different. Too often we forget that because of the narrow, stereotypical ways we tend to see "the others", or "show" ourselves.

We often forget that our individuality is an expression of both the inner and outer parts of our "color spectrum". It's usually just the outer part we see through our cultural lenses. It is the inner part that constitutes our individual talents, and it is these that constitute the universal and perhaps most beautiful part of the symphony humanity can be, when it is at its best and plays in harmony.

Otherwise, I would like to give cred to Anders who is Juno's and TRAX "co-parent" and Espen, both for inspirational friendships and contributions to the first TRAX performances.

Linda who helped me by finding the focus group for the book, Ida who provided my writers jacket, Bjørnar and Ellen who taught me a lesson about trust. Elisabeth for both friendship and contribution to this book. Lille Thomas who was my external reading glasses in the early part of my script work. Marianne who opened my eyes when I thought they were more open than 7-11. Rolf for his technical support. Jan Erik and Anne for my "writers-den" at the Eagle's Nest. Ove and Lisbeth for their hospitality at Hovden. Helge Myrup for the Danish TRAX-translation. Jon Mannsåker for giving me the opportunity to contribute my articles in Parapsychological Notices. Morten for his kind contributions. Hilde in Bergen who taught me to "just pull the trigger". Bente in Denmark who "saw" what I did before I started. Erika at Hardanger Folk High School who is Juno's and TRAX's "Godmother".

And Aunt Eva who is My Godmother and who means so much to me still after she moved on 101 years old. Christian who is literally a walking proof that limitations are overrated.

To Andilon who was both my soundtrack producer in the Netherlands and a soul-friend. RIP Andilon. Although we were unable to complete our concept and ideas, I promise you to give them life! Thanks to my parents Kari and Richard for an impressively good reproduction-result. And to my siblings.

And last but not least, a huge heart felt thank you to Virginia Legere (Ginger among friends) at the other side of the Atlantic Ocean. She has been my faithful companion throughout the creation of the English-language version of this book, which is also the main release. With her knowledge, wisdom and brilliant communication skills, she has left her solid fingerprints on this release. For me, our collaboration has also been a tremendous learning process. To me, Ginger is more than a colleague, she is a soulmate. I look forward to future projects in collaboration with her. One of them is already in the cast.

Finally, I would like to thank all of you who gave me resistance along the way, without you I would not have been the "human warrior" I am today.

ABOUT THE AUTHOR

Richard Bruvoll Jr. is an educated Sexologist from UiA, the University of Agder, specializing in Basal Sexology and Sexological Counseling. He also holds a Bachelor's degree in psychology from UiO, the University of Oslo, with the subjects: Youth Gender and Learning, Gender in Higher Education, Identity and Social Relations, Psychology of religion, Social Psychology.

Social Psychological specialization: Individual and Society, Communication, Language and Social Relations. Developmental Psychological Specialization: Risk and Resilience.

In addition to his formal education, Richard also has experience from both youth psychiatry and social youth work in Bergen, Stockholm and Oslo. He has also undergone a number of communication courses and seminars as well as trained in various therapeutic methods.

He has long experience as a performing musician and infotainer. Richard Bruvoll Jr. and Anders Ringkvist's performance "TRAX", has received media coverage in both VG, Dagbladet (Norwegian National Newspapers), NRK 1 and 2, (National Broadcasters), as well as been covered in a number of magazines, local medias and online medias.

Richard is probably also, like most, "heterocultural". Still, he does not consider himself heterosexual. He identifies himself as freesexual. Or simply: Sexual.

FOREWORD

External Author

PROLOGUE

by Richard Bruvoll Jr

THE TRACKS OF MY TEARS

A child will be born tomorrow,
As open as an empty book
We'll fill it with hope and sorrow,
The very things that messed us up
We'll ask him to join our congregation,
A Hindu Muslim Christian or a Jew
Pretty soon he'll recognize his brothers,
But soon he'll know the enemy too
Someone always hates someone
(Michael Rutherford, Mike and The Mechanics)

January 1971 – The past, part I

I Am 13 years old. I don't understand why all these people say I'm a monster. All those Christian people who say that I am a devil's child, and that I deserve to burn in hell. I pray to God, am I not a Christian then? I just can't understand it, I don't recognize myself in the eyes of those Christian people. I care about all those who suffer in this world, those who are hungry, all those people who are abandoned and suppressed.

I care about baby birds being kicked out of their nests. I just want to make the world a better place for all those who are rejected! I do not understand. Still, there is one thing I am slowly beginning to understand, namely that I am an unwanted child out there. This emerging understanding in January 1971, would eventually have untold consequences for my future.

The Easter 2018

The book you're now holding in your hands has had a long and difficult birth. So difficult that it was about to die at the very moment of births, as if it was wrapped by its own umbilical cord. Well over term it was too. But with countless revival attempts, the pulse finally returned. Barely.

In many ways, the book resembles both my own entry into this reality, which we like to call the world, and my own life here on Tellus, as this planet has been named. It's not a novel I attempted to write. I'm not a novelist. My aim all along was to connect the dots. Trying to add a few more pieces to this great puzzle of knowledge that is out there: Research, studies, considerations (both mine and others).

To use the words of Daryl Bem (Social-psychologist, researcher and author of one of the most comprehensive theories of sexual orientation): "It was already all there, scattered about in the biological, psychological and sexual research." He just needed to put together the pieces. Connecting the dots.

Therefore, I consider myself more of a "Summarizer" than a writer. I also want to use stories from my own life, but also from the lives of others who have crossed some of my tracks. And they are many. I will also describe case-stories from my experiences as a miljeu-therapist, sexological counselor, infotainer and artist.

All the exciting and wonderful people I met during my time as a miljeu-therapist and social worker in Bergen, Stockholm and Oslo. But also the countless young people I have met with in connection to TRAX.

But first a little personal or biographical account of my own early life. My story. I was probably born a bit more curious, wondering and inquiring than most of my fellow sisters and brothers. At least I have retained these qualities well into my so-called adulthood. Moreover, these qualities, or talents, have only become stronger and more pronounced as the years passed by.

We are probably all born this way, but it may be difficult to protect and cultivate these talents, especially when the cultural educators are pointing at you with their threatening index fingers with their subsequent "if you don't obey me"- sanctions. And not least when our curiosity moves into forbidden landscapes, such as the "forbidden" landscape of sexual emotions and feelings.

I began my journey of explorations into this landscape rather early. I'm still on this journey, but now with far better navigational instruments than those I had as a thirteen-year-old in 1971.

I was merely a "seed" when I painfully learned that there was a first, second and third prize in this life. To be better or worse than this indistinct "ideal" that often is referred to as "the others." As a thirteen-year-old, I realized that I was nowhere near winning neither the first, second nor third prize. I ended up at the absolute bottom level of the hierarchy. I had lost before I my life even had begun. I was the "devil's child".

This was confirmed by three religions, based on a phrase uttered by an angry old man more than three thousand years ago. Moses was the name of this man, whose existence never even has been confirmed. In any case, there is no historical evidence of his existence. On the other hand, there is research claiming that the interpretation of some of his "laws" is probably completely wrong. Many of these "laws" have led to a living hell on earth for an endless array of boys, girls, women and men. And still do. I will discuss this in Part II and III of the book.

In addition to the religious condemnation I woke up to when I shockingly discovered that I also fell in love with boys, I also quickly became aware of the cultural judgmental of non-hetero feelings. The condemnation from all those who weren't necessarily Christians. This condemnation was like an invisible nerve-gas that permeated all levels of the culture as I experienced it. Right down to my classroom, my friends and peers, my family. And, myself.

The worst I knew was so-called merry social gatherings, including family celebrations, school parties, and the like. And the recesses. Being in such situations and just waiting for "when will it come"? Not if, but when. "Everyone" had opinions about it, and "everyone" had degrading jokes and "funny" comments about it. It was mental torture. Even worse was that I myself also laughed at all those degrading gay-jokes- and riddles. I didn't dare not to.

And then there was the fear of blushing in those situations, with the inherent danger of revealing my "sick" and "inferior" nature. But, at the age of eighteen, I had become a master at preventing such situations. I had become the first and best to tell the worst and most degrading gay jokes in town. I had become a champion in labeling any behavior or person that could possibly pass as gay. In almost all contexts. In the process I turned into an obedient and "funny" mainstreamer (lamestreamer). But that was only on the surface, I had literally built an armor between the real me and the world.

But let me for a moment rewind back to my earliest childhood. My curiosity was ignited long before I started school. I remember one late night while my family were fast asleep, I sneaked out of the house and climbed over the fence and out into the "wilderness" on the other side. There I was, laying in the grass staring out into the universe, the great unexplored.

Some moments before I had been looking out the window of my room, watching this dazzling and magical starry sky. I just had to go out to see. To get closer. So there I was, out there in the grass, looking up at this magical starry sky, wondering if there might be a boy in the grass on one of the many other stars (which I then thought were planets), and looking down at my star. Maybe he too was lying there in his grass, with the same floating and magical thoughts, and wondered if a boy like me was lying on this planet looking up at his planet?

It was at the same age, as a 5-6 year old boy, that I started on my journey to become a sexologist. At least if I quote Styrk Fjørtoft's comment after I told him the following story between the footage of a TV portrait at NRK in 2003. The story goes as follows:

As a 5-6 year old, my growing interest in anatomy had begun to manifest. When my mom was having her monthly girlfriends club, I was very excited to study them when they went to the bathroom. I did this through my little "microscope" (keyhole). The "microscope" turned out to be perfectly positioned relative to the toilet bowl.

I was able to observe both the downs and the ups from the seat. At one occasion I was a little bit too late to leave the "lab". Suddenly the door burst open, and there I was in a very revealing squat position. Fortunately for me, Aunt Margit was one of the understanding kind. She shook my hair and asked me laughingly, "But what are you doing here Little Richard?" My answer became a bit of an "urban" legend in those circles, my reply was: "Wow, you have exact the same **bowl-formed peeing-thing** as Janne!"

I started out quite early on my creative track too. Probably a natural manifestation of curiosity. One day, while our parents were at work, my brother and I felt rather bored, and couldn't figure out what to do. But all of a sudden we got this brilliant idea of making a stock car. The source of inspiration was an old case clock. Very old it turned out to be. In fact, from the 18th century, and one of very few of its kind.

We both immediately noticed that if we'd cut off the lower part, we could build racing car with a long frontpart/hood and a perfect seating for the driver where the clockwork would be. Our pretty newborn sister's pram had the perfect chassis with wheels. Thus it was history as well. The neighbor's newly acquired TV-antenna also had stylish potensial, which we could use part of it as antennas and various other flashy details on our new and tough creation.

Later that day my parents proved, for the first time, that they are non-violent beings. Barely. My father locked himself into the study when he came home from work and got the news. He was probably struggling to harness his violent temptations. In hindsight, I must say that I have no trouble understanding his temptation. This creative transformation of old useless scrap, didn't get any approval at all by our parents. I no longer recall how many weeks of reduced allowance we had to suffer.

Somehow, one might say that I have continued this trend of trying to transform old "useless scrap" into something new and useful. As I see it. But that's not necessarily the way others see it. Well anyway, both curiosity, exploration and creativity are three talents that have not weakened in me along the life journey. They've grown stronger. And these three talents, along with the magic outlook on life, have been, and still are the driving force in my life's story, and pretty much in everything I do. I was not the most school-savvy when I was in high school, but my curiosity was still with me. Luckily, the school system failed to kill it off.

These above mentioned talents, along with faith and a wider perspective, have changed me radically in terms of my belief in what a human being is able to achieve, when the right intentions are present. This, together with recent research, including the new physics, the new biology (epi-genetics) and neurology (neuro-plasticity), means that I cannot help but think that a radical change in attitudes and behavior is possible. That it works. And it works.

I see it, and I experience it out there in the audiences when I'm on the road with TRAX. I saw it time and again as a social worker and social-therapist. I've seen it as a counselor in many of my clients. And, I experience it in my own personal development. It's an active belief. A belief that I'm also aim to convey with this book.

Originally, I would never write a book. I considered myself to be more verbal in commun-ication than in writing. My first goal when we, Anders Ringkvist, Espen Saga and I, for the first time were on the stage with the performance TRAX, was that this evening at least some of these young souls would fall asleep to the thought that: "There's nothing wrong with me, but human cultures sometimes can be or act in evil ways".

It worked. And it still works. It has ever since been one of my most important goals every time I perform. It is also one of my goals with this book. That someone goes to bed after reading, it with the idea that they're not failures or abnormal, but natural, unique and important individuals, who have talents, and lessons to contribute to us all.

My intentions

I believe in what I do because I see results from it! After a long and sometimes painful journey, I also believe in myself. In addition to my own talents, my greatest inspiration is humanity's many brave individualists. One example is the journalist Gary Webb. Other inspirers are those who stop at step two of Cooley's self-monitoring process (See Concepts Explanations) and see themselves, perhaps for the first time. And who also have the courage to be what they see in that "mirror"! Schindler, among countless others, is to me such a person. It's never too late.

With this book I also want to contribute to both a deconstruction and a reconstruction of categories, which among other things define who you should be based on poorly founded cultural norms. Sexuality is one of them. This latter is all too often poisoned by a fixed and polarized gender-role system, which in turn has been glued to sexual categories.

This categorization of sexualities actually happened just 150 years ago. This is described in Part II. I also want to contribute to a larger perspective, which is free from this blue or pink, mars or venus, them or us thinking. I would also like to show that we all have a lot to gain from such a larger perspective. Whether you are girl or boy, straight or gay, or in the middle of it all.

So, this book is very much about sexuality and gender in all its colors. But no one is going to be held as more or less worthy of protection than the "others". It is, as you've probably already have guessed, also about prejudice and where the prejudice comes from. But most of all, it is about self-identity, love, care, respect and sexuality as important components of your own capacity for love. And that you're good enough, no matter which lane you drive in on the sexual and emotional highway of life. There are no right or wrong sexual-orientations. But there are good and bad ways to apply them.

As mentioned, the idea of writing this book was born in Kristiansand as a student of Sexology at UiA. I and a fellow student, Arne Utne, chose bisexuality and gender role identity as the theme for our 2008 term assignment. The respondents gave some answers that surprised both us and others. Some of the answers unequivocally showed that sexuality is about much more than just sex. Gender-role identity was found to be a far more controlling factor for sexual behavior than sexuality itself.

Actually far more than most of us like to admit. In addition, there were some myths about bisexuality, both popular and professional myths. They were all weakened. Several of our interviewees also asked, "Where can I read about myself?" The latter started Arne and myself on a large-scale search into various university databases, professional literature, libraries in general, professional journals and organizations both locally and globally. It was literally not a cyber stone that we didn't turn. We spent endless days and nights on this research. And the result? It was as surprising as it was disappointing. Bisexuality was basically, well, bi-phrases in most of the writings. Once in a while they were devoted to some paragraphs, and rarely to entire chapters in the professional literature. And in a very few cases, professional books. So few that you could easily count them on one hand, with several amputated fingers.

Otherwise, we found that bisexuality was politically correct when mentioned in various political and organizational contexts, especially those who depended on government fundings. It more or less looked like the bisexuals were wiped out, or at least silenced into non-excistence. It became more than clear that no one had written the book that several of the respondents were asking for. Well, somebody had to write it.

With this book, I'm almost certain to curse in more than one "church" or "congregation". Be it religious, cultural, political, subcultural, scientific and or other ideological "churches" and congregations". It's probably unavoidable with the themes I've chosen to dedicate my life to. None the less, I consider this book to be necessary, and for some even vital. Furthermore, we are currently living in the midst of a chaotic paradigm shift, which requires new angles and new (far greater) perspectives than the narrow and uncomfortable framework most of us are prisoners of today.

A new paradigm

"The Danish sexologist and MD, Christian Graugaard, presents the current paradigm of sexuality as legitimized through reproduction. Descriptions of sexuality in the last couple of centuries can be considered as historical documents that highlight and justify sexual acts for the purpose of continuing the genealogy - or appear to do so. Any other kind of sexuality has been described as sinful, criminal or sick (perverse).

This is a paradigm that started at the end of the 18th century, and it ends now. This means that sexology as a subject is in the midst of a giant leap from one paradigm to a new paradigm. (p-13 Sex and sexology Elsa Almås)

I would like to emphasize that with this book I also address all of you who so generously have given me your time, experiences and life stories. Furthermore, I am addressing the countless number of young people who have not yet been granted the opportunity to speak their stories, as well as all of you thousands of young people who are at the threshold of the long and exciting journey of discovery that life actually is.

But the biggest, and arguably the most important minority I turn to, is You! Whatever lane you find yourself in on the sexual emotional highway matters little. In any case, you will learn something, hopefully you will gain some new and larger perspectives on who you are. And who your fellow-travelers are. Perhaps this book may even encourage you to be just a little bit more of who you are. And to embrace your own unique talents and story, in the midst of this great story we call humanity.

October 1972: The past, part II

I'm sitting here at the dam this windy October morning, like I've done so many times before. I've skipped school .. once again. I have become an expert in falsifying sick leaves. Well, it's really my dad's handwriting that I've become an expert on. I'm sitting here, yearning for a better life, dreaming of leaving for another place. A better place. I pray to God to become normal, like all the others. I don't want to be this way. I hate being abnormal. Please stop punishing me, please take away this spell. I alternately look at the pond behind me, and the Atlantic far away on the horizon. There has to be something better than this. I throw a time-capsule into the pond behind the dam, just like the astronauts on TV did in space I hypnoticly watch the circles as they wave out from the time capsule, which is not visible any more. On the back of this time capsule I have carved a message for the future. Maybe someone out there in a distant future will read the message from this lonely 14-year old boy.

Eventually I forgot this message. Or, maybe I didn't.

The Road Not Taken: Robert Frost

Two roads diverged in a yellow wood,
And sorry I could not travel both
And be one traveler, long I stood
And looked down one as far as I could
To where it bent in the undergrowth;

Then took the other, as just as fair,
And having perhaps the better claim,
Because it was grassy and wanted wear;
Though as for that the passing there
Had worn them really about the same,

And both that morning equally lay
In leaves no step had trodden black.
Oh, I kept the first for another day!
Yet knowing how way leads on to way,
I doubted if I should ever come back.

I shall be telling this with a sigh
Somewhere ages and ages hence:
Two roads diverged in a wood, and I-
I took the one less traveled by,
And that has made all the difference.

THE FUTURE: OCTOBER 2001

I'm on-stage at Hordatun School in Hardanger, together with Anders and Espen, overlooking hundreds of young people in the audience. Teenagers at the beginning of their own life-stories, with their own cultural, personal and mental "backpacks".

A child will be born tomorrow,
As open as an empty book
We will fill it with hope an sorrow,

The very things that messed us up
We'll ask him to join our congregation,
A Hindu Muslim Christian or a Jew
Pretty soon he'll recognize his brothers,
But soon he'll know the enemy too
Someone always hates someone

"Juno was grateful that God hadn't listened and acted on his prayers back then at the dam up on his mountainside sanctuary on the Atlantic coast. Many, many years ago. In another time.

He now knew what he wanted to do with his life: "I'm going to tell everyone what I've seen. I want to tell the stories of those people I've met. I will sing and shout out about their invisible sufferings, yearnings, sorrows and tears. And to you Matthew, Seth and to all of you who no longer cry, who are silenced: You shall never be forgotten. I will be your voice! I'll be more of who I was meant to be in the first place. This is my promise to you"

Excerpt from the show TRAX

CHAPTER 1

A Free Culture – The Written Language and the Wheel

The Pre-modern age: From lust and joy, to prejudice, sin and shame.

"Religion is the single topic that has had the most important and profound impact on the species of human beings." David Fontana. Psychologist.

From the book "Psychology, Religion and Spirituality"

I decided to go all the way back to the beginning of the written language, when I first embarked on this journey of writing this book. Not just my own beginning, but the great beginning, the one we at least know from historical writings and archaeological and anthropological research.

This decision led me all the way back to ancient Anatolia, located in present-day Turkey, and to Mesopotamia, which was located in what is today's Iraq. Much has been written about these cultures. Especially about the latter one.

My focus will mostly be on the inter-human part of the history, and in this chapter, especially the expressions of gender and sexuality in ancient

Anatolia and Mesopotamia. When it comes to the latter, it is especially the urban community of Sumer that I want to focus on. You will be amazed when you discover what this community has meant to all of humanity. All the way up to our present day.

But let me begin with what is considered to be the first urban community in history, namely Catalhoyuk in Anatolia. This society can be dated back to almost eight thousand years before our own time. For a long time there has been an almost unison agreement that all cultures and religions have regarded women as inferior and submissive to men. This historical assumption has led us to regard it as a biological fact.

But in Catalhoyuk there were quite different patterns of human interaction regarding men and women. This urban community tells a completely different story than the adopted assumption of the "order" of the sexes. (1)

Professor Ian Hodder at Stanford University has been researching this urban community for more than twenty years, and discovered, among other things, that they had a very advanced infrastructure. The most interesting observation in this context is that it was a society without defined gender roles. It was built on equality without any kind of hierarchy. It is also interesting to note that they did not organize themselves around biological nuclear families.

The households also served as burial grounds for those who had lived there. They were buried under the floor of the residence. DNA analyzes of these remains reveal that there was no closer genetic relationship between household-members, than could be ascertained for the society as a whole. (2, 3, 4)

This research is also an excellent example of how useful today's technology can be in order to understand ten thousand year old puzzles. But let's fast forward about three thousand years in time, to the rise of Mesopotamia and the urban community of Sumer. Reading about the Sumerian culture and their relationship regarding gender and sexuality, shows that sexuality was as much about fun, play, exploration and joy, as it was about reproduction. Even spirituality was a central part of sexuality.

Sexual acts, even between people of the same sex, were completely natural to the people of this culture. Apparently, sexuality was neither linked to, nor locked into identity-roles.

Masturbation was seen as important for enhancing potency. By the way, sexual categories were not yet invented at that time, they were invented more than five thousand years later. This phenomenon I will return to in Part II of the book.

Sexual acts and rituals were considered to be modes of action, not identities. Unlike the modern era, also women had a free attitude and enjoyed sexual freedom. Ritual intercourses with the female priests were performed anally, to avoid pregnancy. (5) The mythical tale of Gilgamesh, one of the oldest, probably the oldest written mythological story we know of, indirectly shows that contemporary views of the time, with regard to sexual relations between equal sexes, were not only accepted but also elevated to something divine. This is clearly described in the epic about Gilgamesh and Enkidu. (6)

In a commentary on a recent British translation of this epic, John Kavanaugh argues that the heroic dream world of Gilgamesh and Enkidu is based on, and even depends on, the homosexuality of the Sumerian culture of Mesopotamia. He also draws comparisons to ancient Roman culture, where homosexuality was regarded as high-quality morality.

Furthermore, he also draws comparisons with ancient Greek culture, in this case the Thebes, where the war-heroic behavior itself actually depended on the warrior couples' love for each other. This also meant sexual reletaionships with each other. Kavanaugh suggests that perhaps the people in this old Sumerian culture simply were interested in, and liked, sex. (7)

For my part, I would like to add, as I mentioned above, that homosexuality was not a category at that time. And when it comes to Kavanaugh's comparisons, he certainly has a point, but there were also big differences between these cultures. I'll get to that later. Otherwise, I myself believe that most historians are largely making a mistake by using the vision of our own time on historical phenomena and events of that time.

And today's sexual perceptions are very binary; blue-pink, in general categorically two-fold, like gay or straight. This makes all the nuances between these extremes, more or less invisible, or even disappear. The heterosexuals therefore get very busy explaining away behavior that doesn't "look" heterosexual, and the homosexuals tend to become busy in categorizing the same behavior as purely gay.

Homosexual acts and behaviors are far more understandable as bisexual acts and behavior, in a historical perspective. Back then, these people were neither defined, controlled nor judged by standards of sexual categories, identities or gender-roles. Such standards simply didn't exist 5000 years ago. When it comes to hetero-cultural historians, scientists, and cultural mediators of our own time, their hetero-centric bias has given birth a relatively new concept called "Bisexual Erasure" (bisexual acts and rituals are erased).

This hetero-centric bias has become most evident throughout the entertainment industry. Not in the least, the part of the industry that has its base in Hollywood. This phenomenon is explained in more detail in Part III (chapter 19) of the book.

The British Museum also indirectly and partially touches on some of what I wrote above. They state that the term "Homosexuality" (or, for that matter, "Heterosexuality, my addition) as a way of describing certain behaviors is an European invention. But same-sex attraction is not at all a modern Western "invention". On the contrary, historical evidence establishes that sexual attraction between members of the same sex has always been an aspect of human existence and experience. The British Museum also mentions Gilgamesh and the gay erotic elements of that same epic. (8)

The Sumerian culture is also said to have given mankind four very important and revolutionary inventions. These inventions have undoubtedly revolutionized absolutely all cultures equally into our own so-called postmodern cultures. I'm talking about nothing less than the written language, the wheel, mathematics and astronomy. They also constructed what is said to be the first calendar. The plow is probably also a Sumerian invention. When it comes to writing, it is said that it originated in Mesopotamia around 3500 years before our time, and that they were the first people to make full use of this communication-tool. In addition, women and men were granted equal rights regarding; legal-, religious- and business-matters. (9, 10, 11)

But 2300 years before our time, all this changed when the Akkadian king Sargon invaded Sumer. The Semitic invasion was the beginning of the end for equality and human rights in Sumer. Many of the laws that Sargon introduced, we recognize in the later female-hostile and macho-oriented Abrahamic religions. The effects of these changes are to some extent still present in our time. (12, 13)

I often use the fact that the Sumerian culture's creativity shatters one of Freud's coping strategies, also knowns as defense mechanisms, more specifically the one he called "sublimation". In short, sublimation is about "shameful" and "intolerable" sexual energies being transformed into societal, useful and creative abilities. Based on these fantastic Sumerians' accomplishments, I argue that the complete opposite is the truth. Namely, that if people are allowed to explore, cultivate, and enjoy those same amazing sexual energies (among other energies), they will create both good communication (language) as well as useful and universal technologies for all (the wheel and the plow).

I myself think about the ingenious invention of the plow every time I pass Norwegian mountain-crossings during the winter season. And in gratitude, I'm occasionally sending my warm and loving energies to the old Sumerians. Not to mention the wheel, there is hardly a technological gadget that does not have its origin in the wheel. So we should all send our warm thoughts to the Sumerians every time we are out driving. And not least every time we text, tweet and communicate along the way on various social and unsocial media.

As mentioned, the idyll and creativity of Mesopotamia came to an abrupt end. A male-dominated culture took over. And to make a long story short, this ending eventually became the beginning of mono-theism. And mono-theism is a religion ruled by only one god. We recognize this monotheism today as the three Abrahamic religions, Judaism, Christianity and Islam.

However, I would like to add that there is a competing view regarding the origin of a mono-theistic belief system. This occurred in Egypt by a pharaoh named Amonthotep IV. He is known for his attempt to change the belief in polytheism (worship of several gods), to the belief in only one god. (14)

Nevertheless, it was only the three Abrahamic monotheistic religions that reached the level of world-wide influence. Hence, it was only these religions that really came to influence the evolution of the human cultural history. And they still do.

However, through these Abrahamic religions, eroticism was gradually transformed into sin, guilt, shame, and punishment. In the same wake a woman-suppressing view emerged. This view in turn would lead to a shaming and suppressing of female sexuality. Manhood and potency were from then on the governing and controlling factors of all societies that were directly controlled, or indirectly influenced by the Abrahamic religions. This is also very visible in numerous cultures and sub-cultures of our own time.

The early history, the conception, pregnancy and birth of the emotional shame

The dark view on sexuality and women can thus be traced all the way back to the Semitic culture's invasion of the Sumerians about 5-6000 years ago. The Semites are still considered the origin of the cultural understanding of sexuality in our own time. It was, as mentioned above, a strong male-dominated culture that later on also was the founders of the first authoritarian mono-theistic religion, Judaism. The Jewish Bible Torah (or the Mosaic Law) also formed the basis of the other two Abrahamic religions, Christianity and Islam.

The Semitic culture also introduced circumcision of boys, this as a sign of the covenant between man and God. In early Judaism, Abraham promised God that all men should be circumcised as a proof of belonging to the people of Israel. That reproduction early became the main focus of sexual acts, is also made clear by their sacrifice of boys to God for the sake of reproduction in the time before Abraham. (15)

Circumcision was later continued by both Muslims and Catholics. When it comes to ritual circumcision of girls, we know that the so-called Pharaoic circumcision can be traced back to the 5' century before Christ. Pharaoic circumcicison means removing the clitoris and parts of labia. Circumcision of boys and girls is not exclusevly an Abrahamic heritage. Among Muslims, for instance, there is an Islamic absorption of both North and East African cultural rituals after the Islamic occupation these areas. Pharaoic circumcision is still practiced in some countries in North Africa. This custom is in our time referred to as genital mutilation. (16)

As we already have seen, the Sumerian culture was relatively free, liberal, open and creative, but it was also likely to have been non-violent. Archaeological findings have so far not been able to point to weapon-discoveries in early the Mesopotamian cultures. Cooperation was probably more customary than competition. (17)

The expanding Abrahamic culture, on the other hand, was based on domination, violence and competition, and would eventually dominate large parts of the world with its view on sexuality and the gender-hierachy.

However, if the Sumerian culture's influence on human rights and dignity ceased after the Semites' entry into Mesopotamia, they still left us with the most important tool of communication, invention and education, namely the written language. We should all take a deep bow in gratitude for their gift to humankind.

However, maybe some of the Sumerian view on humans as sacred beings survived in the collective conscious shadows for some millennia. There are some striking similarities between parts of the Sumerian culture and the great flourishing of new thinking, knowledge, art and philosophy that took place in Greece for approx. 2500 years ago. This era of Greek culture also became a boom of human creativity and a history-transforming knowledge. In many ways the cradle of our modern sciences. But the origin of scientific creativity should probably be granted the Sumerians.

Another similarity was the old Greeks' cultivation of eroticism. Bisexuality was widespread and was central to education, art, sports and bodybuilding. In intellectual circles, it was common for young boys to have a sexual relationship with their male teachers and mentors. In these circles it was even looked down at if one didn't have a mentor and lover. This is evident in the book "Symposium" (Written by Plato), where they offer their tribute to the God Eros:

"Anyone who is pardoned by this Eros turns to the masculine gender and feels attracted to the manly and prudent. Even within the crowd of boy lovers, one can distinguish those who are possessed by this high and pure erotic drift. They never put their love on underage boys, but wait for the time when the mind begins to apply and the first downs spread beyond the chin." (18)

In the higher strata of Greek society, bisexuality was the norm in the same way that hetero-sexuality is the norm in modern society. They were socialized to perceive it, not only as something completely natural and normal, but also as something high-valued, as a young man to have an older male lover and as an elder to have a young man as a lover. Plato believed that love was a wonderful feeling that made men behave upright. He thought true love was that between an older and a younger man. None of them considered this as abnormal, or unmanly.

Presumably, the warriors of Sparta and Theben also considered these kinds of relationships to be natural and normal. (19)

As for the Thebans, it was common for older and younger men to live in pairs, but they were also married to women. The city even had a holy corps consisting of male soldier-couples. This same army also helped giving the Thebans hegemony over Greece for a period. In Sparta, there were strict rules on how the male soldier-boyfriends should behave towards each other. This kind of love between men in ancient Greece was linked to strict religious beliefs. Some central Gods in that regard were Zeus and Apollon. (20) In addition to the god Eros as mentioned above.

In Sparta, same-sex relationships between young and older men were even mandatory, with the premise that men should marry and produce children. Their conceptions were based on the fact that erotic relationships between a young unexperienced soldier and an older experienced one, would enhance fighting loyalty and motivate heroic actions. But as soon as the novices reached adult maturity, the relationship was expected to be non-sexual. But historians are not entirely sure to what extent the latter was adhered to. (21)

In ancient Greece, the general ruling paradigm, or assumption, was that boys went through a gay stage at puberty, followed by a bisexual stage at young adulthood, and finally reaching a dominant heterosexual stage later in life, when they married and had children. (22)

A very known historical warrior and hero, some would argue, that practicly anyone knows, is the Macedonian King, Alexander the Great. He too was bisexual. His male lover was Hephaestion. There are countless stories and Hollywood-productions about Alexander the Great, but none of them even come close to telling the whole truth. Only the part that fits our modern-era hetero-cultural understanding of gender, manhood, courage and conquest has been told. The lover-part is always filtered out. As already mentioned, this phenomenon has a name among scientists, it's called: "Bisexual Erasure". You will learn more about this in Chapter 19. (23)

In Crete it was considered a shame for a wealthy young man not to have a male lover. Several other well-known cultures also cultivated this sexuality, such as the Romans, Assyrians, Babylonians and Egyptians, just to name a few. The latter two also had their own gods for this, Horus and Set. Among America's indigenous people, sexuality between men was also very common. (24)

Regarding sex between women, it did not have the same status as sex between men, simply because it did not fit in with their (men's) understanding of an active and a passive part in a love relationship. It was thus regarded as unnatural, although everyone was aware that women too could fall in love with each other. In this connection, the female poet Sapfo should be mentioned. She was known for the passionate love poems she wrote to her younger female students on the island of Lesbos. (25)

This kind of love is also found on continents other than the European. We find equal attitudes and the same tribute to the love between men, practicly anywhere on this planet. For instance, not many people know that the Samurais were very liberal regarding same-sex love. Just like the Greek Spartans, they not only accepted it, but they actively encouraged same-sex relationships in their culture. These relationships generally arose between an experienced Samurai and a young warrior-trainee. This practice was known as "Wakashudo" and was common to all the members of the Samurai culture. In fact, it was so common that if you didn't practice "Wakashudo", you could risk being embarrassed, stigmatized or bullied. (26)

Again, this kind of sexual behavior and expression of love, is observed on all continents, in all cultures and at all times of recorded history. It is described as a perfectly natural part of erotic life and friendship, and as we have seen, also among warriors. It is only in "our time" that this part of human emotions and behaviors has been portrayed as sinful, unnatural and morbid.

And, funny enough, when you think of some of the things that have been referred to in this chapter, it seems rather strange that love between men is often seen as "impermanent" with our modern "dark-colored" glasses. And when our modern filmmakers with their narrow lenses retell the classic Greek Epics, all that can be reminiscent of sexual facination between men is erased. "Bisexual Erasure".

Yet there were aspects of Greek culture that were not quite so charming. The women had limited rights and freedoms in a number of areas. The Greeks also kept slaves. A major exception to this was probably Socrates and his wife Xantippe. She was a midwife and enjoyed great freedom in all areas. By the way, one of my favorite Socratic quotes is: "My wife Xantippe is a midwife, and help humans entering into this world. I am the midwife of souls" (27)

It strikes me that the Sumerians and Greeks, in many ways (but not all), are similar cultures. They have both given birth to some of the most precious "Jewels" regarding the development of humanity. Could it be that unrestricted natural unfolding of human talents, like sexuality, freedom and creativity are connected, entangled with each-other? Is it even possible that this freedom is crucial to the development of humanity itself?

In the third part of the book I refer to a world-wide study that in many ways supports just that. This research is done by a rather unknown branch of psychology called Political Psychology. The study is presented in Chapter 15.

Regarding the ancient Greek culture, and what they have given all of us, and the significance this has had for our contemporary universal knowledge, such as philosophy in general, the philosophy of science including all the scientific "spin-offs" from the latter one, cannot be over-rated.

We must not forget what they gave us, and we should also be aware of what became "lost along the way". Or rather, what became lost (erased) in translation.

CHAPTER 2

The Transformation of Dualism

The Birth of Polarization

"Polarization affects families and groups of friends. Its a paralyzing situation. A civil war of opinion." (Mick Jagger)

Dualism can probably be traced back to the followers of Orpheus. This cult arose 700-480 BC. (1) Among their gods, Eros and Sofia were central. The latter was the God of wisdom and it was both male and female. The followers believed that if one lived a "pure" life in accordance with their ideals, the soul would be liberated from the body after death and live a happy life, thereafter. (2)

Also in Pythagorean philosophy and mysticism we find dualism central to the understanding of the soul and the body. They believed in reincarnation, but like the followers of Orpheus, they also believed in the final liberation of the soul as a result of the "pure" thinking. Dualism was continued by Plato, and eventually it also appeared in Christianity, but now with a completely different interpretation of "Purity". Purity for the early Christians, meant abstinence from any kind of sexual behavior. The earlier view on love and sexual pleasure as something beautiful, individual and divine, disappeared. (3)

With Christianity, and primarily with Paul's entrance on the scene, sexuality became the subject of the dualistic distinction between soul and flesh. The flesh was hereafter regarded as something inferior, and man had to avoid the sinful desire of the flesh at all costs. This dualistic sexual outlook was further enhanced when the Iranian religious philosopher Mani entered the scene, two hundred years after Christ. (4)

Manichaeism (named after Mani) became its own syncretic religion, which means a kind of confluence of different religions. (5) It claimed that man had two souls, one for the good and one for the evil. Thus, a kind of religious variation of the psychiatric diagnosis MPD (Multi Personal Disorder) one might say.

MPD means that one has several personalities, which are often contradictory, that they oppose each other. They may also be hidden from one another. (6)

The struggle between these "two souls", the good and the bad (the sexual), was very central to Manichaeism. Even in marriage, sexual desire was considered sinful. Manicheanism had a strong impact on the shaping of the Abrahamic religions, especially Islam, but also on Jewish and Christian fundamentalism. They are still largely affected by Mani. (7)

Early Christianity did not really have a dogmatic view of sexuality. That is, until Paul entered the scene. Paul was strongly inspired by Moses, who in turn already had linked shame to certain types of sexual behavior. Paul was obviously impressed and inspired by the Mosaic Law. Could it be that he saw the potential of power in these "laws"?

Sexual shame is further reinforced in the Christian cultures by Augustine, and eventually also by Thomas Aquinas. Augustine was a follower of Mani a few years, before he broke with Manichaeism and eventually became preoccupied with Christianity. With Augustine's entry into Christianity, reproduction became the only "natural" sexual act. Everything that had to do with desire was seen as sinful and harmful to the soul. Augustine is still considered to be one of the world's greatest church teachers, and he had a great influence on both theology and philosophy in the Middle Ages. His doctrines still have a significant influence in our own time. (8)

Interestingly, the Man from Nazareth did not claim any of these hostile views that would eventually result in prohibitions, injunctions, as well as abuse of power and control of human emotions. This view, which was established long after Christ, has left its destructive footprints right up to this day.

There's a local example of these destructive footprints in the town where I was born. In this small town, Haugesund, there is a place called Utboredalen. The name "Utbore" means carry-out, and it derives from a custom of secretly carrying newborn babies out there. The babies were left there to die because they were born out of wedlock. They were born in "sin", and therefore left alone in this remote walley to die or be taken by predators. (9)

These young girls who ended up in "sin" were themselves victims of an Abrahamic view on women as inferior to men. They were exploited by men in charge, who, of course, considered themselves to be "Christians." This cruelty took place in the nineteenth century. This shows the far-reaching effects these ancient self-proclaimed advocates of God have had on the lives and behaviors of ordinary people in a small Norwegian town nearly 2000 years later.

Surely, not many have as much blood on their hands as self-proclaimed enforcers of the "right faith"

"When religions control human sexual life, they thus control their lives, their identities and ultimately their understanding of what it is to be human."

Dag Eistein Endsjø

Christianity eventually became a powerful political tool in the hands of powerful persons. The moral rules were governed by only one Almighty God. For centuries it was forced upon the people with raw and evil power. Not at least through the introduction of the Inquisition in the twelfth century. Thinkers who would not profess to Christian doctrine were now held to be heretics, sentenced to death, and burned alive. Thore Langfeldt, a Nowegian scholar and author points out that the result of this process was that Religion had now become politics.

It may be worth remembering that it isn't terribly long since we burned women alive during the witch-processes, also in Norway. (10)

Intolerance was further strengthened in the 13th century when Thomas Aquinas reiterated and emphasized the significance of what Augustin had previously claimed, namely that all sexual acts that do not lead to conception were unnatural and sinful. Aquinas is considered to be one of the most important philosophers in the history of Christianity,

The semen was to be used only for reproduction, and even in that setting eroticism was considered sinful. Thus, masturbation, anal and oral sex, as well as sex between two of the same sex were banned. This resulted in perverted outcomes, such as that a man's rape of a woman wasn't necessarily regarded as particularly sinful, as it could lead to the woman being fertilized. (11)

By the way, Thomas Aquinas believed that kissing and touching between two people of different genders was not necessarily sinful, but that it could still be a sin of death if the motivation was "wrong". (12)

One might say that Moses was for Paul, what Mani and Augustine were for Aquinas. Paul, for his part, became a kind of tabloid newspaper variant of Moses' laws. Where Moses had lengthy accounts of the rights of slaveholders, and how to treat the slaves, Paul concluded briefly and brutally that the slaves should submit to their earthly masters in all, period.

Regarding Thomas Aquinas, it is interesting to note that at the end of his life, he completely distanced himself from everything he had written, after an experience that some scholars today claim to have been an NDE experience (Near-Death Experience). After his experience

Aquinas announced that everything he had claimed should be regarded as meaningless and worthless. These were his last written words before he mysteriously died later that year. (13)

It would be interesting to know if this is part of the curriculum of theological studies on our planet. It may also be worth noting that the planet wasn't yet properly rounded in Thomas Aquinas' time.

To gain an understanding of the problems many people are struggling with today as a result of these "Stewards of the word of God" like Moses, Paul, Mani, Augustine and Aquinas (and many others), it is necessary to take these historical steps back in time, to be able to detect possible connections with contemporary cultural condemnations of various human groups and behaviors.

The condemnation itself, as we've already seen, has most of its origins in the Mosaic Laws, which in turn have been reinforced through the Abrahamic religions: Judaism, Christianity and Islam. Here are some examples of religious prohibitions and injunctions taken from the Mosaic Laws of the Old Testament.

All three of the above mentioned religions are, as I said, based on the Mosaic Law, thus this following imperative is reflected in all of these three religions.

"You shall not lie with a man as you lie with a woman, it is abomination" (The Bible, Leviticus, 18:22)

This Bible quotation has recently been given a completely different meaning by some theological researchers. This boundary-breaking science will have a great and long-lasting impact on how we view non-heterosexual individuals. I will cover this new research in Chapter 18. This is important in the light of the 3300 years of harassment and punishment of non-heterosexual people.

In some cultures on our planet, many still pay a fatal price for this Mosaic Law. Bible quotations, as most of us know, have inspired and "justified" genocide, torture, oppression and terror everywhere on this planet.

Some examples are the massacres performed by Europeans on the African and American continents just a few hundred years ago. The Bible's repeated disdain for people and races other than "God's chosen one" is also clearly demonstrated in Deuteronomy 14:21:

"You shall not eat any self-dead animal. You can give it to the immigrants in your cities so he can eat it, or you can sell it to a foreigner. For you are a holy people to the Lord your God."

Another quote from Deuteronomy 23.2 reads as follows:

"He who is born in a mixed marriage shall not have access to the Lord's congregation. Even the descendants of the tenth generation cannot join the congregation."

In another Bible-translation 23.2 reads:

"No one born of a forbidden union may enter the assembly of the LORD. Even to the tenth generation, none of his descendants may enter the assembly of the LORD."

This quotation among others, was used as "justifying evidence" for Ku Klux Klan's treatment of African Americans. And although we would rather see this organization as a racist organization, it is in fact a Christian sect, rooted in the "holy" scriptures. The philosopher Dag Øistein Endsjø calls it "Holy sexual racism."

It has influenced law-makers, especially in the United States, right up to our own time. Probably as a result of the extensive slavery in the southern states of USA. The first American laws against sex across races were introduced in 1662. Except from these laws were the slave owners. They were granted the right to use their assets as they wished. And they did. It is unpleasant to think that when Barak Obama was born, as a child of a mixed marriage, this was still banned in 22 of the

50 US-states. Slavery as such, Americans found support for it both in the Old and the New Testaments. (14)

Muslims do not hold the same racist view on marriage. However they warn against marrying "idolaters", regardless of race. But if you convert to Islam, you will be fine no matter what race you belong to. In addition, Muslim men are allowed to marry women of "those who have been given the Book before you." Which means the other two Abrahamic religions (Jews and Christians). But you have to be a virgin. (15)

In addition to these aforementioned prohibitions and injunctions, there is thus the notion of a master-race, or the chosen ones in these religions. Paul, who also has been honored to be the first missionary, founder and organizer of the Christian Church, said:

"You slaves shall obey your earthly masters in all things" (Colossians, 3.22)

The latter is a paraphrasing of one of the Mosaic Laws, and again, as mentioned above, a kind of tabloid-press version of the far more comprehensive Mosaic Law, which states:

"If a man beats his male or female slave with a rod and the slave dies as a direct result, he must be punished, but he is not be punished if the slave gets up after a day or two, since the slave is his property" (Leviticus 21:20)

In another Bible translation, the last paragraph of the same Bible quotation reads: "the loss of his property is punishment enough". In my research on the Bible, I was constantly surprised by the changes in Bible quotations from one edition to another. And from one language to another, or from one period in time to another. Editing is an interesting sport.

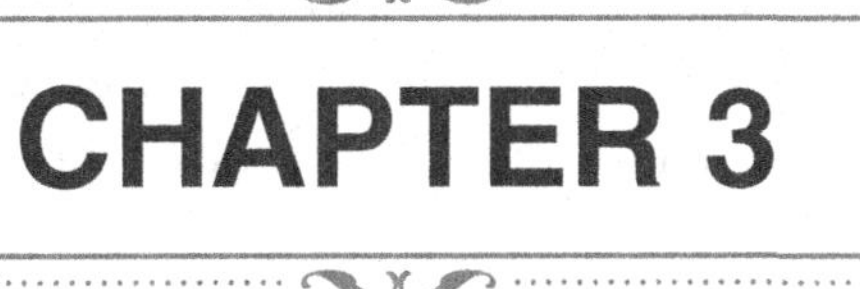

CHAPTER 3

Most Atheists are Religious. They Just Don't Know It

"We're all raised in a cultural matrix, totally molded by religion. Not going to church, synagogue, or mosque, doesn't mean you aren't "religious"."

Professor Michael Ledwith -

It's important to be aware of how some religious imperatives also have become cultural "truths", even for people who do not follow a specific religion. We have to be aware that our culture implicitly expresses much of our religious heritage, sometimes so subtle that it is almost invisible. And just as religion is an important component of the foundation of culture, culture forms the basis for several of the social sciences, such as sociology and psychology.

At the same time, it is strange that this Abrahamic god whom so many worship, and which has left such deep traces in virtually all the world's cultures, was unaware that the earth he is supposed to have created is neither flat nor square with four corners, but round. In fact, Aristotle discovered this 2500 years ago when he noticed that the shadow on the moon's surface during an eclipse would be curved.

Religious "truths" that are repeated and sometimes even indoctrinated by means of power in the form of threats or violence are slowly but surely have become a major part of cultural norms and rules. It has also indirectly colored social and psycho-social norms, and in the end, you and me. In this way, religions have been indirectly "allowed" to decide what is normal and what is abnormal. Even psychiatry and clinical-psychology have been tainted by this process. These three levels; religion, sociology and psychology, have become so intertwined that it's sometimes difficult to see where one of them ends and the next begins.

Another reason may be that many people consider themselves Christians, without really having any particular knowledge of the basis of the faith they profess. I often use to test people on their biblical knowledge of some of the central Mosaic laws, like the 10 Commandments. So far no one has passed the test.

We simply confess to some belief because important authorities in our upbringing have told us that it is a good faith. And we accept it, without even bothering to scrutinize it. In particular, one commandment undermines the claim that the 10 commandments are the foundation of our humanistic heritage:

"*You shall not covet your neighbor's house; you shall not covet your neighbor's wife, or male or female slave, or ox, or donkey, or anything that belongs to your neighbor*" (2)

It is also important to emphasize that the Bible actually consists of several books and that these were chosen by old powerful men. Not God. It is equally important to be aware that many of these books were also censored, some of which were also omitted and rejected. Not by God. (3)

And why was it so important to keep some of these books and scriptures hidden from the public light? Some revealing answers emerged in connection with the legendary discovery of The Nag Hammadi Scriptures in Egypt 1946. Among the books they found was a complete edition of the Gospel of Thomas. Scholars already knew something about it through other historical scriptures. Half of the Gospel of

Thomas consisted of up to then, unknown passages and words of Jesus speaking to his disciples.

These scriptures reveal, among other things, that Jesus does not share Moses' and Paul's contempt for the female sex. It also reveals that at least two of the disciples were women. (4) Some scholars even believe that the Gospel of Thomas is the original, and not The Gospel of Mark's, as previously thought. (5)

The influence of religion on modern cultures is possible to reveal, by studying current cultural beliefs and norms, and then ask the simple question: Where do they come from? With some background knowledge of the three Abrahamic religions, you should be able to find the origin of most of your culture's rules and norms.

The vast majority of cultures have restrictions on the individual's freedom, and his or her ability to live out his or her natural potential and individual identity. These restrictions often express themselves as social conventions on what is "allowed" and "not allowed", or a set of "shoulds" or "not should"t, etc.

If they are deep and rooted enough, these cultural restrictions also often express themselves as indicators of what is "normal" or not in the sense of natural or unnatural. If you're considered not normal (abnormal), you may become a case of clinical psychology, or psychiatry.

In the end then, these "truths", which have gradually become uncritically accepted by the majority, have become norms, rules, laws and in some cases mental diseases that must be treated. One simply becomes "blind". We do not see the world with our eyes, but through our eyes. The filters are far behind our eyes and are often called world-views or belief-systems, or as in the language of science, they're called paradigms.

These built-in cultural limitations can be seen as an analogy to the blind spots we have on the retina. They're there, but you can't see them. To use a bad analogy; You wear your cultural lenses in the same way as a pair of sunglasses. The external reality is filtered through your cultural lenses and stored as "truths" according to the prevailing paradigm in your culture and in your mind.

One is so conditioned by cultures teachings of right / wrong, normal / abnormal that it is almost impossible to "look behind" one's own judgments, and thus unable to see the origin of these judgements. But it is not impossible. As a sexologist, I often experience this phenomenon at a "micro level" in conversations with my clients.

With these "blind spots", it also becomes hard to see the pain and sorrow you can inflict on other people with your own "straightforwardness" and righteous-ness. What others may perceive as hurt and unjust persecution, you may see as a universal truth that must be enforced and adhered to.

That words can kill is far from a cliche. I have experienced that in my own work during the years. People who have tried to end their lives because they've been rejected, ostracized and shamed. It is therefore of the utmost importance to examine your own cultural beliefs, your own "glasses," in order to discover the origin of your "truths."

In our modern age, these religious injunctions and prohibitions are not necessarily as clear-cut as they were in ancient times, but the footprints are obviously still there. Some of them are of course benign, and based on respect and compassion.

A somewhat harmless example is the Norwegian celebration of St. John on June 24th. Here in Norway, Christianity was introduced somewhat late compared to most of the European countries, and because of that we still have some strong fingerprints from the Norse mythology. This very day was an annual celebration in Norway, long before Christianity was introduced. We lit a bonfire to chase away evil spirits, and this ritual was otherwise marked in a rather tipsy way to put it mildly. Today the bonfire is used for grilling sausages instead of evil spirits, but otherwise most people are getting as drunk today, as the Vikings back then. Maybe it's not a suitable way to celebrate a Christian Saint, you might say, but some "fingerprints" don't come off easily.

If religion failed to influence the culture in this case, even though it was intentional, it is an example of the influence of these historically "invisible fingerprints". Although most people in the free world today do not directly relate to Moses' injunction and prohibition, there are still too many people who, with their attitudes and actions, are clear reflections of Mosian doctrines. Some "fingerprints" are difficult to remove, but no "fingerprints" are impossible to remove.

"When religions fight for secular authorities to force through their religious-sexual beliefs, they know that this may involve the naturalization of some of the most central religious principles. Even if they are unable to repent you directly, managing your sexual life can make you live almost as if you were a follower of religious dogma." Dag Øystein Endsjø

Non-heterosexual behavior is still considered by many to be abnormal and even pathological or sinful, in many cultures it's even punishable. In Norway it was forbidden for men to have sex with each other until 1972. Why was it not forbidden for women to have sex with each other, you might wonder? Well, because it never was a topic in the Mosaic Law. With regard to the statute which prohibited sex between men in Norway, it was attempted to be repealed for the first time in 1954. The Norwegian church, by the way, went strongly against this.

The highest clergy council in Norway stated that a repeal of this law would lead to the legalization of a perverse and disruptive relationship that is contrary to the interests of society and Christian morality. They also felt that the existing law should rather be extended to include sex between females. (6)

Homosexuals still run the risk of death-penalty in these countries: Mauritania, parts of Nigeria, parts of Somalia, Sudan, Iran, Saudi Arabia and Yemen.

In these countries they risk imprisonment: Algeria, Botswana, Burundi, Egypt, Guinea, Cameroon, Comoros, Morocco, Oman, Senegal, Swaziland, Syria, Togo, Tunisia, Zimbabwe, Belize, Antigua and Barbuda, Jamaica, Afghanistan, Bhutan, Brunei, Indonesia, Kuwait, Lebanon,

Oman, Pakistan, Myanmar, Singapore, Sri Lanka, Turkmenistan, Uzbekistan, St Kitts and Nevis, Palau, Samoa, Solomon Islands, Cook Islands, Ethiopia, Ghana, Kenya, Libya, Malawi, Seychelles, Sierra Leone, Tanzania, Zambia, Uganda, Bangladesh, United Arab Emirates, Malaysia, Barbados, Dominican Republic, Grenada, Guyana, Papua New Guinea, St. Vincent and the Grenadines, St. Lucia, Trinidad and Tobago, Kiribati, Nauru, Tonga, Tuvalu, Palestine, Gambia, Lesotho, Liberia, Namibia, São Tomé and Principe, Qatar and the Maldives.

In the following countries homosexuals are punished with fines or forced labor: Angola and Mozambique. Countries with unclear penalties: Iraq and India. In Algeria and Chile gays are mentally ill. (7)

Go through the list once again, and then try to identify which of these countries were subjected to "Christian" Western colonization and, or missionary work.

What we so far have learned from available historical material shows that prejudice, persecution and suppression of non-heterosexual behavior, first started with the introduction of the Mosaic Laws and the dogmatic Abrahamic religions. Prior to this, most cultures had a far freer and more natural view on these topics.

The reason may be that their natural religions did not include dogmas that opposed naturel expressions. In addition, they also had very good knowledge of the widespread same-sex sexual activity among many of the animal species. This I will thoroughly discuss in the third part of the book, including a discussion on key findings in this field. Findings that for many appear revolutionary, and for some people rather disturbing and terribly annoying. Bruce Bagemihl is the name of the scientist behind probably the largest of studies in this field.

Sexuality between men at all times seems to have flourished in conditions where women were not present, armies, wars, campaigns, prisons, etc. At times, and as we have seen a bit of in the previous chapter, one has actually found that sexuality between men has been most prevalent among warriors, Norwegian Vikings are not an exception. The Vikings were even accused of introducing homosexuality in France when they visited, invaded or settled (pick your choise) in Normandi.

And, apropos prisons, a survey done in the Sing-Sing prison in New York concluded that 30% of the prisoners were so-called actively gay, and a large proportion of the remaining were passive gays. (8)

What the percentage was of this large proportion of the remaining "passive gays" they didn't mention. In any case, absolutely none of the above examples testifies to the popular claim that these inclinations are a manifestation of "feminization," or lack of "masculinity," which it became so common to claim towards the end of the second millennium.

For my part, I do not know if I would dare to appear as heterosexual in the aforementioned armies or the Sing Sing prison, simply because the fear of not being able to pass as macho enough.

Speaking of which, perhaps the "modern" human problem is that we feel trapped in different categories where heterosexuals and gays actually only make up two of them. And that these categories seem more inhibitory and exclusive than humane and inclusive, and thus also to "imprisoning" for most of us.

This is not just the legacy of dogmatic and judgmental religions, but probably also the legacy of the early sciences introduction in the cultural arena. And first and foremost the medical and social sciences, which, with their exaggerated belief in categorization, also greatly contributed to reinforcing and cementing of the narrow Abrahamic view and perception of man.

When it comes to suffering afflicted on minorities in our immediate past as a result of such prejudices, I will remind you of the crimes committed during the interwar period and during World War II. Not least those who had to suffer due to racial persecution, developmental disabilities, and sexual orientation. These wrongdoings were justified by "research" from both the medical science and some of the social sciences.

Along with the Jews, homosexuals were among the first to be interned in concentration camps, as early as 1933. In total, it is estimated that approx. 10,000 homosexuals were interned and between 3 and 6,000 died as a result of "scientific" experiments. Among others, hormone injections. (9)

When the surviving prisoners in the German concentration camps were liberated by the Allied forces, several of the homosexuals were forwarded to other prisons for execution of the sentences given by the Nazi regime. In other words, the Nazi persecution of the homosexuals was recognized and approved by the "Christian" Allied forces. (10)

Fifty years later, in the capital of my own country, Norway, homosexuals were denied to participate at a ceremony in memory of the victims of German concentration camps before and during the war. This on the ground that it could be offensive to other participants.

"The married women shall submit to their husbands as under the Lord Himself" (The Bible, Ephesians, 5.22)

Another example of oppression and prejudice rooted in the Bible, and which has set a solid "fingerprint" both in the past and the present era, is that of women's lack of the right to participate in societal life, and their ability to formally influence the laws. The fact that women have gradually been granted these rights is of a relatively recent date. Norwegian women were first granted the right to participate in elections in 1913. They were also among the first women in the world to receive these civil rights.

As mentioned above, homosexuals were not decriminalized in Norway until 1972, the diagnosis itself was not removed until 1977. And it was not until 1990 that it was removed from the WHO's official diagnosis manual ICD. (11)

As I see it, it's very problematic, to say the least, if one is to adopt an inclusive human rights and equality perspective for all, if one should place the prohibitions and injunctions of old Abrahamic and dogmatic religious laws as grounds and guidelines for social relations. With that in mind, it seems rather hard to refer to the Abrahamic religions as the "religions of love", as long as they suppress, reject and explain a significant portion of "God's Children" as inferior.

Yet, there are other historical (and less dogmatic) writings and interpretations of these three Abrahamic religions. Writings that are as old as the religions themselves, that neither promote oppression or hatred. They are in fact more inclusive than polarizing. These alternative historical understandings and interpretations exist within Jewish, Christian and Muslim writings.

You will learn more about these writings in the last chapter of the book, along with some of the most controversial research of our time.

PART II

The Modern Era

CHAPTER 4

The Transformation from Sin to Disease

"A sexual behavior becomes less excessive if it is recognized, accepted, and made appropriate in a given context - rather than prohibited. Needs and sexual desires cannot be suppressed. They must be channeled into appropriate forms of expression"

Isabelle Hernault - Canadian psychologist and sexologist.

"Juno was on a mission. He started studying at the university and became deeply absorbed in the literature relevant to his quest. He studied psychology, the psychology of religions, social-psychology and sexology. All the topics that might shed some light on the phenomenon, origin and history of sexual orientations. What interested Juno more and more was the phenomenon «sexuality» in general, not only the religious and cultural banning of unwanted sexual orientations."

Excerpt from TRAX

The transformation from being sinful to becoming mentally disturbed. From now on, "God" appears in a white coat carrying a diagnostic manual.

"The Abrahamic religions turned biology upside down:" if it feels good, it's bad - and if it hurts, it's good" - James William Prescott –

The Modern Era doesn't describe as much the variety of sexual behaviors as it describes the continuing limitations of them. This is true regardless of whether one talks about the religious, legal or scientific regimes. But this same era (see description below) is also the birth of sexology as a science, and its turbulent history until now.

Sexology suffered greatly during the Nazi-regime's period, but also in the post-war period, where a not so sexuality-friendly American psychology was to dominate the field. However, one great and very important exception must be mentioned, Alfred Kinsey. He made a big contribution to the field of sexology, and as a consequence, also impacted psychology. Today, Kinsey is still regarded as the person who rescued the field of sexology after the "latency period" from 1933 to 1945. Regarding the latter; the sexological research literature was among the first to be burned when Hitler and his men came to power.

But behind it all, the dark and gloomy tones of the Abrahamic religious dogma still sounded. Influences in this era were both direct and indirect via religious, cultural and scientific paradigms. Sin was still the meta-theoretical point of departure. Common to these two seemingly different paradigms, the religious and the scientific (sin or biology), is that both generate guilt, shame and dysphoria, instead of magic, joy and euphoria. Any sexuality that did not produce children was "wrong" in either case.

In Part I, I pointed to the most important, central historical trendsetters with the subsequent important paradigm shifts. The history of sexuality can also be roughly divided into three eras; the Premodern-era, which I briefly described in the previous section The Modern-era that I will address in this part. And lastly, the Postmodern-era to which I will devote most of the third part of the book. The latter era is poorly defined in terms of content, rather chaotic I'd say. And thus a subject of great discussions. As I see it, it is a relatively empty concept, an era just waiting to be filled with content. New Content.

One might say that we are in a transitional phase, simply in the midst of a paradigm shift. Or in the midst of a leap forward, as the professor in sexology Christian Graugaard puts it. If so, we are living in a time of a unique historical opportunity to influence the content of the coming epoch, and thus on a way forward towards a freedom humankind may never have experienced.

The start of this transition to the Postmodern-era is dated to the 1980s. According to Christian Graugaard, more precisely 1985. The date and the exact time of the day he didn't reveal. He also uttered the following inspirational words at one of the first lectures I attended as a student of sexology:

"It is now possible to rediscover" America "." (Lecture by Graugaard, UiA-September 2007)

I totally agree. I think Graugaard is right in his claim that sexologists have a better oppor-tunity to "see" these shifts, than other scholars. Precisely because sexology looks right into the most important driving factors for both individual and cultural liberation.

When it comes to the Modern-era, which most of the time dates to the beginning of the 19th century, it has given rise to most of the sciences of our time. (1) Such as the natural sciences, including physics, biology and medicine, as well as the social sciences. At the same time, some of these sciences have collective "unconsciously" acted as indirect promotors of religious dogma. Still, in the same era, sexology also emerged as a science. But as mentioned above, it had a very turbulent "gestation", "birth" and dramatic "childhood", until now.

"Bisexuality is the ghost in the binary machinery". (N.N)

It's no exaggeration to say that sexology has been the enfant terrible of social sciences, just as bisexuality has been, and is still is an "disobedient child" for both of the mono-sexualities (heterosexuals and homosexuals) but also for the mono gender-role identities (Thc Blue-Pink, Mars-Venus syndrome). You will learn more about the latter in Chapter 12 and 13. As for the term *enfant terrible,* it's French, and mostly referred to in the meaning of being a prodigy, and more often than not, prodigies are not obedient to cultural "truths".

Christian Puritanism is the meta-theoretical (Metatheory: See Central Concepts) starting point for both prohibitions, theories and treatment methods in relation to everything that had to do with sexuality from the end of the 18th century. These laws, theories and treatment-methods had all in common that they would keep at bay "the dangerous and dirty sexuality." Above all, it was masturbation, which also was referred to as "self-contamination" as the British author of "Onania" called it, and homo-sexuality that were the main-focus from then on.

And we shall eventually see that these two latter behaviors would also be seen in relation to each other. This is largely due to Rousseau's seduction hypothesis, which I will return to below.

The masturbation or "self-contamination" would eventually reach epidemic heights. It is also conceivable that the "contagion" (masturbation) in itself was seen as self-love, that is, love for one's own gender instead of the other. The scientists of this era showed a sexual fantasizing ability that human history probably never have witnessed, neither before nor after.

As mentioned, the "seed" of sexual shame can easily be traced back to the Mosaic Laws and the Abrahamic religions. And this shame was greatly amplified in the Christian cultures by Paul, Mani, Augustine and eventually Aquinas. One might wonder if there is anyone at all who manage to get through the narrow sexual needle's eye into the "Abrahamic paradise". I have made some "mathematical" calculations on this, you can read the results in chapter 17.

Masturbation becomes harmful, life-threatening, fatal and epidemic

"This is what we know: When it comes to sex, masturbation is the most common act. It is the least dangerous, the most controllable by a person's own wishes, and

the least likely to lead to misunderstanding. But masturbation is certainly not the most socially accepted sexual practice. The simple answer is religious taboo."

Pepper Schwartz & Virginia Rutter.

"Masturbation is sex with someone I love" - Woody Allen

Scientific theories of sexuality emerged in the 18th century, but they brought with them the legacy of the ancient religions into the "free" world. The legacy largely consisted of the view of sexuality as purely a reproductive method and nothing else. And thus became the only normal expression of sexuality. As a result of this meta-theoretical view, all other expressions of sexuality was considered abnormal, eventually also clinically pathological. In other words, something that needed to be diagnosed and "repaired".

Some of these "abnormal" expressions of sexuality were even considered potentially harmful and in some cases, even life-threatening. This view permeated the theories and treatment-methods that emerged from the late 18th century. Especially masturbation became the subject of an enormous and sickening focus. At the same time, women gradually began to be a-sexualized.

Yet, masturbation had once been a high-quality sexual act. An example of this is the Egyptian god Atum. This god, who was regarded as the first power of the universe, rose from the original darkness, masturbated and became the sun god Ra. And from his seed arose the first divine creatures, Shu and Tefet. These gave life to heaven (Nut) and earth (Geb). An ancient papyrus shows the earth's self-sustaining fertility by Geb sucking himself and swallowing his own semen. This is the oldest known illustration of the sacred power of masturbation. (2)

So to all you guys out there who have tried to suck yourselves (and there's many of you), can see it as a sacred act (or for most of you, an attempted sacred act). Or maybe some kind of spiritual yearning?

But the Abrahamic religions did not share this spiritual view of masturbation. Even though they had long held that masturbation was a great sin, it wasn't deemed dangerous or lethal until the 18th century. This transformation from sin to danger probably began with a book published in England in the early 18th century. The book bore the title of:

"Onania, or the Henious Sin of Self-Pollution, and All its Frightful Consequences, in Both Sexes, Considered. With Spiritual and Physical Advice for Those Who Have Already Injur'd Themselves by This Abominable Practice".

The book was published under a pseudonym, but it has been claimed afterwards that it was the self-proclaimed doctor John Martens who was the author. Fortunately, he also had a cure, a fortifying mixture that he sold for 12 shillings per bottle, which of course could cure the terrible spiritual and physical consequences of masturbation. (3)

"Doctor" Martens should probably be awarded the prize of being the founder of modern-day marketing. The creation of needs is, as we all know, the first commandment of marketing. Often needs we weren't aware of, that luckily can be met with various variants of "snake-oil". "Snake-oils" that suspiciously often are produced by the same person or institution that initially invented the error, defect, or ill-ness.

Although Marten's book-title probably wouldn't be a preferred tabloid bestseller-title for the promotion of a book in our days, it was back then. And it absolutely caught the mainstream's attention. Apparently, content involving sexuality sold just as well back then as it does today.

With this book, the concept of "masturbation" (onania) was born. "Masturbation" comes from the biblical story of Onan, a story that is not about masturbation at all. In short, Onan refused to fertilize his late brother's wife to save his late and childless brother's honor. Instead, he let his seed fall to the ground, and God therefor decided that he should die. Onan should instead have been honored for having "invented" the first method of contraception.

As we have seen, activities involving masturbation was far from harmless, even here in "liberal" Norway. In Aschehoug's Conversation Lexicon (Encyclopedia) from 1907, the following warnings were stated. They were not as scary as "Doctor" Marten's warnings, but still pretty scaring. Here they are:

"Onania, masturbation, self-contamination, is an unnatural satisfaction of the sex drive, especially at the time before sexuality is fully matured. Masturbation is most common among boys, especially where many are gathered. In adulthood, masturbation is usually performed only by the degenerate individuals, who, most often later in life, suffer from self-blame for their past weakness and fear of its consequences. As a rule, there are no direct consequences."

Aschehoug's Illustrated Norwegian Conversation Lexicon, 1907.

In a very short time "onania" (masturbation) became a concept of serious discussion both among religious followers as well as among "scholars ". As Thore Langfeldt puts it: "This notion of masturbation brought religion and medicine indelibly together into a new discourse". And from now on, masturbation and homosexuality became the main focus. (4)

During this process, "self-contamination" was transformed from sin into pandemic propor-tions of danger through the dissertation of a Swiss physician and epidemiologist. His name was Samuel Auguste David Tissot. Together with his entrance on the scene, masturbation became a medical diagnosis. This despite the fact that no serious attempt was made to substantiate this claim. (5)

One might say that Dr. Tissot and his hysterical contemporaries marked the beginning of Scientism. Scientism is a term that was created by some sociologists ca half a century ago. A term they used to describe a phenomenon where theories were transformed into belief-systems and ideologies. Theories that are based on assumptions or convictions without any substance. They seemed so credible that no-one even bothered to question them. "Just So Stories" as Rudyard Kipling probably would have called them.

However, there were honorable exceptions, such as a British doctor named John Hunter. He asserted from his own clinical observations that if anything at all was dangerous regarding masturbation, it was the inflicted shame and guilt. Unfortunately, Dr. Hunter's later releases of the book in which he stated this view, were censored. (6)

Masturbation was also alleged to be the cause of tuberculosis, insanity, epilepsy, death at a young age, and blindness just to name a few. Or, as Dr. Benjamin Rush, who also has been honored for being the father of American psychiatry, stated:

"Masturbation causes impairment of semen, impotence, urinary incontinence, spinal cord disorder, pulmonary tuberculosis, indigestion, weakness, dizziness, epilepsy, hypochondria, memory loss, insanity, weakness and death." ("Medical Studies 1812")

It is a good fortune that glasses have become so affordable in our postmodern era. Otherwise, it must be described as a wonder of Divine proportions that there are any humans left at all on our planet.

By the end of the 19th century, it had become common to circumcise boys in the United Kingdom and in the United States, in order to prevent this sinful and life-threatening "self-contamination." All based on short-circuits and beliefs, which in turn became a "scientific" theory and eventually an academic paradigm. It was all built on sandy ground. A meta-theoretical legacy from the Abrahamic religions became a medical paradigm. Scientism.

No scientists on the American continent questioned this collective madness. Another person who had a great influence on this discourse was the Swiss philosopher Jean-Jacques Rousseau. Rousseau is probably most famous for writing "Du contrat social", best known as the catechism of the revolution. Or the French Revolution user-manual one might say.

But in the same period of time, Rousseau also published a work on child rearing. There, he argued, among other things, that the adults harmed the child regarding their morbid relation-ship with sexuality and exposure to it. He considered the child a "Tabula Rasa". Tabula Rasa is Latin and means a blank slate, or unwritten page. The term originates from the philosopher Aristotle. (7)

Shortly after this release, he also became acquainted with Dr. Tissot and his dissertation on masturbation. Rousseau, by the way, was himself an unhappy sadomasochist. He claimed that his sexual inclination had its root-cause in a childhood experience, where he at the age of 8 had been lying naked on his governess's lap while she spanked him. The "marriage" of "Tabula Rasa" and his own childhood experience were seemingly sufficient for Mr. Rousseau to form the basis of what has since been called the seduction-hypothesis. (8)

As a comment to Rousseau's sadomasochistic fetish or paraphilia, this has most likely been established much earlier in his life. So even if it wasn't particular nice of his governess to spank him, she doesn't deserve the blame of having caused his paraphilia. You will learn more about paraphilia in Chapter 19.

The seduction hypothesis, was by the way, finally put to rest and buried in 1981. It's death-sentence was executed by one of the most comprehensive studies of sexualities and sexual behavior ever conducted. Bell, Weinberg et. al's study has since been simply referred to as "The Bay Study". An abbreviation for "The San Francisco Bay Study". (9)

Nevertheless, this idea that one can be seduced into a sexual orientation or sexual behavior still lives among many people to this day, but is in the Western World perhaps most prevalent in the United States. In this connection, it may also be interesting to note that "Behaviorism" also called "The Second Force of Psychology", has had and still has a strong foothold in the United States. This psychological direction is largely based on the view of the individual as a tabula rasa. (10) Or with a more modern example, empty hard disk. Roughly explained as: everything is learned, hence also sexual orientations.

As I mentioned earlier on, at this time they also began to associate masturbation with homo-sexuality. This is probably because gay acts often consisted of mutual masturbation. This fit perfectly with both the seduction hypothesis as well as the understanding of man as a "Tabula Rasa". Hence, masturbation wasn't only harmful in itself, but also led to the spread of homo-sexuality. And with this, masturbation had now reached alarming pandemic proportions.

It was the Anglo-American cultures who were the most avid masturbation-fighters beyond the 19th century. One of the American pioneers for combating this self-contagious masturbation, Sylvester Graham, argued, among other things, that the diet was important to overcome this plague. Among other things, he proposed that one should avoid white bread, pork and tobacco, and replace these with whole-grain products. (11)

It is possible that Sylvester Graham was an involuntary precursor of the popular current raw food wave. By the way, whole-grain products and cereals work perfectly well for all contemporary masturbators. In addition, happy vegetarians masturbate at least as much as chain smokers and raw-food followers. So here Mr. Graham missed his targets in every direction. He should rather have recommended overdoses of alcohol, cannabis and tobacco, if he was to have the slightest chance of achieving his bliss-less goal. It should come as no surprise that Mr. Graham, like the rest of this league, never was questioned about his insane claims. Another "Just So" story.

On the contrary, his madness inspired other "professionals" and authorities to move beyond his imagination. Scientific fundamentalists can be as little charming as religious fundamentalists. Among those inspired by Sylvester Graham was Doctor John Harvey Kellog and his brother, who in the late 1800s launched a cereal to reduce sexual desire and thus prevent masturbation.

This cereal is today known as Kellogg's Cornflakes. This may seem innocent enough, but far worse is that the same Dr. Kellogg recommended circumcision of boys in order to cure masturbation. This should preferably be performed without anesthesia, as the pain of the procedure also would have a reinforcing effect on the desired result. For girls, he suggested the use of pure carboxylic acid directly on the clitoris to dampen these abnormal sexual tensions. (12) It is quite interesting to note that to this day, circumcision of boys is the most widespread of all surgical procedures in the United States.

Circumcision of boys in USA have admittedly declined from 95% in the 60s, to less than 70% today. The number is still high when taken in to account that the overwhelming majority of the US-population are Protestants. Protestants are not being circumcised elsewhere on this planet. (13)

In Norway in the year 1846, the famous psychiatrist Dr. Sandberg published a study which showed that masturbation was the main cause of mental illness among those admitted to Gaustad hospital in Christiania (today Oslo). (14)

The psychiatric training in Norway back then, probably consisted of having completed the Christian confirmation-curriculum. And a weekend-course consisting of Dr. Martens, Graham, Kellog and Tissot's "research literature".

During this same period, Ludvig Dahl, the first Director of Medicine in Norway (the pre-cursor to which currently is called the Minister of Health), launched gymnastics as part of the education in the Norwegian school-system. Not at all a bad idea, but his over-arching goal by this move, was to counter sexual desire. He claimed that the blood accumulated in the head and abdomen when pupils were sitting still for too long periods of time. This, god forbid, would stimulate the desire to masturbate. (15)

Ludvig Dahl could possibly not have been familiar with the art of rope-climbing. This morbid attitude against masturbation still lives on in some cultures and in certain environments to this day. In 1994, US Secretary of Health, Jocelyn Elders, was fired because she suggested that masturbation should be part of sexual education in American schools. (16)

One can safely state that neither prayer, raw-food, cornflakes nor physical exercise has worked entirely according to its original intentions. But the side effects are not bad at all. Exercise is healthy, rope climbing is fun and cornflakes taste very good. Don't you agree?

CHAPTER 5

The Birth of Sexology

"It was a pure incident that brought me into contact with this field of work. As a very young physician, in 1930, I undertook to answer medical questions in a weekly magazine. Already in the first small pile of questions, one or two were touching the topic of sexuality. In my answers in the magazine's column, I sought to deal with these questions in the same way as I dealt with other questions, that is, provide simple information, built, as far as my knowledge went, on the results of the medical science at that time. The result was unexpected. It was as if I should have pressed my finger against the trigger of a machine gun and held it down. The flow of questions increased like an avalanche, and common questions about health and illness drowned in the mass of sexual issues raised." (1)

These words were written by Dr. Karl Evang in 1948 in the prologue of his book "Seksual-opplysning" (Sexual Enlightenment). Karl Evang was a pioneer regarding public education based on the research of sexology and the knowledge it had been able to produce in his time. He was also a pioneer internationally, not at least because of his courage to address these "dangerous and sinful" issues. He was certainly ahead of his time, putting "dangerous" topics on the agenda long before Kinsey made his entrance into the sexological arena. He should at least have a street or avenue named after him. People with less achievements than him, have had their names immortalized on Norwegian streets and squares.

Dr. Karl Evang was one of my first heroes, mentors and inspirators, when I as a frightened and desperate thirteen-year-old, set out on my own quest into this dark and forbidden jungle. I found Dr. Karl Evang tucked away in a bookshelf. I would eventually discover many other teachers in the back shelves of the local library. Teachers who never found their way to Haraldsvang Junior High School in Haugesund.

The establishment of the sexological science in The Modern-era can roughly be divided into two directions. On one side you'd find Jean Jaques Rousseau, Richard von Krafft-Ebing, Alfred Binet and Sigmund Slomo Freud among others. These were clearly influenced by the Abrahamic heritage. The other side consisted of sexologists such as Wilhelm Stekel, Albert Moll, and Iwan Bloch, who, with their wider perspective, may be more aptly described in a "Sumerian tradition". It was also this latter sexologicial discurse that became too threatening to the Nazi-regime.

With modernism also came the Gaussian curve (the normal distribution curve). And so the "normality" was established, more or less at the expense of much of the natural and individual variation. The Modern Era was in many ways the beginning of the explosive urge for measurement, differentiation and categorization. Typically, homosexuality as a concept actually first emerged in 1863, even before the category of heterosexuality was claimed. The sources differ a little with regard to the exact dating. However, this affected everyone, and for the first time, sexual attraction began to take the form of becoming an identity. These two categories, heterosexuality and homosexuality, were quickly adopted by the physician Richard Von Krafft-Ebing, and he is probably the "clinical godfather" for these sexual orientations. (2)

In the zeal of categorization and splitting, bisexuality eventually became "invisible". It was more or less denied, displaced and banished, far into the darkest corners of the scientific closet. Still, one might say that it had an indirect comeback as identity-confusion in Freudian psychoanalysis. This idea of bisexuality as identity-confusion still lives on among many people to this day.

As usual, the normal and abnormal were clearly differentiated, and non-heterosexual attraction turned into personal identity disorders. And with this, the seeds of homophobia were planted. Homophobia, by the way, first became a concept a hundred years later. The concept was first launched by George Weinberg in the 1960s. Homophobia will be discussed in more detail later in the book. (3)

Today it might be more fruitful to use the term biphobia instead of homophobia. It may be that it is bisexuality that is the real threat and enemy of hetero-normality. I think Naomi Mesey elaborates and substantiates such a claim quite well:

"Heterosexual people collectively try to preserve a heterosexual ethic, that is, an ethic that implies that heterosexuality has a kind of monopoly on sexual virtue. But in order for this heterosexual ethic to present itself as congruent with this virtue, homosexual ethics must be presented as congruent with immorality. The existence of this heterosexual ethic therefore depends on a view of reality based on "right and wrong", "health and illness" or heterosexual and homosexual. Mesey claims homophobia thus arises as a result of the dependence on this ethic. But, she says, the real enemy of this heterosexual ethic is not the named homosexuality, but the unnamed enemy bisexuality. By deconstructing hetero / homo binary, bisexuality reveals that it cannot be isomorphic with the virtue / immorality binary. Thus, bisexuality threatens the heterosexual ethics at the collective level, while also threatening the heterosexual identity at the individual level." (4) (5)

Richard von Krafft-Ebing was among the first to become interested in sexual "deviants". He viewed these "deviants" as people suffering from identity disorders. This was in line with the modern differentiation of humans, but also in line with Rousseau and the rest of this discourse' pathologizing of natural functions. Krafft-Ebing's theory claimed that perverse instincts were brought to life through various social factors. Not unlike Rousseau's claim, he too believed that excessive masturbation in adolescence and mutual masturbation in boarding schools could lead to homosexuality. (6) Perhaps Sylvester Graham should have thought of banning boarding schools?

But Krafft-Ebing nevertheless saw the people behind the suffering and gradually gained a more open mind in relation to their suffering. He was also willing to change his theories as he became acquainted with the people behind the diagnoses and their stories. His application of the Case-method probably made him understand things in a slightly larger and more nuanced perspective. (7)

The Case-method is perhaps one of his greatest contributions to the sexologists who succeeded him, as well as to psychiatry and psychology. We should also keep in mind that it was Dr. Richard von Krafft-Ebing who discovered the syphilis-bacterium and thus the cure for the same disorder.

When it comes to homosexuality, Krafft-Ebing changed his viewpoint radically throughout his career. Towards the end of his life, he portrayed homosexuals as completely healthy and emphasized even their importance as cultural and societal supporters and contributors. One of those who probably contributed most to this change in his view, was Dr. Carl Heinrich Ulrich. Ulrich, who was a physician too, theorized that homosexuality could be genetically conditioned. (8)

Sigmund Freud was another scientist who greatly influenced both psychiatry, psychology and sexology. And eventually also mainstream thinking in Western cultures. Freud constantly found himself in conflict with many of his contemporaries, partly as a result of his version of "The seduction hypothesis". As I mentioned in the previous chapter, this hypothesis was buried by Bell, Weinberg and Hammersmith. You will become more familiar with them during this book. All three of them have greatly contributed to the sciences of psychology and sexology.

In his theory, Freud argued that behind any neurosis lay a suppressed seduction. By seduction he meant all kinds of acts that arouse children's sexuality. This was completely in line with Krafft-Ebing's theory of "perverse instincts" that were awakened. It was also in line with the view of Jean-Jacques Rousseau. (9)

In other words, Freud spoke of these inclinations as innate and which therefore also could be aroused. Before Freud came up with his theories on child-sexuality, it was already recognized among his colleagues that children were sexual. If anyone is to be awarded the pioneer title and the Nobel Prize in that regard, it should be Dr. Albert Moll. (10)

Although Freud also found that children from the very beginning have a general desire for pleasure that gradually targets the environment, especially the parents, it was the sexologist Albert Moll (1862-1939) who asserted that children had a natural sexuality with which they were born. Not innate perversions that had to be tamed, like Freud and his followers would have it (11)

Freud also believed that masturbation led to neurasthenia (see explanation below) and that cessation of it led to anxiety neurosis. His theory that the child was born polymorphic pervert (see below) meant that all sexual preferences were innate. And that it was the development of shame that made the child suppress the "sickly" sexuality. (12) Meaning all sexual expressions except conventional heterosexual desires. He claimed that it was through shame that sexuality was directed at reproduction. In a brutal way, one may say that shame through Freud had been "transformed" into both an educational- and a "therapeutic" method.

Neurasthenia means nerve impairment, neurotic fatigue both psychologically and physically, as well as experiencing unclear body pain. Polymorphism means multiple forms. As an example: The elemental carbon can act as both diamond and graphite. (13)

"Contempt is always nourished by self-contempt" – Dr. Finn Skaarderud

Later in life Freud wrote to a friend and colleague of his, Dr Zandor Ferenci, that he had overcome his own homosexual tendencies. Moreover, he gradually became uncertain regarding what to think about bisexuality. (14)

But Freud's claims about the "polymorphic perverse" child meant that all "perverse" sexual talents were innate, including bisexuality.

Interestingly, this has had to include himself too. Perhaps it was his own bisexuality he referred to in his letter-conversations with Ferenczi. Could it also be that he along the way became aware of his own projections of his denied or suppressed sexual feelings? Who knows?

In his excellent book "Eroticism and Fundamentalism", Thore Langfeldt points out that Freud eventually found that boys masturbating together did not necessarily become homosexuals. At the turn of the 20th century, Freud's theories on sexuality were in stark contrast to the views of the social radicals and the new sexology, among them Stekel, Moll and Bloch.

Contrary to Stekel et.al, Freud believed that sexual intercourse was the only normal expression of sexuality. He also believed that women had a weaker identity than men, and therefore were more easily seduced into perverse acts than men. (15)

CHAPTER 6

The Old Order is being put Under Hard Pressure

"By this I know the scholar: What he does not understand is disbelief; what he has not touched doesn't exist; what he has not measured is illusion; what he has not weighed, has no weight..."

From Goethe's Faust

If a woman is soulful normally developed and has received a good upbringing, her sex drive is very small. If it were not so, the whole world would be transformed into a brothel and it would be impossible to marry and start a family"

Dr. Joseph G. Richardson. Professor of Hygiene
at the University of Pensylvania. 1909

Sexological entrepreneural spirit

As we have seen, the field of sexology can be roughly divided into two directions: those who followed in Rousseau's footsteps who believed in the "epidemical" seduction and the life-threatening masturbation, such as, Binet, Krafft-Ebing and Freud, and on the other hand Stekel, Moll and Bloch who claimed that the child was born with an innate natural sexuality. The latter ones also asserted that mutual masturbation was harmless.

Dr. Wilhelm Stekel claimed that if a child ceased masturbating it was because the parents, or others in their environment punished them for it. Dr. Stekel thought most children masturbated from when they were young, but kept it hidden from the time Freud called "The Latency Period. Stekel also claimed that we are all born bisexual. (1)

Iwan Bloch was one of the first to introduce anthropological and ethnological methods (see concepts) to better understand sexual phenomena. Such an interdisciplinary approach contributed to a far more nuanced view, knowledge and understanding. Albert Moll, in turn, rejected both the seduction-theory and the claim that masturbation was harmful. Furthermore he documented that Freud was wrong. (2) Dr. Moll was later supported by Bell, Hammersmith and Weinberg's extensive research in the late 1970s.

Historical and anthropological studies documented already at that time, the prevalence of bi- and homosexuality. The Greeks' tribute and cultivation of this kind of love was obviously on par with other high-valued cultural expressions. Thus this was good enough evidence that they were not ill. If so, one would also have to judge the fruits of Greek philosophy as madness (!) Observations which showed that men who for various reasons at various times had sex with each other, were neither ill nor degenerate. They were most likely bisexual.

It's safe to say that some of the above mentioned pioneers helped lifting the field of sexology from a belief-system (scientism) consisting of assumptions and prejudice, to a much higher and more professional level based on scientific knowledge.

While Stekel, Moll and Bloch and their followers struggled against the sexual oppression of women and homosexuality, as well as being supporters of birth control and free abortion, Freud and his disciples continued the suppression of women's sexual life, among other things.

I don't want to let go of Freud quite yet. Sigmund Freud divided the development from child to adult into what he called the psychosexual stages. He described the development of the child through 5 such different stages. The first stage he called *The Oral stage*, where sucking is the sexual form of expression. The second stage, *The Anal stage,* in which defecating is a sexual pleasure. The third stage, *The Phallic stage,* where the genitals become central. By the way, *Phallic* means erect penis. The fourth stage, *The Latency stage,* during which Freud assumed that the child was asexual. The fifth and final stage he called *The Genital stage.*

His formulation of this last stage is interesting: "The genital stage is the stage in which the genitals are developed and matured, and the individual is enabled to assume *the sexual role that the child's culture outlines.*" (3) (My italics)

In other words, he argued that heterosexuality is learned, it is what culture shapes the child to become during this genital psychosexual stage. He must have meant that since most cultures are hetero-culturally organized. After all, he also claimed that all children were born "poly-morphically perverse", meaning born with all sexual desires as potential opportunities.

If heterosexuality is learned, and at the same time claiming that homosexuality among adults is the expression of failed cultural indoctrination (or learning), then it's logical to assume that bisexuality is the foundation, and that both hetero- and homo-sexualities are the result of external influencing factors. In other words, environmental factors.

His claim that children were sexually inactive during the latency period was probably due to the fact that they had gone "underground" (under their bed-quilts) with their sexual desires, solidly infected by feelings of shame and guilt due to adults' judgmental index fingers.

This Freudian psychosexual stage has become one of the great false notions of sexuality, both psychologically and sexologically in modern times. A performance that still lives on in many cultures and in many people's minds to this day.

Sigmund Freud's psychoanalytical view of bisexuality, was to see it as an arrested development during the psychosexual stages from child to adult. The result of this has been a solid denial and suppression of bisexuality on all levels, from religious through, cultural, subcultural, psychosocial and individual levels.

Freud's psychosexual stages have thus become a solid psychosocial stigmatization of many different sexual feelings in a large part of the population. In parallel, this has led to the indoctrination of heterosexuality as the most healthy, normal and desired orientation. In short, these so-called psychosexual stages have become a crash-course in shaming, denying and suppression of sexual feelings that do not fit into this narrow view. The psychosexual "Latency stage", along with the "Genital stage" begs to be renamed as: "The Psychosexual Stages of Denial and Suppression".

Sexology becomes dangerous

It was otherwise a very important scientific work that was done in the field of sexology in Germany during this period. Especially during the 1920s and until the Nazis took over. Germany was a pioneering country in the advancement of scientific sexological research until 1933.

During this same period, doctors, sexologists and artists focused on, among other things, the woman's situation. They promoted equality between the sexes and the right to free abortion. They believed that masturbation was healthy and that the ban on homosexuality should be decriminalized. It was a fruitful period for scientific sexology that the world had never seen before. For the first time, world congresses were held in sexology. Scientists from all over the world had become concerned with this subject. (4)

It is discouraging to think of the Nazis' extinction of all the sexological research literature that did not support the narrow reproductive Abrahamic-inspired view. There are similarities to the persecution of the Jews. But unlike the latter, there is little mentioning of the annihilation of the sexological research literature, and the persecution of the researchers, in textbooks. The persecution of these scientists also led to a shortage of professionals to pursue the sexological science after WW2.

The persecution and terrorizing of the non-heterosexuals as well as the people who defended them, is also absent in the literature used in our schools today. It's difficult to find other historical examples where almost an entire science with its scientists nearly was exterminated because of a warped ideology and a bitter and frustrated young man who in the first place wanted to become an artist, and who probably was homosexual himself.

At least according to Dr. Lothar Machtan at the University of Bremen. Dr. Machtan is a Professor of History, specializing in modern and contemporary history. In 2001 he published a book entitled "The Hidden Hitler". In his book he claims that Hitler was homosexual.

One of the sources Machtar refers to is the memoirs of Hans Mend, in which Mend, who was one of Hitler's fellow soldiers during World War I, says that he, Hitler, was the lover of a soldier named Ernst Schmidt. And that they were almost inseparable lovers while being soldiers at the front during W.W1. Hitler was also arrested by the Vienna police after the war for his homosexual inclinations. At that time, Hitler was a completely unknown person. Dr. Machtar also claims that Ernst Rohm, the leader of Hitler's storm troops during World War II, as part of an extortion threatened to reveal Hitler's gay orientation. And that this allegedly was the reason for the execution of Rohm. And many others. Rohm himself was gay too. However, there is a great deal of disagreement regarding Dr. Machtan's claims. (5) (6)

The Norwegian psychologist Astri Bastiansen included in her book "Den tusende dråpe" (The Thousand Drop) a psychological profile of Adolf Hitler. Here she points out, among other things, Hitler's intense hatred towards Jews, Catholics and Czechs, among others. Although she doesn't mention anything about his homophobia in her analysis of Hitler's hatred, she suggests that his hate is based on projection (See Concepts).

She justifies his hatred on the fact that Hitler was abused as a small child, but also despised by his stepfather, who was a Catholic. Hitler also held an incomprehensible hatred towards Czechs. Which in turn led to his desire to wipe out all of Czechoslovakia as a nation. This despite the fact that his only friend as a young man was a Czech boy!

His intense hatred towards Jews may be related to the fact that his biological father, who never was present in Little Adolf's life, probably was a Jew. Hitler's mother served with a Jewish middle-class family when she became pregnant with Adolf. In that case, Adolf Hitler was partly Jewish himself. (7)

If we add Hitler's intense homophobia, along with Lothar Machtan's claims into Astri Bastiansen's "equation", then it's far from incomprehensible that Hitler actually was gay or bisexual. This along with the fact that he lied about being impotent as a result of syphilis and therefore could never start a family. Syphilis has never been confirmed in any of his medical records after the war. And if we finally brings the Czech boy into the same "equation", then his incomprehensible hatred towards Czechs might be a little bit easier to see.

In a later chapter I will illuminate the phenomenon of homophobia as a function of projected homosexual feelings, in a broader perspective. And among other things, you will become acquainted with another Nazi, a contemporary Nazi.

After World War II, the world felt such an intense hatred and disdain for everything that was German that the scarce research and sexual knowledge that survived, was soon "forgotten". By now it was the American culture that greatly started to influence both the psychology and the sexology in the "free world". (8)

CHAPTER 7

The Early Research on Homosexuality

"Scientific fundamentalists are no more charming than religious fundamentalists"

Richard Bruvoll Jr.

Von Krafft-Ebing and Freud were, as we have seen, among the first to study the phenomenon of homosexuality, but then as an abnormality. Although both Krafft-Ebing and Freud changed their points of view later in life, their early fingerprints are still visible.

On that note I will present a psychodynamic explanation of homosexuality as a diagnosis. This psychodynamic diagnosis is a result off Freud's successors being "frozen" in several of his previously ill-founded hypotheses. These successors of Freud are largely to blame for what has now become a relatively widespread general explanation of male homosexuality. This despite the existence of a considerable amount of empirical research which totally rejects this hypothesis. The hypothesis is called "The Triangular Situation".

"The Triangular situation", in short, claims that men become gay as a result of a dominant mother and an absent father. It was as late as 1992 still maintained by many psychoanalysts, among them Dr. Otto Kernberg. The author of this hypothesis, Irving Bieber, found that this situation was typical of his gay patients. It was later refuted by Bell and

Weinberg's research. Later studies from Germany, Australia and the US also asserts that such a situation is no more typical for homosexuals than for heterosexuals. (1)

This hypothesis can also serve as a frightening example of unsustainability by generalizing findings from clinical data to entire populations. This phenomenon is not uncommon in both psychoanalysis and the more recent revised version, psychodynamic-theory. Whether psychoanalysis can be classified as a scientific theory at all is disputed by many. Among them is the psychologist Barbara Engler.

Barbara Engler explains an important difference between a scientific and a philosophical theory in her book "Personality Theories". Here she emphasizes that scientific claims can be falsified through observations and experiments, while philosophical assumptions are always associated with their underlying epiphany visions, it just has to be that way, it seems so natural. (Just so stories). Furthermore, it is impossible to design a test or set up an experiment to confirm or debunk a philosophical assumption. Just as it is with religions and ideologies. (2)

From conversion to weaning, or from exorcism to reparative "therapies"

In a positive sense, homosexuality was now placed on the scientific map as a phenomenon that should be a subject of further investigation. In that regard, Sigmund S. Freud somehow made his contribution. One might say that the knowledge of homosexual behavior, on its path from sin to pathology, had been hidden under the bed-quilts of the provisional "Latency-stage".

It may seem that Krafft-Ebing's construction of homosexuality as a diagnosis, and Freud's early conclusions about the origin of homosexuality, have contributed to a meta-theoretical view that homosexuality should be studied as a pathological phenomenon, implicitly; "To find a cure".

This resulted in a later approach, used by clinical psychologists and psychiatrists to determine the presence of a mental disorder. "The

Family Resemblance Approach" it was called. This approach shows how easy it has been to conduct individual pathologizing and suppression of what can often be proved to be a cultural rather than an individual abnormality.

"The Family Resemblance Approach" was based on a cultural view of what is normal or abnormal. Abnormal behavior means deviations from "normal" behavior in the mainstream of the current culture. What has been classified as abnormal has changed as much from time to time as from one place to another. And therefor it doesn't have any universal relevance, nor universal scientific relevance. The model consists of criteria such as:

Suffering - Misalignment, (to what? To heterosexuality? To the culture?) - Unintelligible and irrational behavior - Unpredictability and loss of control - Unconventional and lively behavior - The observer's discomfort, (many people may still feel discomfort by watching two men, or two women kissing in public) - Violation of moral and ideal norms, (Who's moral norms, and what is an ideal norm?)

(My comments in parenthesis)

This method was still in use when I was a psychology student. I even chose this as an exam assignment back then. And I failed the exam, because I had strong opinions about it, which I was not allowed to have at that level of the study. When I search the web these days it is hard to track the literature on this subject, I will assume it is scrapped. I hope so. Some definitions of the above can be found in the source references in the appendix section. (3)

Especially the latter: "Violation of moral and ideal norms" can very easily be abused. In most cultures, this criterion would be sufficient to categorize homosexual behavior as a mental disorder. In some cultures this can also be used to label certain religious followers or political opponents as mentally disturbed. That is exactly what the psychiatry in the former Soviet Union did. As well as many other regimes have done, and unfortunately some still do.

According to this model, not all the criteria needed to be met. One single criteria could be sufficient. This type of thinking, along with cultural rejection and religious condemnation, has led to persecution, oppression and death for an unknown number of culturally disobedient individuals. And this is too often done in the name of science. The disobedience itself has often been reason enough to "cure" the deviant ones.

In this connection, it is worth warning about the danger of generally accepting dogmatic explanations coming from both psychiatry and clinical psychology. Neither of these are exact sciences such as physics. There are few objective or absolute answers to questions concerning individual human behavior.

One terrifying example that makes most of us freeze is lobotomy. Lobotomy was practiced in Norway between 1941 and 1974. Lobotomy is a surgical procedure that involves destroying the frontal lobe of the brain. In most cases, the ability to feel, as well as to reason, was destroyed. Some also showed a zombie-like behavior after the procedure. This was used as a treatment method for anxiety, but also in most cases of schizophrenia and in some cases of homosexuality.

Regarding homosexuals, psychiatry also utilized castration. Perhaps the most perverse use of lobotomy was to bring calm to psychiatric wards. Moreover, the procedure itself was life-threatening. Up to the mid-1950s, every fourth patient died as a result of the procedure itself. Or rather, the abuse. Gypsies were also exposed to these and other abuses from both psychiatry, the church and other societal authorities. (4) (5) (6) (7)

And to complete this madness, let me finally add that Doctor Antonio Egaz Monis was awarded the Nobel Prize in 1949 for his "invention" of lobotomy as a psychiatric treatment method. (8)

CHAPTER 8

Identity – Heterosexuality and Homosexuality

Theory and research

Part I: Who am I, and why am I

"Juno increasingly recognized this" invisible "pain in others. He decided to do something about it, get an education, authority. He needed to be heard! Juno had his wake up-call. He was also terribly tired of waiting. Waiting to be accepted, waiting to be respected, to be seen. But most of all, it was probably himself he was most tired of waiting for (!) He had to do something ..."

Excerpt from TRAX

To be degraded and harassed for something you cannot change is the worst thing a person can be socially exposed to.

"Theater Bjørn Erik is over for this time, the last act is playing now. The curtains will soon fall. It's a relief to finish it. It takes its toll playing this role. I don't wish to live anymore, I don't want to act anymore, I resign the role of Bjørn Erik. It's over. The final Curtain-fall." (1)

These words are the last words Bjørn Erik wrote in his diary before he ended his life. In his diary he also wrote that he did not belong to God. He fell in love with boys, and hence felt like he was constantly sinning. He thought that this kind of sinful thoughts were the worse. Bjørn Erik considered himself as a Christian. He was a boy who just wanted to spread joy to others. But because of his unaccepted sexual-orientation, he called himself "Dirty, Sinful Me".

The story about Bjørn Erik eventually became a movie. In this movie we get a very close look at the evil he was exposed to. Not at least from a preacher in Seiers-kirken (The Victory Church) in Oslo. It seems like this preacher's life-mission was to "cure" homosexuals and save them from this sinful way of life. (2)

Bjørn Erik obviously despised his own identity. He is a tragic example of internalizing others contempt for him, and then ending up by being the main-perpetrator of himself. Unfortunately this is far from uncommon among young non-heterosexuals. It is also common among non-white minorities in white majority cultures. I will elaborate internalized homophobia more thoroughly later in this chapter.

Let's have a look into the concept of identity, there are several definitions of this term. I will not elaborate on all of these, but use a definitions that I believe is relevant to understand some of the topics in this book. This relevant definition is:

Identity as personal identity: Here we distinguish between *I* and *Me*. Self-identity is what every person perceives as typical of him or her. The activity of the *I* constantly changes the *Me*, which in turn changes the way the *I* perceives it. This dialectical interaction between *I* and *Me* is crucial to the development of the personality. (3)

Let's try to elaborate the term *Identity* at the intersection of nature / nurture. A lot of research have been done to uncover the cause of homosexuality. There are some studies that show a fairly stable correlation between a-typical gender-role behavior (gender-non-conformity) and homosexuality. But there are various explanations for gender role-typical behavior and gender-role atypical behavior. Some believe it has to do with pre- and postnatal hormonal development. (4)

Others are looking for direct genetic causes. (5) But the various biological explanations are poorly founded. Some of them have been completely rejected by scientists within those same disciplines. I will get deeper into this in due course.

Some have tried to look for the genetic missing link among mono-zygotic twins, such as Bailey and Pillard. They searched for homosexuals who were also twins. They found that if one in a mono-zygotic twin-pair was gay, the chance of the other also being gay was 52%. Part of the problem with this study was that they specifically searched for gay respondents. The research was not based on a general selection of mono-zygotic twins. (6)

Another interesting observation regarding this study is that if an exclusive gene for homo-sexuality exists, then every single twin in this study should have been gay. And if there exist a gene for heterosexuality? Well, then all the twins in this study should have been heterosexual. What about the environment? Well, it's an established fact that mono-zygotic twins share all environmental factors. Unlike their siblings.

In this case, epi-genetics might be an explanatory path to follow. But if this mono-zygotic riddle has an epigenetic explanation, then that would mean that we all have both hetero- and homo genes in us. And that these genes can be switched on or off. Or, as in the case with bisexuals, all the switches are on, "or all lights are lit"?

Still others are searching evidence for "The gay brain", not unlike the desperate pursuit of "The female brain". Speaking of the latter chase, so far no convincing data has been found to support such a claim. In a comment on the continued pursuit of "The female brain", neuro scientist Marcel Kinsbourne stated that it seems that this desperation is so great that if no differences are found, they have to invent them. (7)

The fact that this pursuit of female and gay brains has been devoted to such enormous interest among researchers, is probably due to the fact that, culturally speaking, we have "glued" sexual orientations to the gender-role identities. Most research done by old hetero white men, but not all, the following researcher is an exception to the rule.

Simon LeVay is one of those researchers hunting for "The gay brain". He examined the brain structures of 42 deceased individuals. Their brains were compared and he claimed to have found a difference in a brain structure called the anterior hypothalamus. This part of the brain is the size of a grain of sand. He concluded that this tiny part of the brain was twice as large among those in the sample who were considered as heterosexual men, compared to the homosexuals and the women in this sample. (8)

Some of the criticisms regarding LeVay's study were that they had neither counted the amount nor measured the density of the brain cells in this study. In addition, five of the nineteen homosexuals, as well as two of the six women, had equal brain-structures as the heterosexual men. All the gay men in the study died as a result of AIDS, and it is well known that AIDS is a disease that also affects the brain. A later study found similar differences regarding deceased transgender people and others. They probably had the same "small" anterior hypothalamus as LeVay's deceased women and gay men. (8)

However, in this transsexual study, which also included heterosexual and homosexual men, they found that the transsexuals had smaller anterior hypothalamus than the rest. But, they found no differences in the brain structures between the heterosexual and the homosexual men. Regarding the transsexuals, they had undergone massive hormone therapy, which is also known to affect the brain. As a prelude to these studies, researcher Marc Breedlove reminded that if one were to find structural brain differences, one cannot know for certain whether they are causes or effects. (8)

And then we have all the testosterone hypotheses regarding homosexuality. I'm not going to go into details here, just state that they've all been discarded. But some of this research can be somewhat entertaining. Like in a study where they injected solid amounts of the hormone testosterone into gay men. Result, they didn't become more straight, they simply got much more horny with men. (9) Is it fair to say they became more gay than they were before the "cure"?

Another problem with biological research has been the causal assumption. It seems like it's far too tempting to assume a causation from physiology to psychology, just because of a correlation between them, biologist Ruth Hubbard reminds us.

She argues that if a society arbitrarily divides the children into two groups, one being dressed in short skirts and being told that they must move in manner that avoids exposure of their panties. Whereas the other group is dressed in overalls and encouraged to climb trees, play ball games and other (instrumental) activities.

Then let's fast forward to puberty, where those wearing trousers are encouraged to eat like a growing boy, whereupon the other group is warned to mind their weight. Then both those who have tottered about on high heels, as well as the other group that have run around in sneakers, will both be biologically and socially different. Sociologist Michael S. Kimmel's sarcastic comment is that we have yet to find the gene that carries the belief in nature over nurture (10) What a great idea for a genetic study, anyone?

Still others, such as the social constructivists, believe it is only the environment. (11) And yet others take a middle perspective, such as social psychologist Daryl Bem with his theory: "Exotic Becomes Erotic". Before I dive into Bem's theory, I will briefly refer to different types of temperament and the significance these may have for a heritage-environment interaction.

Research shows that as newborns we are quite different, these inequalities have been measured and graded along three different temperament dimensions: the social, the emotional and the active dimensions. As an example, one child may be shy and anxious and another outgoing and uninhibited. These are both examples of the social dimension. This social dimension may also be a precursor to introvert or extrovert behavior in adulthood. (12)

It's said that our genetic inheritance, our genotype, in interaction with the environment is influencing our personal traits and behaviors. This process will later on determine our phenotype. From the very first moment, we trigger reactions in the environment around us, which in turn confirm and reinforce our basic traits. (13)

Three different types of interactions are mentioned: Passive, Evocative and Proactive. The passive is the one that is already present in the form of inheritance from the parents. Both directly, but also indirectly, in that they themselves organize an upbringing environment in line with their own preferences and interests.

The evocative interaction consists in other people's tendency to respond in line with the child's genotype. For example, a social child is more likely to attract the attention of other people than a shy and withdrawn child. The third, the proactive interaction, occurs later on as a result of more independence and thus also opportunities to seek out and choose environments that better match one's own genotype. (14)

It is believed that part of the personality is well rooted in the genotype. Good examples of this are found in twin studies where mono-zygotic twins who are separated at birth and thus are being raised in different families and environments. Nevertheless they score very similarly in tests of personality traits as adults. I will go into more details about this phenomenon in chapter 19.

Has anyone done research on heterosexuality? What's the origin of heterosexuality?

Why do some become heterosexuals? Is it a choice?

"The fish is the last one to discover water" Chinese proverb

"When did you discover that you are heterosexual?" How did you react, honestly, when you became aware of it? Did you tell anyone? Did you tell your parents? If so, how did they react when you confessed that you're heterosexual? Have you ever come to some kind of reconciliation of being heterosexual?"

When on the road with the show TRAX, I once in a while do the above mentioned "quiz" in the audience. This shows how blind most of us can be with regard to our own observation, or lack of taking the others perspective, out there on the great ocean of "normality".

Let's get back to Dr. Bem. In his theory "Exotic Becomes Erotic", Daryl Bem has based his theoretical research on a wide range of existing research, including much of the above mentioned. From this pool he has constructed a theory which he claims can explain both homosexuality and heterosexuality. The latter is possibly the most revolutionary with his theory. Not many researchers have posed the question: How did heterosexuality emerge? What is its origin?

In short, Bem's theory claims that biological variables in themselves, including genetic, hormonal, and neurophysiological variables, do not directly lead to a heterosexual or a homosexual orientation, but to childhood temperaments that influence the child's preference for normative or deviant gender behavior.

These preferences lead the child to feel different from the opposite gender, or in some cases different to it's own gender. Later in the development process, the child will then experience this difference as "exotic". This in turn will lead to an elevated physiological arousal which eventually will be "eroticized".

When it comes to homosexuality, Bem points out that all previous theories on the causes of homosexuality received virtually zero support from the most comprehensive study done in this field. I referred to this study in a previous chapter, the one conducted by Bell, Weinberg and Hammersmith. In 1981 they interviewed 1000 gay and 500 heterosexuals of both sexes. In their study they tested several theories on the causation of homosexuality, including the behaviorist theory (2'Force) and the psychoanalytic theory (1'Force). None of them were supported by the findings in Bell, Weinberg and Hammersmith's comprehensive research (15)

However, Bell, Weinberg and Hammersmith's study did lend some support regarding the correlation between deviant gender behavior and non-heterosexuality. (Bisexual or gay) Respectively, 71% and 70% of non-heterosexual men and women felt different from their own gender normative behavior in childhood. Only 8% of heterosexuals felt the same way. These findings have also been confirmed by a meta-analysis (See Concepts) conducted by Bailey & Zucker in 1995, based on data from 48 other similar studies. (16) (17)

Let me emphasize that the reports of feeling different from their own gender-role in Bell et. al's study did not necessarily mean that they identified themselves more with the opposite gender's behavior. It's also important to note that these data were retrospective. That is, the experiences they had as a child, were observations done with their adult's "eyes".

Regarding Bem's theory, it implicitly points to a "neutral" sexual orientation as the basis for hetero- and homosexuality, by arguing that none of the biological factors directly leads to a specific sexual orientation. We will take a closer look at this in Chapter 19.

The EBE theory (Exotic Becomes Erotic) Daryl Bem claims, is also an attempt to unite the two "trenches" within this research, namely essentialism and constructivism (Nature versus Nurture). These two perspectives are thoroughly described in the third part of the book.

Another claim for the link between "deviant" gender-typical behavior and non-heterosexuals, was promoted by a psychiatrist named Richard Green. In 1987 he presented a new study based on research on gender-role behavior and the development of homosexuality. In this study, 27% of the 55 participants, were submitted to therapy in order to be treated for their so-called deviant gender-role behavior. (18) (19) (20)

All of the 55 boys that Dr. Green selected for his study were what Green himself called "sissy-boys". They enjoyed playing with dolls as well as doing household chores in general. Dr. Green claimed that these children had a four times greater risk of developing gay behavior than those he called non-feminine boys. The purpose of his study was to prevent homosexuality.

In addition to therapy, the boys in the 27%-group ("The sissy-boys"), were all influenced or coached by their parents to participate in gender-specific activities under supervising from Dr. Green. And all to no avail. The result showed that 75% of them still "became" bisexual or gay. In fact, there was a one percentage-point higher proportion of those who went into "therapy" who later acknowledged gay attraction, compared to those who were not treated, 74% of them later acknowledged gay attraction. (18) (19) (20)

The only thing of importance that Dr. Green's study revealed, was that individual therapy and behavioral group-therapy methods do not work at all regarding conversion, or suppression of sexual orientations. Not even in children. This despite the well known fact from psychological research, which asserts that children are far more malleable than adults on most levels. Green's study was later omitted from Bem's later publications of the EBE theory (!)

Green's findings should be a sign of warning to everyone who is still obsessed with the idea of "repairing" non-heterosexual love. Nevertheless, this kind of "therapy", or rather clinical sexual abuse, still exists in several countries. Fortunately, most of the countries in the Western world have abandoned this practice, and many of them have also totally banned this form of intervention, or as I prefer to call it, abuse.

When it comes to the selection of participants in Richard Green's study, one of the central, almost unison criticisms, was that the behavior of these boys was very rare. So rare that Dr. Green had great difficulty finding participants who would fit in with his "sissy-boy" definition. The critics therefore claimed that this study did not in any way reflect the majority of homosexual behavior in the population otherwise. (21)

If we try to see the attitudes and behaviors of young non-heterosexuals through Cooley's "Looking-Glass Self" (see below) and how this may affect their self-esteem, we will also see a process in which the inner conflicts and mental pain are being reinforced. One might call this a psychological form of "Hexing."

Charles Horton Cooley argued that pride and shame are the primary social emotions, and that they are largely related to our relationships. He regarded them as the social self-feelings, which included every feeling that we direct towards our own selves. We don't think much about it as long as we are fairly accepted and confirmed by our surroundings. (23)

Self-monitoring he suggested, was made up of three basic elements: 1) The imagination of our appearance to the other person 2) The imagination of his judgment of that appearance 3) And as a result of the previous two, some sort of self-feeling such as pride or shame. And finally the self-esteem as a result of this. He also pointed out that our social monitoring of ourselves is going on constantly. Even when we are alone. And social self-monitoring always involves an evaluation of ourselves, which will eventually culminate into one of the two social self-feelings, either pride or shame. (22)

This process may be a bit easier to understand in the light of both William James' and C.H Cooley's theories. William James, one of America's most important contributors to the field of psychology, and Cooley, both mentioned that if we were to study ourselves we would have to study our inner selves. James distinguished between two types of self-awareness, a subjective and thinking *I*, and an objective *I* as *me*. (The *I* and *Me*). Self-perception can thus be described as what we think of ourselves, the characteristics of *Me*. He also asserted that our self-concept is affected by our relationships. (23)

However, according to these dynamics, the young person may become involved in the stigmatization and traumatization of himself or herself. In such a perspective one can only wonder how much mental pain Dr. Green's "Sissy-children" have been suffering, caused by the psychiatrists, psychologists and parents in these studies. And ultimately, of their own internalized self-contempt.

If we add what the psychologist and sociologist Thomas Scheff writes about low-status individuals in subdominant groups, we get a pretty good description of the stigma and degradation many of these young non-heterosexuals undergo every day. Not only do they experience a lack of dignity in the outer world, but in order to get through the day they also have to take the dominant group's view: This is how Dr. Scheff describes it:

"A powerful source of self-generated shame". "In order to get through each day, they must often take the view of the dominant group, thus view themselves through the eyes of the scornful others" (24)

Assuming a purely environmental causation perspective, as hardcore behaviorists and social constructionists do, it becomes difficult to explain why these young bisexuals and homosexuals do not become heterosexual, especially when you think about all the massive heteronormative influences they are bombarded with from day one. To the extent that they might be affected by this heteronormative brainwashing, must be that they become actors. Namely, pretending to be heterosexual, combined with a solid dose (overdose?) of self-denial in a desperate attempt to gain acceptance from the others out there in that big stage-performance we call "reality".

In some cases, it can lead to the suppression of their own sexual feelings, and with respect to the latter, this can result in projected self-contempt expressed as homophobia. Disowned or suppressed sexual feelings, which in turn are being directed outwards as hatred and disdain towards others with the same tendencies, or supposedly the same tendencies. As a result, they become active participants in the entire traumatization process. This have been confirmed by several studies.

Part II: Internalized and externalized homophobia

Dr. Henry Adams, an American psychiatrist and his research team, conducted a laboratory experiment based on the above. He wanted to test this hypothesis whether homophobia could be an expression of repressed homosexual feelings in people who either did not realize it or who denied such feelings. Homophobia is defined as: horror, anxiety, anger, discomfort and aversion to homosexuality. The presence of homophobia was measured by using a self-report scale called "The Index of Homophobia".

The experiment involved 35 homophobic and 29 non-homophobic men, all of whom reported to be exclusively heterosexual. In the laboratory, they were mounted with an instrument that measures blood flow in the penis. Then they were shown three four-minute erotic videos with hetero, lesbian and homoerotic content respectively. As many as 80% of the homophobic men showed signs of erection when watching the homoerotic video. 54% of them full erection. The results for the non-homophobic men were 34% and 24% respectively. (25)

Everyone reacted more or less alike to the other two videos of lesbian and heterosexual content. When they were subsequently asked to give their own assessment of the reactions, the homophobic men typically underestimated their physical reactions on the homoerotic video. Thus, Adams et.al received support for the hypothesis to test. (25)

The loudness of some homophobes also becomes a little more understandable in the light of Psychologist Helen Lewis's famous words:

"Some people rather turn the world upside down, than themselves inside out."

There is also another hypothesis which claims that anxiety can also cause such reactions. But if homosexual stimuli were to cause anxiety in the homophobic men, which in turn caused erection, then this hypothesis should be ruled out by the non-homophobic men who also experienced erections. Anyway the hypothesis is widely debated and in this case not convincing. (26)

What about the 20 percent of the homophobes in Dr. Adam's study who didn't experience erections at all? It is conceivable that the kind of eroticism presented in this study was wrong for them, or maybe the age of the porn-actors were wrong? Not everyone get turned on by the same things. This applies to all sexual orientations. Just google the porn sites on the web, and you'll soon find that there are endless many hetero-sexualities, homo-sexualities and bisexualities. And then there is the endless variety of para-philias. The latter is discussed in more detail in Part III.

Another criticism of the Adams study is that the sample was small, and that they should also have included women, as well as a control group consisting exclusively of homosexuals.

Regarding the anxiety hypothesis, it seems to me a bit too "exotic". Probably very few of us get erected when we discover that the neighbor's psychotic Rottweiler is on the loose. But, of course, it can be a hitherto undiscovered paraphilia.

There are studies and laboratory experiments that show that being exposed to anxiety-producing film-clips can lead to increased sexual arousal. Afterwards. (27) This was not the case in the Adams study, they were measured while they were watching the erotic videos. Not afterwards.

It is also interesting that the homophobes in Dr. Adam's study physically reacted much like the non-homophobic men while watching the hetero-erotic and lesbian videos. This may indicate that the sexologist and endocrinologist John Money's description of homophobia as "malignant bisexuality", may not be very far from the truth.

Otherwise, there is more recent research on the phenomenon of homophobia that I find far more interesting than Dr. Adams'study. Especially because of the creative design and the experimental layout. It also reveals the participants' unconscious reactions:

Netta Weinstein, William Ryan, Cody DeHaan and Andrew Przybylski examined six studies from the US and Germany with a total of 784 respondents. Participants were asked to rate themselves on a ten-point scale to what extent they were heterosexual or homosexual oriented. The participants were then measured, using a computer-controlled test, to confirm their implicit (actual) sexual orientation. During the test itself, they were shown pictures and words indicating heterosexuality or homosexuality. They were asked to sort them into categories such as queer or straight (gay or straight) as soon as possible. The computers then measured their response time. (28)

What participants did not know was that in front of each picture and word, the word "me" or "others" flashed across the screen for 35 milliseconds. This is long enough for it to be treated unconsciously, while it is impossible to see or perceive it consciously. The method is called semantic association and assumes that if the word "me" flashes up before pictures or words that reflect your own sexual orientation, you will sort these pictures or words into their proper category faster than if the word "me" appears before a picture which does not conform to your own sexual orientation. The method has in previous attempts proved to be reliable by being able to distinguish self-identified heterosexuals, homosexuals, bisexuals and lesbians. (28)

Using this method, they were able to identify a subgroup that indicated degrees of same-sex attraction, despite the fact that the same people graded themselves as predominantly heterosexual. In fact, more than 20% of the self-identified heterosexual participants showed same-sex attractions. This same group was also far more likely than the other participants to flag anti-gay attitudes, as well as being willing to impose far stricter penalties for insignificant offenses, if committed by supposed homosexuals, i.e homophobia. The latter was also measured using the same method. (28)

They also found that those of the participants who had supportive and inclusive parents were more in touch with their basic (implicit) sexual orientation, and also less homophobic. In contrast to the group that self-identified as heterosexual but showed same-sex attractions. The members of the latter group were far more often raised by parents who were controlling, unaccepting and prejudiced toward gays. (28)

Regarding the part of this study that identified upbringing patterns as a contributing factor, there's extensive research to support this. Research which unfortunately is relatively unknown to many psychologists, psychiatrists and sexologists. You will learn more about this in Chapter 17.

The famous American TV-preacher, homophobic and anti-gay activist, Billy James Hargis, may serve as a glaringly example of externalized homophobia. He also fits like hand in glove with John Money's hypothesis of homophobia as malignant bisexuality.

Mr. Hargis' projected malignant bisexuality was revealed by a young couple whom he himself had previously married. On the wedding night, this couple revealed to each-other that they, many years earlier, had been sexually abused by the same Mr. Hargis. The case attracted a great deal of media-attention throughout the North American continent. (29)

It probably doesn't come as a shock that his career as a charismatic TV-evangelist and anti-gay activist abruptly ended. Billy James Hargis case represents only the top of a giant repressed sexual iceberg. Eventually, he was followed by an army of evangelical preachers and priests. As well as countless other religious or non-religious "gurus", whom all turned out to be not quite as heterosexual as they claimed to be.

Incidentally, there are strikingly many people, most often religious people, who believe that acceptance of same-sex sexuality will cause "everyone" to become gay. In my eyes, such anxious statements are rather self-revealing. At least with regard to the following revelations. (30)

"You, therefore, have no excuse, you who pass judgment on someone else, for at whatever point you judge another, you are condemning yourself, because you who pass judgment do the same things." Paul, Romans Chap. 2, 1

The founder of the Christian church, Mr Saul, or Paul, whom he called himself after he became a Christian, could not possibly have understood the meaning of his own statement in Romans 2: 1. Paul himself denounced a great many others, including women, drunkards, slaves, men who loved men as well as an endless number of others.

Let's try to see the young invisible non-heterosexuals in a perspective where it becomes easier to spot the various contributing factors, mechanisms and processes at play in the traumatization many of these children and adolescents are exposed to daily. Traumatization in this context explained as loss of meaning and helplessness.

My Head teacher in social psychology at UiO, psychologist and researcher Astrid Bastiansen, says as a summary of the research on the subtle aspects of trauma, that it is the interpersonal trauma which creates the most serious problems. A traumatic situation that persists over time can deprive the victim of their own identity and self. (31)

It is crucial to see these potential traumatizing factors in a dynamic ecological perspective such as Bronfenbrenner's. Cooley was an early pioneer with regard to such an expanded perspective. (32)

Bronfenbrenner's theoretical framework is an interactionist-model, because it focuses on the interaction between the individual and its surroundings. He argues that human perception of the environment is often more important than the objective reality, and that this perception influences both our expectations and actions. (33) This has also been confirmed by the famous Asch study, which I urge you to read. You'll find a link to this famous study in the appendix-section. (34)

Bronfenbrenner hierarchically distinguishes between the Micro, Meso, Exo and Macro systems in his theory. The micro-system represents the individual and its direct social interactions with family, friends, school etc. The macro-system is the supreme, and represents among other things the laws, attitudes and ideology of a culture. In addition, he describes a Chronosystem which involves the time factor, which means historical influences and changes in a longer time perspective. (35) Religion is one of those influences.

A good reason for describing the historical processes is that they often show how problematic it can be to explain an etiology within narrow time frames. (Etiology is the study of causation or origination).

Just as Astri Bastiansen points out: What exactly defines a situation, where does it begin, how long is it, and where does it stop? She also reminds us that most human phenomena are subtle, that is, difficult to detect. They are complex, dependent on many factors that work together. In addition, they are vague, and thus problematic to place in one category over another. (36)

The themes of biphobia and homophobia largely represent the challenges that Bastiansen mentions: It is subtle in the sense that especially the youngest non-heterosexuals, try to hide their suffering and thus do not immediately reveal the underlying problems. This may lead to a focus on symptoms, such as depression or drug-problems among others, rather than focusing on underlying causes. Symptom-treatments never deal with underlying causes.

It is complex, in the sense that it can be contingent on many different underlying factors, which may work more or less together. It becomes no less complex when the aggressor and the victim may be represented in the very same person, which is the case regarding many homophobes. Finally, it's vague, because bisexuality in particular, is not immediately easy to classify, considering that most of them define themselves as heterosexuals. One pervasive exception to this "rule" is a comprehensive new British study. I will introduce this study in Chapter 19.

It is vital to clarify the processes and mechanisms that are in operation when it comes to the traumatization of invisible minorities. Such an approach must seek to avoid polarized thinking and labeling, such as hetero versus homo, or micro versus macro etc.

Whatever minorities we're talking about, the smallest unit in any group is the individual, you. And we all have an equal right to be respected and included in the greatest of all groups, the majority which spells humanity.

Nevertheless, the prejudice against non-heterosexuals is far less now than just a few decades ago. The first Norwegian comprehensive survey on attitudes, which included general views on homosexuality among other topics, was conducted by Scanfact in 1967. It revealed, that 72% of the men and 81% of the women meant that homosexuals should do what they could to combat their sexual inclinations. (37) You can read more about this in the Nova-report in the appendix-part.

But even if things have improved since then, in some environments, prejudices still prevail. For example in many religious communities, in some sports environments such as football and hockey, as well as in some immigrant communities based on orthodox Islamic cultures, orthodox Christian cultures or orthodox Hindu cultures. The prejudice is also more evident in specific age groups, mostly among the older part of the population, but also among the youngest.

We live in a hetero-cultural reality, where most symbols reflect the heterosexual ideal. In fact, we are all treated as heterosexuals until the contrary is "proven". In this frame it is easy to feel lonely and isolated for these young non-heterosexual individuals. Especially during the most vulnerable phase of life, namely childhood and adolescence. Too many of them struggle with mental health issues such as anxiety, depression, but also with substance abuse problems. (38)

It is reasonable to assume that, as a result of these problems, young non-heterosexuals are also over-represented in social care and psychiatry. Nevertheless, this often seems to be a non-issue among many therapists.

This invisibility may have fatal consequences. A “blind” therapist may inadvertently contribute “the thousandth and final drop”. Simply because the client cannot withstand the stress of not being seen, once again. The story in the next chapter may be representative of invisible suffering.

CHAPTER 9

A Child Welfare Educator's Considerations

"Love is the only way to grasp another human being at the innermost core of his personality. No one can become fully aware of the very essence of another human being unless he loves him. By his love he is enabled to see the essential traits and features of the beloved person; and even more, he sees that which is potential in him, which is not yet actualized but yet needs to be actualized. Furthermore, by his love, the loving person enables the beloved person to actualize these potentialities. By making him aware of what he can be and of what he should become, he makes these potentialities come true."

From Victor Frankl's book: "Man's Search For Meaning"

Elisabeth's Reflections: (Will be adden In a later edition)

"There ain't no cure for Love"

Prejudice in a Social Psychological Historical Perspective

As we have seen, science has also contributed to the prejudice regarding some of the sexual orientations. Not at least with its research-focus on the cause of homosexuality in order to find a cure for it. This is something that other minorities largely have been spared. For example, there is no research on ethnic Africans' pigmentation in order to develop a medical therapy that can change their skin color.

In particular, the bisexuals became "invisible" as a result of the construction of the mono-sexualities in the late 1800s. Hence it's difficult to identify the individuals who make up this "minority". And at a very young age, everyone is invisible. Both homosexuals, heterosexuals, lesbians and bisexuals. During the early development phase, everyone is assumed to be heterosexual.

It's not very common that thirteen-year-olds are "coming out". Therefor the youngest ones also constitute a powerless minority among the minorities. Powerless because of their invisibility, but also because of their lack of social connection and support. Other than what they may seek out on internet forums.

They largely lack the ability to influence their own situation as a group in relation to the majority. Something other minority groups have as a result of their visibility. When, in many cases, the sciences themselves are the premise-providers of discrimination, this becomes a potent source of prejudice among people at large.

Prejudice as a topic of scientific research, is also the story of the science's own prejudice:

Just over a hundred years ago, there was almost a universal tendency among scientists in both the United States and Europe to accept racial inferiority. The idea of the superiority of the white race, with the white man at the top of this hierarchy, was deeply rooted in most western people at that time.

This is probably due to the Europeans' colonization of both the African and American continents. Which in turn led to the subsequent abuse of Africans and slavery. The idea that a certain race had been given a divine power over other races, is part of the Abrahamic heritage, and eventually also as a result of Darwinian-theory. Thus, they did not see the immoral aspects of their evil treatment of the Africans and Native Americans.

This is also a daunting example of a collective cultural dehumanization of other colors. These attitudes were clearly reflected in the early social sciences. These "researchers" began studying and explaining racial differences based on the assumption of other races' inferiority.

They regarded the supremacy of the white race as a natural starting point for studying the "inferior" races. These biases were also reinforced by comparisons of intelligence tests conducted among white, also called Caucasian, and African-American individuals. (3)

The one who contributed the most to change this largely unscientific focus was psychologist Floyd Allport. In 1924, he stated:

"The difference in mental abilities between white and black Americans is simply not large enough to explain the exclusion the blacks are exposed to". (3)

Thus, all of a sudden the focus was on white racist-attitudes instead of the "inferiority and mental limitations" of the non-Caucasian races.

The social-psychological research that underpinned such a racial vision in the early 20th century was the differences they found in some intelligence-test measurements. In those cases where they didn't find any differences, they often insisted that further research would prove this. Does that sound familiar? Did you read about the term "Cognitive Dissonance" in Central Concepts at the beginning of the book? Anyway, among researchers today, this tendency to dismiss research-findings that doesn't confirm your theory, is coined "The File-drawer syndrome or problem."

Two important events is said to have contributed to the change of this this biased racial focus. The first one was the burgeoning Black Civil Rights movement in the 1920's. The second one was the widespread protests regarding the Europeans dominance in the African colonies. (4)

By the way, there is currently no evidence to support the difference in intelligent between races. Recent research has revealed an environmental impact on IQ. For example, in a study on IQ, Scarr and Weinberg found that Afro-American children who were adopted into white middle-class families with a satisfactory psychosocial climate, actually scored higher on IQ-tests than the average of the general population. (5)

The paradigm shift, first triggered by Floyd Allport, may serve as an example of the start of a new era in social psychology, where the focus was shifted to underlying psychological processes, such as group dynamics and social processes. This trend was further reinforced as a result of the Nazi abuse before and during World War II. Social-psychological research on prejudice had now become a phenomenon that both deserved and received a great deal of scientific as well as public attention.

Regarding sexual orientations, the early psychoanalysis, psychiatry and psychology have heavily contributed to the prejudice against non-heterosexuals, just as social psychology contributed to the oppression of non-Caucasian races one hundred years ago. With one difference, the non- Caucasian races didn't have to go through the mental torture of conversion "therapies" on top of their social suffering.

Countless "scientific" attempts have been made to "cure" non-heterosexuals. As we have seen, these methods have their roots in psychological and medical theories. One of the most widespread conversion-"therapy" has been aversion-therapy. In this "therapy" "patients" are shown erotic images, when images depicting homo-erotic situations are displayed, they are subjected to electric shocks. (6) It's otherwise called torture, and in this case, in addition to physical torture, there is also the aspect of mental torture.

In 1998, APA (The American Psychiatric Association) issued a warning of the risks by using reparative therapy to "cure" homosexual behavior. The risks include: Applied depression, anxiety and self-destructive behavior. They also emphasized that there is no published scientific evidence to support the hypothesis that sexual orientation can be changed. (6)

Let me also add that the ultimate consequence of self-destructive behavior is suicide. Besides the people who have been directly exposed to this degrading treatment, this has also indirectly contributed to the stigmatization by the general population. Priests, doctors and psychologists have always been basic and important premise-providers to the general understanding of what is "right" or "wrong" regarding human behavior. And they still are.

A grotesque example of how homophobia can lead to unnecessary suffering for heterosexuals too, is a well-known case from Canada. A boy named Sheldon Kennedy was sexually abused more than 300 times over a few years. When they asked him in court why he hadn't report the abuse earlier, Sheldon replied that he didn't dare to reveal the abuses because he was afraid that people would think he was gay. (7)

It is quite daunting to think that a teenager prefers to be physically, emotionally and mentally abused rather than suspected of being gay! This would probably not have happened in a society which accepts, respects and includes all sexual orientations as both equal and natural. In this case, Sheldon's hockey coach emerged as a heterosexual man in a sport considered to be among the most macho-centric and homophobic subcultures alongside football.

So it appears that anyone, no matter sexual orientation, risks paying a high price for this cultural homo-anxiety.

The Norwegian sociologist and scientist Hannah Helseth says in a comment to one of her surveys that boys and men lose in all areas where their masculinity ideals clash with the demands of society. She further points out that boys in the school yard are terrified of being called, sissy or gay. She also mentions that most of the 14-year-old boys she has interviewed have this as their biggest fear: "It's the nail in the coffin" as one put it. (8)

These findings are further corroborated by a large American study among high school students, where 70% of the boys (N-3500) responded that they would rather be beaten up than accused of being gay by their peers. (9)

An example of famous people who were probably both gay and no doubt homophobic, is J. Edgar Hoover. Rumors about the FBI-commander's gay tendencies were pending as early as the 1940s. Some biographies reject this, while others see it as proven. (10) Regardless, many had to pay a scary price for Hoover's homophobia, both hetero- and homosexuals. But would it happen if the culture had been accepting and including regarding all sexual orientations?

A more recent example from our own continent is the British neo-Nazi, Nicky Crane. Nicky Crane was considered the most violent neo-Nazi England had ever seen. He was a role model for all younger Nazis especially in London. What nobody knew was that he was living a double life ala Dr. Jekyll and Mr. Hyde. Or maybe one should say Dr. Jekyll and Mr. Hide. He ended his life because of complications associated with AIDS. Just like the famous German neo-Nazi, Michael Kuhnen. He also died of AIDS, but unlike Crane, Kuhnen was not revealed as homosexual before post-mortem. (11)

Jon Schmid, too, is a terrifying example of projecting one's own secret and dis-owned sexual feelings out as hatred and contempt for others. He is one of the many who have damaged and ruined the lives of many children with his contribution to the aversion "therapy" terror. With the help of "God," he and his congregation claimed that they could cure homosexuality. They created a program to change children's sexuality. Today Jon Schmid is married. To a man. (12)

So did John Paulk and Alan Chambers. Two of the "pioneers" and founders of Exodus. Eventually they both showed remorse, and had the courage to ask for forgiveness for the harm and terror they had inflicted on these young souls, including those who committed suicide as a result of this "therapy". I will share some of their public apology below. I do this because it is both inspiring and very important to others. Especially young people who are struggling. I have great respect for Paulk and Chambers for doing this. Not many would dare to do such a complete reversal, acknowledging the injustice and harm they have inflicted on others. I call it "Schindler-courage".

Here are parts of Chambers and Paul's public apology: Chambers: "I'm sorry for all the pain and hurt many of you have suffered as a result of what we did. I am sorry that we have deceived parents into believing in our propaganda to be able to change their children's sexual orientation, and thus to have stigmatized their parents as well. More than anything else, I'm sorry that many also left their faith because of what we did - and that some also took their lives as a result." (13)

John Paulk: "I have made many mistakes during this journey and I have injured many people, including people who were close to me. I am sorry that I have communicated that you and your families are worth less than mine. I'm sorry that someone chose to take their lives because of this." (14)

These are only brief excerpts from their official request for forgiveness. The excuse in its entirety can be found in the source references: Chapters 9: 13 and 14. Let me add that both were revealed as gay long before taking this bold step of asking for forgiveness for the pain and damage they inflicted on these young people. Most of them children. Projection can in some cases have terrible and fatal consequences.

"Is it genetic? I mean, can you actually be born a hypocrite?" - Bill Maher

American pastor Ted Haggard is another, and in my eyes, one of the most grotesque examples of projected self-hatred in our time. He was the head of more than 45,000 evangelical churches in the United States. He was also a close friend of President George Bush, and a frequent guest at the White House. He was an evangelical "rock star", as talk-show host Bill Maher describes him. He was also a frequent guest in not quite as "white" houses as the house of the American President.

Haggard was revealed for both using drugs and whore-houses. Whore-houses homosexual people. (15) (16)

Ted Haggard has deceived millions of people, and he too has probably injured millions of children with his fiery anti-gay appearances on both TV and summer camps for children across the North American continent. Yet, there is no sign of remorse for what he as the United States' most celebrated and leading evangelist has spit out about homosexuality as a sin and the work of the devil. It is more than likely that he indirectly has the lives of many young people on his conscience. Amazingly, he has been accepted back into the evangelic circles again, because he regrets being tempted and seduced into sin, by the "devil," at a feeble moment. There are no gays in the evangelical-Christian backyard. Only heterosexuals who have been tempted by the "devil". (15) (16)

Many of the same evangelical churches in the United States are engaged in something they call hell houses. These are built up like something familiar to the ghost-tunnels found in theme parks and amusement parks. These hell houses are aimed at children, to scare them away from any "sinful" thoughts and actions, such as sex with peers. Here, for example, you meet boys who writhe in pain in hell after having died from AIDS. The suffering and violence in these scenes have prompted psychologists to issue public warnings. But to no avail so far. (17) (18)

It is high time that the research-resources that have been spent on an endless search for the cause of and the "cure" for non-heterosexual love, to turn their focus and their resources towards the causes of contempt and condemnation. In such a perspective, it will be easier, especially for the youngest, to recognize and justify their own existence. That they, just like everyone else, are born with a capacity for love. And that the ability to love, no matter the colors of love, is the most needed talent of all. It's both a blessing and a gift.

Knowing that many of the major societal changes in history have come about as a result of the persistent struggle of small minorities, it seems promising. Very often such historical changes have been triggered by one single individual. It should suffice to mention Mahatma Ghandi, Mother Theresa, Nelson Mandela, Rosa Parks and Claudette Colvin.

Rosa Parks became famous around the world when she refused to give up her seat to a white man on a bus in Montgomery, Alabama, 1955, after the Supreme Court repealed the law of segregation (read the law of apartheid). (19)

But the real hero of this story is Claudette Colvin. She was the first person to refuse to respect the segregation of white and dark-skinned Americans. But since Claudette was seen as both big-mouthed and emotional in addition to being pregnant with a married man, Montgomery's Leaders for African-American Rights chose instead to front Rosa Parks. (20)

Unfortunately, prejudice still seems to thrive, even among those people who are working to combat prejudice. Anyway, Rosa Parks was also arrested, and the rest is history.

Finally, we must not forget the wise and brave individuals in the sciences themselves. Like Floyd Allport and many others. An incredible amount of courage is required to speak up against "Rome", even when you see and know that the "Roman Empire" is founded on sandy soil. Sometimes even on mercury sand.

At the very end of this second part of the book, I will quote a not completely unknown minority-leader and "rock star", who lived two thousand years ago:

"This is my command: Love each other."
John 15:17

PART III

The Postmodern Era – A New Order – The Way Forward

"Every time you are tempted to react in the same old way, ask if you want to be a prisoner of the past or a pioneer of the future."

Deepak Chopra

The era we're now somewhere in the beginning of is called the postmodern era. Although not all seem to agree on what this really means, or where it's going to lead us. However, one thing that scholars seem to agree on is that deconstruction is a central part of this new "paradigm". I myself see it as a big mess, a post-millennium chaos, but chaos may not be the worst base for new beginnings. Never the less, many people are still holding on to some old modernist "truths", which may not work that well anymore. Change is "dangerous" for most of us.

One phenomenon that may be helpful to describe the beginning of this new postmodern era, is the concept of "exponential development". Exponential development can easily be explained by the developments in data technology. One example is the storage capacity of a computer, or a smartphone. This capacity has doubled every 12'months in recent years. This exponential growth looks like this: 1 + 1 = 2, 2 + 2 = 4, 4 + 4 = 8 and so on. This is in contrast to a linear evolution, which is slow, like chronological aging: 1 2 3 4 5 6 7 8 and so on.

Exponential growth, or development, is a curve that looks pretty much like a linear curve at the beginning, but it won't take many stages of development before it takes off and points steeply upwards relative to the linear curve.

The audio media may serve as a good example. From 2001 to 2013, the record industry sales in Norway dropped from over one billion to 116 million. (1) This is due to an exponential development of other media on the Internet, like streaming, Youtube, google and the explosive (exponential) spread of smart-phones etc. We have never seen anything like this exponential development and growth in recorded history. Most things have developed slowly, safely and linearly. Until now.

Peter Diamendis points out that we are living in an exponential era, where at the same time we are still largely thinking linearly. Thus, such exponential growth can seem overwhelming and daunting to us. (2)

While writing this, I'm sitting here in Blokhus (Denmark), without having to move a meter in order to gather the data to what you are now reading. With my laptop, the world, wide, web and the spider (me), I have access to all the sources I need. When I started out studying psychology way back in the modern era, I spent days at the university library in writing a 20-page essay. Sometimes the sources (books and research-articles) had to be ordered from other libraries around the world. That being said, this technological exponential development has generously given me a lot of time, and saved me a great deal of energy.

But this exponential development also presents many new and major challenges. One example is population growth. It has doubled four times since it passed the first billion earth-citizens in the 19th century. (3) This, in turn, requires exponential solutions with regard to agriculture, alternative energy sources, educational systems, infrastructures and social organization, just to name a few. Linear solutions and ways of thinking are outdated.

But unfortunately, we are still largely stuck in a linear way of thinking. Also regarding our cultural views of the individual, gender-roles, or roles in general, we still hold on to the modernistic ways of linear thinking. We have to think again. On the societal level, conventional jobs are disappearing at express-speed, as a result of artificial intelligence and robotization. This is also increasing exponentially. Fortunately, some are at the forefront, trying to develop solutions to this. One example is citizen pay, which is currently being experimented with several places on the planet.

We need all the contributors that exist in order to find the best postmodern solutions for all of us. Maybe we should take a new look at the Sumerians again (I wrote about them in Chapter 1.) They showed us that human freedom breed creativity, and that creativity is an absolute necessity for both individual and collective development. The Sumerian society was based on freedom and individual equality. Both the Sumerians and the ancient Greeks, may have been precursors of the exponential development phenomenon, with their thinking, wheels, languages, sciences and inventions.

Chaos-theory may be relevant to our new age. The Canadian biologist Bruce Bagemihl argues for this and several other theories in his monumental work "Biological Exuberance". You will find out more about Bagemihl and his research in the last two chapters of the book.

In the first chapters of this third part of the book, I address, among other things, the sciences' treatment of gender, gender-roles and sexuality. And it is a modernist approach most of these scientists takes regarding cultural expressions of being human. But you will also see new and larger perspectives, new ways of seeing individual-beings and their collective "straitjackets".

In this part of the book I will try to show some new paths to new understandings, using new perspectives. Simply by wearing new "glasses" on both existing knowledge and data, as well as all the new research that is piling up at an exponential speed. Old road maps are becoming more or less useless. We need new road maps, not new terrain.

As you will see in the last chapters of this book, I am far from alone in thinking so. And as I mentioned in the introduction of this book, some might think that I'm in over my head here, but luckily I do not suffer from aquaphobia (fear of water). And deep-diving has always appealed to me. Both myself and my inner six-year old child.

INTRODUCTION PART III

"Merely complaining without posing an alternative offers nothing"

Jaque Fresco

Much of what has been conveyed in the previous two parts of this book may seem like a bit of a misery-description regarding both past and present conditions of naturalness. And it is, to a large extent too. But after all, it is impossible to find the way to Rome if you do not know where you are. And besides:

"A journey of a thousand miles begins with a single step"

And once you know it, you can take your first steps on the new road. So what can we do to make the future easier, more enlightening and thus evolving, simply how to create the future as a better place for ALL of us! Or rather, how can we make it easier for all to become who they actually are. Not what "others" mean we should be, whether those consist of self-appointed religious administrators, politically ideologues, marketers, or pompous and self-proclaimed moralists. Or even worse, a combination of these.

In this third part of the book, I will gradually outline a new architecture, a new and alternative understanding based on data and empirical evidence that has been referred to in the previous two parts. A new interpretation and understanding of this research, in addition to all the new research that doesn't fit into the old paradigms. Knowledge that until now has been called anomalies. Knowledge that simply does not fit into the classic theoretical strait-jackets or into the minds of their makers. I'm far from the first to outline a new architecture, but I do it from my own vantage point.

This is my contribution to the postmodern era, which we are at full speed into. I'm not into de-construction of the individual. I'm rather suggesting a deconstruction of some of the Abrahamic and social-Darwinian dogmas, which are the most prevalent narratives of our time. It's also an attempt to deconstruct the wide-spread value-apartheid and polarization that has been a curse, and still is a curse to a large part of humanity. Values and ways of thinking that still leave their clammy imprints on too many people, with the sole purpose of getting individuals to fit into forms and categories that should have been thrown on our historic landfill ages ago. Values that have led to oppression and death of so many people.

Above all, children and young people of today have to pay dearly for this in the form of all too often sick ideals, which are often impossible to reach. This in turn has led to bullying and harassment between them, in order to appear the most successful, the coolest, in order to be accepted by "the others". They are manipulated into playing roles in a stage-play directed by adult modernist actors who convulsively follow their own outdated scripts. Scripts that may look different on the surface, but which for the most parts are based on a common mantra, competition. A mantra that values some as better individuals than others.

The ones who suffer the most from this above-mentioned inhumane pressure, and who all too often succumb to this, are often referred to as the weak ones among us. I would argue that they are not the weak among us. They are the empathetic among us. They are the ones to teach and guide the rest of us to become human. More human. These empaths have a lot to teach to the many apathetics among us. And remember, it's the apathetic people that make up the silent, and all too often, dangerous majority.

In the following chapters of this part of the book, I will address these issues:

Chapter 10: Juno Enters the World. An Emotional Refugee
Chapter 11: Julian's Story
Chapter 12: Gender Roles in a Developmental Psychological Perspective
Chapter 13: The Infectious Obsession of Gender Differences
Chapter 14: Gender Roles - Sexuality – Identity
Chapter 15: Classical Science and Meta-theoretical Straitjackets
Chapter 16: Everything Revolves Around Sex - And Sex is Selling Everything
Chapter 17: When Sex Itself is the product - The "Free" Market
  Part I: «Sex, Lies & Phone-calls»
  Part II: Aggressive Versus Non-Aggressive Sexualities
Chapter 18: Abrahamic Dogmas - A New Interpretation
Chapter 19: From Sexual Straitjackets to Freesexual - A New Perspective
  Part I: We Need a New Role-liberation
  Part II: The Liberation From the Mono-sexualities
  Part III: How come so few have done Research on Scientists
Chapter 20: NDE – And a New Spiritual Paradigm
  Part I: Juno's Journey to Freedom
  Part II: The NDE Visions – A New and Liberating Worldview
  Part III: No Fingerprints are "Normal" – They're All Natural
Epilogue

CHAPTER 10

Juno Enters the World. An Emotional Refugee

"The woods are lovely, dark and deep. But I have promises to keep, And miles to go before I sleep, And miles to go before I sleep."

Robert Frost

THE TRACKS OF MY TEARS

"A child will be born tomorrow, as open as an empty book,
We'll fill it with hope and sorrow, The very things that messed us up,
We'll ask her to join our congregation, A Hindu Muslim Christian or a Jew,
Pretty soon she'll recognize her sisters, But soon she'll know the enemy too,
There's so much love for everyone, still somewhere someone hates someone"

"There was a storm that night, when Juno came into this world. A cold winter-night in a small town on the ragged coast of the North-sea, he grew up in an average Norwegian family. Juno preferred to play on his own, he didn't care much to join the other boys in the neighborhood when they played ball. He was a somewhat insecure little boy, who already then felt like a stranger in this world.

When Juno turned 13, he slowly began to understand why he had always felt so different. It was in junior-high he had his first real serious experience with falling in love...with a boy. Although this wasn't his first encounter with romance, he had also felt strongly for June, but to have feelings like this, for a boy…

One day at school he appeared from nowhere, just standing there at the main-gate. Juno had never seen him before, his eyes were radiating. Juno was thrown into a turmoil of intense emotions, it felt like his soul was electrified. For a long time they were just standing there, like frozen in time and space, neither of them daring to speak. They were incapable of exchanging anything more than the yearning expressions, mirrored in their sad eyes. It remained that way. It had ended as quickly as it had begun.

Juno often fantasized about them being lovers. It shamed him to think of them being in bed together, making out. He withdrew even more from those around him, sinking deeper into his dark and lonely universe.

He started reading, trying to find answers...to understand. While in the background the media was flooded with social debates over the equality of civil rights for gays. Why were the religious authorities banning the kind of love felt by Juno?

It's not as if Juno sat down one day and decided that from now on, he was going to be attracted to boys. This wasn't simply a decision that HE made, it stemmed from a place much deeper than that, and it took life the moment he was born!

Juno started to pray, begging God to redirect his loving desires, so that he could be like the other boys, begging God to relieve him from this curse and punishment.

From now on, Juno often skipped school. He spent most of the time in his secret hiding place in the mountain-side overlooking the small town where he was born. There he could spend hours and hours looking out over the Atlantic horizon, wishing he was another place, in another time, in another life. He tried hard to piece together the purpose of his miserable destiny. What was the meaning of his life? Why didn't he feel like other boys? Why weren't his interests like those of the other boys? Why wasn't he like them? Why, why, why?

When Juno did attend school, he spent most of his time looking out the window, daydreaming. But when he wasn't immersed in his own little world, he transformed himself into the proverbial Class Clown, much to the great amusement for his classmates, but to great despair of his teachers. You see, Juno had discovered how he could acquire the admiration of his peers, the feeling of being respected! Yet, deep inside he knew that it wasn't really him they admired, but rather the various roles that he played. Because no-one really knew Juno, no-one really knew that sad and scared little boy hiding behind this clever disguise.

Still, behind his noisy mask, if you had just looked close enough, you would've been able to see the tracks of his tears, tears that often appeared when he was all alone by himself."

Excerpt from TRAX

How many young people like Juno have had to suffer because of other people's distorted views and attitudes, nobody knows. That they can be counted in the millions is beyond any doubt. The oblique view of the authorities quickly becomes the "truths" of the masses. Finally, it is called common sense. After all, it is the authorities that manage both the divine and the scientific "truths." Unfortunately, many of these "truths" comes at a grat expense for others, like for instance Juno.

In a historical perspective, sexuality has had many expressions, and sometimes quite different conditions. Whoever manages the cultural "truth" of what sexuality is, or how it is to be exercised, also has great power to make people either happy or unhappy. (1)

"The boxes that define straight, gay and bi can get too tight. - And obviously they are restricted. After all, they were established to sort the sick from the healthy, the criminals from the law-abiding and the sinners from the saved"

Agnes Bolsoe

As the church began to lose its power to define sexuality as a sin against God, medical science took over and diagnosed much of the "sinful" sexuality as disease, with subsequent inferiority and shame as a result.

Even to this day, this shame is a powerful player in many people's lives. Not at least in terms of regulating who you have sexual acts with and how you perform them. Fear of sanctions from society and neighbors, if you should reveal who you really are, can be unbearable in itself. This causes many to become prisoners in their own personal jail. Shame can be life-threatening.

The Norwegian psychiatrist and author Finn Skaarderud says something that in my opinion, is very insightful and informative about this "nerve-gas" that shame actually can be. He bases his knowledge on the research-literature, but also on the experience of his clinical practice as a psychotherapist. He also points out the difference between guilt and shame, something that many people confuse. Unfortunately, also therapists. Among other things, he says:

"The feelings of shame are largely about the notions of what others think of one. We all want to be included, accepted and respected. But if you are ashamed of who you are, then the personal identity itself is threatened." (2) Sexual shame can affect anyone, both heterosexuals and non-heterosexuals, who struggles with "unusual" sexual fantasies, fetishes and para-philias. The latter is also discussed in chapter 17 and 19.

While shame often is linked to the disclosure of your real self, or the fantasy of being disclosed, guilt is more related to unacceptable actions or behavior. You can make up for the guilt, and thus get rid of it. Shame, on the other hand, is paralysis, because the shame is about who you are. The deep shame is the pain of seeing oneself as someone who does not deserve to be loved. The overgrown shame is suicidal. Those who, on the other hand, experience anxiety or grief, serious illness, accident or loss will experience the care from the others. *The shameful expect nothing but judgement and contempt.* (2) (My italics)

Based on this, it can be said that many non-heterosexuals suffer from a double overdose of both shame and guilt. Shame of who you are, and guilt for your fantasies, feelings and actions. Skaarderud also points out that shame is linked to self-observation, in the form of seeing oneself with the gaze of others. Cooley called this process "The Looking-glass Self". I described it in part II of the book. (See also Central Concepts)

"The difference between a serial killer and a saint is environment. That is a very hard thing to accept because it raises a lot of questions"

Jaque Fresco

As described above, shame can lead to deep self-contempt, but also denial. The ultimate consequence of the suicidal shame is suicide. And in some cases murder as well. When self-contempt is projected as contempt for others who act as exponents of it, tragedies like the attack and murder of 49 people in a gay club in Orlando in June 2016 can happen.

The perpetrator himself was a frequent guest at the same gay-club. Growing up in a strictly religious Islamic environment, he has probably experienced the homosexual scorn as particularly strong and outspoken. (3) (4) The perpetrator in Orlando also brings up associations with the Norwegian terrorist and mass murderer on Utoya. He too had a pronounced disdain for homosexuals, rooted in old Christian-orthodox ideals. Nevertheless, he also was a frequent guest in the gay community in Oslo. On one occasion he even participated in Oslo Gay Parade. Several of his friends had long suspected that he was homosexual. (5) (6)

Chapter 17, Part II and Chapter 18 may provide some clues as to why these two turned out as monsters, and did what they did. They are off course individually responsible for their hateful and grotesque actions!

But, we others are also to a certain extent co-responsible as social "gardeners" of the "soil" in which they were raised. Have you ever seen a newborn monster? (Think again)

Sexuality, together with the gender-role issues and various ideological and religious systems, is something that bothers me a lot. Not only as separate phenomena, but also as interactive dynamic processes. These themes are much more interconnected than most people would think. For example, bi and homosexuality is not an isolated phenomenon that affects only those who sort under these labels. Unfortunately, for many people they also threatens the general definition of "being a man". An example of the latter, is the Canadian hockey-player Sheldon Kennedy, whom I wrote about in Chapter 8.

Thus, many heterosexuals suffer from homophobia. Besides, the male gender-role is unfortunately still much narrower than the female gender-role. Helseth and Slaatsveen illustrates this quite clearly:

"It is about the liberation from a kind of macho ideal". She further calls for men who can do the same liberation-job that women did in the 70s, but now for men (boys; my addition). Both Hannah Helseth and Anders Slaatsveen (sociologists), completely agree that; "One of the most negative aspects of young boys' relationships, characterized by strict rules, is the fear of homosexuality." Helseth goes on to say: "I have discussed sexual harassment with very young boys. The worst thing they can be is to be gay, it is compared to the same loss of dignity as being called whore for girls". "The harassment of 14-year-olds is about proving that you are a man, by proving that you are not gay!" Says Helseth. Slaatsveen, for his part, also believes that the image of the gay man as something very feminine is part of the problem. (7)

The above shows why it is so important to see this Abrahamic imprint throughout history in the form of limitation, sin, and shame. In addition, we must take into consideration research that has been left out, that actually can shed a fruitful light on human sexuality and gender roles (how to be a man and how to be a woman). Not at least the research which is done under conditions and in cultures where the absent of shame hasn't led to sexual behavior going underground (or under Freud's quilt) and thus becoming "invisible".

You will find out more about this research in the following chapters, as well as in chapters 19 and 20. Among many other academic disciplines, you will also see this through the glasses of anthropological and biological scientists. Glasses that you have never seen on the cover of your local, regional, or national newspaper. Or in your "News" feeds.

CHAPTER 11

Julian's Story

"Is all mankind divided into races, congregations, categories and roles? Juno had become so tired and fed up by the tyranny of shoulds, and all the divisions and labeling of people, which ultimately only lead to prejudice, polarization and role-playing."

Excerpts from TRAX

Someone once said that growing up in a dysfunctional culture or dysfunctional family is like getting into the second half of a movie and thus never get to understand the plot.

Juno had really set out on a long, painful and winding road in order to discover the truths and finally being able to accept his own true self. My goal is for this road to be made short and exciting instead of long and painful. In some ways, Juno had lived through the dysfunctional story of humanity until, as a young adult, he finally could begin to live his own unique story.

When Arne Utne and I were doing our pilot study on bisexuality, there was one answer that stood out from most of the others in that he (the respondent) embraced most of this problem- complex with his own observation and reflections. Not at least regarding many of the dysfunctional and fixed views we have on both gender-roles and sexuality. Much of it as a result of historical "invisible" fingerprints. His answers shows how these imprints have even marked a young man in the capital of one of the world's most liberal societies today. Norway.

I quickly realized that he had so much on his mind and in his heart that the interview with him (originally stipulated for 15 minutes) actually required several hours and meetings. Despite the length of the answers in this interview, I have chosen to reproduce large parts of it. Here is "Julian's" story, his own experiences and considerations:

"How did you discover your sexual orientation?"

"It's not that I discovered my orientation, it's always been there. We live in a heteronormative world where love between people of the same sex is seen as unnatural. I think it's very strange that people think it's not natural. I think it's just as natural to be in love and to sit on the coach with my arms around a boy, as it is with a girl. The only thing that separates a boy and a girl are the genitals."

"Being bisexual or homosexual consists in far more than just having anal sex with a boy. And by the way, many heterosexuals have anal sex today too. I think the world would be a better place if we weren't put into different categories. It's not because my big goal is for more men to have anal sex, my goal is for guys to care for each other, to be able to hug each other, etc. Masturbating together or having oral sex is not dangerous either for that matter. You don't have to be a stereotypical gay for that."

"I think it's sad that guys can't show compassion for each other. During most of our upbringing, and much of our adult life, we spend most of our time with people of the same sex, whether it be friends or colleagues. But then there is this invisible rule that we should act in a masculine or macho way, without exposing feelings or compassion towards those who happen to be born with the same genitals as you. What does it do to us humans? Today even 7-year-olds are homophobic. Homophobic in the sense that they use "Homo" or "Faggot" as "weapons" when harassing other children."

"I believe the most important thing for all people is to feel loved and cared for. What does it do to you if you don't dare to show love and compassion to those you spend most of your time with, because if you do, you run the risk of being labeled homo or sissy. And what characterizes most psychopaths? Lack of perceived love and compassion. Basically we all need to be loved and appreciated, regardless of gender."

"When I was 15-16, I was frustrated, very frustrated because I had feelings for some of my friends. In my head I thought that it was only the genitals of the guys I was attracted. But I now see in retrospect that it was not what I missed most throughout my childhood. What I clearly missed the most was being able to hold around each other, simply cuddle with each other, the physical contact, etc. It was far more important to me than having sex."

"It is ironic that among mates it is seen as less gay to suck each other than to lie close to each other with all their clothes on. Because if you suck a mate you do it to as a "service". And if you choose to do it, it will not be a good experience either, because you have to constantly hide that you enjoy it and you are then automatically labeled as submissive and feminine."

"This whole charade results in too many males walking around like "ticking bombs", despite the fact that there are many like-minded people at school and among your friends. This leads to sex where the genitals are the most important focus, since you have lost the hope of being allowed to "cuddle" with the same sex. And this continues into adulthood. People are seen as a piece of meat instead of a human being, because they in their childhood were not taught to show compassion and closeness.

"How do you interpret the term bisexual?"

"Being bisexual is when you're sexually attracted to both sexes, but only fall in love with the opposite sex. A relationship with someone of the same sex is not that interesting."

"How do you interpret the term biphilia?"

"Biphilia means that you fall in love with both genders. It is not the gender you fall in love with, but the personality and the person regardless of gender."

"Do you have suggestions for measures at the community level that would make it easier to be bisexual?"

"Open bisexual nightclubs and cafes, because at the gay venues there are, in my opinion, a lot of over-feminized gays that I cannot identify with. My experience is that you have to be like that in order to fit in and be accepted. I also think it's sad that you are not allowed to flirt and socialize with girls there. Because everyone assumes you are 100% gay."

"We need more focus on the fact that boys too are emotional-beings just like the girls, but already from childhood, boys are trained to suppress their feelings, which means that these feelings eventually might explode with fateful outcomes such as rape, violence and murder."

"I think it's a shame that society owes it only to the biological make-up as the reason why it is almost always boys who practice violence, rape and murder, and who are least involved in children's lives, who perish in traffic accidents etc. I mean the gender-roles must take at least 90% of that blame. Why are there 3 times more men who commit suicide? When women, according to the research, experience more psychological problems in life than men. And so it is all over the world, not just in Norway and Europe".

"A society free from gender-roles will lead to fewer divorces and children suffering from their parents' conflicts. One hardly dares to think of how many men who, on the basis of society's terms, have chosen hetero-relationships and who are deeply unhappy, and how many men and women who lives alone that are desperately longing for someone to love. In an open gender-free society with less prejudice, it would be easier for these people to express their love. This in turn would lead to bisexuals and gays having fewer sex partners, seeking out less casual sex such as gay saunas, etc. Less insecure sex and more stable relationships in other words."

"Another important thing is to stop the prevailing macho-pressure, which leads boys to talk about girls as a piece of meat, all the bragging about when was the last time you tricked a girl into bed, and if you say that it's more than two weeks ago you're a jerk.

"Greater focus on the importance of children and adolescents feeling good both mentally and physically, simply by eradicating the assumption that you can "only" be friends with members of the same sex, and "only" experience sexual relationships with the opposite sex"

"Those who live in a homosexual relationship and who are not biologically able to have their own children are a tremendous potential resource for all those children who lack competent care-takers in their lives. Our society suffers greatly from the fact that many children's biological parents are not competent enough. Gays (whether girls or boys) can be just as good caregivers as others. I think of foster homes, etc."

"Is there anything you think such an investigation should emphasize that has not been a part of this one?"

"Yes, the vast majority of those who are attracted to the same sex are not 100% gay, and the vast majority do not work as hairdressers. That you are less likely to be unfaithful as a bisexual if you are open about your orientation and know which gender you want to share your life with. That many people's perception of bisexuals is wrong, in that they think most of us are only sex-focused, while in reality it is more about closeness and intimacy with someone of the same sex. That many bisexuals would prefer to have a same-sex relationship, but finding such a person is difficult since most bisexuals are hidden in the closet."

"Anything else you want to highlight?"

"For me, it has always been natural to mostly fall for boys, of course it has been a mental strain many times. But all boys are born with sexual feelings. You create fantasies in your head that turns you on. Those feelings are more important to me than the shame I have for turning on my own gender. The big question is whether my mental health is getting worse by fantasizing about boys when I masturbate. I constantly work in my head to defend these feelings for myself. It's maybe an attempt to suppress these feelings of shame in order to maintain some sort of self-respect."

"But I must be honest to say that it affects my mental health even though I like to think that it doesn't bother me. It gives me a feeling of loneliness because I know I'll never be an "open" and proud bisexual person, and at the same time I have to hide perhaps the most important part of me as a person. The society prefers people who turn on the opposite sex."

"But why do I turn on boys more often than girls? Boys have more muscles than girls, I guess it gives me a sense of security over a slim girl body. And those feelings I can do nothing about. I can try to suppress them, but they will always be there in the unconscious. But having said that, I do enjoy having sex or intimacy with a girl too."

"One thing I find very strange is that I think I will be happier with a girl because of the sense of victory I would feel by being in heterosexual relationship."

"I would also like to add that in this struggle for gay rights, many people believe that all this attention will lead to more openness and less prejudice. I disagree, I believe that when stereotypical feminized gays are fronting this movement, it will lead to more prejudice. Because those who don't like gays get confirmed the stereotype that "all" gays are crazy and different. Something only 8% of those who are attracted to the same sex really are.

"I also believe that many gays and bisexuals feel that this stereotyped identity is not representative of who they are. They can't identify with this way of being. I can't identify myself with this, because I don't have a personality nor look like a stereotypical gay person."

"Some believe that one can be sexually "re-oriented". What do you think?"

"No, I can deny it, but how will it work in practice? The problem is that you interact with the same sex every day, you see the same sex in magazines, on TV, in traffic, at work, in school. The only way to avoid it is to lock yourself up in a basement and spend the rest of your life alone."

"Any closing considerations?"

"Many girls are fed up with desperate boys out on town who are just hunting for sex. If the gender-roles were abandoned, many boys would be "allowed" to be attracted to each other, it would also lead to less violence because "the market would be bigger". The big problem for both boys and girls is that the boy is seen as the conqueror and the girl as the victim, it's obviously not love that is the most important. Why is it that the countries with the most rigid gender-roles, also are the countries with the most problems on all levels of their societies?"

"I experience that bisexuals are not taken seriously, neither among heterosexuals nor homosexuals. It seems like both groups believe that bisexuality is a prelude to becoming properly gay. The orientation I have is not accepted as a real orientation, I am somehow not completely out of the closet, completely in balance. This is something that bothers me! Why do they think they have the defining power to decide that I'm halfway out of the closet because I see myself as bisexual? Why should they tell me how to practice my love?

"We should also keep in mind that children who experience anxiety regarding their own sexuality can react in two ways: They either withdraw or become aggressive." (My italics)

"Julian"

"Julian" certainly had a lot on his mind. My questions triggered an avalanche of thoughts and viewpoints that he had been wrestling with since his childhood. He had many thoughts regarding the distortion of gender-roles and their impact on sexual orientations. There is nothing wrong with "Julian", he is a healthy and reflected soul in a dysfunctional culture based on ancient myths and "Just so stories". "Julian" is pointing his fingers on some damaging and psychologically dysfunctional systems. He is angry, and has reasons to be so.

Many may respond to his anger at what he regards as the stereotyped features of the gay-movement. However, one should be aware that this element in queer environments reflects both the historical Stonewall uprising, but also the fact that some of them actually fits in to this "stereotype" without role-playing. They should therefore be respected. In addition, there are few who mention female stereotypes in those same environments, presumably because of the broader range of expression women are culturally allowed to play since the women-liberation gained momentum in the 70'tees.

Speaking of Stonewall, it was, in fact, first and foremost the transgendered people and the transvestites, who started the movement in the streets of New York back then. It was they who started the rebellion. A riot that has led to annual gay parades all around the world. They therefore deserve our respect for their historic human-rights struggle, and their impressive courage. They are the true heroes.

Let's get back to "Julian," one daunting example of this systemic dysfunction that he points out during the interview are (among many others), 7-year-olds who are homophobic. Homophobic in the sense that they use "Homo" as a "weapon" of harassment of other children. They do not necessarily know what it means, but they do understand that there is something horrible and degrading about being gay, which hits hard.

On some occasions I have asked 7 to 10 year olds whether they are heterosexual, but only in cases where I've caught them in verbal homophobic behavior. Well, I don't stop children on the street with this "survey", for the most part I've done this among friends of mine who also happen to be the parents of these "innocent" little creatures. It's probably not very popular when mom and dad are present. But without exceptions, these parents have experienced an "unwanted" epiphany when they discover that their children have no idea about what heterosexuality is.

By the way, the kids know perfectly well what being homosexual means, and that it's viewed as something inferior, something to dislike. However, these episodes can also be fun, at least for me. I remember an episode in Bergen a few years ago, when this 10-year old, who couldn't answer my question, after a moment of brooding that probably was a bit embarrassing for him, finally asked: "Well tell me then Richard, what is this heterosexual thing?"

Anyway, It's sad that too many resigned adults don't have the courage or strength to ask themselves: "Where in the world does all this contempt come from? Am I a part of this? Am I transmitting this view to my own children?" We could at least stop transmitting and inflicting these delusions and "Just so" stories on our children. Even if we through our own upbringing have been brainwashed with these stories, whether it's through our parents, priests, ideologists or through the media.

Apart from children being homophobic, "Julian" addresses many other interesting issues during the interview. One red thread throughout the conversation we had was the poisoning feelings of shame. Another one was the gender-role "strait-jackets". Regarding the latter two, he is an exponent of the vast majority of the respondents in our pilot study. In fact, even we were surprised by how central these issues were to the majority of the respondents in our study. (You can read more about the central findings of our pilot-study in Appendix I)

These rigid gender-roles also affect others than the non-heterosexuals. This is also evident in "Julian's" considerations. He talks, among other things, about the boys as conquers and the girls as victims. He also points out that countries with the most rigid gender-role systems, are the countries with most problems on any societal level.

"Julian's" claim is actually spot on. In fact, one of the largest studies ever conducted by an academic discipline called political-psychology, confirms by far his observation. The study was conducted in no less than 133 of the countries on our planet. You can read more about their findings in Chapter 15. Some of these findings will surely surprise you.

I would like to thank both you "Julian" and the other respondents in our pilot study, for giving us so much of your time and your deepest feelings. I would also like to add that many of your questions have had a profound impact on the content of this book. From the deep of my heart, thanks a lot, all of you.

"When someone pulls away the rug beneath your feet, and then they blame you for falling"

Vaarin Albrigtsen

Too many people like "Julian" end up in the psychiatry ward because of their feelings of being outcast. But healthy people like him don't belong there. Moreover, as we have seen through the previous part of this book, both psychology and psychiatry are largely responsible for this systemic dysfunction. They have both been powerful premise-providers at all levels of the culture.

During my work as a youth-worker, sexologist and infotainer (entertainer with a message), I have encountered many examples on how psychiatry in many cases reinforces some of these people's sufferings, rather than reinforcing their identities and sexual orientations. But to be fair, there are also many examples of this needed support being given.

Still, a treatment system should not be based on an ideology, or anyone's personal belief. I think it's important to point this out, precisely because both psychiatry and psychology have been, and still are powerful premise providers. Here are some cases that each show a frightening lack of insight (including therapeutic self-insight), as well as both deliberately and subtle prejudice.

A few years ago I received a call from a young boy who was very worried about one of his friends who had tried to commit suicide several times, because she couldn't deal with her sexual orientation. The boy who called me is himself homosexual and well informed by my work in the field of sexology. It turned out that "Maria", as I choose to call her, didn't only struggle with her own acceptance, but with her family's acceptance too.

Among other things, it turned out that her family were devoted members of an evangelic congregation. Eventually I got to a meet with "Maria", which led to a four hours conversation at a cafe in Oslo. I will never forget this meeting. She told me about her sister who reacted with nausea when she, after a long time, dared to come forward with her sexuality. She told me about an older brother who turned his back on her, and refused to have anything more to do with her. But the worst part of the story was probably when she was thrown out by her own father. He told her that there was no place for sinners in their family.

«Maria» suffered a major breakdown. She was eventually admitted to a psychiatry ward, but they had little to offer her but drug treatment. While she stayed at the ward, she even tried to talk about her sexual orientation as one of her main problems, but according to her no-one would even listen to her. They treated her breakdown, which obviously was a symptom of a dysfunctional family.

By the time I met her, I was fortunately well acquainted with the Abrahamic religions. And parts of the research on the Torah, the Bible and the Koran. She also told me that after being discharged from psychiatry, she contacted a local GLBT group. They told her that she had to get rid of her religious beliefs, otherwise she would only have herself to blame for her continuing problems. Just for the record, let me add that there are groups within this same organization that support the religious members. However, I had long since understood that one cannot simply "take" a religious conviction away from a human being.

Thus, much of the conversation we had was about religion and various condemning biblical quotations and many of the misinterpretations and contradictions regarding these Abrahamic religions. But by all means also all the good quotes, not at least those of Jesus. I also told her about the Gospel of Thomas, which was banned in early Christian history. And that it may have been banned precisely because it equated women with men. I also told her that the Bible doesn't condemn sexual love between two women. In fact, it's not a theme at all, neither in Judaism, Christianity nor Islam. What actually happened was that she re-framed her faith, and slowly she began to accept her own sexual talents.

In the aftermath of this story, I have often wondered what it was that did the trick. Was it that Bible does not condemn the love between women? I don't know. However, she told me that the reason for wanting to end her life, was that she "knew" she was going to burn in hell and that she couldn't stand the torturous time of waiting. She just wanted to get it over with. No, we're not talking about the dark middle age, we're talking about the modern era, in Norway.

The last thing she said still makes me shudder to this day. By the way, eventually it all went well for "Maria". The last time I heard about her she was studying at the university, she had embarked on one of her most important future dreams. Moreover, she had finally been accepted by her family.

"Maria" wasn't ill, but the context she experienced herself in, including her own parents and siblings, was a seriously dysfunctional one, one that was in a dire need for treatment.

"Time and time again, I've seen both depression and other so-called psychiatric diagnoses evaporate when one is allowed to live openly with one's talents."

E. E Pirelli Benestad

Another story I experienced, which is about "Siv", is somehow a bit funny, but it could easily have led to tragedy, if it wasn't for a highly attentive acquaintance of mine who worked as a miljeu-therapist at the time. Let's call the therapist "Steve". "Siv" was referred to a clinical ward because of an uncontrolled, and often irrational anger. Her fury could come as lightning out of a clear blue sky. She went through an endless series of clinical examinations by numerous psychiatrists and psychologists. "Steve" was one of the few who managed to get under her skin. "Steve's" empathy and care eventually made "the ice melt". "Siv" slowly gained confidence in "Steve".

During one of their conversations, "Steve" randomly touched the topic of homosexuality. He talked about it being as natural as heterosexuality, and that he had several friends who were gay. Among others, he mentioned me as an example of being both. He also told her about my work. This conversation with "Steve" caused "Siv" to open up. She sensed that "Steve" was inclusive, and that he showed genuine interest, even though he was heterosexual. On a later occasion, "Steve" told me about this episode, and that her irrational outbursts of rage from that day on had evaporated like snow on a warm sunny day.

"Siv" later stated that she would like to meet me, so we did. We talked for hours, and she told me about many episodes she had experienced, including a psychologist she met with on a regularly basis. She had gently begun to move forward about her sexuality, hoping that the psychologist would come up with some liberating questions. Her shame prevented her from talking about it directly. Nothing happened. Finally she decided that on her next appointment, she would hit her psychologist with a vase she had spotted in the corner of the office, if the psychologist was unable to take her hints.

Fortunately, both the psychologist and "Siv" avoided this scenario. Before this potentially violent visit to the psychologist, "Steve" came to her rescue. As mentioned above.

My personal experience of "Siv", was that of a strong, committed and not at least humorous person. It wasn't very difficult to like her. I was told that she later got a girlfriend, and that her problems had mostly been reduced to everyday challenges. Challenges that we all have to deal with in life. No matter sex, race or sexual orientation.

The following story is about one of our respondents in the pilot study. First, let me add that we received inquiries from all over the country regarding our study. But due to both finances and time, we had to limit personal attendance to the south of the country. The rest of the interviews took place online. This following interview took place at a parking-lot in the respondent's hometown. The interview lasted several hours, this is the short version.

"Victor" grew up in a religious family, but he told me that his family never spoke negatively about homosexuality. "Well, they never talked about sexuality at all," he added.

The problems for "Victor" escalated the day he enrolled at a Christian boarding school. This school obviously had homosexual contempt as a central theme of the teaching that dealt with religion. The principal in particular, constantly touched on this topic in his devotionals. "Victor's" shame and fear of revealing his sexual orientation, had by this time built up to dangerous heights. But it was one of the principal's devotional speeches that became the triggering factor. "Victor" decided to end it all. Fortunately he was rescued by a fellow student who happened to stop by his room. One minute later, "Victor" would probably not be among us anymore.

As a result of the suicide attempt, he was admitted to a psychiatric ward at the regional hospital. There he went through endless conversations with a clinical psychologist. "Victor", was so ashamed that he did not dare to approach the real reason why he wanted to end his life. His shame was simply too overwhelming. So he talked about the symptoms, anxiety, depression, etc. After more than twenty hours of therapy, "Victor's" father contacted the ward to ask them whether it might have something to do with sexuality. He wondered whether "Victor" might prefer men, as he put it. From that moment on "Victor" received the help he needed.

"Victor" is alive today, not as a result of the psychiatric ward at the regional hospital, but because of a random visit and a vigilant and caring father. It is shocking that a trained psychotherapist with six years of education failed to get into the topic of sexuality. Today, "Victor" accepts his sexuality and is open about it to both friends and family.

I have often wondered whether psychiatric patients might be the healthiest among us. They are often involuntary whistle-blowers regarding the dysfunctionality of our modern systems. Some of them, such as those mentioned here: "Julian", "Maria", "Siv" and "Victor" are potentially our teachers. They make us aware that something is very wrong, even within some of the systems that are initially there to help.

When both therapeutic context - and text, makes you "blind"

To end this chapter I want to mention an episode I experienced some years ago when I was working as a milieu-therapist in Stockholm. One evening I got a call from a former colleague at another institution. My former colleague felt he needed some "professional" advice regarding a dramatic and difficult situation that took place at his institution.

The opening of the telephone conversation went as follows: "Richard, you who define yourself as bisexual might have some advice regarding the following problem. We came over two of our 15 year-old boys the other day while performing oral sex on each other in the basement. We've had emergency meetings, a psychologist is connected, all in all it has become difficult to deal with the situation, we don't know how to handle it!"

My first impulse and response was: "Well, what about you, did you ever happen to get horny when you were 15? And were you among the lucky ones who actually experienced this as a teenager?" A moment of silence appeared at the other end of the line. Then he asked me a little hesitantly what I would do in a situation like this.

I replied that if it was me who accidentally came upon these two, I would quietly withdraw, that is if they hadn't already discovered me. On the other hand, if they should discover me, I would have done my best to acknowledge that it was perfectly ok, and pardoned me for inadvertently having broken into their private intimate sphere. I would of course make sure that the act of love was founded on mutual consent. Observing the act would normally be sufficient to confirm that. I would not have engaged the rest of the staff and made a case of it, or dramatized it in any way.

I went on to say that both you, the rest of the staff and the boys are lucky if you haven't stigmatized them more than they already are by being disclosed in a private moment of intimacy. Since you are calling me, I guess you haven't gone that far yet. You now have the opportunity to stigmatize both of these two young boys, with whatever it may cause of possible damage to their self-images, love life and self-esteem.

By the end of the day, it all went well. They managed to de-dramatize it in due time. However, the embarrassment remained in both the boys, for a while. But embarrassment is neither a disease (diagnosis), nor something that kills you.

It is both interesting and important to note how all behavior can be interpreted as diagnosis when, for example the arena is a juvenile institution or a psychiatric ward. Then everything from tooth brushing to being angry, or having natural sexual desires and dreams, can be analyzed and interpreted as symptoms based on the diagnosis they may have been assigned.

In fact, some studies have been done on this phenomenon in the United States, by a psychologist named David Rosenhan. The results they came up with were pretty scary. So surprising and scary that it became a mainstream news story.

Dr. Rosenhan and his colleagues turned to psychiatric clinics across the United States, where they faked psychiatric symptoms, such as hearing voices in their heads among other things. They were admitted without exception. As soon as they were inside, they behaved like their normal selves. Nevertheless, the context (here the institutions) meant that their completely healthy behaviors were largely interpreted as symptoms of the diagnoses they had received at hospitalization. (1) (2)

Especially those of you who work in institutions and child welfare, I strongly recommend that you familiarize yourself with this type of research. Tunnel-vision is only useful when driving 200 km. per hour on the highway. In treatment, one should drive slowly, so slowly that one are able to observe all of the surrounding terrain. And remember, you too, are part of the terrain (the environment). You are not necessarily an objective observer, even if you have put on your "white coat".

CHAPTER 12

Gender-Roles in a Developmental Psychological Perspective

A little story about boys and girls

"If gender difference was so natural, why does it have to be so methodically and continually forced on our children"

Michael S. Kimmel

"Children still need to take a look between their legs to find out what leisure activities are advisable for them. On Facebook you can choose gender yourself. First I chose to be female. It didn't matter whether I was single or in relationship, I was nevertheless peppered with advertising for dieting and plastic surgery. Then I chose to be single male. The ads were immediately filled with dating services with light dressed ladies. I eventually switched to married male. Now I get a daily dose of advertisings for tools, private guitar-lessons and active vacations."

Guri Fjeldberg, author (1)

In their book "The History of Girls and Boys - Gender Socialization in a Developmental Psychological Perspective" Bjerrum Nielsen and Rudberg go deeper and wider with their developmental perspective in explaining the causes of gender-identity and gender-roles than what has been the case among most prevalent gender researchers. Their perspective probably belongs in an integrative approach. What is also interesting about their approach is that, like John Money's definition of gender, they differentiate between the unconscious and the cognitive processes. In addition, they also look at the interactivity between them. In this perspective, the individual is both a conscious and an unconscious actor.

Gender-researchers have mostly been sociologically oriented in studies of the origin of gender socialization. They have largely focused on societal conditions and limitations. They also assume that everything is constructed. In addition, they focus primarily on women's opportunities (or lack of opportunities). But sociology, like biology, cannot explain the whole "picture" alone. Bjerrum Nielsen and Rudberg point out that the inequalities and limitations regarding gender can be partly explained as reproduced in a psychological sense. They further argue that we must see this in a three-part interactionist development perspective. Such a perspective must then attempt to understand gender socialization as a result of both cognitive development as well as an underlying depth psychological perspective, in addition to the sociological. (2)

Bjerrum Nielsen and Rudberg believe that parts of gender socialization go deep, and in order to see and understand the whole picture, cognitive-psychological and psychodynamic theories must also be applied in addition to the sociological perspective's theories. They argue that socialization and identity formation must be understood as a process in which the individual is an active participator, trying to create both meaning and structure in the reality into which he or she is born. This view is firmly rooted in cognitive theory, which states that when the child has arrived at the age of two and discovering that they belong to one of two categories called gender, it tries to make sense of this gender difference. Reality and the child itself are from this moment on, interpreted by gender as the most central cognitive scheme. (3)

A scheeme is a theory of reality, which one uses to understand new experiences from based on what one already knows. This is called *assimilation*. If there is a conflict between old and new experiences, this either results in new information being denied, because the old knowledge seems safer, or that one changes or expands the scheme in line with the new experiences. This latter is called *accommodation.* (4) Not unlike scientific paradigms, which you'll learn more about in chapter 15, 19 and 20. It's also related to the concept of *cognitive dissonance.* (See Central Concepts)

One might say that the cognitive perspective describes the reason-oriented aspect of the individual as a rational actor. But as most of us have experienced, being human is as much about irrational thoughts and actions, based on feelings and deeper emotions. Which in turn can be expressions of unconscious structures and processes. To be able to understand and explain these, one must apply in-depth psychological theories and models.

As mentioned, Nielsen and Rudberg use psychodynamic theory to explain these aspects. This theory shows how the earliest experiences we have in our lives, form the basic structure of our personalities. One might call this a kind of an unconscious scheme.

These schemes are already established when we begin our cognitive mapping of our reality at the age of two. These unconscious schemes are so deeply ingrained in us that a later change of them will be very difficult and demanding. These basic unconscious schemes reflect phenomena such as closeness, separation and what the environment accepts or does not accept regarding the child's expressions of needs.

The object-relation theorists, which the above researchers mostly refer to in terms of psychodynamic theory, recognizes that the child is fundamentally socially oriented and therefore has a need for connection with other individuals. The child's relationships with others develops from day one, where the boundaries between the child and other individuals are blurred. It continues to develop until the age of three, when the child is able to perceive itself as a separate and independent individual. From this age the child is able to stand in mutual relations with other individuals. This process of psychological interaction eventually leads to the development of the child's self. This self, in turn determines the child's ability to form relationships and separations from other people even later in life. (5) See also Chapter 19 where I write about Ainsworth's research on attachment-styles.

One might therefore say that the early childhood's unconscious schemes play an important part in the adult's "symphony" of emotions, thoughts and actions, and therefor an important part of our basic subjectivity. Thus, psychodynamic theorists also see the individual as an agent, but at this level the agent is not conscious. In this context, it is very important to note the differences in reactions adults show regarding girls' versus boys' behavior in early childhood.

Nancy Chodorow, a sociologist and psychoanalyst, studied how children developed behavioral patterns based on their earliest relationships. She claimed that this idea of gender- differences that defines us as men and women is produced. It is a social, psychological and cultural product. Produced by people who live in and create this social, psychological and cultural world. (6)

It may also be interesting to refer to Kate Milletts, who believes that an androcentric societal perspective (andro = Greek for man) is why these stereotypical gender roles become psychologically internalized in both boys and girls already in early childhood. She argues that both mass media, literature, and the sociological and psychological sciences help to reproduce and maintain these stereotypes, by prescribing what is "natural" male and "natural" female These latter factors are very central in adolescence. (7)

An example from the psychology of religion may also be relevant to include. A researcher named Petra Junus proposes in a dissertation on women's identity and religiosity, a model that explains the above-mentioned internalization of the stereotyped gender roles. Junus claims that the masculine image of God in the Jewish, Christian and Muslim culture is internalized at the same time as the gender-identity is being fortified in the child (2, 3 years of age). This masculine image of

God becomes important for the child's self-representation. Boys' self-representation is reinforced by the fact that God is the highest authority, while at the same time God is culturally portrayed as a man. This same masculine image of God also contributes to a downgrading of the female gender. This leads to a negative impact on the self-representation of young girls. (8)

Jean Baker Miller writes in Towards a New Psychology of Women that, since the norm of human behavior is based on an androcentric understanding of reality, men themselves have attributed their own "inferior" characteristics, which they define as weak, not only to women, but also to children. Such qualities include, among other things, underdeveloped thinking, emotional dependence, lack of initiative and an emotional life that is not controlled by reason. Miller further states that such traits are intuitively therefore to be perceived as survival strategies for all those who have no power. (9)

What Miller talks about is strongly reminiscent of projecting one's own unwanted traits onto others. Psychoanalysis describes projection as one of several defense-mechanisms. Projection is also the defense-mechanism which is most documented and confirmed in psychological experimental research. (This coping-strategy or defense-mechanism is also explained in Part II of this book, and in Central Concepts). This is also the defense mechanism which is most frequently used. Both consciously and unconsciously. (10)

Nielsen and Rudberg argue that human psychology is an important "engine" for society's reproduction of gender inequalities at different levels of behavior. They further say that a baby-girl in pink clothes will not necessarily mean anything for her own active and cognitive socialization. But if the pink clothes causes adult people to treat her differently, for example, with more tenderness and caution than if she had been dressed in blue, and thus been perceived as a boy, then this can have consequences for her first experiences of who she is in relation to other people. (11) Nielsen and Rudberg's observations have later been confirmed by two studies conducted in Sweden and the United

Kingdom, respectively. (You can learn more about these studies in Chapter 19)

In this context, psychologist Hanne Haavind's research is equally important. She found that adults' perceptions of a child's behavior are accepted with a much higher tolerance when the behavior is seen as gender-typical, than when it actually is an expression of the child's individual personality. Boys are more punished than girls when such behavior is considered to be outside the norm of expected gender-behavior. (12) The boys, in other words, are more punished than the girls when they move outside the trodden paths. One might say that they are punished if they "leave Mars" to explore space!

Bjørnar Moxnes is a person who obviously see the problems this can cause for young boys of our time. He has taken the initiative to start a gender-role course for men.

When Bjørnar Moxnes asks the students in his gender-role course about what would have happened if the guys had started sewing or knitting? "You would be accused of being gay or sissy!" are the most common answers he gets. Besides, it would be completely unthinkable for these boys to cry in the movie theater. "After all, we should be aware that gender-roles are barriers to us. In a way, we can't do what we want, we are tied up in a role, or locked up in a cage", one of the participants said. "The whole society is losing out on it", says another participant. The boys in Moxnes' courses doubt whether they had raised such topics in other contexts, but think it is important to have this opportunity to talk about it. Because they usually don't do that, out there. (13)

So it is not so much about sex as it is about being accepted as a "man", and indirectly how women are and should be treated. In addition, it should be mentioned again that the most used bullying / harassment strategy in Norwegian schools today is the gay and bitch / whore stigma.

This male-gender straitjacket affects everyone, girls, boys, heterosexuals, homosexuals and in-betweens! So it's not so much about sexual-orientations, it's mostly about being accepted as "man", and that includes a long list of does and don'ts. Indirectly it suggests how women should be treated, and what "woman-ness" is. In addition, let me once again mention that the most widely used bullying or harassment-strategies in Norwegian schools today are the gay and bitch / whore stigma. As it is in the rest of Europe. (14)

As mentioned, this also affects the girls! They suffer just as much as the boys from these hopeless macho ideals. The less we allow boys to feel, and the more we treat them as "strong" conquerors, the less emotional they dare be. In many ways they are trained to be "egophiles" instead of empathetic beings. But it goes both ways, even girls are trained in "egophilia", as the study below shows.

A survey conducted among Norwegian high-school graduates in 2008 showed frightening results, almost half of the girls had had very unpleasant sexual experiences on the verge of abuse, with peers of the opposite sex. More than 30% of the boys reported the same! Psychiatrist Mette Hvalstad, who conducted the survey, believes that lack of communication is one of the main reasons. She points out that this generation communicates sexual feelings even worse than their parent's generation. (15)

VG-Magasinet (Norwegian newspaper) recently put the spotlight on many of the same issues, and the consequences this will have for young people. Judging from the trends described in this article, it doesn't look good. It may even seem that the situation is deteriorating from year to year. Something radical must be done. One cannot just continue with "fire extinguishing", trying to limit the damage. Radical changes in attitudes are needed. Massive preventive forces must be deployed. At all levels, and at the earliest possible age. For all genders (!)

The above-mentioned VG article was entitled "Sex Without Borders". The article writes about party-rape, which has increased by 45% since 2011. It goes on about intimate-images and video-clips that are spreading exponentially on many social-media channels. Both voluntary and involuntary admissions.

"This is a nationwide trend. Young people share photos and movies, abuse takes place without the youngsters being aware of it" says Laila Sondrol, section manager of the national police. Rita Parnas, police attorney in Oslo says: "My impression is that much of what is filmed is boundless sexual acts where pleasure and love don't seem to be the focus. The girls are subsequently negatively labeled as whores, bitches etc, while the boys are given credits." (16)

What is mentioned above is not derived from what we call extreme subcultures, or criminally charged environments. This is about ordinary young people in what we might call mainstream youth communities in Norway today. I often hear stories like this when I talk to young people in one to one conversations. This results in a lot of anxiety and not least, lots of low self-esteems and broken souls.

In the same VG article, we also hear some of the young people's own experiences as a result of this malignant culture. Perhaps one of the things that made the most impact on me was "Emma's" story. She experienced a party-rape as a 14-year-old. She was dragged into a room, despite the fact that she refused. She even tried to appeal to the boy's conscience by shouting out that she was a virgin. To no avail. Eventually, she could no longer bear this humiliation and pain alone. (16) Here are her own words:

"When I finally told my dad, I cried, but I refused to report it. Then I would have everyone against me. Maybe I could have won a trial, but then I would be left all alone without any friends." Her reason for not reporting the rapes is heartbreaking, but at the same time very scary. It tells a lot about the prevailing attitudes among many of the young people today. As well as a lack of unity and mutual trust between what was meant to be friends. (16)

In the article "Emma" and her friend "Caroline" also describes the general climate as being poisoned by pressure among their peers.

Pressure to lose your virginity. "If you're a boy in the 8'grade, you start to stress if you haven't done anything yet" says "Caroline" (16)

The journalists also interviewed a boy named "Christian". He says that he and his mates like to show off, be the coolest ones, and that they party hard every weekend. "The guys go out for sex," he says, and at parties they take pictures of it, which they post on closed Facebook-groups. A few days later there is an award. Those who win are seen as loose. This applies to both girls and boys, but it is the girls who are most often called sluts, he says. When asked by the journalist why they are called sluts, "Christian" replies: "It's just the view of women, t's a little weird to talk about." (16)

This is a terrible "picture" with regard to sexual behavior and gender-roles. Some of what I have referred to above shows that everyone, both girls and boys, are subject to this gender-role hysteria. One effect of this is the lack of emphatic communication. Another one is that boys are seen as conquerors, and the sexual language they use is filled with war and sports metaphors: "Get meat on your bone, prey, hunting pussy," and so on. Affection, empathy and respect are wiped out of this "language". It is beginning to resemble a generally accepted collective sociopathic behavior. An offline war-game.

We are running the risk of bringing up a generation of bad lovers, but "good" porn actors, and terrified people who don't trust their own "friends". And the girls? They often respond that they dare not communicate their bad experiences in fear of hurting their manhood. This I've heard more than once from female clients.

"Where have they learned this? Is this too the fault of feminization of the schools? Boys account for 70% of the behavioral problems among students today. If this trend is not reversed, it could have more serious social consequences than we like to realize today! This situation is more serious than you think!"

This is from an editorial in Haugesunds Avis, a regional newspaper in Norway. Among other things, it claims that boys are learning in other ways than girls, that the schools are feminized, etc. (17) But this can be a dangerous dead-end! This wasn't a problem a generation ago.

The same reasoning and discussion has also appeared elsewhere, including in the state of California. There, six schools were opened where they separated the genders. Girls and boys schools. A systematic study of this pilot-program yielded rather depressing results. In fact, traditional gender-role stereotypes such as "good girls" and "bad boys" were reinforced in these schools. This is not exactly good news for those who set out to save the boys from feminization. Already after three years, five of the schools were closed down. (18) Maybe it's time to bury this polarized view of "feminism" and "masculinism"? Could it be that human-individualism is a possible third way to explore? Individual talents instead of cultural straitjackets?

But how did it all begin? This was not such a widespread problem in the 70s. It's probably a result of the acceleration of categorization and polarization in the following decade. Homosexuality began to be seriously associated with feminine behavior, in the sense of being weak, passive, etc. Again we see the link between gender-role identity and sexuality. This gender-dichotomy reinforced it all, supported by the film and media industry. And this despite the fact that most lesbians and gays cannot be associated with either a "feminine" or "masculine" behavior.

It wasn't until the late 1970s that the term "homophobia" emerged. This increased the homo-anxiety and became a propeller both for differentiating the roles of women and men, but also for the sexual-identities. We will take a closer look at this phenomenon in the next chapters.

It can safely be stated that the gender-role identities are unfortunately still the most central organizing principles, also regarding the sexualities. And all the pressure to fit into these gender-roles are to some a nightmare in which they brutally suppress sides of themselves in order to satisfy "the others." That this happens at all is a cultural sociopathic problem, which in turn often comes through as individual psychopathic traits. It's produced, it's not genetic. And the producers are you and me.

We saw this in both "Julian's" and Sheldon Kennedy's stories. But neither "Julian" nor Sheldon is the problem. We are the problem! You and I.

CHAPTER 13

The Infectious Obsession of Gender Differences

"Pink was once a color associated with masculinity, considered to be a watered down red and held the power associated with that color. In 1914 The Sunday Sentinel, an American newspaper, advised mothers to 'use pink for the boy and blue for the girl if you are a follower of convention. The change that contributed to the reversal of this claim began after World War II." (1)

The process that contributed to the reversal of this claim began first after World War II. For some reason, it became even more important to reinforce gender differences. But this time the colors were changed. Some claim that it started with Barbie, but it is probably wrong to blame it on only one player. With the post-war media revolution and the advancement of the popular industry, with all its influence, advertising and trendsetting that followed, one can perhaps say that it is the most "successful" PR stunt of all times that has caused, or at least spread this dubious message worldwide. This campaign has been so "successful", that the "wrong" color on the "wrong" sex today can lead to everything from hysteria to gender-behavioral restrictions and unfortunately also harassment and bullying of children.

It's also worth mentioning that during the war, women had to work away from home as they were needed in the war industry. But when the men returned home from war, women were stuck back in the "kitchen", back to where they "belonged." Advertizing got pretty strong about women's roles in the home. T.V programs such as "Leave It To Beaver", "I love Lucy" and so-forth, in the early 1950's glorified house-wives, wearing dresses, pearls and bringing slippers, pipes and beverages to their husbands when they came home from work.

However, today, the power of propaganda has reached staggering heights. Now, there is talk of women from Venus and men from Mars. This virus has crept into our everyday lives, to a degree that it has become a pandemic, spreading it's viral code right into our bedrooms. For the first time in history, we may be talking about extra-terrestrial sex. And it's not even a paraphilia, yet. Some men are even building "Man-caves". It has become as popular as "Exes on beaches" and "Cup-cake wars". Maybe it's time to "worry" about 30, 40 year old extra-terrestrials, who, both online, offline and in between are setting superficial standards for their so beloved children. (See Chapter 19 regarding the concept of paraphilia).

By the way, almost all well-known societies over the last millennia, right up to our own postmodern era, have based almost unison their rules, norms and policies on the *assumption* of a great gender inequality. But also a gender difference (2) (My italics)

In other words, such an assumption also implies an element of competition between these Mars and Venus immigrants. One of these tribes is "better, more important, more credible" than the other. This is also reflected in the way we discuss gender; we don't say the other sex, or the neighboring sex, we say the opposite sex. It's a bloody competition we're talking about. And it sells very well. Just ask John Gray, he became a multimillionaire with his book: "Women from Venus, Men from Mars" We simply just love the great divides: Male-Female, Homo-Hetero, Black-White, Christian-Muslim. Polarization is perhaps the greatest pandemic of them all. A cross-cultural folk disease?

While the earthly representatives of the gods, the clergy, had long dominated mankind with its "truth" about the differences between races, genders, and more, it was in the late 1800s that the new science after Darwin took over the stage. All of a sudden, "everyone" had become biologists. And by God (!) how all-knowing and biological they were. Especially regarding gender differences. In 1879, French sociologist Gustav LeBon concluded:

"In the most intelligent races, as among the Parisians, there are a large number of women whose brains are closer in size to those of gorillas than to the most developed of male brains. All psychologists who have studied the intelligence of women recognize today that they represent the most inferior forms of human evolution and that they are closer to children and savages than to an adult civilized man. They excel in fickleness, inconstancy, absence of thought and logic, and incapacity to reason. Without doubt, there are some distinguished women, very superior to the average man, but they are as exceptional as the birth of a gorilla with two heads." (3)

Gustav LeBon was far from alone in this "scientific" view on the genders at that time. For example, psychologist G Stanley Hall was also quite clear in his determination of the abysmal difference between men and women. Hall, by the way, is also held by some as the father of American psychology. There were no such thing as psychological mothers at that time. You probably understand why.

Hall was perhaps a little more caring in his statements about the "weak" woman than LeBon and many others were. Smart as he was, he also saw the danger of an epidemic development of the scary homosexuality, if girls were allowed into the classroom with boys. It would not only harm the girls or take away their fragile femininity, it would also "feminize" the boys. The end of it all would be that the mysterious attraction of the opposite sex would be erased, thus causing all the boys to become gay. (4)

It's weird that Hall didn't warn against the same homo-danger for the girls. By the way, maybe it's not so strange, after all the girls were not viewed as sexual individuals at the time. Regarding the boys, It's possible that Hall would have changed his mind about this "homo-danger" for the boys, if he had paid visits to the local prison, or boarding schools for boys. Well, it's been a while since LeBon and Hall and his contemporary colleagues dominated the scene. Fortunately, it has changed considerably since then.

However, the big difference between men and women is still the theme on which movies, fashion, flirting, porn, ideals and family structures are based on. Nevertheless, most of the research on this topic shows that there are far greater differences within the sexes than between the sexes. Gender equality is far greater than the popular industry is trying to have us believe.

If you look more closely at this research, you will see that only a small part of the population is sorted by these gender role stereotypes that are described in virtually all media. The large proportion of the male and female population share a large common middle zone. (5)

And if one depicts the inequalities and the similarities graphically in the form of two circles, or planets, where let's say we call one Mars and the other Venus, they will almost completely overlap, like an eclipse. One will find that the similarities actually cover at least 96%. This applies to almost every aspect of the psyche, human experience, but also sexual norms and habits. The outer edges that reflect inequalities in form of hyper-masculine or hyper-feminine behavior are negligible. Nevertheless, these are most often inflated. Psychologically, this phenomenon is called the accentuation-effect. (See Central Concepts)

Psychologist Carol Tarvis argues that this binary thinking regarding this cosmic abyss between women and men leads to what philosophers call "The law of the excluded middle". Namely the excluded field that is located between the outer edges. Tarvis also reminds us that it is precisely in this field that most women and men find themselves in terms of personality traits, psychological qualities, values, abilities and more. (6)

When one sees this distribution of human behavior, which, for the majority does not lie on these fringes, it is perhaps not surprising that many men and women feel that they are unable to live up to these expectations of "normal" female or male behavior. This also applies to the sexual arena.

This can also lead to a conscious accentuation-effect, with the result that most men and women consciously are drawn to these reinforced extremes of this vast field, because it is often these extremes that is highlighted as ideals for gender behavior, and thus culturally expected. At the same time, one avoids the discomfort of standing out too much from the masses. In this way, one becomes a psychological co-creator of something that is perceived as biology. In other words, this is far more cognitive than biological. (See Central Concepts)

Not long ago, I had a lecture for some teachers, where I, among other things, addressed some of the above. As an example of male accentuation, I mentioned the term *macho*. I then asked the audience if they knew what this term meant. There were many answers, but to my great astonishment none of them knew the correct definition of the term. Macho simply means exaggerated masculinity, in other words it is a highly cognitive thing. It is deliberate role play.

When brain research is presented as evidence of innate, unchanging gender differences, the mistakes of the past are repeated, claims Harvard psychologist Cordelia Fine. As an example, she mentions an experiment where math skills were to be measured:

Women at a university take a math test. A group of women are only told that this is a test to find out why some people are better than others in math. Another group is told the same thing, but here the researchers add that the test has been done on thousands of people, and no gender differences have been found. The women in the second group do better than those where gender is not commented on. The prejudice that women are bad at math is so strong that the subjects do not need to be reminded of it. They are still underperforming. (7)

Here we see an example of how both supposed "scientific truths" and prejudices actually turn into self-fulfilling prophecies. The myth that men are better at technical and logical problem solving than women is tenacious. And it is nowhere near true.

This social psychological form of self-fulfilling prophecy has another and more malignant clinical relative, namely implanted "truths". In Norway, the Bjugn-case is a tragic example of this phenomenon. Bjugn is a small community where a significant part of the male preschool teachers were accused of sexual abuse, based on rumors. The therapists' assumptions became the children's "truths" during the process. An entire community had to pay dearly for this scientific ignorance. One would like to expect that they at least had some knowledge of Elisabeth Loftus's extensive research on this phenomenon. Everyone, both laypersons and scholars, should familiarize themselves with this well-documented phenomenon.

If you are interested, you can find a link to her research in the appendix section. (8)

Regarding the sexual arena: Why has sexual orientation been so poisoned by these gender-role stereotypes? The reality is neither blue nor pink. It is probably rather shades of grey (not shades Gray). Men do not come from Mars, and women do not come from Venus. We all come from planet earth, or Tellus as it is named.

"Homo is femi," many claim. Well, one thing is for sure, this claim does not find much biological support anywhere. On the contrary, if one looks a little over the shoulder and studies the sexual activities of various warrior societies, which I discussed in chapters 1 and 2, one sees that sexual activity between men has been particularly prevalent in the warrior cultures. And warrior cultures are rarely referred to as feminine or pink cultures native to Venus?

Homosex is probably more of a macho phenomenon in that context. Maybe homosexual macho warriors come from Mars? Because when it comes to the Samurai, Spartans or the Vikings (and many more), none of them are seen as weak sissy-boys from Venus, right?

But what different factors actually contribute to the development of gender-identity, gender-roles and gender differences? In this book, I try to focus on a battery of studies, underlying factors and different angles, which together may help to explain why gender roles and differences emerge only after the human child has been given a language. I think it is important to shed light on all the explanations and interpretations of the various perspectives in this field, in order to someday reach a conclusion regarding the possible innate differences.

Hetero, gay or in-between. Sexual behavior as identity

Sexual desire, arousal and sexual behavior may or may not be synonymous with one's sexual identity. That is, people can identify as heterosexual, but still feel attracted to the same sex, and vice versa. In the western world, the vast majority of people tend to identify as either heterosexual or homosexual. Other cultures have no distinction between these two sexual orientations. Our western cultures mostly embrace the essential (biological) perspective, the either or perspective. Whether one is heterosexual or homosexual, we consider it an innate orientation. (Polarization)

For the essentialists, it is obviously important to establish an either or understanding of orientation. As well as to build a whole world around the one or the other identity. Just like the identity-building regarding the two races that come from Mars or Venus, respectively. In Western cultures, for example, homosexuality has evolved from being a sexual behavior to an identity. In earlier times, people could engage in same-sex sexual acts without building an identity and a lifestyle around these desires and behaviors. (9)

Psychologist and researcher Michael Bailey and his colleagues studied identical twins who were divorced at birth and reared apart. These separated identical twins thus grew up with different conditions and environments. Identical twins, as is well known, share completely identical genetic material. The studies found a probability that was far greater than coincidence, that if one of the twins was homosexual, then the likelihood of the other being the same would be high. (10)

Since the twins in this study did not share the same environment, but the same genetic material, one would expect that if only the genes controls sexual orientations, it would be logical that all identical twin-pairs reflected that. They didn't. Thus, other factors also come into play.

Subsequent genetic twin studies have pointed out the fact that having a particular genotype, DNA-encoded for a particular characteristic trait, will not necessarily develop or result in a corresponding phenotype (the physical expression of this characteristic trait). Scientists wonder whether the environment and individual history can influence the expression or the suppression of genotypes. (11)

In a relatively new research discipline called epigenetics, they talk about genes that turn themselves on and off. For my part, I think it is more accurate to say that they are turned on and off, due to both internal and external environmental factors. In other words, according to this research discipline, we are all endowed with both hetero- and homo-genes. You can read more about epigenetics in Chapters 19 and 20.

If biology does not decide whether one is hetero- or homosexual (or March - Venus immigrants) or in-between, does it mean that sexual orientation is a choice? Not really. It is not like you can place an order of the preferred sexual orientation for your child at the local orientation store. It is conceivable that physical and social structures along with individual biography work together to inhibit or open up various sexual desires and behaviors in an individual.

Due to basic strong and strict social norms when it comes to sexual peace, most people will probably follow a single sexual (monosexual) orientation as their beaten path through the adult part of their lives. In any case, a large part of the scientific data still supports the idea that biology is a contributing player in the big game of sexual orientation. Or as Scwartz and Rutter put it: "But it's not the only game in town". (12)

Alfred Kinsey opened the door to think of sexuality as sexualities. Most people use dichotomous (either / or) terms regarding sexual orientations, but the recognition that many people also have the ability to have sex with both men and women at some point in their lives, is greatly to the thanks of Kinsey. Using a scale that measures sexual behavior between the extremes (heterosexuality and homosexuality), Kinsey clarified the existence of bisexuality.

The latter is probably troublesome for the classical essentialists and determinists. Nevertheless, biology also proves the existence of bisexuality in the animal kingdom. (13) (14) Bisexuality will be thoroughly covered in Chapter 19, in connection with some studies that reveal a surprisingly large and so far hidden prevalence of bisexual variation.

The fact is, as I mentioned in an earlier chapter, that if we do not know the biological origin of homosexuality, we do not know the biological origin of heterosexuality either. Although biologists claim that it is caused by hormones, chromosomes and genetic information, it is far from proven. For many, the origins of heterosexuality have not been questioned at all, because it appears to be given and rooted in the imperative of reproduction. (15)

"If a plant is not allowed to live in accordance with its nature, it dies. The same goes for a human being"

Many years ago I wrote an article in an Australian magazine (fanzine) with the headline: They Don't Grow Tomatoes in The Sahara, with an angle on the environment as a significant factor for human growth and development. This was a long time before I could even spell the word psychology, and even less was able to speak this complicated language "psychologish."

The article I wrote at the time had long been forgotten until I saw a Swedish short-movie entitled "Man tenkar sitt" ("It Makes You Think") during the New Year's weekend 013. This movie was about life in a "sleepy" suburban street viewed through the eyes of a 10-year old boy. It touched on the "terror" of normality in mainstream-culture. (16) The words that appeared on the scrolling text at the end of the movie have literally etched into my mind, probably forever:

"If a plant cannot live according to its nature, it dies. So does a human being"

These words sort of reframed the underlying message of the movie in a new way, at least for me. I definitely recommend you to watch it, and perhaps watching it with the quote above as an imaginary "3D glasses".

The partner therapist and relationship educator, Bjoerk Matheasdatter, gives us some excellent descriptions and metaphors regarding not being allowed to live in accordance with one's own nature, by ignoring the individual's uniqueness when it comes to upbringing, influence, respect, acceptance and nourishment. All of these five aspects fall under what psychology call environmental impact. Nurture. By modern biologists they are often named Epi-genetic factors.

"We can all flourish if we're allowed to be the flowers we are," is the headline of an article she wrote in her column in the Norwegian magazine (Dagbladet). The subtitle was "In Good Soil". Here she uses pictures from her own interest in plants and gardening in a brilliant way. Among other things, she writes: "For several years I have been trying to plant raspberries in the soil outside my house. I have brought with me plants from where ever I have been able to find some, and replanted them outside my house, but always with disappointing results.

The last time I planted, I tried something new: I brought some soil with me from where I found them. Then the plants thrived, grew and gave me berries for breakfast and dessert. It wasn't the plants' fault that they withered and died. It was I who had not provided the right soil and nourishment. Gardeners know this. They do not blame the plant if it does not grow and thrive. They ask themselves: Is this the right nutrition? Will this plant thrive here? They don't expect a cactus to become a rose, or a rose to endure the same as a cactus." (17) She continues:

"Imagine if we could look at humans the way a skilled gardener looks at the plants. It is said that we live in the age of individualism, but when I speak with my clients, and hear about the challenges they meet in their daily lives, I wonder if we rather live in the age of conformity. Have we forgotten that we are different "plants" that need different soil and nourishment in order to flourish?" (17)

She concludes at the end of the column that: "As adults, we must take responsibility, know ourselves and know what we need in order to flourish. As children, we depend on others to ensure good growth conditions. When the child shows dissatisfaction in kindergarten or school, is too quiet, is too restless or scores poorly on tests, then we search for errors with the child. When the error is found, the child is given a label, which in the worst case becomes an identity marker for the rest of his or her life. And when the label is ready, the child can be helped to grow, where it does not thrive." (17)

Finally, she points out: "Others, both children and adults; can invest so much force to adapt, that top grades, careers and super-trained bodies become camouflage for a cracked soul." (17)

There are many "cracked souls" left in the wake of the adaptation and categorization hysteria. Not at least when it comes to narrow gender roles and sexual straitjackets. Have we created cultures and societies where we plant everyone in the same "poisoned soil", then use "pesticides" and "herbicides" and other manipulative "tools" in order to make all appear "healthy" and "fresh" from the outside?

Based on what I have written and referred to in this chapter and chapter 12, it is worth noting that no one today knows for sure which are the most potent influencing factors when it comes to gender roles and sexual behavior patterns. What we do know, however, is that all of these perspectives, each with its own focus on their respective levels, also are in an interactionist relationship with each other.

The "conductor" can thus make changes at virtually any of these levels, with the exception of any basic biological quality, and at the same time influence the entire "symphony". This gives hope for a developing potential influence, and release of individual human talents, qualities and opportunities. And who knows, maybe this can even help more children to grow... where they thrive (?)

And perhaps only when this development has reached its "end point" will we possibly be able to claim that there are some psychological gender-differences as a function of biological gender. But not before! Social-Darwinian Stone Age scenarios may be intriguing stories, they may even appear convincing, but they have no scientific explanatory power at all. They are "Just So" stories.

CHAPTER 14

Gender Roles - Sexuality - Identity

"You'd think we were different species, like say lobsters or giraffes, or Martians and Venutians. In his best-selling book, pop psychologist John Gray informs us that not only do women and men communicate differently, but they also think, feel, perceive, react, respond, love, need and appreciate differently. It's a miracle of cosmic proportions that we ever understand one another."

Michael S. Kimmel

"Girls get girly and boys get boyish because that is what they have received praise and encouragement for, while opposite behavior has either been ignored or punished" (1)

Harriet Bjerrum Nielsen & Monica Rudberg

The interplanetary theory of women and men: Women coming from Venus and men coming from Mars. By comparison, this must be the absolute greatest cosmic migration-wave in human history.

Biology, Sociology or Psychology? - Or the question of gender as "hardware" and gender roles as "software"? It's more about role liberation, not sexual liberation

Gender or gender-role identity is a social characteristic that often corresponds to biological gender. Both animals and humans are identified as male or female in accordance with the genitals. But only people are described as male or female with all the labels that come with it. (2)

Gender can also be understood as psychological gender. When we say that something is "gendered", we mean what social processes have decided should be appropriately masculine or feminine behavior. And while biological sexes varies very little, gender role identities vary enormously. What it means socially and psychologically to be a man or a woman, can mean very much different depending on where you were born and what era you were born into. In other words, it means that there are far more than biological variables that come into play. They are possibly part of the symphony, but no one knows for sure which violin biology might play.

As soon as a child is born, it receives a host of signals about gender roles and sexuality. In the United States, children are provided with pink or blue diapers, respectively. In case people should be unsure whether to treat the child masculine or feminine, the diapers will guide them. This gender dichotomization continues through childhood and into adulthood. Thus, this gender difference treatment from infancy is repeated and reinforced as gender role differences well into adulthood. (3)

This also affects the child's sexual behavior from young age through adulthood. Currently there are three competing perspectives and explanations regarding differences in sexual desires between men and women. *The biological explanation, the sociobiological and evolutionary psychological explanation* and *the social constructionist explanation.* These perspectives present their respective explanations as complete and mutually exclusive. (4)

But there's also a perspective that goes beyond these three, which seeks to integrate findings from all three of the above into a larger perspective. It's called *the Integrative Approach.* I'll come back to that.

Although biology may seem more or less constant, there are still many examples of how social reality appears to shape biology regarding human sexuality. Each society has its own rules for sexuality, so how people experience their biology can vary greatly. In some societies, women are very passionate and active in sexual contexts. In still others, women do not even have a concept for orgasm.

The latter was something anthropologists discovered in parts of Nepal. Here it is quite clear that it's culture, and not biology, that governs. We know for sure that female orgasms are physically possible. Even male ejaculation can be culturally dictated. In some cultures it is considered healthy to ejaculate early and often. In still other cultures, ejaculation is considered healthy only when it occurs rarely. In some of these cultures, men are even able to experience orgasms without ejaculation. Sometimes the dictates of culture are so strict and rigid that they completely override some of the so-called laws of nature. (4)

Social anthropologist Margaret Mead found after extensive field studies of cultures in New Guinea, that gender differences could not be as deeply biologically rooted as generally thought. In New Guinea, she studied three very different cultures in depth. These were the Arapesh, Mundugamor and Tchambuli cultures, respectively. The first two cultures showed surprisingly equal relations between women and men. Masculinity and femininity were obviously not the dimensions that organized and governed individual behavior. (5) Men and women were not the opposite sex.

For example, the members of the Arapesh culture appeared to be emotionally warm. Both men and women shared child rearing. They were trusting and they also raised the children equally, regardless of gender. Aggressive behavior was not tolerated by either the boys or the girls. In addition, they were also sexually equal. It all seemed to be characterized by cooperation instead of competition. (5)

In contrast to the Arapesh people, the Mundugamores were a warrior people, although they too were equal. They expected both women and men to be equally aggressive and violent. The women did not show any of what we like to call "maternal instincts", they strongly disliked being pregnant, and were not very affectionate towards their children. Just like the fathers. Margaret Mead stated that both men and women were violent, competitive and very sexually aggressive. But, they were equal. (6)

The third of these cultures, the Tchambuli people, was more like what we are familiar with in the Western world. Here, an extreme difference between the sexes' behavior was cultivated and encouraged. One gender was very concerned with care, social interactions, jewelry and clothing. The other gender was the main providers and breadwinners, who controlled both the economy and other instrumental activities. They were also the ones who took the initiative for sex. And they were women. Mead wrote that it was the only culture where she had observed that among children at the age of eleven, it was the girls who were the initiators. The boys were the passive ones. (6)

The only thing that was exactly the same among all these three cultures was that they all claimed that all their behavior was a natural consequence of their biological sex. Of course.

In Chapter 17, I will also consider the research of neuropsychologist James W. Prescott. His research focuses on the upbringing practices of different cultures, where he goes into both the breadth and depth of this. Among other things, he has researched the relationship between sexuality and aggressiveness. His findings are both surprising and revealing. He also does not quite fit into conventional academic echo-chambers, which is probably why his research has been more or less silenced by both biological and social scientists. By the way, I would argue that the findings of his research are more relevant than ever.

Other examples of culture overriding sexual arousal-patterns are found in many tropical cultures where women do not cover their breasts. This doesn't make the men walk around in constant arousal. Breasts are simply not seen as sexual stimuli in these cultures. (7)

Not to forget the Trobriand Island people where women are seen as insatiable, and are at the same time the gender that takes the initiative for sex. Or the Tukano-Kubeo people in Brazil, where women are the sexually aggressive ones. They even avoid getting pregnant as it interferes with the frequency of sex. To top it, they are very unfaithful, commit adultery and justifying it by stating that it was just sex. Their husbands secretly give them anti-aphrodisiacs to "cool them down." (8) All these cultures, of course, conclude that it is natural and that they are the normal ones. Does it sound familiar?

Sociobiology and Evolutionary-biology

The research in previous decades, including the research on sexuality, has brought about a new school with regard to the understanding of human sexual behavior. Sociobiology and evolutionary psychology explain most gender role differences as strategies for sexual reproduction. The key assumption within this thinking is that humans have an innate impulse to pass on their genes through successful reproduction. This impulse they call reproductive adaptation. (Popularly called the adaptation program, which by the way is scientifically rejected). (9)

They further claim that humans, and other animals, experience immortality by having children who live long enough for them to be reproductively mature and produce children themselves. Socio-biologists and evolutionary psychologists try to demonstrate that almost all female and male behaviors, and especially sexual behaviors, are governed by this simple yet powerful innate impulse. (9)

Socio-biologists and evolutionary psychologists simply say that men inseminate and women incubate. They further say that the differences in reproductive abilities and strategies also determine sexual desire. The evolutionary psychologist Buss goes so far as to claim that reproductive strategies shape most categories of desires. Older men generally choose younger women because they are more fertile, and younger women seek older men who have status, power and resources. So that they can protect and support themselves. Evolutionary psychologists also claim that men's propensities for casual sex and multiple partners are a result of this inherent drive to maximize their offspring. They even claim that rapid ejaculation has a reproductive advantage. (10)

Well, the latter statement is probably not entirely in harmony with what many men with this "advantage" experience. Nor do their partners view premature ejaculation as a "blessing", especially if their partners are women. For those concerned, this is often perceived as very difficult, and it's a frequent feature among sexologists' clients. However, this is a problem that can be corrected by the guidance of a skilled sexologist. Does this latter then mean that sexologists are overriding an evolutionary "advantage" for these men and their partners?

The socio-biologists and evolutionary psychologists' stories of how male and female differences in reproduction shape sexuality are fascinating. In order to accept these arguments, one must accept the premise that the behavior of most animals and humans is driven by the instinct to reproduce itself and improve the gene pole. A serious weakness of this theory is that it cannot be tested empirically scientifically. (10) In addition, epi-genetic research comes in as a very disruptive factor. (See Chapter 19)

Gender role behavior as a "natural" effect. "The Genes Hold Culture on a Leash"

In our time, there is almost a religious belief that most things can be explained by biological heritage. "The Genes Hold Culture on a Leash" has become a universal thesis in sociobiology, but also among mainstreamers. This claim also implies an assumption that our cells behave "feminine" or "masculine" as a result of millennia of evolution.

The claim "The Genes Hold Culture on a Leash", by the way, originates from one of the most central figures and founders of the socio-biological perspective, Edward Wilson. Dr. Wilson, a professor of entomology ("insectology") at Harvard, has generalized the field of study on insect-behavior to human behavior. Wow, what a bold generalization. (11) Amazing!

This perspective, based on Darwin's theory of evolution, claims that gender roles are the result of genetic inheritance, and the above-mentioned principle that everyone is governed by the urge to pass on their own genes. And that these genes are gender-specific. This perspective further argues that a successful evolutionary process depends on the need for all members of a species, consciously or unconsciously, to pass on their genes to the next generation. And that this, among other things, causes a marked difference between male and female behavior and sexuality.

Since a man cannot be sure that he is the father of an offspring, he needs to spread his sperm to the greatest extent possible to be sure of the transmission of his own genes. (Egophilia?) Women, on the other hand, know for sure that their own genes are represented in their offspring. (Egophilia?) Based on this theory socio-biologists claim that this explains the promiscuity of men. (11)

But there is more, this same theory even explains why men rape. The rape-hypothesis, as it's been called, explains rape as a reproductive adaptive strategy for men who are otherwise unable to fix a date in the usual way according to socio-biologist David Barash. He, and several other socio-biologists, further explain that men who rape only succumb to their genetic drives to reproduce themselves. Sociologists Thornhill and Palmer have even written an entire book on this topic, in which they claim that rape is a natural biological phenomenon, and that it's a result of the human evolutionary heritage. The book is called "A Natural History of Rape". (12)

This sociobiological perspective, which has also resulted or reincarnated into a psychological offspring, called evolutionary psychology, is, as we have seen, problematic to defend from a purely biological perspective. This is problematic especially due to the observed differences between gender roles from culture to culture, and from one era to another, which historians, anthropologists, sociologists and social psychologists have demonstrated through their respective research disciplines.

Moreover, the sociobiological and evolutionary-psychological perspective is closer to a philosophical theoretical direction than a scientific theoretical direction. Sociobiological and evolutionary-psychological views are based more on beliefs and assumptions than computerized knowledge. A philosophical theory is based on an epiphany (aha experience) and in the world of socio-biologists and evolutionary-psychologists this epiphany spells: "The survival of the fittest".

Psychologist Barbara Engler explains this important difference between a scientific and a philosophical theory in a simple way in her book "Personality Theories, An Introduction". Here she emphasizes that scientific claims can be falsified, while philosophical assumptions are always associated with their underlying epiphanic visions and revelations like: "It just has to be that way, it seems so natural." Such as for example: "Survival of the fittest". I also touched on this topic at the beginning of chapter 7. Otherwise, I recommend those who are particularly interested to read Barbara Engler's introductory book on psychological personality theories. (13)

What works "best" with this sociobiological and evolutionary-psychological perspective is that it both underpins, glorifies, and promotes social-sociopathic behavior as the best and most natural strategy for development and survival. Thus, men in this social-Darwinian universe appear as sociopaths, while women are portrayed as helpless victims or apaths. As for the rape hypothesis, it is so loosely grounded in the real world that even a middle school student with some social knowledge can torpedo it.

For instance, most rapists already have female partners, many of them are even married with own children. Another thing to consider is that a significant number of those who are raped are outside the menus cycle. Either they are too old or too young to contribute to reproduction. Moreover, it is not very uncommon for a violent offender to kill his victim, which doesn't exactly support the rape-hypothesis regarding reproduction. Finally, the rape-hypothesis doesn't explain men who rape men. The latter is actually common among prisoners, especially in violent cultures. (14) (Once again, see Chapter 17, Part II)

Another solid nail in the coffin for the rape hypothesis was provided by researcher Diana Scully. In a study where the participants were convicted rapists, she found that these men actually had more consensual sex than their law-abiding "brothers". In addition, it turned out that the probability that these rapists were fathers, was just as great as among other men in their society. (15)

Since socio-biologists and evolutionary-psychologists base their hypotheses on biology, it will for obvious reasons be necessary to consult biologists to find empirical and scientific studies that may explain or support their perspective. Professor Inger Nordal at the Department of Biology at Blindern (the University in Oslo), says something about this social-Darwinian perspective in her comment to Bjørn Vassnes, one of the Norwegian defenders of the sociobiological perspective. Among other things, she says:

"I, as a biologist, would argue that there is no critical and serious biological research on man that can tell who we are (i.e what lies in our genes) and who we become (i.e our personality, which is shaped by an infinite amount of signals from day zero). In the Stone Age scenario of sociobiology, men go hunting. According to the theory, the most successful hunters have a few more children than those who tend to miss. Men are therefore selected for space vision, it is claimed (how they can fail to bring the postulated genes to their daughters they don't explain)" She further says that the socio-biologists' so-called "adaptation program" is impossible to support by scientific methods, and is thus labeled unscientific, and therefore rejected. (16)

Nevertheless, the sociobiological perspective is gaining more and more popularity among both laypersons and scholars. Perhaps because pure biological science has made enormous progress in many other areas in recent times. Its widespread popularity could also be because many of us want it to be true. It seems so credible, it sort of fits, right? In addition, this belief-system has been a media-bestseller during the recent decades. So, ultimately, it might be just another "Just so" story.

And we have probably all been daily "brainwashed" by this sociobiological view through the popular media, including the porn industry, which by the way is mostly male-dominated. Even to the degrees that most lesbian porn-movies are produced by men. For men. It's again worth remembering that from the moment you entered this world you have been washed with signals from your cultural environment about what is normal and what is not normal in relation to what sexual organ you were equipped with. As a result, people who grow up in different cultures and circumstances will tend to develop different sexual behaviors.

Another sign that sociocultural influence may play a greater role in shaping sexual behavior than biology, is the historical changes in male and female sexual behavior. At times, women have been described as horny temptresses, and men as hesitant participants. A well-known example is found in the biblical story of Adam and Eve, a reflection of the culture of the Middle East some few thousand years ago. (17)

At other times, women have been seen as "pure" in thought and virtue, while men have been branded as greedy sexual beasts. These changing ideas about gender role behavior are the social "clothing" for sexuality. The similarity between these perspectives is that they all believe in the idea that there are enormous differences between men and women and male and female sexuality. (17) It may seem that the latter is the only thing these different perspectives, beliefs, theories or discourses can agree on.

However, social constructionists believe that society influences and regulates behavior through its norms. Some of them even claim that everything we see as either male or female sexuality is culturally constructed. (18)

But if one uses either the social constructionist or the essentialist (biological, sociobiological and evolutionary-psychological) approach to understand sexuality, one get at best only half stories. In my opinion, there is sufficient evidence that gender role differences are to a far greater extent the result of sociocultural and psychological processes than of pure essentialist or pure constructionist explanations.

Nevertheless, a social constructionist, sociological and psychological approach is more powerful if it takes in to account the essentialist approach. This perspective is called an integrative approach. Biology is just one part of the interaction that culminates in sexual desires. Sociological and social psychological factors such as family relationships and social structures also influence sex. Biology is neither where sexuality begins nor ends. One might say that social and biological contexts help define sexual possibilities. (19)

The integrative approach largely follows what many sexological researchers have observed. But first, let us consider the following example. A study conducted a few decades ago sought participants for a laboratory experiment with the following headline: "How physical arousal and tension affect a man's preference for one woman over another". (19)

The researchers connected male students to a monitor where they could hear their own heartbeats while looking at photographs of various female models. The men were told they would be able to hear their own heart rate in response to each photo they viewed. A higher heart rate would then indicate an increased physical attraction. The participants were then shown photos of a dark, blonde and a red-haired woman, respectively. Afterwards, each of the men was asked to select the photo of the woman he would prefer to date. (20)

In every one of the cases, the participant selected the photo of the woman, who he claimed to arouse him the most. At least they thought they were choosing the models that made them most horny. In reality, they had all been listening to fake heart rates that was randomly being speeded up or down. In doing so, they all believed that they had actually chosen the models that aroused them the most. Or whom they believed aroused them the most. In this case, in other words, the imaginary attraction of these men was in fact more controlling than their own "gut feeling" (20)

Or rather, the external sociocultural influence determined their desires in an indirect way. Their minds, which by the way is a very potent sexual organ, told them that their bodies should respond to a particular photo. And that's exactly what they did.

In other words, the participants' physiological experience of arousal was overshadowed by the social context. So then one has to ask: When social circumstances (social influence) have an impact on sexual taste, is it then real? Absolutely. Social reality is as much a fact as the biological reality in the lives of individuals. (20) As a matter of fact, in some cases fiction can become subjective facts.

Even biological research supports, presumably involuntarily, the integrative perspective on the testosterone hypothesis. Some decades ago, researchers found that a group of gay men had lower testosterone than a similar group of heterosexual men. (Kreuz, Rose, and Jennings 1972). The traditional interpretation was rooted in the meta-theoretical assumption that homosexual men were less masculine than heterosexual men (that they were "lesser" men), and that the low testosterone level thus explained why they were homosexual. (21)

A group of active military men were also tested for testosterone, as a control group. Probably with the assumption that military men are "more" men than homosexuals, and therefore have higher testosterone levels. But to the great astonishment of the researchers, the military men also measured low on testosterone levels. The researchers thus tricked themselves into believing that an unusually high number of military men also were homosexuals. (21)

Eventually, they came up with an alternative explanation for their findings, namely that stress, anxiety, and similar emotions affected the hormone levels of men in both of these groups. They claimed that the stressful context of either being homosexual in a heterosexual culture, or soldier in a potentially dangerous and aggressive war culture, had influenced the biological response in both groups. Thus the hormones all of a sudden and magically became the "cart", rather than the "horse" in both of the groups. (21)

So, if one doesn't like the outcome, just invent a new interpretation that fits in to the equation without disturbing the meta-theoretical belief too much. The above mentioned research-story is a funny one, but at the same time also a frightening example of how a meta-theoretical belief can lead to lies and the reinforcement of myths that should have been eradicated long time ago. In this case, homosexuality as an androgenic-hormonal "deficiency disease". And that homosexuality is biologically less masculine than heterosexuality.

It would be interesting to know whether these researchers subsequently tried to cure both homosexuality and war-anxiety with testosterone on the basis of their findings. Hopefully they went home to watch TV.

Much of this obsession with testosterone is probably related to the fact that this hormone is also associated with aggression. And that aggression in turn is most associated with men and thus masculine behavior.

This despite the fact that research has established that testosterone does not trigger aggression or instrumental behavior in men, unless aggressiveness already is present as a personality- trait. An overdose of testosterone changes nothing regarding the behavior of non-aggressive men. However, increased testosterone levels have been demonstrated in winners of sports competitions (regardless of gender) after they've competed and won. Not before or during the competition. (22)

So, what does it mean to use an integrative perspective in the approach to sexuality? First, an integrationist will ask questions about biology when the social context is not satisfactory as cause, and vice versa when biological causes become thin. Regardless, the point is that all sexual and physical experiences occur and make sense in a social context. (23)

However, social control of people's sexual behavior, often leads to a limited, and limiting expression of love and sexuality for many people. Cultural authorities have great power when it comes to regulating the most intimate spheres of the individual. Too often too much power. It's important to remember that neither love nor sexuality are "merchandises" of scarcity. Although it can sometimes seem like this when this area of human life so all too often becomes the subject of politics.

As an apropos to the fact that cultural myths have power, one myth is that men are more easily aroused by porn than women. So powerful is this notion that women reinterpret their physiological responses (probably more or less unconsciously) when exposed to pornographic media.

Several experiments have been done on this topic, where the participants were measured both psychologically and physiologically. Psychologically by reporting on the subjective experience, and physiologically by measuring blood flow in the genitalia (as in the Adams study in Chapter 8). It was not possible to detect physiological differences in sexual arousal between the males and females in these studies. The difference first showed up when the participants were asked to describe their experiences. Men tended to exaggerate their reactions, while women reported none, or only slightly sexual arousal in half of the cases. (Julia Heiman 1975) (24)

One can speculate on the reasons for this under-reporting among women. But it's reasonable to believe that these are the reflections of the traditional beliefs, that men are the most sexual, combined with the fact that women have almost always been accused of being easy, slutty, etc. when they publicly expose as much sexual desire as men. What do you think?

Throughout the history of modern science, there has been a tendency to be blind to many different factors that may help shape what we call masculinity and femininity, or expected masculine or feminine behavior. It has been assumed that these gender differences are a result of nature, that we are biological "created" into these gender roles. Again, a "Just so story."

As we have seen, it's not quite that simple. Recent research, including gender research, has produced a wealth of data that tells some completely different stories. One perspective that I believe is fruitful for being able to understand how gender differences occur and how gender role identity develops, is Harriet Bjerrum Nielsen and Monica Rudberg's developmental psychological perspective. (I described it in Chapter 13). They also take an integrationist approach in their research.

It's also important to be aware that during the first few years after we are born, 30 000 nerve synapses develop per second within every square centimeter of the cerebral cortex. In other words, the brain is far from developed as a newborn. It's plastic. This means that the brains of our first years of life are also built and developed by external (social) stimuli and impulses. (25)

It's more than obvious that the pink or blue blankets and diapers we equip our new born babies with, are influencing adults' differentiating treatment of these cute newly arrived citizens, and thus also has a strong effect on these children's early neuropsychological development. Especially when it comes to "proper" gender-behavior. With referral to the above mentioned research (in both this, and earlier chapters) it will be on the verge of idiocy to claim that "The genes hold everything on a leash".

The sociobiological perspective has received a lot of attention in recent times. Not at least in the popular media, where the focus has largely been uncritical regarding this perspective. It has all too often been presented as a "natural truth." One can rightly question the thoroughness of many journalists when it comes to journalistic research and source criticism regarding this field. Perhaps they have some lessons to learn from their colleagues in the sports newsrooms?

I would argue that there must be a much broader research-focus than the one we have now in order to gain a greater understanding of the factors that influence, maintain and reinforce these different patterns of behavior. An interdisciplinary scientific approach is absolutely necessary to understand these forces. Not at least in order to be able to isolate the biological factors that may or may not be the basis for different social behaviors.

In order to be able to find this possible fundamental biological difference, we still have a long way to go, and an endless series of "Just so" stories to get rid of. The detoxification of these "Just so" stories (or myths) may be the biggest challenge of them all. For my part, I believe we owe such a detoxification process to those who come after us. And in that regard, the detoxification of homophobia is actually important.

In fact, the detoxification of homophobia is very important for all genders. Many people have become aware that homophobia negatively affects people's same-sex experiences and relationships. But what may not have been equally obvious, is that that homophobia also has a major impact on heterosexual experiences and relationships. And then mostly heterosexual men.

For heterosexual men, to be seen as unmanly, even worse "feminine", or perhaps worst of all, being suspected of being gay, can be a huge threat to the perception of their gender role identity. A significant proportion of heterosexual males spend a lot of time and energy promoting their masculinity, precisely to ensure that others do not get any "wrong" ideas or perceptions about them. An incredible amount of energy is spent on avoidance strategies. Energy that could have been spent more "environmentally friendly" to put it that way. Do you use any avoidance strategies? (Be honest!)

In his book "The Gendered Society", Michael S. Kimmel refers to a study in which this very phenomenon is confirmed. The study he refers to is called: "Nice Women Do Not Say Yes and Real Men Do Not Say No". The researcher behind this study, psychologist Charlene Muehlenhard, found, among other things, that many of the heterosexual men in this study sometimes had sex just to prove that they were not gay. Because of this widespread notion of homosexuality as something "feminine", it means that homophobia also is one of the strongest re-enforcers of the gender-role identities. Heterosexual men then tend to be hyper-masculine, and heterosexual women hyper-feminine. (26)

In this regard it's also important to remember that before the 20th century, homosexuality was described as actions, something one did, not as an identity (something one is). And as homosexuality became entrenched as an identity, it also had consequences for male friendships. Thus, it became important for heterosexual men to distance themselves, not only from female identity markers, but also from homosexual identity markers. Heterosexual men became more and more wary, in all directions. And more and more it resembled the form of war games. Not interactions.

Psychologist Robert Lewis identified four barriers to emotional intimacy between male friends: Competition, the need to be controlling, homophobia, and the lack of positive role models for male intimacy. These four barriers, in turn, hindered the ability to convey vulnerability, openness about deeply personal matters, as well as the ability to show emotion and tenderness in relation to other men, to mention a few. He claimed that men in particular avoid appearing "weak" and vulnerable, in order to maintain their competitive edge. (27)

At the very end of this chapter, I would both add and emphasize that women, including mothers, are also co-responsible for the upbringing of boys, in addition to the girls. And this with far greater authority today than just 40 years ago. I think it's worth recalling this fact in today's climate, where there is an excessive tendency to "shoot" at boys and men for the state of "all" affairs. They are not "monsters". In many cases they are boys and men who are not allowed to be emotional human beings. They are as culturally and psychologically "brain-washed" as any other gender. We have all been "brainwashed". Furthermore, it is not a prerequisite to have a penis in order to become a "monster".

If we nevertheless were to insist on this abysmal difference between the genders, we should at least have so much respect for equality and justice for all, that we employ equal proportions of men and women in all those professions that perform power over individual destinies. Such as employees in preschools, schools, colleges, universities, psychiatry, law, child welfare, police, etc. (Fill in the blanks). This would provide a fair representation for both Mars and Venus immigrants, and other extraterrestrials and aliens on this beautiful planet.

CHAPTER 15

Classical Science and Meta-Theoretical Strait-Jackets

"The American philosopher of science Thomas Kuhn claimed that most scientists are still trying to reconcile theory and facts within the routinely accepted materialist paradigm, which he describes as essentially a collection of articles of faith shared by scientists. All research that cannot be accounted for by the prevailing worldview are labeled "anomalies" because they threaten the existing paradigm ..."

Pim Van Lommel - Dutch Cardiologist
and Consciousness researcher

A very needed and interesting approach in this chaotic transition to the postmodern era, is the critique of all the sciences that try to explain human behavior solely from a classical scientific paradigm. The classic Newtonian "clockwork-universe" paradigm has long been adjusted and complemented by the new physics. Especially the quantum physics' abolition of, among other things, determinism, objectivity and locality. Professor Elsa Almås also mentions some of the latter in her introductory book in sexology: "Sex og Sexologi" ("Sex and Sexology") (1)

It is both useful and important to try to shed light on the background of the various sciences' meta-theoretical views (assumptions) and what consequences this may have for people who are affected by this research.

This is an important topic because an unconsciousness about one's own subjectivity as a researcher, can even have fatal consequences when the research object itself is a human being. And not at least when it comes to minority people. Scientists have all too often been blind to their own prejudices and their own subjectivity, precisely because of the belief in "objectivity". To believe that one is objective as a researcher is an illusion. If one is aware of this, one will be much more aware own hidden (unconscious?) agendas and prejudices.

Some of the most grotesque examples of the above are thoroughly exemplified in Part II of the book, especially the prevailing meta-theory of the first half of the last century, that Africans and Latinos were inferior races. The scientists themselves were totally blind to their own prejudices. Fortunately, psychologist Floyd Allport dared to question this collective "scientific" madness. This was also the starting point for research on prejudice itself.

Today's diagnostic systems, and their anchoring in a therapeutic tradition, are based on a classical paradigm in which sexuality has had reproduction as its primary function. Whereupon sexual expressions that move away from this have automatically been considered abnormal. This is another example of a meta-theoretical starting point. In other words, a "truth" that it is based on an assumption, a belief. An assumption that has colored the scientific research and harmed an infinite number of people who in the first place were completely healthy individuals.

In this context, it is again important to point out that the same therapeutic systems, with the same meta-theoretical assumptions, are also heavy suppliers of premises to all other social actors. This view is thus reflected in culture, teaching arenas and psychosocial environments, at all levels. And ultimately also become the general public's perception of true and false. (Healthy and unhealthy)

An example of downright dangerous medical assumptions known to most of us today, is the Hungarian physician Ignaz Philipp Semmelweis who in the 19th century discovered the cause of childbed fever. He introduced antiseptic to the medical staff as the cure. And was ridiculed and ostracized, because his revelation didn't fit with the current medical paradigm. Today we all wash our hands, surgeons too.

But a lot of new knowledge has been added, especially during the last 30 years. It must be one of the great tasks of postmodernism to apply this new knowledge, as well as sort out old and useless "heritage" from the modern era which still leaves its "invisible" fingerprints on the various institutions of our time. We must apply the new knowledge and new methods that also promote the subjective, healthy individual development. For once, perhaps for the first time, the individual should be put at the center.

Regarding the further development of new methods based on this new knowledge, the interdisciplinary perspective is completely inevitable. There is much to be gained and learned from the science of sexology regarding the interdisciplinary approach. Sexologists have been using this perspective for more than a century. They should therefore serve as examples and guidance into this new era. The sexologists are probably the first to adopt an integrative approach (as described in the previous chapter) with regard to understanding individuality in a non-fragmentary way.

This is not least important when one considers that sexuality is also one of the most important driving forces in both the individual and society. Psychology, like most other social sciences, has more or less ignored sexuality. Developmental psychological literature up to the 1980s (the early beginnings of the postmodern era), is almost chemically purified of sexuality as part of the child's development, and thus human development. (2)

As the picture becomes larger, the meanings also change.

Niels Bohr, The Father of Quantum Physics

Niels Bohr believed that the findings from quantum physics should have consequences for all sciences, including the social sciences. Social science research is not a closed system. Therefore, interdisciplinary and complementary analyzes and approaches are the only way to go in order to obtain the truest knowledge about man.

Niels Bohr also believed that we had to live with permanent contradictions. There is no way to express all of nature in a single description with the language people have at their disposal. The only way to grasp reality is to tell about it in different ways, and put them together so that they complement each other in a comprehensive overlap of different descriptions. This also includes seemingly contradictory concepts. (3)

As an example, the effects of a melody can be analyzed in many ways like: physically, neuro-physiologically, emotionally and psychologically. How can these ways of understanding be linked? The melody can also simply be absorbed as a whole, by listening to it. And sometimes, maybe enjoy it.

A great example of an integrative approach is the model described by the American internal medicine and psychiatrist, George Engel. His model operates with different levels, which also reflects different professional and knowledge levels. Each level is also represented by its respective theories and research methods. These may in turn interact with other levels and their respective research methods. Engel believes that it can be fruitful to develop specific methods at each level just to gain more accurate knowledge. (4)

The point, he argues, must be that one does not describe the whole of reality only from one of these levels, but that one develops collaboration and communication channels and arenas across these levels of research and knowledge. George Engel describes two hierarchies where the individual forms the bottom of the upper hierarchy and at the same time the top of the lower hierarchy. The actual levels in the hierarchies are, from the top of the upper hierarchy through the lower hierarchy: Biosphere - society / nation - culture / subculture - network / family - dyad (two people) / nervous system - organ systems / organs - tissue - cell - organelle - molecule. (5)

It is therefore important to see these different levels of scientific knowledge, not as competing levels, but as complementary knowledge. All of them are in fact overlapping and can therefore provide us with new and valuable knowledge, which in turn can give us new and more comprehensive methods of understanding and treatment.

Let me give you an example: Biology has little knowledge of sociology, and vice versa, but even though they have their own respective research requirements, it does not mean that they are mutually exclusive. On the contrary, they affect each other. (5) The sexology, which in principle considers itself to be interdisciplinary, is a good example of the recognition and importance that the various academic directions should, or rather have to work together to see the dynamics and interactivity between the different levels. As exemplified in George Engel's model.

Basically, human beings different and unique genotypes must be seen and accepted as rare seeds, which with the help of good "gardeners" can contribute to help them growing into beautiful plants (phenotypes), all of which can all help to develop and bring forward the diverse and beautiful "flora". that we together constitute as human beings.

The New Physics and the Post-Modern Era

"A new scientific truth is not usually presented in a way to convince its opponents. Rather, they die off, and a rising generation is familiar with the truth from the start." Max Planck

The difference between sciences that falls within what some call "hard sciences" or "soft sciences", respectively, are the "absolutes". Hard sciences, such as mathematics and classical physics, can generally provide absolute answers. They can be experimentally tested everywhere and will usually produce the same result as their theories predict, unlike the "soft" sciences. When it comes to soft sciences such as psychology, one must be far more cautious regarding scientific predictions. Soft sciences change greatly in relation to society, time in history, individual uniqueness and more. Not everything can be forced into a "clockwork", or be measured by metric methods.

"If you wish to set up the law that all crows are black, you must not seek to show that no one is; It is enough if you prove one single crow to be white"- William James

The fact that a good theory must be falsifiable also means that a prevailing theory does not have to be a truth either.

I think we are facing a paradigm shift, although according to Kuhn, this cannot be seen until after it has happened. I also believe that this new paradigm is going to eliminate some obsolete worldviews, and at the same time give us an opportunity to correct old "sins".

The new physics can serve as an example that we are moving into a completely new understanding of reality. Quantum mechanics has shown us that at a fundamental level, nature behaves so strangely that our classical conceptual apparatus simply does not suffice. This forces us to use philosophy to help us at least make an effort to understand. But, as I mentioned above, there must be an open minded approach, not a deterministically closed "religious" unwavering belief in a fundamental truth, a meta-theory that excludes all other perspectives or attempts to gather new understanding.

When it comes to the old "inherited sin" and its "abnormalities", try to replace "abnormal" with "natural", then you may see old absolutes with new glasses and a clearer vision. I think "normality" is toxic because it obscures "objective" scientific thinking. By the way, do you know the full title of Darwin's main work? (The Academic "Bible" of the Modern Era). And if you know the title, do you manage to see a fundamentally philosophical belief, a meta-theory, assumption or epiphany on which this new "religion" is based?

In my opinion, this "religion" of the modern era is potentially as harmful and dangerous as premise provider, as the Abrahamic religions were. The "religion" of modernity has increasingly become a Darwinian "encyclopedia", providing deterministic explanations of all human behavior. It is based on a meta-theory which, among other things, involves competition, gender discrimination and in fact also racism. Darwin's theory of evolution has become a "social-religion" popularly called social Darwinism. The racial hygiene that emerged almost a hundred years ago is based on this very view. Adolf Hitler, Joseph Mengele and their men were far from alone in this.

By the way, the complete and original title of Darwin's "Bible" is: "The Origin of Species by Means of Natural Selection, or *Preservation of Favorite Races in the Struggle of Life*". The last paragraph of the title has probably inspired many blind "objectivists", and unfortunately it still does. (Ps. My italics)

The rape hypothesis, which I discussed in the previous chapter, is a good example of how psychological brainwashed "objective" researchers can become from their own "religious" "isms." The rape hypothesis would probably never been invented had it not been for the underlying social Darwinian assumption.

And speaking of classical science and Newton, a deterministic world-view to say the least, most people have forgotten what was somewhat sarcastically called "The ghost in the Newtonian machinery". What Newton could not explain with his model he blamed on "the intervention of The Almighty God". I talk more about this in Chapter 20.

As far as quantum physics is concerned, it alone should have revolutionized several of the other so-called "soft sciences". Among them psychology. Also keep in mind that in the diagnostic manual DSM

II (1968), all the diagnoses were based on psychoanalytic theories. Not particularly testable and scientific theories, but still full of deterministic absolutes. (6)

As mentioned, psychoanalysis is more a philosophical theory than a scientific theory. Just like the psychological version of the theory of evolution, evolutionary psychology. I recommend you read Barbara Engler's explanation of the differences between a philosophical and a scientific theory once again.

Political Psychology - A study

Violence, sexual violence, oppression and war, are over-represented in regions with a lack of human rights and human respect.

In this part of this chapter I will present a research discipline that is rarely mentioned in connection with other social sciences. This study can also serve as another great example of an integrative approach, as well as the interactivity in George Engels's two-hierarchy model. This research discipline is called "Political Psychology". Without going too far into the description of this branch of research, I will briefly describe it as an "operator" in the border-region between social psychology, sociology and political science.

I will here only refer to some central and very interesting findings and conclusions this research came to in a very comprehensive study during the nineties. This study covered no less than 133 of the countries on our planet. The research aimed to uncover indicators that point to the tendency and danger of state authoritarianism.

Those who had the best protection of human rights, fewest deaths due to violence: enjoyed freedom of speech, had the highest standard of living, most welfare goods, less oppression of women, can be predicted on the basis of various factors such as presence of gender equality, sexual orientation and more.

The factor that was the strongest indicator of a well-developed and free democracy was, in fact, statutory equal rights for heterosexuals and homosexuals.

The seven who scored highest in this study were: Denmark, Sweden, Norway, The Netherlands, Canada, New Zealand and Australia. (The study is more than 10 years old, so many more European countries would have scored high on this list today, if it had been repeated.

The researchers identified 10 indicators which they in turn divided into 3 levels of analysis. The first level they called. "Authoritarian Belief", which represents the following indicators:

1. 'Stats faith or ideology. This was determined by using a scale from all faith tolerated to one faith implemented.
2. From law-abiding and tolerated attitudes regarding homosexuality, to prohibition and oppression, to denial of homosexuality and homosexual acts. The latter is almost always present in authoritarian societies.
3. 'The statutory status of abortion. This scale went from legal abortion to only possible if the danger to life (the mother's life). Here too, the latter is almost always the case in authoritarian societies.

The second level, which they called authoritarian submission, they divided into 4 indicators representing the suppression of criticism and opposition, and the imposition of authoritarian hierarchy and leadership.

4. 'The state's suppression of deviations from official social norms.
5. 'Censorship
6. 'Suppression of the opposition
7. 'The statutory status regarding trade unions. Here the scale went from legal to illegal.

The third level they called the Authoritarian Aggression

8. 'Status and application regarding the death penalty. This scale went from abolished for all crime, to retained and used for ordinary crime.
9. 'State terrorism or official human rights violation. This scale went from, no violence reported to terrorist states that practiced disappearances, torture and executions.
10. 'And the last indicator, which measured military investment in relation to investments made regarding citizens' health and welfare, the health system. (7)

Anthropologist Peggy Reeves Sanday's research largely supports some of the findings in this political-psychological study. She found in her own research that one of the most important predictors of rape tendencies in a culture was the levels of: militarism, macho ideologies in general, and weak father-child relationships, to mention a few. (8)

According to Thore Langfeldt, there are many indications that the degree of sexual puritanism is associated with a high rate of violence. This is especially evident in the most fanatical religious cultures, such as fundamentalist Islamic cultures and fundamentalist Christian and Jewish cultures. Sexual oppression in adolescence also appears to lead to adult sexual abusive behavior. This is clearly seen in countries that operate with statistics. In the West, USA, Ireland and England are found at the top of these statistics. (9) Those same countries are also among the most puritan western cultures. Thus, the findings in the above political-psychological study also receive support from sexology.

From my point of view, it may otherwise seem that in our time we "glorify" and stretch ourselves towards the bad examples mentioned above. At least when it comes to the increasingly glorification of violence in most media. This applies not least to the media that cater to the youngest among us. We risk brainwashing them by promoting aggression and violence as the solution to societal, social and relational problems.

Neuropsychologist James W. Prescott's research also supports the above mentioned studies. He studied numerous different cultures and their ideologies in order to discover which indicators in the upbringing of children and adolescents in these cultures that possibly maintained and reinforced aggressive or non-aggressive adult behavior. You will learn more about James W. Prescott's revolutionary research in Chapter 17.

Anthropology and Homophobia

As a comment to the strongest indicators of a well-functioning and free democracy in the comprehensive psychological study above, namely statutory and equal rights for heterosexuals and homosexuals, I want to quote anthropologist Walter Williams.

In an article, the anthropologist and researcher Williams points out that in the most cultures studied by anthropologists find elements of eroticism between same-sex people which at the same time is socially accepted in these cultures. He further argues that acceptance of same-sex sexuality can enrich a society. He himself has researched indigenous peoples on the American continents and found that social acceptance of same-sex sexuality provides better religion (spiritual systems), better families, better relationships with children, better friendships and a better society in general, because the suppression of sexual diversity as rule results in social rebellion. (10)

Philosopher Dag Øystein Endsjø also points out that anthropologists and historians have shown that homosexual behavior has been, and *is* very widespread in many cultures. (11) This does not mean that homosexuality as an identity necessarily is socially accepted in these same cultures. Nor does it mean that homosexual behavior is always equally valued compared to heterosexual behavior. More on this in the next chapters.

If one is to use socio-economic arguments to explain why the heterosexual family must be protected by suppressing non-heterosexual tendencies and behaviors, as well as women's rights and individual freedom in general, then one is, to put it mildly, on thin ice. Had this socio-economic argument been true, then the worst dictatorial and theocratic nations (which, without exception, rank at the bottom of the UN list of corrupt nations and poor socioeconomics), would have been rock solid socio-economic paradises. They are not.

It may be high time to put aside these paranoid notions that non-heterosexual love threatens family values, society and so on, when it is so clear that the exact opposite is the case.

CHAPTER 16

Everything Revolves Around Sex – and Sex is Selling Everything

"Did you think sex is just about sexuality?" Well, think again. There is hardly a psychological problem where sexuality is not central. Despite this, sexuality is still not a central theme in psychiatric and psychological treatment or counseling. At the same time, sexuality is what occupies, challenges and engages absolutely all people the most, at all times. Whether it is a question of inhibiting it or promoting it. Thus, sexuality is as central in asceticism as in promiscuity, and most of what is between these two extremes. Shame, guilt and performance anxiety are recurring themes in many people's lives, especially when it comes to sexuality. These problems are very often expressions of psychologically internalized socio-cultural attitudes (the external voice): "You should not, do this or that, what would other people think, it's abnormal, etc.". This in turn is transformed into the inner voice: "I should not feel this way, I'm abnormal, I'm sick, I'm wrong, etc."

Richard Bruvoll Jr

"The most powerful shame and guilt providers are: Religious systems (it's a shame) Legal systems (it's criminal) Scientific systems (it's a disruption) Together, these systems are also the most important premise providers for cultural and psychosocial attitudes".

Espen Esther Pirelli Benestad

Sexuality is at the core of everything

It's all about sex. It should suffice to mention religion, porn, fashions, prostitution (in all variations), social media, nuns, monks, priests, imams, popes, marketers and so on. They all have sexuality as the most important and central part of their systems, whether they inhibit it or promote it. By the way, sexual orientation is also the only human talent that can lead to the death penalty without using it. But to say that sexuality is easy? Not at all. Beautiful? Yes, it can be, and it should be, when sexuality is not separated from love.

Imagine if we could begin to see these "drives" as valuable talents, as abilities to express love, with their many different and unique colors and variations. Some talents may be a little more unusual than others, but still abilities to express love, and as an expression that, just as valuable as the others. But unfortunately and all too often, sexuality is expressed in verbal communication as if it were competition and war. As mentioned, just notice the sports and war metaphors that are often used when people talk about sex, shagging, meat on the stick, hunt. Just to name a few.

Many young people think they are very open and liberal when it comes to sex. They are usually not. By the way, they are very skilled at talking loudly about fucking, doggie-style, blowjobs and so on. They master the porn language at their fingertips. By the way, blowjob is a term that comes from American prostitution. Dirty talking and blue-movies are concepts that are direct reflections of a pornographic communication style. The latter originated in American culture, more precisely from one of California's film industry's most lucrative genres, the porn movie industry. Moreover, this style of communication is more or less locked into old outdated notions of gender. It is neither open nor liberal. Where do you think "dirty talking" originally comes from? Some of the above is also confirmed to a large extent by Eivind Myhre's research.

Eivind Myhre has analyzed the view of men, sexuality and love in girls 'and boys' magazines. He did this in connection with a master's thesis in interdisciplinary cultural studies. He analyzed a selection of the girls 'magazine Cosmopolitan and the boys' magazine Mann from 2009 and 2010. Among other things, he hunted for ideas about male sexuality and love. Heterosexuality was a natural starting point in the magazines. But he also found that girl sex and cuddling between girls was viewed as perfectly fine and natural. One of the girls (in Mann) put it this way:

"If you have a boyfriend, and tell him that you want to have sex with another girl, then he will not be surprised. It's a more like, yes, of course you want." Sexual relationships between girls are written into the magazines as a natural part of heterosexuality. Sexual relationships between boys are not understood in the same way, says Myhre. (1)

«Sex and cuddling between boys is interpreted as homosexuality, as opposed to similar acts between girls. Instead of being accepted as part of heterosexuality, boys run the risk of being accused of not being manly when cuddling with other boys. Girls don't risk to be associated with un-femininity when participating in same-sex." Myhre continues. (1)

Myhre points out that the acceptance of sex and cuddling between girls can be interpreted in several ways: "On the one hand, it can be seen as a form of objectification because it seems that the point is for others to watch it. The man's gaze is central. Girl sex has become mainstream through porn, and girls seem to be influenced by this. On the other hand, it can be seen as a form of "girl-power", because girls have greater freedom to express sexuality than boys. Girls can include intimacy in friendships in a way that there is no room for in boys' friendships." (1)

For Myhre, the concepts masculinity and non-masculinity became central to understand these differences. He calls them dominant performances, performances that are linked to something traditional. These performances are taken as given by the young, and they consider them completely natural. (1) Not very liberal attitudes to trace among the young in this regard.

One of the main findings of Myhre's study was the great difference in the representation of women's and men's orgasms. Women's orgasms were both explored and discussed. Men's orgasms were most often reduced to a mechanical act. There was also a great focus on men giving women the best orgasm possible. On the other hand, it was not seen as women's responsibility to give men good orgasms. (1)

"I place representation of orgasm and sex in the context of what I call the male performance. By this I mean that it becomes a way for boys to formulate and confirm their masculinity when they give girls orgasms", Myhre says. (1)

Myhre also found that anal sex could be perceived as both masculine and feminine. Masculine if the boys are the active part, but feminine if they are the recipients. It seemed that both genders agreed on that. They also agreed that if a woman plays the active role, for example, by using a strap-on, she reduces his manly-hood. (1)

Myhre also revealed something that does not exactly portray the girls in a charming light. He found that girls seek advice from each other about boys. Sometimes they band together in order to manipulate the other sex. A reader's letter in Cosmopolitan illustrates this:

"He is perfect, but uses too feminine jewelry. My boyfriend looks good the way he dresses up, except for the accessories he uses. It looks like they should be in my jewelry box and not his." "Monika 29". Solution suggested by the columnist ("The Oracle"): "Ask one of his female friends to make fun of him the next time he wears jewelry, that's a brilliant weapon. He will probably not be in discord with what's accepted as normal." (Cosmopolitan) (1)

Here, Myhre rightly points out that Cosmopolitan is actually helping to legitimize girls joining forces to ridicule what they perceive as femininity in boys. He also found that the central message of these trend magazines is the idea of the differences between men and women. Men should be masculine and women should be feminine. And besides, that heterosexuality is the very framework around the notions of men, sexuality and love. (1)

Also note the language used by the "Oracle" in her response to "Monika": "Ask one of his female friends to make fun of him the next time he wears jewelry, that's a brilliant weapon. He will probably not be in discord with what's accepted as normal." Again we see war metaphors in the communication between the genders. In this case the word "weapon". As I mentioned before, this is more reminiscent of a battlefield, a wargame rather than interactive cooperative communication.

The only thing that separates these young "liberal" people from their great-grandparents is that they can talk the language of porn. That language was a foreign language in the 19th century. All too often I see in my work how devastating it can be when communication about sex is reduced to a meat market language, consisting of war and competition metaphors, as well as an overdose of manipulation. A language that is totally robbed of honest emotional content.

This was also pretty well exemplified in the large survey among High-school graduates conducted by psychiatrist Mette Hvalstad, which I mentioned in Chapter 12. However, I would like to remind you once again about the disappointing results it showed. The survey revealed a prevailing lack of communication regarding sexual issues. This in turn led to a lot of sexual boundaries being violated. Interestingly enough, the violators weren't just the boys.

A new report on youth and rape emphasizes how dangerous this inability to communicate clearly can be, and how dangerous it can become when toxic gender role hysteria dictates communication. The report is called "The one who joins the game, has to accept the pain." (Roughly translated). I for my part, believe that we produce a great deal of these problems precisely by our constant insistence on gender differences. "The great divide": Blue - pink, Mars – Venus, and so on.

The report touches on a very sad and recurring fact, that many rapes and a lot of abuse is committed between young people, between «friends». And that young people lack a clear understanding of what rape and abuse really mean. It's very easy to get hung up on "The Stranger

Danger" (scary monsters in the park), but all too often the biggest threats are to be found among your peers.

It is also interesting to note that the young people themselves say that they must challenge and fight the gender roles. Especially with regard to boys getting credit and status when they sleep with many, while girls considered sluts if they do the same. (2)

Silje Berggrav, who made the report, also says that it is a widespread opinion that the boys should take the initiative and that the girls should be the ones to tell how far they could go. She goes on to say that although the boys agreed that a no should be respected, this is not necessarily complied with in practice. The boys often go further than the girls want them to, the girls' no are often not respected, and sometimes the girls just give in to it. (2) This echoes the VG article I quoted from in chapter 12.

However, It's interesting to note that the young people themselves say that they must challenge and fight the rigid gender roles. For example, the boys are given credit and status when they sleep with many girls, while the girls are considered sluts if they do the same. (2) It should be noted that not only the girls, but also the boys agreed that combating and challenging the gender role stereotypes is central, if one is to solve this serious problem.

An example of how this gender role pressure, as a result of the gender role stereotypes, strikes in both directions, I experienced not long ago with a client. Let's call him Adam. Adam was 19 years old when he approached me, because he was afraid that he had contracted chlamydia. Why do you think that? I asked. He then told me that he had performed unprotected sex with a girl who was rumored to have chlamydia. I told him there's only one way to find out for sure. Then I told him that he also had a moral obligation to inform everyone he have had sex with after this episode, that is, if his suspicion would be confirmed by an MD. Chlamydia may lead to infertility.

Then I asked him why he had had sex at all, and even unprotected sex with this girl despite this suspicion. His answer did not surprise me, but it probably surprises many others. Adam described the situation as follows:

He and his friends had been out on town, and eventually ended up at a private party. Late at night, two by two they vanished into other rooms to have sex. Back in the living room sat Adam, and this girl with a possible venereal disease. According to Adam's description, she had a rather vampy demeanor, played a lot on sex, both in language, behavior and facial expressions. And "everyone" in his peer group had had sex with her, he claimed. By the way, she wasn't even Adam's type, which he also tried to show her without hurting her. However, she did not take a no for a no, she teasingly asked him if he rather preferred men, then began to massage his genitals. Eventually she removed his pants, and they were on. "But why did you not stop her?" I asked. "I was afraid she would think I'm gay, and that she and the others would start harassing me," Adam replied.

There are several things that strike me with Adam's experience. First, he described these people as his friends. Secondly, this homosexual anxiety, which despite the fact that Adam is not homosexual, drove him to have sex with a person who did not appeal to him in the first place, and who on top of that could have cost him a venereal disease. Had these roles been switched, she would most likely have been on the indictment bench. Therefore neither she, nor her "sisters" with similar manipulative behavior, appear on any criminal statistics of sex-offenders. They simply go under the radar.

And last but not least, Venusians and Marsians, women and men, mothers and fathers, uncles and aunts, football coaches and make-up artists, are all complicit in Adam's humiliating experience. They are indirectly responsible, in their insistent dogmatic belief that gender is glued to two abysmal-different modes of behavior and communication.

Another example I want to include in this same context is the experience of one of my female clients, let's call her Eve. When Eve approached me, she was in deep despair. She was about thirty years old, she was well educated with a good and job, she was charming and had an appealing appearance. I reckoned she would have no difficulties in invoking the interests of most men, neither socially nor sexually. It turned out that It was the intimate experiences with men that had repeatedly caused her this despair, and which ultimately led her to approach me.

To make a long story short, the basic problem was (again) "inter-stellar-communication-problems". She listed up a number of dates that had all started so well, but ended in despair, at least on her part. Here's one of them. Eve had been out on town, and at a bar she met a handsome young man with an appealing appearance. He also seemed intelligent and humorous, some of the qualities that Eve held high in men. They eventually ended up at his apartment, with common goals in mind.

It all started off well with a delicious foreplay, that is, until he started performing oral sex on her. As Eve explained to me: "I love oral sex, but I have a super sensitive clitoris". The lover was probably a little too "hard-tongued," and as a result she began to moan, not from lust, but from an incipient pain. He obviously interpreted this as a sign of her enjoying it, after which he just indulged in even more of what didn't work. She ended up faking an orgasm just to get it over with, to stop the "torture".

When I asked Eve: "But, why didn't you tell him, why didn't you stop him?" I didn't want to hurt his manhood" she answered. Well, Eve's reaction is unfortunately not uncommon, and faking orgasms is actually quite common, for many different situational reasons, but always the same underlying cause: Dysfunctional communication! Let me add that both women and men make use of this way out, the fake exit.

The causes of Adam and Eve's dysfunctional communicative experiences began way before their night on town. It began before they even had a language. The toy stores, the fashion industry, the film and music industry, and eventually the online porn sites, had all "prepared" them for this. These cultural "mentors" are all proponents of this rigid difference in gender performance. This in turn leads to a lot of dysfunctional communication, dysfunctional sexual behavior and too many sad experiences for the members of both of these "extra-terrestrial" tribes.

It is said that history is both shaped and written by the winners. And until a few decades ago the "winners" were mostly men. But we do not need "victorious" women either. Victory is a war-term, it does not belong in communication or love. This battlefield rhetoric may not turn out well, neither for Mars nor Venus residents. We live in a time where everything is getting more and more polarized, but polarization always ends with war. A battlefield where no one walks out "victorious". On the contrary, in the wake of "victorious" men or women, there will always be many broken souls.

When it comes to the media, they play an increasing role in the upbringing of girls and boys. Unfortunately, this is not only for the good, nor in the spirit of enlightenment. Although it can be that too of course.

Psychologist and sexologist Thore Langfeldt points out that in the last decades, the tabloid media has become more and more concerned with and focused on violence, and at the same time we see a new sexual puritanism. There is almost no censorship of violence while at the same time natural sexuality is still a taboo phenomenon. With the birth of the internet, the acceptance of violence has been utterly strengthened, also through violent porn. (3)

Note that Langfeldt points out that natural sexuality is still a taboo phenomenon. Porn, on the other hand, has become public property. The porn sites are right there at the fingertips of everyone, including children. This is one of the consequences of the exponential digital revolution. At the same time, it may seem that sexuality is becoming more and more aggressive. Is it people who mirror the violence in media and porn, or is the violent media and porn mirroring the people?

The United States is at the top of the statistics for sexual abuse in the West. In Europe, Ireland and England top these statistics. In the US, one can show gross authentic scenes of violence in prime time on TV, while nudity is taboo. (4) This is also in line with the findings of the comprehensive psychological-political study, which I wrote about in Chapter 15.

But similar trends are also emerging here in Norway. This is probably an indirect import from the Anglo-American cultures. Not only have we started to "bleep" sexual words or swearing, but also scrambled mouths of people who talk about ditto. The latter is probably to "protect" deaf children too. But we have yet to see the scrambling of blood carnages. It's amazing. However, nudity was not uncommon to be seen in Nordic TV-productions just a few years ago. Today nudity is censored out. Tits and genitals are dangerous, not at least for innocent "asexual" children.

This was also confirmed by Lise-May Spissøy, editor-in-chief at NRK, a major TV-channel in Norway. In connection with the 40th anniversary of one of the most popular Norwegian TV-shows, they did a review of the features during this 40-year period. One of the things they discovered was that they dared to show naked bodies earlier. Among other things she mentioned a feature about nude volleyball, which would have been unthinkable to air today, she says. (5)

Now it is violence that dominates the prime-time broadcasts. At the same time, one sees this hypocrisy regarding the censorship of, among other things, nudity. And thus naturalness. It is quite clear that many believe that children are better informed by watching scenes of violence than nudity and swearing. In addition, violence is the number solution of conflict, even in TV series aimed at children. The natural attitude regarding nudity has disappeared. Even in the locker room at school.

While children become accustomed to violence through popular media, natural sexuality becomes something they must be "protected" from.

The message is that conflicts are resolved by violence. By not relating to sexuality and pretending that it is not part of children's lives, they may experience powerlessness in relation to their own sexuality. This according to Thore Langfeldt, who is an expert on violent perpetrators. He also adds that all this may contribute to the development of abusive behavior further down the track. (6)

While pretending to protect the children, we invade them with violence, among other things, also through internet porn, with all their false portrayals of body and performance. Whore and conqueror, pink and blue. The consequences of this may be greater than we imagine. It may be worth remembering that neither smartphones, Youtube, Facebook, Instagram, Twitter, nor other social web-tribes existed prior to the year of 2006. Actually, it's a big experiment we're doing, with children and young teens as guinea pigs, or "lab-rats".

It is also depressing that today girls, starting at the young age of nine, want reconstructive labia plastic surgery (surgical correction of the genitals). Where do they get it from? Certainly not from sex education at school. If they have someone who teaches them about sexuality at all. (7)

In a commentary in the Norwegian newspaper Dagbladet, author Agnes Ravatne points out how this blue-pink perspective in fact is depriving the children of our time of both individuality and freedom of choice. Her headline is: "Pink Princesses and Male Losers". She starts out by how she experiences a toy store before Christmas, in search of gifts that can suit her nieces and nephews aged one to seven. She describes these children as already emerging free individuals and useful citizens. And as she so painstakingly puts it: "Only to be sucked into a gender-segregated universe of cute, obedient housewives and tough pirate guys?" (8) She goes on to say that it's not only the toy manufacturers who have an explanatory problem:

"A number of studies done with video cameras show how kindergarten staff unknowingly, but systematically, treat boys and girls differently.

Boys get attention and talk time while girls are ignored and hushed on. Boys take the room while girls are made into the staff's little helpers. But while the public conversation is largely about what such differential treatment does to the girls: do they become more reticent as they get older? Will they become obsessed with their own appearance as a desperate cry for attention? One seldom asks the question: "what does it do to the boys?" (8)

As an apropos to my concluding comment in Chapter 14, that women too are gender role educators also regarding the boys, I will add that in Norwegian kindergartens and preschools, the education staff consists of 91% women. (9)

Further down in the article Ravatne quotes Helga Aune, a gender equality researcher, who in an article in Better School No. 3/14 says: "Today, boys have lower grade point averages than girls, they drop out of school, and are a minority in higher education. Who would have thought just some few years ago that today there's a serious discussion about quoting male students for veterinary, dental and psychology studies, to ensure that there will be elements of testosterone in all these former male bastions?" (8)

She continues: "What does it help with quotas, when the new reality at the universities may be the result of what is happening in kindergarten and primary school?" She (Aune) further points out that «When the boys are sent out to play (to cool down) by their mothers, while the (mature) girls have to do their homework before they are allowed to go out. Then it's the boys who miss out on competence such as discipline, following orders and cooperation. Similarly if this becomes a pattern already in school or kindergarten, that the noisy boys are allowed to go out and play, while the (mature) girls are to do school assignments. Then the boys are missing out on concentration and learning-skills too." (8)

Agnes Ravatne further points out that: "It's common to claim that today's school is not designed for boys, but might it just be the opposite? That today's boys are not prepared for school?" She concludes the article with the following sigh regarding her experience in the toy store: «For which toolbox should one actually choose when your niece dreams of becoming a carpenter, preferably wearing a princess dress, and all the toolboxes have pictures of guys on them? And what kind of toy plane should she buy for the nephew, when his favorite color is pink, and all the planes are blue? Shouldn't toy manufacturers soon realize that today's kids are shopping for identity like hardcore post-demographic consumers?" (8)

Both Ravatne and Aune's observations are interesting. Much of what they point out is supported by two recent studies done in Sweden and the United Kingdom. You'll learn more about them in Chapter 19.

As I mentioned earlier in this chapter, the toy industry has in fact become a very central provider of gender role identities in our time. I myself have for several years done "observational studies" of this when I am out touring with TRAX. I have lost count of how many toy stores and chains I have visited both here in Norway and Denmark. The first thing that strikes me is that they are divided into two departments, and that the color pink and blue is what separates the departments.

They are not signposted with boys 'and girls' departments, respectively. It is not needed, the color symbolism has taken over. One doesn't need to be able to read to understand. I have more than once observed parents grabbing their hopefuls as they are on their way into the "wrong" department, often with the explanation: "No, honey there are no boy toys here, we have to go over there", and vice versa. And it starts as we have seen, early on. Very early. In order to be approved for the sexology education in Norway, one must complete a supervision process led by an approved clinical sexologist or psychologist. For my part, this guidance was carried out at Haugesund hospital together with two colleagues, Elin Johannesen and Gunnhild Hildrum.

It also happened to be that both Elin and Gunnhild worked as midwives at the same hospital. One day we had some spear time before the tutorial started, they insisted on giving me a guided tour. During this tour we met a young couple with a "shopping cart", equipped with a pink flag in one of the corners, and a newborn baby wrapped up in a pink blanket between the corners. As soon as they passed, I looked at my two colleagues and baby suppliers and said: "Please, tell me that what I just witnessed, isn't happening in Norway 2010?" "Oh yes," they replied with a grin, well aware of my preoccupation regarding this phenomenon. "Not only that" Elin added, "The parents also receive a greeting card from the maternity ward, which is colored either pink or blue, according to the gender of the newborn."

This is really incredible when you think about the origin of this practice, as I mentioned earlier in the book. Another example of how culturally constructed this femi-macho marker is, comes from the Renaissance. Back then, high-heeled shoes for men, often red, were considered very masculine. For the upper class of the day, this apparently gave them the pre of being macho and virile. (10)

Another effect of the blue-pink "world view" is pointed out in a chronicle written by Mari Grinde Arntzen. The chronicle carries the headline "The Tyranny of Beauty", quoted from the book «Perfekt. Skapelsen av det plettfrie mennesket». Translated to English it reads: "Perfect. The Creation of the Immaculate Human Being". Grinde Arntzen writes:

"In 2014, the first consequences of today's ideal were put on the table. More and more young girls get mental health problems due to beauty pressure and the desire to perform to the maximum. Boys of primary school age eat protein powder to build muscle. Pregnant women eat less in order to have babies under normal weight and thus a flat stomach right after birth. Several children are diagnosed with unexplained musculoskeletal disorders due to full schedules and excessive pressure. The culture of perfection, performance and achievement is about to wear us all out". (11)

This is another effect of the same hysteria. It almost looks like boys are getting bluer and girls are getting more pink with each passing day. What is new to this millennium, is the explosion of social media, blogs and other online media channels, together with the marketers' enormous and growing power over these media. Guidelines for how to be a perfect girl or a perfect boy are poured out, literally 24/7, with subsequent products on how to become just that, perfect. Exactly like the self-proclaimed doctor I talked about in Part I, the one who first pointed out the numerous dangers of masturbation, and then presented his fantastic (snake-oil) cure. First they tell you that you are "wrong", then they prescribe the cure to become "right".

We are all affected by this mass hypnosis' post-hypnotic indunctions about the "right" ideals in all channels daily. As Mari Grinde Arntzen also points out in her article: «The market's magic formula is to hang the ideals so high that no one can actually reach them, while at the same time as the advertisers claim that buying this particular product can make you reach the ideal. The dissatisfied person is the most profitable one."

Maybe we can learn something from the bonobos? According to the evolution theory, they are our closest relatives among the primates, and they can neither read, deny, repress, nor spell the terms: role, macho, femi or the toxic word "should". Or as psychologist Karen Horney puts it, "The Tyranny of Shoulds". Well, I would off course not encourage illiteracy. I need readers for this book.

However, there are actually some things that we can "learn" from dolphins, bonobos and some other primates, namely that the more complex their social systems are, the more potentially freesexual they are as well. They use their sexuality in relationship building, as confirmation and strengthening of friendship. And like us humans, they also use sexuality as pleasure. In other words, not just as a reproductive strategy, which is unfortunately too often spells out as "competition" in some social Darwinian tribes. You will learn much more about this topic in Chapter 19.

For my part, I see sexuality as something more than just pro-creational or recreational. I also see it as a creative and loving force, or a talent. Not just as "egophilia" or as a multiplying force. The problem is not sex, the problem is rather that sexuality has been split off from love and then glued to gender role identities. "The Selfish Gene" is a myth, and to me not a very convincing one. The same goes for "The Selfish Gender". They both create a lot of un-productive competition and destruction, instead of compassion.

The vast majority seem to have forgotten the emotional and spiritual significance of sexuality. Today, it has become a commodity, or a marketing method and all too often a "weapon" too. We are all brainwashed.

Psychiatrist Finn Skaarderud exemplifies the latter quite well in his book «Uro» (Unrest), in which he describes a situation where he's watching a woman at a café in Rome. After a while he takes himself in being fascinated by her well-trained abs as she raises her glass to the mouth. He then asks himself if he had reacted the same way just ten years ago. He finally concludes that aesthetic criteria are not free choices. For as he puts it: "We are daily being washed in the waters of norms, through pictures and languages." (12) I just love the way Dr. Skaarderud defines brainwashing.

I myself use a slightly more erotic example of how influenced (brainwashed) we are by culture, images, advertising and aesthetic criteria. Especially when I face people who stubbornly claim that they are not affected by advertising, pictures or any other media. I then remind them that back in the eighties, men's briefs were perceived as sexy, whereas boxers were called "old men's undies", and were considered as gross turn-off, for both girls and boys. Sometime during the nineties, it all turned upside down.

Now "suddenly" boxers became sexy, and men's briefs became a turn-off for most people. Think about it. It tells us, among other things, that we are so strongly affected by all forms of media, that it even has the power to change our erotic preferences (paraphiles?). However, this influence is not powerful enough to change our basic sexual preferences, or basic orientations. Never the less, pop media and advertising do work. Maybe we could do with some brain cleansing in this media polluted age?

CHAPTER 17

When Sex Itself is the Product – The "Free" Market

Part I: Sex, Lies & Phone-calls

"Unexpressed emotions will never die. They are buried alive and will come forth later, in uglier ways"

Sigmund Slomo Freud

"The most important kind of freedom is to be what you really are. You trade in your reality for a role. You trade in your sense for an act."

Jim Morrison

A few years back, I read a blog post by a young American woman, a phone prostitute. She claimed that most of her clients had fantasies they would never dare tell their spouses or girlfriends. She further wrote that the majority of her clients had fantasies that they had no plans to turn into actions, because they would most likely not be able to deal with the consequences of these in their social lives, if they were to realize them.

She further claimed that the majority of them had sexual fantasies about everything from children, other men, wet-sex to submission (masochism) and other fantasies, where most of them were not exactly perceived as mainstream. Fantasies that they themselves perceived as forbidden to like or masturbate to. However, these fantasies were "lived out" in the form of role-playing with "Liz".

One type of these fantasies could be that she would play "Daddy's litle girl", whereupon she would seduce them with a made-up childish voice, and then preferably with "dirty-talking". Or the "Mommy's little boy" fantasy, where, for example, she "touched" his erogenous zones while she "breast-fed" him. These are just a few examples of variations of role-playing games she would perform with her clients.

Perhaps just as surprising was the large element of homo-erotic fantasies these men had. She claimed that if she'd got a dollar for every man who was preoccupied with dark-skinned men with large penises, she would be a "rich bitch" as she put it. Such fantasies could, for example, involve her worshiping and sucking a big black cock. Others liked to masturbate to the fantasy that she was a cute little teenage girl who had group sex with black men.

Another variant of homo-erotic fantasies that was quite common, centered on "compulsion". For example that she would "force" the customer to "suck" her strap-on, or "force" them to suck her male boyfriend. Such fantasies also came in transsexual variants, as well as "forced" anal penetration, or forced to "swallow another man's semen."

She had more than once wondered about the large element of gay-erotic fantasies among her clients. Not at least, she wondered why they called her, a woman. She eventually came to the conclusion that clients who had such fantasies, in which she "forced" them to perform homosexual "acts", did not have to deal with their bisexual feelings directly. After all they were "forced" to perform these acts, thus they were "helpless victims" (!) She also mentioned that fantasies that included submission and pain (masochism) were not uncommon.

After having read her story, it struck me how narrow these gender roles really are. I also remember a thought that immediately dawned on me after reading her story: Could it even be that these limiting ways of gender-performance could in themselves be a contributing factor to the growing prevalence of various fetishes and arousal patterns? And that this male-gender "closet" is so narrow that it does not allow for much more than male macho-hetero porn myths. In that case, it is not entirely surprising that homophobia is as prevalent as it is.

As for "Liz", I guess she's more of a sexologist and "Catholic priest" for these men, than a "telephone whore". She probably contributes greatly to ease the pressure on them, she is probably a safe haven for these desperate men's "forbidden" feelings. By the way, she also claimed that she loved her job. (You will find the entire blog-post in the Appendix-part)

Before I continue, I would like to emphasize that "forbidden" sexual fantasies among women do not lag far behind those of men. They are not quite as pink and soft as the mainstream media would have us believe. To put it that way.

In 2005, sexologists Frida Kahlisto and Eva Henriette Mohn gained access to 980 Norwegian women's sexual fantasies through a study they conducted, which later also resulted in a book. Among the fantasies that probably challenge some people's perception of "normality", they found discovered, among others, fantasies about: Anal sex 57%, exposure 11%, sex with demons and monsters 6%, sex with horses 11%, sex with prostitutes 8%, wet-sex (peeing) 17%, sex with strap-on 26%, sex with younger men 28%, sex with a relative 3%, to be raped 60%, to rape 8%, to be fisted (penetrated with the fist) vaginally 41% anal 8%, bondage 53%, dominance 32%, SM (sadomasochism) 41%. All these, as well as many other discoveries, they refer to in their book «Venus. Norske kvinner sett nedenfra», translated" Venus. Norwegian women seen from below ». (1)

Another interesting finding Kahlisto and Mohn made, which is also supported by many other studies, was that 46% of these women also fantasized about lesbian sex. This is discussed in more detail in Chapter

19. It may also be that this is not at all as gender-unique as many scientists have believed, or perhaps, wanted to believe?

.

A small curiosity in this connection is that Norwegian women's top search on Pornhub is actually "Lesbian porn". And yes, women too are avid porn seekers online. (2) And by the way, Pornhub had 42 billion visits in 2019, so it's a huge "data-bank". You weren't one of them, off course.

And speaking of culturally "forbidden" fantasies in general, and same-sex sexual fantasies in particular, I would like to briefly mention that the absolute largest consumers of gay porn per capita worldwide are Pakistan, with Nigeria notch in the heel. By the way, "she-male" is a common search-word too among google searches from these two nations, which also happen to be among the world's most homophobic (and homo-denying) nations (!) (3) (4)

Could it be that she-males represent a kind of "gay valve" for people who turn on male-genitals, when this is not accepted? Boobs and penises as a kind of bisexual "all in one kit"?

It's well known that transgender people are overrepresented in the prostitution industry (5), but why are so few questioning the other side of the trade, the customers? They must be astronomically numerous (!) And they are almost always men.

For the sake of religious and cultural balance, let me add that Mississippi and North Carolina (two of the most conservative and gay-condemning states in the US), are also among the largest consumers of internet gay porn. And that Utah, the holy land of the Mormons, is a major consumer of she-male porn. (6) (7)

Back to "Liz", while her stories are from one of the levels of prostitution, below you will hear a story from someone who has worked on several levels of prostitution. She has worked as a call-girl, street prostitute and as a phone sex hostess. Actually, the only level of prostitution she has not performed on, is as an actress in the porn movie industry.

Here she will be referred to as «Coco». Her account also involves the darker sides of what is often called the sex market. This story is about her way into prostitution, but also about her way out. She told me her story during a meeting I had with her on a late and dark October evening in 2016.

I had planned the conversation as a semi-structured interview beforehand, but pretty soon she "took over the stage", and her story came more or less effortlessly without my planned questions. The few exceptions were when I asked her to elaborate on some of the events she experienced. From the first moment I became aware that I was dealing with a very strong personality.

Coco didn't have an easy start in life. At the age of 12, she had already started using cannabis and sniffing (glue). As a 16-year-old, she had also been subjected to rape. The first of several. She lived an insecure and unstructured life. A somewhat older female acquaintance of her noticed this, therefore she often took Coco home to her and her partner, and allowed her to stay there for periods. It became a kind of refuge for her, a place where she could find some security. But it didn't last long.

Again she was raped, this time by someone she trusted, and who she perceived as a support in this foaming sea that her youth can really best be described as. It was committed by the husband of her older friend. He even managed to shift the entire responsibility for the rape onto Coco. Because she lubricated during the abuse. Therefor he claimed that it must have been voluntary on her part.

After yet another frightening and humiliating experience, this time with a violent boyfriend, she moved, or rather fled her hometown. This would also be the beginning of a budding career as a prostitute. At first it was an economic necessity, simply to survive. But over time it also became a necessity in order to finance an escalating drug addiction. An addiction that slowly developed into a cocktail consisting of amphetamines, cocaine and heroin. She was caught up in a vicious circle.

She eventually got an assignment as an escort, and with this she also became an expert in hiding her drug addiction. At this level of prostitution, drug addiction is usually not accepted. This meant, among other things, that she learned how to do the injections where no one would notice, for instance in the groin. And she did it with the precision like that of a skilled nurse.

There's a relatively widespread opinion that the escort business is the most "proper" part of the sex market, but that was perhaps where she had the worst and most degrading experiences as a prostitute. As an escort, the majority of her clients were often middle-class men in their 50s. But there were also groups of younger men on weekend-visits in the city who hired her for shared experiences. Preferably in a hotel room that was booked by the customers for the occasion. Some of the experiences she told me about are so engrossing that I will share a few of them here.

On one occasion, she was held captive in a fashionable hotel room in Oslo. For two days. Chained and tied to the bed. During these two days, she was raped by handsome young successful men. They inflicted wounds and injuries on her, among other things she tore as a result of clothespins that were attached to her genitals. But they paid, and therefore they probably didn't consider it as rape.

As a part of their "order", she was locked into a coffin, with holes large enough for a hand to be able to reach in and touch various parts of her body. But it turned out that it wasn't just the touch that was the purpose. She was burned, or tortured as we otherwise call it, with cigarettes, completely unable to defend herself. The latter was not part of their "order", she wasn't prepared for that at all. But as she put it, one find oneself getting into more and more self-destructive and degrading situations by constantly pushing the boundaries.

Eventually, Coco ended up as a street-prostitute. And after a while, she was once more subjected to rape, of the worst kind. It almost became the last experience of her life. However, in the last minute she was saved by her husband. Coco had by this time become married. Her husband, who also was addicted to drugs, knew the dangers of the game, and was constantly concerned about Coco's health and safety. He was therefore often in the proximity to make sure, if possible, that everything went as agreed upon between his wife and her customers. But for obvious reasons he could not join her in various "hotel rooms."

On one occasion it went terribly wrong. When Coco did not come out as usual, he went in, and found her severely wounded and in an unconscious state. He quickly got her to a nearby hospital's emergency ward. Luckily she survived. She later wanted to report the rape, but the police-officer advised her not to do so. She would not get anywhere with it, it would be words against words, allegation against allegation, the police officer claimed. The attitude, the way he spoke and his body language, more than indicated that he thought she had only herself to blame for what had happened in that shady hotel room.

After many years in the sex-industry, Coco managed to get out of both prostitution and drug addiction. The beginning of the end of her career as a prostitute and drug addict, is in one sense a tragedy that turned into an adventure. However, by this time, she had been struggling with depression and suicidal thoughts for quite a while. When these suicidal thoughts appeared, they were often preceded by a tone in her head, a tone most reminiscent of the sound you get when you stretch a guitar string, much like an archer would do, and then letting it go. This sound (or signal) was followed by a sensation of the brain being divided into two horizontal parts, which finally led to a subsequent internal scenario that played out in the upper one of these two parts.

This internal scenario always consisted of a "trial", and in this recurring "trial", all those who had hurt her over the years, told her to take her own life. Because if she didn't do it herself, they would have to kill her. And then they themselves would be convicted.

At one point, she decided to end it all. She forced herself to reduce her heroin doses to a level that was bearable for a short period. During this period, she visited her family in her hometown to say goodbye. In her own way. Everything was planned. She didn't tell them about her decision, only she knew that this time was the last time she would meet them. She also knew that when she returned to Oslo, her tolerance threshold for heroin would be significantly reduced. One single shot would result in an overdose, and thus it would all be over. But a few days before she was to return to Oslo, something completely unexpected happened. All of a sudden and out of nowhere, he appeared, the man of her life. It was wild infatuation and love at first sight.

She had rightly in between felt and experienced this with her boyfriend, and she had also on some occasions experienced orgasm with her clients. But there was nothing near this new resurrected intensity, which she vaguely recalled having had as a youth.

However, the way out of the abuse and addiction was still tough. Perhaps the toughest of all was all the extreme changes that occurred in both the psyche and the body after the first drug-free days and weeks. At first, it was the enormous desire for sex and physical closeness that woke up again after a month or so, something she hadn't felt that intensively while being on drugs. Although she admittedly had felt and experienced this with her boyfriend, and on some occasions even experienced orgasms with her clients. But that wasn't even close to this new resurrected intensity, which she only vaguely recalled that she had experienced as a youth.

And then there was the menstruation, which reappeared after having been absent for several years. It was as if both her body and her mind had almost become electrified, and the feelings she experienced when touching her skin were so intense that they almost seemed frightening. Fortunately, her boyfriend was neither controlling nor dominant. She felt both loved and safe with him, she also felt free to express this cocktail of intense feelings in his presence. Coco herself believes that these extreme changes that occurred during this period were some kind of a mixture of psychological and biological factors and processes. Or perhaps rather the reawakening of these.

After the conversation with Coco there is something that strikes me as brutal, and which is obviously not particularly unusual in this industry, I'm talking about the brutal elements of bondage and sadism occurring in the sex-industry, usually in combination. Nevertheless, she emphasized that the majority of the customers were nice, ordinary men of all ages, and from all walks of life. When she worked as a prostitute on the street level, she found herself in many cases to also be "a shoulder to lean on". To some of them, she was a kind of mixture between a "Catholic priest", a "mother" and a "therapist". Regarding the brutality, she emphasized that this almost never occurred in cubicles (sex shops) or in sex clinics. Those places were relatively safe.

In the light of reflection, Coco has more than once wondered why she is not as injured as other people with similar stories. The best answer she has to that is that she has never fully come to terms with the role of being a victim. She has never had what she calls a victim mentality. But her non-victim mentality can paradoxically also provoke others. There are in fact many people who want her to be a victim, both among professional and non-professional helpers.

But she can also face these same attitudes in others with the same background. In addition, it seems that society expects her to feel ashamed. She may in between feel some sort of shame, but this is mostly about herself feeling different from others, from the mainstream. Especially among facade-perfection-oriented people. After saying these words, she looked at me, looked me straight in the eye and asked, "Is the world expecting me to be hurt, to be beyond rescue?" She also added that several of her former colleagues in the field of prostitution, actually enjoy their job.

I also asked Coco if there was anything she could recognize in terms of the "phone whore" reproduced above. I sent her this for reading for comments well in advance of our meeting this October evening. She chuckled a bit when I asked her this question, and then replied: Oh yes. She had, more than once wondered why there were so many men who wanted her to stick a dildo up their anus. By the way, this was a far more common order as an escort and at sex clinics, than on the street, she added.

In retrospect, Coco sees that the most brutal experiences she had as a prostitute were probably planned assaults and rapes, including the gang rapes. In addition, they often brought drugs, probably to lower her threshold of resistance, as a part of their brutal plan.

Coco had many stories and experiences to tell. I have only included a small selection here. A selection that can stand as representative of what she experienced during her years as a prostitute. A funny revelation she made, which is certainly not quite as funny for avid users of sex phone services, went as follows: When horny customers asked her to masturbate and penetrate herself, she used a mascara bottle. By inserting the cap with the brush in and out of the bottle, she achieved desired sound effect. This, of course, accompanied by loud moaning while she checked the latest news online, or her Facebook feed.

Another thing she told me, which is also almost a universal protection among prostitutes, is that she never let the customers kiss her on the mouth. She also told me something that shows how powerful and profound some experiences can be, regarding both cognitive-, unconscious- and cell-memories. Memories that can be triggered just by a special scent. Coco still can't handle the smell of Old Spice, or related male perfumes. This evokes memories of unpleasant experiences she had with middle-aged men while she worked as a young escort.

In a phone conversation I had with "Coco" a few weeks after the interview took place, I asked her if she had any thoughts and reflections on the topic of prostitution, things that may not have emerged during our meeting that dark October evening. She replied: Yes, there are two things. One is the hidden prostitution. The second is the increase in sado-masochistic desires and among sex customers.

As an example of the first, the hidden prostitution, she mentioned the interchanging of services among teenagers. She knew girls in high school who gave blowjobs in the school toilets in exchange for, for example, a bottle of vodka, because they did not have money for the upcoming weekend party. The girls she talked with, did not see this as prostitution. She also mentioned "sugar-daddies".

Most of us are probably familiar with the term "sugar-daddies" from various documentaries about students who supply their economy with paid-for sexual services. As well as those who simply exchange sexual services for chick clothes and fashionable trips abroad. Such things probably often go under the radar of what we otherwise call prostitution or the sex market. (8)

The other thing Coco mentioned was the increase in sadomasochistic desires among customers in the sex market. She emphasized that these were her own observations from her time as a prostitute. From the beginning of the nineties, it had been largely the same wishes and orders from year to year. But around 2007/2008, there was an explosive increase in this type of desires and wishes from the customers. This despite the fact that she and her colleagues did not "market" themselves directly to this segment of customers.

Some claim that porn is to be blamed for this increased sexual brutalization, and even claim that abuse and rape are a result of this. I will not go deep into this controversy, but confine myself to quote a few of the actors in this debate. One of the studies that has been taken into account for this brutalization, especially of women in porn, is Ana J. Bridges and colleagues at the University of Arkansas.

In their study, analyzing 304 different situations in popular porn movies, they found that 88.2% of them contained physical aggression, while 48.7% of the scenes contained verbal aggression. The perpetrators of the aggression were mostly men, while those exposed to it consisted overwhelmingly of women, who, moreover, often showed pleasure in response to the aggression. The remaining women responded neutrally to the aggression they were subjected to. (9)

Many have taken this study, among several other similar studies, as proving the cause of the brutalization and oppression of women. Thus, this type of porn is the cause of oppression, abuse and rape of women. On the other hand, there are those who claim the opposite, namely that the increased exposure to porn in general, has led to a decrease in sexual abuse and rape.

Such as Michael Castleman. He has, with the support of abuse statistics from many countries which previously had strict restrictions on porn, but where it now has been legalized, looked at rape statistics before and after these restrictions. His conclusion is: "More porn, less rape". He also uses statistics that measure the same before and after the internet's entry on the planet. Among examples he uses, we find Denmark, Hong Kong, Japan, China and more. (10)

The debate over whether porn has become more violent and aggressive in our time is still going on, rather loudly. Some claim it has become so, and perhaps it has. For my part, I am more concerned with the long-term effect in terms of attitude and behavioral changes this may have on the youngest, those who started watching porn at 10. This is a phenomenon that was not very widespread before the internet. Today, children and teenagers are shopping a lot of sexual "lessons" from the web, as they shop other "lessons" on how to be "normal", from all popular media-produced entertainment. The main-question should be: How does all of this impact the attitudes and behaviors of the youngest generation.

As we saw above, Coco observed an explosive increase in the desires and wishes for violent sex among sex-customers around 2008. And what we also saw, regarding both "the phone whore" and some of Coco's own experiences, is that the aggressive elements are however strongly present. And why are these elements part of our sexualities at all? Could there be some deeper cultural and psychological reasons for sexuality to become aggressive?

Part II: Aggressive versus Non-Aggressive Sexualities

"The greatest threat to world peace comes from those nations that have the most depressing environments for their children and who are most repressive of sexual affection and female sexuality. Violence against sexuality and the use of sexuality for violence, especially against women, has very deep roots in Biblical tradition."

James W. Prescott. Neuropsychologist

One who has done a lot of research on the relationship between sex and aggressiveness is the developmental- and neuropsychologist James W. Prescott. He has spent most of his career and life studying the relationship between violence and pleasure.

The conclusion of his research is that deprivation of physical sensory pleasure is in principle the main cause of violence. His interest in this research was aroused by the famous Resus monkey studies of Harry F. and Margaret K. Harlow. Prior to this, he also knew of laboratory experiments with animals that showed that pleasure and violence had a mutual connection. That is, the presence of one excluded the other. An enraged and violent animal will immediately calm down by electronically stimulating the pleasure centers in the brain, and vice versa. When it comes to humans, it turns out that a personality that tends toward pleasure rarely shows signs of aggressive behavior. (11)

This interrelated relationship between pleasure and violence is very important because certain sensory experiences in early childhood and puberty will create a predisposition for either violent or pleasure-oriented behavior in adulthood. (12)

Prescott was quickly convinced that deprivation of body touch, body contact and movement (rocking, etc.) was the cause of later abnormal social and emotional behavior, including such as deviant sexual behavior, aggression and violence. (11)

In Harlow's experiments, they separated the babies from the mother at birth. They were then placed one by one alone in cages, but in a common environment with other baby monkeys. In other words, they were deprived of the opportunities for body touch, body contact and movement. The only way they could develop social relationships with each other was thus limited to the senses of smell, vision and hearing. Both these and other studies indicated that deprivation of touch, body contact and movement resulted in a number of abnormal and emotionally disturbed behaviors in these monkeys. (11)

Although there were many studies at the time that confirmed this association between sensory deprivation and abnormal behavior in monkeys, it was not as easy to find similar studies involving humans. Admittedly, there were many studies that showed a connection between juvenile delinquency and dysfunctional families and / or physical abuse, but few of them had measured the degree of deprivation of physical tenderness in childhood. (11)

However, two psychiatrists at the University of Colorado, Brandt F. Steele and C.B. Pollock, had done just that. They studied physical abuse of children through three generations and found that parents who abused their children had themselves been deprived of physical tenderness in their own childhood and that their sex-lives too were dysfunctional. As an example, they found that all mothers who abused their children, without exception, had never experienced an orgasm. The men in this study also reported dissatisfaction regarding their sexual experiences. (11)

Prescott made early use of other scientists' studies, regardless of research discipline or subject, which also characterizes modern sexological interdisciplinary approach. Among others, also demonstrated by Daryl Bem's research in chapter 8. You will get more examples of the fruitfulness regarding this type of approach in chapters 19 and 20. But now we come to the most interesting part regarding Prescott's research, namely his use of the treasure trove of research data produced by anthropologists and ethnographers.

To further validate the hypothesis that deprivation of physical pleasure leads to physical violence, Prescott had to find studies that dealt with child-rearing practices, sexual behavior, and physical violence among humans. And the anthropological research provided him with these "missing links". Prescott found 49 cultural anthropological studies that contained the variables needed to predict aggressive versus non-aggressive behavior among adults. And it showed that adult physical violent behavior could be accurately predicted in 36 of the 49 studies, based on the "The Infant Physical Affection Variable". (I will hereafter call it the IPA variable). He found that a low IPA-variable resulted in high physical violence in adulthood, and vice versa that a high IPA resulted in low or absent physical violence in adulthood. (11)

But it was his findings on closer examination of the remaining 13 of these 49 cultures, that would lead him to his two-step model of somatosensory deprivation as a cause of aggressive behavior in adulthood. 6 of these 13 cultures had both high IPA and high aggressive and violent adult behavior, while the remaining 7 had low IPA but also low aggressive and violent adult behavior. (11)

On closer examination he found was that in 5 of the 6 cultures that deviated from the high IPA hypothesis, also represented oppression or prohibition of sexual behavior during puberty, high appreciation of virginity and prohibition of sex before marriage. Conversely, he found that in the 7 remaining cultures that had both low IPA and low physical violence among the adults, at the same time recognized sexual behavior during puberty. Thus, they also accepted sexual behavior before marriage. (11)

These findings revealed that the good benefits of high IPA were literally erased by denying physical sexual pleasure and joy during puberty. And conversely, that the devastating consequences of low IPA can actually be reversed precisely because of the recognition and consent of sexual pleasure and joy during puberty. One of my favorite concepts is called sexual healing, and James W. Prescott's findings actually reinforce sexuality as a potentially powerful and healing "therapy."

These highly interesting findings by Prescott have led to a revision of "The Somatosensory Deprivation Theory" from being a one-stage, to a two-stage development theory. In short, violent behavior in adulthood can either stem from deprivation of pleasure in infancy or deprivation of pleasure in puberty. The latter also with the potential as a "behavioral therapy" regarding damage in the first stage, and thus perhaps the most important finding.

With this two-step development theory, Prescott could actually predict aggressive and physically violent behavior among adults across 48 of the 49 cultures he studied. And as he stated himself:

"I am not aware of any other developmental variables that have such a high degree of predictive validity". To read the complete research article with all the different variables and tables, check the link in the Bibliography section. (13)

James Prescott also reflects on our closest "relatives" among the mammals, the bonobos. Prescott points out that there is only a 0.9% difference between the human genome and the bonobo genome. He also points out that while violence against offspring and females is non-existent among bonobos, the opposite is true of the human race. Sex is also the social "glue" in the bonobo communities. (14) One might say that they live by the motto: "Make love, not war."

One should perhaps not get so hung up on this genome, because as we have seen throughout this book, there are countless examples from various research disciplines which show that the environmental factors also play a significant role. Something that recent epi-genetic research also support. As for our closest genetic "relatives", Prescott fails to mention that all of them are also bisexual. You will learn more about this in Chapter 19.

The outcome of the studies referred to above, namely that cultures that punish children or suppress sexuality are violent, do not support the values of the major traditional religions and cultures. Especially the values that deny tenderness in relation to children and loving sexual relationships for young people. In our own western cultures, Prescott claims that it is the Judeo-Christian traditions that are responsible for the aggressiveness and violence.

He points out that the Judeo-Christian traditions both condemns the flesh and promotes pain and punishment as character-building. (11) Something that is in direct conflict with his own findings. That is, if one does not hold ideals such as aggressiveness, warfare and violence as high-quality character traits.

Actually, it is the pleasure they have problems with, it is the very pleasure they see as immoral, Prescott claims.

I would add that what Prescott refers to as the Judeo-Christian tradition, should apply to all the Abrahamic religions, since all three of them originally are based on very rigid and equal values. Not at least regarding sexuality. You'll see examples of this in the next chapter. Like Thore Langfeldt, also Prescott mentions the cultural panic regarding nudity in the media, as well as the cultivation of violence (including sexual violence) in the same media. Actually, it's the pleasure they have problems with, it's the very pleasure they see as immoral, Prescott claims.

James W. Prescott developed and led the Developmental Behavioral Biological Program at NICHD (The National Institute of Child Health and Human Development) from 1966 to 1980. In an interview with Arnell Dowret January 8, 2006, Prescott was asked how the federal government in the United States responded to his research, and why this research is still unknown to most people. This is despite the fact that his research has been referred to by authorities such as Carl Sagan. To this he replied that in 1974 they got a new department director who did not really like that the topic of child abuse and neglect of children should be the focus of their research. This evolved into a confrontation that eventually led to Prescott being fired. The official reason they gave, was that this type of research was a misuse of public resources. (15)

It is far from the first time that "unpleasant" research results are concealed, distorted or suffers loss of funds for further research. It's certainly not the last time either. Some other examples you can read about in Chapter 19. Echo chambers are not a new "invention".

The last question he was asked in the aforementioned radio interview was about the prevailing tendency for most people to reject environmental factors as influencing agents, and that genes seem to have become "the darlings" among both humanists and biologists (essentialists). To this he replied that the environment is far more important than genes. And added that there are no living organisms that can develop into healthy, functioning organisms by living in a toxic environment. In addition, the environment regulates and controls the genetic expressions. (15)

With this last phrase, he obviously referred to the new research discipline called epi-genetics. That said, there are probably no pills for dirty water. It needs to be cleansed.

CHAPTER 18

Abrahamic Dogmas – A New Interpretation

"See, this is my opinion: we all start out knowing magic. We are born with whirlwinds, forest fires, and comets inside us. We are born able to sing to birds and read the clouds and see our destiny in grains of sand. But then we get the magic educated right out of our souls. We get it churched out, spanked out, washed out, and combed out. We put on the straight and narrow and told to be responsible. Told to act our age. Told to grow up, for God's sake. And you know why we were told that? Because the people doing the telling were afraid of our wildness and youth, and because of the magic we knew made them ashamed and sad about what they'd allowed to do with themselves"

Robert McCammon

I will begin this chapter with an excerpt from some thoughts a friend of mine, Thomas S. Svendsen wrote in an exam paper at UiO (University in Oslo). At that time (2003) he studied Christianity at the Faculty of Theology. The thesis was entitled: "The Norwegian Church's view on homosexuals" - The Episcopal Council's decision from 1995. Excerpt from the thesis:

The Episcopal's minority is also allowed to express itself and make statements such as "Consideration for the congregation and its situation must be decisive." In other words, the individual must not come forward with other personal information (such as identifying as homosexual), than what is generally accepted within the congregation. I suppose this is said in fear of the church losing its solid attachment in the Bible, and that it must take into account the problems and issues that are relevant in today's society."

"This, of course, is a frightening thought for the religious elite. The Episcopal Council concludes that it has not been possible to reach a common view in this case. Jesus is highlighted in the afterword as a unifying body within the church. Jesus deliberately avoided the rich and prosperous, He mingled with whores, thieves and beggars. Had Jesus lived today, he would definitely not drink coffee with the Church Council, he would probably be sitting outside the church's locked doors and talk to individuals who are not yet accepted in our church. For according to Jesus it was they who should inherit the kingdom of God."

Lost in translation

What if the Episcopal Council actually has based its contempt of same-sex sexuality on a basis of misinterpretations of central passages, in the book of which they base their contempt for non-heterosexual human emotions? This chapter will be about what they overlooked, denied, and thus never became part of their theology curriculum.

Another friend of mine, Morten Wattøe, who both grew up in a Christian family and considers himself a Christian, a few years ago made me aware of a branch of biblical research that may indicate the latter. That precisely the top trustees of the biblical faith have despised non-heterosexual people because of misinterpretations and thus wrong conclusions. I myself didn't know about this research, despite the fact that I since 1998 have spent a great deal of time studying religions and religious research in general. In addition, the psychology of religion was one of the subjects I studied at UiO.

Somewhat amazed at this, I went to the sources, and I was, to put it mildly, surprised by these findings. At the same time, I was a little bit embarrassed by the silence of this in religious circles, and perhaps most of all their leaders' ignorance of this research. I have chosen to devote this chapter entirely to this research.

This research could have an impact on the millions of young non-heterosexual people within the Abrahamic religions who struggle hard with both shame and guilt because of their sexual orientations. As well as religious people in general who suffer from sexual shame for their sexual feelings and guilt for their sexual behavior. In Chapter 20, I will also turn to research, which, regardless of individual religious belief, will put many self-righteous religious moralists in a strange light.

Furthermore, this research can have an enormous significance for all those who have placed themselves on their high Abrahamic pedestals just to condemn, judge and make the lives of different others a living hell of anxiety, if they take into account these amazing findings.

As a little quirk, before I continue, I will share a little story that happened to me while I was going through this above mentioned research. I was doing this in Denmark, more specifically in Thors Minde, although most of the script is written in Blokhus (Denmark), and at Hovden (Norway). Hovden is a ski-resort situated at the "roof top" of Southern Norway. Both these places counts among my personal «Sanctuaries».

That aside, one morning in Thors Minde there was a loud knock on the door. I was sitting in the kitchen, which for the purpose of studying and writing was turned into a giant vision board. I opened the door, and at the other side of the threshold appeared a smiling middle-aged man, nicely dressed in dark blue. He had something that looked like pamphlets under his arm, I immediately guessed he was a Mormon or a Jehovah's Witness. So, before he got the chance to make his case, I asked: "Is it the Watchtower you want to sell me?". It was, or as he put it: "I'm not selling it, you can have it for free." I told him I wasn't interested. Then I did something I had never done before, I invited him in for a coffee and a chat. He accepted my invitation.

Once inside, he looked curiously around at all the notes covering most of the wall surfaces, as well as the cabinet doors. Then he asked cautiously, "What are you doing?" I replied that I am working on a book script about gender roles, sexuality and worldviews, and that I am, among other things, also a sexologist. He looked like an alien's first visit to an unknown universe. I also told him about this new research I was studying, which might put 3300 years of prejudice and persecution of, among other things, non-heterosexuals and women, in a very bad light.

I briefly referred to some of this new research, and then asked him about his own personal thoughts about this, including his views on non-heterosexuals, and which Bible-passages he anchored his own personal views in. He had the traditional view that it was a sin to practice non-heterosexual love or behavior. But he became very unsure of what to believe after my brief introduction to this new research. He also added that his neighbors were a homosexual couple, and that he certainly not did condemn them. "They were after all such a sweet and helpful couple", as he put it. He was a nice man. I liked him. And he was certainly a good human too.

In retrospect, I've been thinking that I actually went a little beyond my own prejudices this morning in Thors Minde. I haven't had the habit of inviting Jehovah's Witnesses into my home, to put it mildly. At the same time, I smile inside myself with the thought that this windy morning, there had suddenly been a change of roles. That day, it was I who was the "witness" with a message to "sell".

Let's turn to this aforementioned research, starting with some well-known concepts.

Greek, on which the New Testament is written, is a far more descriptive language than, for example, English. Both the English and the Norwegian language, has only one word for love, respectively *Love* and

Kjærlighet. The Greek language have *agape*, *storge*, *philia* and *eros*, each of which describes different expressions of love. It can easily become confusing when poor western languages are trying to force many shades and facets of love into one color. This is important to keep in mind when reading translated scriptures as literal truths. The messages can easily become "Lost in translation".

Homosexuality and The Old Testament: It is not about homosexuality, but idolatry.

The Old Testament of the Bible contains two Bible verses that refer to men having sex with men: Leviticus 18:22 and Leviticus 20:13. If we want to understand what these Bible verses mean, we need to look at the context, both in relation to the text as it is written, but also in a historical perspective. We must understand what these rules were about at the time when the Old Testament was actually written. And why they were written. Without seeing it in such a context, it is impossible to conclude whether these rules concerned men in committed loving relationships. (1)

If we read the entire text of both chapters, we get a hint: No less than three times we are explained that the rules in chapters 18 and 20 are specifically meant to prevent the Israelites from doing as the Egyptians and Canaanites did. Thus, we also have to examine what kind of homosexual acts were common practice among the Egyptians and Canaanites. (1)

Biblical historians tell us that the Canaanite religions that existed at the time of Leviticus, often included fertility rituals that also involved sexual rituals. These rituals were said to please the god or goddess who was worshiped, in such a way that the fields and livestock were blessed. In some such rituals, entire families performed sex with one another, both husbands, wives, mothers, fathers, sons, daughters, and so on. Temple-prostitutes were also included in these rituals. In short, there were a great many sexual acts performed in connection with these rituals, including sex between men. (1)

For example, historians tell us that many Canaanites and Egyptians worshiped a goddess of fertility and love named Astarte or Ishtar. In her temples there were special priests, called Assinu, who were thought to be able to protect one from evil and bring happiness. These priests were a kind of living good luck charms, and worshipers at the temples often touched them ritually as part of the worship. Sexual intercourse with these priests was considered particularly effective in receiving favors from the goddess, since the man then offered her his most personal possession, sperm, through her priests. Having an ejaculation in one of the priests of the goddess was something they believed guaranteed them eternal life. (Semen was believed to be the essence of life). Similar cult-based sexual rituals were very common in connection with many other gods in ancient times. (1)

What we see from this is that the form of sex between men that was common in Canaan and Egypt at the time of Leviticus, was "temple prostitution". Leviticus 18 starts with: "You shall not do as they do in the land of Egypt, where you lived, and you shall not do as they do in the land of Canaan, where I am bringing you." (18:3). (1)

Chapter 20 is even more specific in that it begins with an order not to associate with a god named Molok. And both chapters contain long lists of sexual practices that were common in cult rituals like those mentioned above. However, neither of them mention whether two people of the same sex can have loving relationship with God's blessing. (1)

What historians, on the other hand, tell us about the kind of homosexual relationship that was based on love between two people of the same sex, is that this did not exist in any meaningful way in the Canaanite culture. The Canaanite was a tribal culture where it would have been virtually impossible to form such relations. Children were an essential part of survival in this primitive agricultural society, where one was dependent on being able to grow one's own food in order to survive. Furthermore, there were rigid rules that determined what men could work with and what women could work with. (1)

If two men had chosen to live together, one of them would have been placed in the role where he had to perform the woman's work, and one man's presence among the other women in the village would simply not be tolerated. (1)

It's thus unreasonable to believe that the author of Leviticus intended to forbid a form of homosexual relation, which simply did not exist as an institution at the time the book was written. When reading the book in this historical context, there is little doubt that the injunctions given refer directly to homosexual acts as a ritual part of the worship of fertility deities in the form temple prostitution. In other words, it was idolatry that was central to these injunctions. And it is obvious that idolatry fitted very poorly into the establishment of a monotheistic power structure. (1) (Monotheistic means only one god)

Below I will present excerpts from Dale B. Martins's research on the New Testament and their references to non-heterosexual behavior. Martin is Professor of Religious Studies at Yale University.

"I don't get it"

"Parents teach their kids to love but can't deal with it when their son loves another boy. Religion teaches of an all loving God yet the churches condemn homosexuals. When will the world open its eyes to the double standards it's made up of?"

A 14 year old Christian, suicidal boy's
reflections on a Tumblr blog in 2017

The New Testament

The New Testament in the Bible provides very little ammunition for those who may wish to condemn the homosexual relationships of our time. Compared to the New Testament's very clear condemnations of aggression, wealth, infidelity, or disobedient wives and children, the few Bible quotes that can be interpreted as condemnation of homosexuality are, to put it mildly, very ambiguous.

It is therefore not exactly surprising that the translation and interpretation of only two words has received almost unreasonable attention. Both words, *arsenokoités* and *malakos* appear in a list of sins in 1 Corinthians 6: 9, and *arsenokoités* is repeated in 1 Tim 1:10. The translation of these words has varied over the years, but in the twentieth century they have often been translated to mean homosexual acts between men. (2) The result of this has been that the New Testament (or rather Paul) condemns homosexual acts.

People are often seen referring to these Bible verses, shrugging their shoulders and saying "I do not condemn homosexuality, I only refer to the words of the Bible!" Such statements can, however, be challenged by examining what the original texts actually contain. (2)

The attempts of conservative Christians to establish their ethics based on a "simple" reading of the Bible have unfortunately just provided more grounds for hatred and condemnation. By simplifying everything down to finding all the answers by "just reading the Bible", without a closer look at historical contexts or different ideological desires of the priesthoods throughout history, this has led them to read their own destructive ideologies into the Bible. (2) This has rarely been more evident than the condemnation of non-heterosexuals by the church in the modern era.

Arsenokoités

This word has throughout the ages been given many different meanings and interpretations. However, it is only in modern times that the word has been translated to mean homosexual acts. Modern commentators have even interpreted *arsenokoités* to mean the "active" part (he who penetrates) in anal intercourse, whereas *malakos* means the "passive" part (he who is penetrated). (2)

Still others have interpreted it as simple as meaning "male homosexual". Some have in an attempt to separate the "sin" from the "sinner", referred to it as "practicing homosexuals". It is interesting to note that the change in meaning of this word occurred sometime between the end of the eighteenth century and the middle of the twentieth century. (2)

Before the nineteenth century *arsenokoités* almost invariably referred to a "perversion": a perverse act or inclination which they claimed to be sick and abnormal. This shift in interpretation did not happen based on historical criticism of language translations, but as a result of changes in modern sexual ideologies. (2)

The most common mistake made in translating the word *arsenokoités* stems from the fact that Greek language experts are uncertain about the meaning of the word. In order to disclose what the word might mean, one has in recent times looked at the composition of the word. *Arsenokoites* consists of two known words. These two words are *arsLn* and koitLs, which means *man* and *bed* respectively. (2) And the interpretation must then "obviously" be two men having sex. In a bed (!) I mentioned in a previous chapter that sexual fantasizing knows no limits, especially among the men and women of the church.

The approach referred to above, is linguistically not valid at all. An example of how wrong such a approach is easily explained by the word *understand*, which certainly in no way means to *stand under*. The basic meanings of *below* or *stand* have nothing to do with the word *understand*. The two words have simply no connection. (2)

The only reliable method define a word, is by analyzing the use of the word in as many texts and contexts as possible. Unfortunately, the word *arsenokoités* is a word that is rarely used. The few places it occurs are in the context of lists of sins, mostly in the Bible. None of these provide any explanation of what the word means. Still, there are a few texts the word is used in that are not directly referring to the list of sins in 1 Cor 6: 9 or 1 Tim 1:10. In those texts, the word is mentioned in lists that describe various sins related to exploiting others. (2)

In ancient Greek texts, the word appears in lists of sins such as, "Do not make arsenocaine," meaning: "Do not neglect information, do not kill others, pay the one who worked for you, suppress not the poor, with more ». In this context, it would be more appropriate to refer this term to exploitation and financial crime. Why murder appears on this list may have something to do with prostitution and pimping. (2)

It is of course possible that the original meaning of the Greek word also relates to men's sexual exploitation of other men. However, it is difficult to claim that two men who love each other exploit each other. (2) On the contrary, the importance of mutual loving excludes both exploitation and aggression.

What we can conclude is that we're not able to prove what *arsenokoités* really means. We can however, prove that no one knows the meaning of the word. (2) It is therefore completely unacceptable to conclude that the word refers to "men who make love to men," as too many of the interpreters of the Bible claim.

However, it is possible that *arsenokoites* may refer to a situation where one person sexually exploits the other. This happens both in heterosexual and in same-sex relationships, in which case the concept must have a universal meaning regardless of sexual orientations. (2) Then it may be that *arsenokoite*s simply refer to any form of exploitation of other human beings.

Malakos

The translations and interpretations of the word *malakos* provide an even clearer case where we can clearly see that ideology has played a strong role. Unlike the word *arsenokoités*, we find many occurrences of the word *malakos*, and we can therefore be confident of its meaning.

Furthermore, we can also follow the changes throughout the history of how the word has been translated, and then clearly see that these are changes that are closely linked to historical changes in ideologies regarding the view on sexuality. (2)

In the early English translations, *malakos* meant "weaklinges", meaning a general weakness of character or being degenerated. *Malakos* had several meanings, but they all had an underlying common denominator in the sense that it referred to "weakness". From the end of the16th century to the twentieth, the preferred English translations of *malakos* was "effeminate. (2)

This can easily be put into historical contexts where the women were seen as "the weaker sex", which the men had to take care of. If one goes a little further, the historical view of women was also that their existence were to please men. And if one goes all the way out, the women were only there for the men's pleasure, so that they would have someone to penetrate. And so it became, that a man who allowed another man to penetrate him was translated as *malakos.* (2)

The result of such an understanding is actually evident in homosexual acts in several cultures in our own time. (All of them Abrahamic). You will learn more about this in the next chapter.

However, interpreting *malakos* as being penetrated nevertheless becomes a misuse of the word for several reasons. First, there is a Greek word that directly means to be penetrated: *kinaedos.* Second, *malakos* refers to the full range of actions, objects, etc. that we associate with femininity. This can be seen in historical context by looking at the different situations where all feminine men were referred to as *malakoi.* Regardless of sexual orientation. (2)

To illustrate this: Men who were too weak to do heavy work, men who are lazy, cowardly men, men who live decadent lives, drink too much, have a lot of sex (regardless of gender), are weak in war, thrive on luxury, etc. The list goes on. Today's nerds, who spend a lot of time in front of their PC screens with little physical activity, or emo-boys who dye their hair and wear make-up, would thus quickly be categorized as *malakoi* based on the original translations (2). These groups do not necessarily represent men who like to be penetrated by other men, right?

A strange change in the content of the interpretation of *malakos* occurred from the mid-20th century. The translation of *malakos* as "effeminate" was almost universally suppressed, and replaced with content mostly referring to homosexual acts, sodomy and male prostitution. This happened in most Bible translations from the late 1950s. (2)

Why have modern translations of this word been almost universally used incorrectly? There is a high likelihood that the reason for this is that it becomes much easier to condemn non-heterosexuals, who are after all, minorities, than to point their finger at all so-called "feminine" men. Not at least because the word also directly refers to men who love luxury and pretty clothes. (2) By the way, have you taken a look at how Popes, Cardinals, Bishops, and priests in most churches dress lately?

In modern times, very "feminine" men can face adversity based on the fact that some find it tasteless or have prejudices against it, (and this too can of course be questioned when we look at how the man from Nazareth met all his fellow human beings). In any case, it would probably be difficult to find priests who condemn stereotypical male interior designers or fashion designers to eternal torment in hell. (2) (My brackets)

Fortunately, for most modern Christians, being feminine is not a sin, so it becomes difficult for them to condemn something that is not considered more than perhaps a passive way of being within the church's own ranks. Therefore, it is easy to conclude that the original translation of the word *malakos* had to be changed, on ideological grounds (ie not from a historical basis and research and analysis), but simply to protect the church's own interests. (2) And possibly to avoid condemning the majority of people in our time.

Consequences

Thus, in conclusion, we are facing Paul's condemnation, and we must therefore ask ourselves what the consequences of this are. If we want to deal with this from a rigorous historical perspective and return to the original meaning of the word *malakos* in the Bible, then we have, to put it mildly, a great challenge in explaining what this will mean. (2)

As you now have seen, the word has many meanings and uses, but as mentioned, the common denominator is "feminine" or "immature". Beneath this lies a solid historical contempt for, and degradation of, women. Perhaps one in such an interpretation must be masculine (or preferably macho) in order to have a chance at all to enter through St. Peter's gate.

Speaking of the masculine-feminine dichotomy, it is not a very long time ago, that Christian missionaries in the north of Norway did not care to convert women, because they were convinced that women didn't have souls. Since women were not to enter Paradise, the probably deemed it as a waste of time. This took place during the christening of the indigenous people in Norway, the Saamis.

Furthermore, sexual acts, such as being penetrated by a man (or a woman), can be added to the list! It will be very difficult to treat *malakos* as a "weapon" of condemnation. Unless one wish to condemn the majority of all people living today. Of course, many of these things in our modern world are not considered "feminine." But what should we choose? The original or the modern interpretation of *malakos*?

If we are to follow a modern interpretation, then what should we regard as sin based on this word? Ballet dance? Drag Queens? Or priests and bishops? Wearing a garment that is considered a woman's garment? Having long hair? Shave? Drink tea? (Unless of course one is British or Australian) (2) Fill in the blanks.

We can, of course, follow the church's interpretation, and relate to the fact that it only applies to homosexual men, but then we are faced with another challenge, namely that being penetrated becomes somewhat degrading. If so, what does this tell us about our view of women? That the word was historically connected to sexual penetration was only possible because the culture at the time already had a view of women as far less valuable than men. (2) A view women in many parts of the world, still struggle with to this day.

In this context, it becomes quite obvious that all this is driven by a macho-infected culture where the man is the ideal, and women, homosexuals and feminine men are inferior.

The conclusion must be that since there is so much uncertainty about the meaning of the word *arsenokoités*, and obviously major changing cultural problems with the meaning of another word, *malakos*, then the only way (as a Christian) to look at this is through the "lens" which according to Christians themselves are the main message, namely love. You know: Love Thy Neighbor. Those among the Christians who condemn fellow human beings as inferior because they love in a different way, would be wise to listen to the main visionary in their religion, the Man from Nazareth.

If we do this, we can conclude that any interpretation or translation of the Bible that causes us to harm, oppress, or directly destroy other people must simply be wrong. Not only that, it must also be a cardinal sin. It is indisputable that the Church's views on women and non-heterosexuals have led to oppression, loneliness, violence, disease, and even the murder and suicide of millions of people on this planet. (2)

If the church wants to maintain its traditional interpretation, the church must also prove, and not just claim, that there is more love in condemning than accepting. The burden of proof now lies with the church and its authorities. Can the church point out that same-sex love is harmful to those involved? Can the Church give compelling reasons to believe that it would really have been better for all non-heterosexual Christians to spend their lives alone? Is it really better for non-heterosexual teens to hate themselves and to pray desperately to God that their very personality needs to be changed? (2) By the way, the latter has never happened.

The vast majority of non-heterosexuals are neither sick, perverted nor for that matter so-called "feminine". The harmful thing in this context is that religion and culture have traditionally told us that loving someone of one's own gender is wrong. And thus made people feel sinful, feel sick and feel inferior.

The burden of proof lies with those who insist that non-heterosexuals would have a better life if they had chosen to jump back into the closet and deny their own ability to love (2). Which in turn also means denying and mocking God's creation.

And when it comes to the concepts of *feminine* and *masculine*, they are more limiting than a promoting of our individual identities. Something the psychologist Sandra Bem (among many others) has clearly shown through her pioneering research with regard to feminine and masculine traits. I will discuss this in the next chapter.

By reading this, you have hopefully gained the insight that blindly relying on the statement: "The Bible says" is problematic. (2) Or for that matter all other religious and ideologically dogmatic writings. And if you claim to be a follower of the man from Nazareth, you will have to run absolutely all interpretations of the Bible through the same man's "love filters". One of them, perhaps the most important "filter", is John 15. 17. You must also dare to look at the consequences of your own 'interpretations of your faith, and what they mean to the lives of your fellow human beings.

Still, even if you insist on reading the Bible with literal glasses, you will have serious problems. First, it is full of contradictions. Secondly, you will find at least one Bible quote that condemns yourself to eternal torment, no matter who and how you are or what you do. You will see many examples of this below. In any case, the most important question should be: "How do I maintain love in all I do?" I think the man from Nazareth would agree. Have you learned to love?

If you want to do your own further research on how *arsenokoités* and *malakos* can be understood in different contexts, you may read Professor Dale B. Martin's entire original text in the Appendix part. To those of you who work as priests, or other Christian youth leaders: You have a great moral responsibility, and should therefore immerse yourself in this research. At the end of Professor Martin's paper, you will find a comprehensive source reference of the research he based his thesis on

I am forever grateful to Morten for that phone call a few years ago that led me into this new, exciting and not least important track, which I believe can only point into a new and more inclusive future.

A little peculiarity regarding Leviticus 18, 22 "You shall not lie with a male as with a woman; it is an abomination", is that Jewish authorities have actually discussed how much penetration it takes to be interpreted as sex between men. Some have suggested that the entire penis head must be inside, others have suggested that just a bit inside is sufficient. Philosopher and expert on religion, Dag Øistein Endsjø believes this reinforces the view that the Bible does not really prohibit same-sex sex between men as such, only anal sex. (3) In some metric measurable sense.

If you are a true Bible follower, and have had sex with your neighbor's wife in a hot moment, you have every reason to worry. In Deuteronomy it says: "When a man is caught having intercourse with a married woman, they shall both die, both the woman and the man who had intercourse with her. Here's how to clear out the evil among you." (4)

The Law of Moses also called the Mosaic Law, primarily refers to the Torah or the first five books of the Hebrew Bible. According to Mosaic Law, women are also at risk of being stoned if they have extra-marital sex with another man, even when raped. The law requires the death penalty for the women anyway. As for Mohammed, he also anchored the death penalty for wrong sex in the Mosaic Law. The Law also represents the divine tradition of Islam. (4)

I must admit that I am not particularly good at mathematics, but I have nevertheless tried to calculate how many of today's 5 million Norwegian women and men would be alive if these religious prohibitions were enforced by the letter. In the calculation, I have included most actions that can lead to the death penalty, including: Masturbation, same-sex love (between men), intercourse with menstruating women, sex before and after marriage, and rape (for those who are raped). My calculations indicate that it would probably remain only a few thousand Norwegians alive. The biggest cut would probably be masturbation, roughly about 4 million people. But if we also count prenatal masturbation (which has actually been proven on ultrasound images), we are probably talking about a total annihilation of Norway's population.

It is obvious that the Abrahamic writings condemn most things that have to do with loving, bodily pleasure and tenderness. As I mentioned in the first part of the book, Greek dualism, by Abrahamism, was transformed into the split between the purity of the soul and the sinfulness of the flesh.

It is obvious that the Abrahamic scriptures condemn most things that have to do with loving, and bodily pleasures. As I mentioned in the first part of the book, Greek dualism, was transformed by Abrahamism, to mean the purity of the soul and the sinfulness of the flesh.

Where Aristotle preached the relief of bodily pain and discomfort through somato-sensory pleasure, Paul, among others, preached the opposite. James William Prescott suggests that the latter has led to alternative forms of "relief" through painful stimuli such as hair-shirts, self-flagellation, self-harm and harm to others. As we saw in the previous chapter, he points out that deprivation of somatosensory stimuli in animal experiments leads to self-harm. They also develop an aversion to being physically touched by others. The roots of this Pauline view, Prescott believes, permeate the Old Testament. Ever since the expulsion of Adam and Eve from paradise. He also points out that the first consequence of Eva's "transgression" was that nudity became shameful. This could also mean the beginning of men's contempt for women. (5)

Another Bible passage that, oddly enough, is also taken into account for homosexual condemnation, is Genesis 19:1, 11. The same passage also implicitly states that rape of women is acceptable, but that rape of men is a malicious act. The passage I'm referring to is the story of Sodom and Gomorrah:

1The two angels arrived at Sodom in the evening, and Lot was sitting in the gateway of the city. When he saw them, he got up to meet them and bowed down with his face to the ground. 2"My lords," he said, "please turn aside to your servant's house. You can wash your feet and spend the night and then go on your way early in the morning." "No," they answered, "we will spend the night in the square."3 But he insisted so strongly that they did go with him and entered his house. He prepared a meal for them, baking bread without yeast, and they ate.

4Before they had gone to bed, all the men from every part of the city of Sodom, both young and old surrounded the house. 5They called to Lot, "Where are the men who came to you tonight? Bring them out to us so that we can have sex with them." 6Lot went outside to meet them and shut the door behind him 7and said, "No, my friends. Don't do this wicked thing. 8Look, I have two daughters who have never slept with a man. Let me bring them out to you, and you can do what you like with them. But don't do anything to these men, for they have come under the protection of my roof."

9"Get out of our way," they replied. "This fellow came here as a foreigner, and now he wants to play the judge! We'll treat you worse than them." They kept bringing pressure on Lot and moved forward to break down the door. 10But the men inside reached out and pulled Lot back into the house and shut the door. 11Then they struck the men who were at the door of the house, young and old, with blindness so that they could not find the door. The same story is also repeated in the book of Ezekiel 23:1, 49 and the book of Judges 19:22, 30. (6)

This chapter describes Lot's hospitality for two male travelers (in some interpretations they are described as angels). In the rest of the story, these angels escort Lot and his family out of the city, then lay the city in ruins for their sinfulness. Still, it is not mentioned in a word that Lot should be punished for offering to surrender his two daughters to a gang rape. (7) In the same way one can interpret verse 5 as a will to rape!

Nevertheless, the core message of the story is obviously that it is the lack of hospitality and inclusion which should be punished with death and total destruction. This is also pointed out by many religious scholars. Although this story is repeated in all of the three Abrahamic religions, it is probably the Muslims who mostly take the story of Lot as condemnation of homosexuality. Even Jesus did not interpret this as a condemnation of same-sex acts. Jesus used Sodom as an example of a lack of both hospitality and true faith. (8)

Hospitality is also the inclusion of the so-called "others". It's easy to show hospitality to our friends. It is maybe not quite that easy to show it to "strangers". As mentioned, the Quran interprets the Sodom narrative as condemnation of men who have sex with men. (9) Young Muslims should carefully read it again, it may probably help many of the young among them who are struggling with their sexual feelings.

As mentioned in one of the preceding passages, the Mosaic Law represents what is called the tradition in Islam. And the laws of infidelity are still strictly enforced in many Muslim countries to this day. Women and men are still at risk of being sentenced to death for adultery and "wrong" heterosexual behavior in countries such as: Iran, Saudi Arabia, Pakistan, Nigeria, the United Arab Emirates and Sudan. (10)

As regards the influence of belief systems on cultures, in this book I have focused mostly on the Abrahamic religions. Precisely because it is these three religions that have most influenced human history over the last 3300 years. This doesn't mean that Buddhism and Hinduism and other belief systems are of no significance. Nor does it mean that these are necessarily particularly sex or female-friendly.

For example, the Buddha believed that heterosexual intercourse was the worst sexual karmic act. And the Buddhist view of women was neither impressive nor respectfully. The Buddha believed, among other things, that the punishment of a man who lies with other men's wives, or who uses forbidden body parts in connection with sex, could risk being reincarnated as a woman. (11)

The same can be said for large parts of the African continent. (12) It is also Western Christian colonial masters, and eventually Western revival preachers, who are the cause of the harassment and violence against non-heterosexuals one sees in the vast majority of African countries today.

In the case of Hinduism, equal sex between men is prohibited. But that has not always been the case. This ban is actually a result of England's colonization of India. Thus, a result of the influence of the Christian colonial rulers. The same can be said for large parts of the African continent. (12) There, as in India, it was Western Christian colonial rulers, and eventually missionaries, who are the cause of the harassment and violence against non-heterosexuals in the vast majority of African countries today.

In the concluding words of his book: "Sex and religion", Dag Øistein Endsjø, an associate professor of religious studies, suggests that since it is difficult to find any definite common norms for the various religious sexual views, we must use the rules that regulate the boundary between religions and between religions and society. That is, the democratic values, human rights and the inviolability of the individual and free choice. Then it is up to the individual whether he or she chooses to follow their religion or not. (13)

The UN Declaration of Human Rights must take precedence over any belief systems. One is not born with a belief system, but into a belief system. We all come to this world as unique individuals, with different colors and combinations of these. Both in terms of external and internal colors.

At the very end of this chapter, I would like to point out once more that there are probably no negative references in the Bible regarding same-sex love. Perhaps the contrary is the truth. There are in fact several positive descriptions of the love between two individuals of the same sex in this collection of books which is called the Bible. And again, I would like to remind you that sexual categories were first introduced more than three thousand years after the Mosaic Law was written, and that sex between women was never mentioned in that same scripture.

One of the positive references to same-sex love is found in Samuel 1:26, which states:

"I am distressed by you my brother Jonathan, very pleasant you were to me. More wonderful was your love to me than the love of women"

CHAPTER 19

From Sexual Straitjackets to Freesexual – A New Perspective

"That's the modus operandi of orthodoxy. They smother a blooming, dangerous young brain in the manure of doctrine for a few years until it goes to seed. Then when the last dandelion fluff of creativity has blown away, they graduate the initiate and rely on him in his dotage to perpetuate the holy book. That's the way it works, isn't it?"

Author and psychiatrist Dr. Irvin D. Yalom,
on psychoanalysis and other professional "sects". The
quote is from his novel: "Lying on the Couch".

Part I: We need a new role-liberation

"Haha, halfway out of the closet, identity confusion? It is freesexual these people really are, they simply refuse to be forced into a role, a role or a script that has been written by others. By external authors."

Excerpt from the performance TRAX

We may all need a little freedom from both gender-roles and sexual straitjackets, but also a little more freedom from other categories and roles. These straitjackets have mostly just two applications, and that is either inclusion or exclusion, as well as all too often an "amputation" of the individual's many different and unique talents.

Categories come in handy when it comes to establishing hierarchies. Just as racism ascribes values to particular races, though often, but not always, with the Caucasian (white) race as the highest valued in the race hierarchy. And just as racism often assigns high status to whiteness, sexuality favors heterosexuality as the highest status, using the existence of homosexuality as a category. First as a sin, then as both sin and diagnosis, as we saw in the second part of the book.

For the phobia to disappear, hetero-sexualities need to be changed and gender role identities expanded, or significantly revised. I showed this in both breadth and depth in chapters 12, 13 and 14. Sometimes it is unfortunately the case that a divorce is needed in order to be able to move on. Perhaps the biggest and most fundamental mistake we make in our time is precisely this dichotomy of abilities and talents that are either "masculine" or "feminine." The Polarizing syndrome, which I also have been highlighting through most of the book, both indirectly and directly.

All this inhibits individual uniqueness and development, far more than it promotes healthy development. A healthy development for everyone, both on the personal and the societal level. In fact, changes are now slowly beginning to take place with regard to free children from these gender role straitjackets. At least on a "micro level". But as we all know, most changes start at this level. And if it turns out that they bear fruit, they often also assume an exponential development. We used to call it "The snowball effect" before technologists and economists "occupied" the language. Examples of this change on a micro-level can be found in both Sweden and the Great Britain.

Lotta Rajalin is a Swedish educator who introduced a gender-neutral environment in her kindergartens. Both in terms of the physical and the educational environment. She wanted to do something about the limitations we place on both boys' and girls' behavior, but also the adult educators' behavior. As an example of the latter, she mentions the tendency to use different adjectives in relation to whether it is girls or boys we turn to. Girls are often spoken of as being sweet, kind, helpful, sensitive and caring. And the boys as strong, brave, mischievous, fast. Just to name a few examples. The play activities also reflected this. In short, we divide them into two polarized groups, where girls tend to be classified as passive and boys as active, or proactive (1) Or Instrumental, this last term I come to below.

Rajalin mentions that even expressions of emotions were characterized by this dichotomization. One might call it "mono-emotionalities". She also points out the striking difference in how we dress these little ones. The girls in pastel and the boys in blue, gray, black and brown. In addition, the girls are often dressed in tight-fitting clothing, while the boys are dressed in spacious clothing suitable for everything from running and jumping to climbing trees. This phenomenon was also addressed in Part II.

Lotta Rajalin's project led researchers at Uppsala University to conduct a study on this, to see if it could have any effect on children's attitudes, development and behavior. And that's exactly what they found. The study was also published in the Journal of Experimental Child Psychology.

Some of the key findings of this research were that children in the gender-neutral preschools compared to other preschools scored lower on gender-role stereotyping. They were less likely to judge their own and others' behavior based on gender role stereotypes. They also played more with children of the opposite sex, even when they did not know them. In addition, they were no more "gender blind" than other children. The study included 80 children aged 3 to 6 years. (2)

In a TED talk, Rajalin pointed out that they did not take away anything from any of the children, on the contrary, both sexes were allowed to expand their scope of behavior. Although the sample in this study was small (N-80), the trends are clear. Ben Kenward, one of those who led the study, also mentioned this. Further research is needed. And it's probably coming.

There are many studies that have investigated gender role stereotyping of behavior and the consequences of this in school teaching. They also conclude that this has equally damaging consequences for both boys and girls. For example, girls are expected to comply with adult directives, which in turn are associated with better academic performance. It also turns out that when both teachers and students think that most boys can't sit still long enough in a structured setting, such as a teaching situation, this shows up again in lower grades. (3) (4)

In other words, this is a "loss-loss" situation. They lose on both sides of the "gender-fence". A divide we unfortunately still insist on, and cling to. And separation in the form of girls 'and boys' schools in order to improve academic skills, proved to be a huge failure, as we saw in Chapter 12.

A study at least as interesting as the Swedish one, was recently conducted in England under the direction of Dr. Javid Abdelmoneim. This study was also followed by a team from BBC TV 2 and recently shown on TV in the UK. Some of the viewer reactions were rather odd. I'll come back to that in a moment.

Dr. Javid set out to explore whether the ways we treated girls and boys could be the root of the stubborn inequalities between men and women as adults. He had also observed that the culture had been exposed to a "tsunami" of pink and blue clothing and toys for the two genders over the past ten years. His study involved 23 7-year-olds from a school on the Isle of Wight. The experiment ran over six weeks where the students were treated gender neutral. (5)

Before the experiment began, all participants underwent a series of psychological tests, all of which were repeated after the six weeks had passed. During these weeks, the students used the same toilet, read the same books and participated in the same sports activities. In addition, the teacher was instructed to avoid gender-stereotypical ways of addressing the children. For example, by avoiding terms like "mate" when talking to the boys, and "luv" when talking to the girls. At home, parents were encouraged to remove gender-stereotypical toys, as well as neutralize language use and to be aware of the distribution of household tasks. (5)

Prior to the experiment, the students were asked for descriptions of men and women. Some of the answers Dr. Javid received were: "Men are better than women, because they have more jobs", "boys are better than girls because they become presidents". One girl said that the words that characterized most girls were: "Pretty", "dresses", "hearts" and "lipstick". (5)

The first round of tests revealed that the girls thoroughly underestimated how good they were. They also showed low self-esteem. The boys, on the other hand, were more likely to over-estimate themselves. But the tests also revealed that the boys were slightly better than the girls in disciplines that require spatial awareness. Dr. Javid points out that boys often develop this skill because they have been encouraged to play with Lego and building kits, which in turn give them better conditions when it comes to solving mathematical challenges, as well as reading maps. (5)

A small ad hoc experiment Dr. Javid did outside the classroom with adult participants, only reinforced this gender dichotomization. In this experiment the participants played with babies wearing clothes from the opposite sex. This led the participants to automatically choose soft toys and dolls for what they assumed were baby girls, and cars and robots for those they thought were boys. It is precisely this "unconscious" tendency we have to transfer our own stereotypical perceptions of gender to children that Dr. Javid wants to change through his gender-role free classroom. (5)

After six weeks, the children were tested again. Another class was used as a control group. The results were, to say the least, surprising. The difference in self-esteem between the girls and the boys had dropped from 8% to 0.2%. For the boys, caring for others increased by 10%. None of the girls used words like "ugly" to describe themselves, they were now replaced with adjectives such as "unique" or "happy". But the absolute biggest difference was the changes in the boys' behavior. It showed a 57% reduction in bad behavior. One of the boys stated that it was better to express his thoughts and feelings than to just get angry. It's Also interesting to note that already after two weeks, the top ten achievers in the class were equally distributed in terms of gender. (5)

In a comment on the experiment, Gina Rippon, professor of cognitive neurology at Aston University, stated that there is no such thing as a female or male brain. The structural differences are so small that it is not possible to look at a brain scan and say that this is a girl or a boy. But the brain is very plastic, and we know that different experiences affect the brain structure. She does not believe that feminine or masculine behavior is built-in biological quantities, but learned. Our plastic brains are influenced and shaped in childhood by cultural and social expectations around us. (5)

Part of the criticism after the program was shown on British television was that the experiment put too much focus on gender, given that these were easily influenced young children. Dr. Javid's reaction to this criticism was that the whole point was to give all children the opportunity to develop and achieve what they want. And that he will challenge any of the adults who do not want just that for their children. And the teacher, Mr. Andre, what was his conclusion? He has continued, and says that the changes have come to stay. The self-confidence he now sees in all these children, which they did not have before the experiment, means that he now aims for the whole school to become gender stereotype free. (5)

Mr. Andre seems to be getting good help from higher levels in British society. The Financial Times writes in an article on July 17, 2017, that the Advertising Standards Authority (ASA) advocates stricter regulation of gender-stereotypical portrayals in advertising. Guy Parker, the director of ASA, says that while advertising is just one of many factors contributing to this bias, tougher standards can play an important role for both individual financial opportunities, but also for society as a whole. (6)

An interesting example in relation to fixed gender roles is found in some Muslim cultures. There, it seems that the most important thing is not to move away from the norm of the governing male gender and the behavior that is attributed to it. For example, it is very disturbed by same-sex sexual acts, but also by transgender people. In Iran, a law was introduced in 1979 that gave the right to gender reassignment surgery for transsexuals. This has led to that not only transgender people are reassigning their sex, but also homosexuals are taking advantage of this opportunity to gain access to legal sex. (7)

This is also a way of maintaining the old bipolar gender roles. Iran is the country that performs the most gender-correcting operations in the world in relation to the population. Gender reassignment thus also becomes the easiest way for many homosexuals to be able to live out their sexual attraction, without disturbing the male role. (8)

From Polarization to Individualization

A scientist, researcher and psychologist named Sandra Bem conducted some interesting research on so-called feminine or masculine traits. Her purpose was to find out to what degree and how many people possibly scored on both scales (feminine and masculine). She wanted to find out if this was perhaps more fluid than previously thought. She did something that had never been done before. Instead of seeing masculine and feminine traits as a bipolar dimension, where one characteristic excludes the other, she saw it as two different dimensions where one could score on features from both dimensions. She also wanted to find out if someone was androgynous, that is, if they had a fairly even distribution of so-called feminine and masculine traits. (9) (10)

People who are very gender role-stereotyped in the perception of themselves, also show this in their behavior. They are motivated to limit their behavior in order to be safe within this gender role perception.

This often leads to denial and suppression of other traits they may have, especially if these should conflict with the prevailing gender role stereotype, regardless of the gender in question. (11) And why should we at all call some of the most important human qualities either feminine or masculine? Traits or characteristics such as love, tenderness, caring ability, ambition and determination are all human qualities. They should be treated like that, and not being glued to the genitals.

In any case, the changes are underway, and the momentum will probably increase considerably during the next decades of the third millennium. As Michael S. Kimmel puts it, it's all about "desexualization" of human traits, not of the sexes. We will still continue to be women and men. (12)

Now it must be said that women are less trapped than men in these stereotypes, probably as a result of the struggle for women's liberation in the recent decades. Nevertheless, they are still also largely prisoners of this dichotomous system. Many of them are also involved in cementing them by passing these limitations on to their "pink princesses" and "blue pirates."

Professor Bem suggested that a completely new system had to be constructed to measure feminine / masculine and any androgynous traits in humans. She divided this system into 60 character traits distributed into three different categories: Masculine, feminine and neutral traits. I will not mention all these traits here, but as examples of masculine traits we find among others: Aggressive, ambitious, leadership behavior, analytical, independent and risk-taking. Among feminine traits are mentioned: Caring, modest, warm, loving, loyal and sympathetic. Among neutral traits, she mentions: friendly, tactful, adaptable, conscientious, jealous and helpful. As I mentioned, these are just an excerpt of all these traits. (13) (14)

All these traits are based on independent assessments of what is considered masculine or feminine traits. In other words, this is not her personal opinion about what are feminine or masculine traits. If you are interested in a summary of all these traits, you will find the link under source references (13) in the appendix section.

In personality psychology, being masculine is associated with an instrumental orientation and behavior, an active way of relating to the environment. Where feminine is associated with an expressive or expressive emotional orientation, a more passive reactive way of being.

In the field of personality psychology, being masculine is associated with an instrumental orientation and behavior, an active way of relating to the surroundings. Whereupon being feminine is associated with an expressive emotional orientation, a more passive reactive way of being.

In my opinion, we should completely refrain from categorizing traits as masculine, feminine or, for that matter, as neutral. All three are involved in cementing stereotyped behaviors or ready-made role scripts. Had one gone on to describe only traits as either instrumentally-proactive or emotionally-expressive, we would feel freer in terms of our talents and interests, as well as being less judgmental and categorical towards other people's talents, desires and behaviors. I would go so far as to claim that it would benefit society and humanity as a whole, because this would unleash the talents and suppressed potential among many more of us. This in turn would result in increased creativity, and thus problem solving. We all need that. Just think about what the Sumerians gave us. (See Chapter 1)

This makes me think of a performance I had with TRAX in Northern Norway a few years ago. It was a pretty big performance for me with five hundred teenagers in the audience. Both the local high school and a boarding school were present this Saturday. As usual, I talked a lot about sexuality and gender roles, among other topics. As it turned out, it proved to be a very good fit for the high school students, which prior to my performance had had a theme week on gender roles, society and gender equality. The principal was very pleased with my performance, both as a summary, but also an additional dimension to what his students had been through that week. But it should also turn out to result in a somewhat unusual experience for me at the boarding school later that evening.

I spent the weekend at this boarding school. Usually we like to have an overnight stay when we attend these kind of schools, which is called folk high schools in Scandinavia. This is to get closer to the youth and the social environment. This time I received a somewhat unusual request from the students, obviously inspired by the performance in general, and sexuality and gender role behavior in particular. I was asked if I would like to be the moderator of their weekly debate that evening. "What is the topic of the debate going to be?" I asked. Gender roles and sexual orientation they replied. Since it just so happened to be one of my favorite topics, I answered yes.

The discussion and the questions were both engaged and pretty much on fire I would say, and as always I was impressed by how reflective these "horrible" young people nowadays can be. That is, when their voices are allowed and the room feels safe and big enough. One question was slightly different from the others. It was a boy who looked like he could be around eighteen years old. I had noticed him in my "side glance" for a while. I often notice when someone has something they have an urge to air, but which at the same time can be perceived as difficult or revealing. There is something about the gaze and an alternation between absence and intense presence in the same gaze.

Finally he raised his hand. And then it came. He began by asking me if I (and the others) considered it unnatural for men to have female interests. I asked him what he meant by female interests, and what he meant by "unnatural"? I mentioned, with a twinkle in my eye, that I for my part know many men who do the dishes and change diapers, and they are still natural men. The mood became a little lighter, and he went on to say that since he was 10 years old he had enjoyed knitting and embroidery, and that was only his mother who knew about it. Nor had he told his friends at the folk high school, before now. He further went on to say that it had made him depressed because he didn't feel particularly masculine having those interests. But also because of the fear of what his peers would say and think about it, if they had known. He had really struggled with this since the age of 10.

This evening also happened to be the first time I talked about Sandra Bem's research, and my own opinion about scrapping the entire battery of masculine and feminine trait-categories, and then burry them on the historical graveyard for failed projects. And finally replace them with instrumental and expressive personal qualities, talents or traits, without "gluing" them to the genitals. For a moment the assembly went quiet. A girl broke the silence and exclaimed: "It is completely sick and hysterical, that we have fallen prey to these thoughts at all, to think like that, and that we've allowed these categories to limit our own individual expression and behavior." Then came the applause, it was like a collectively liberating aha experience, a catharsis. I will never forget the following comment from the boy: "If you had told me this when I was 10 years old, I would probably experience a good childhood without self-doubt, I would probably have been happy and even proud. Because you see, I'm actually skilled in this field!" He said with a big beautiful smile.

By the way, later that fall I was told by the study inspector that he had got a girlfriend. I'm pretty sure that his girlfriend had no problems with his fine adjusted motor skills. Stories like this still bring out tears of joy in me.

On my way home from that performance, an anecdote that Michael S. Kimmel often quoted suddenly came to mind. Michael has a son, Zakarias, who at the time of the following episode was between three and four years. Michael often played word games with his son. One of them he called "the opposite of"-game, and then the son would have to answer, what is the opposite of high, etc. One day Zakarias' grandmother joined them for a walk in the park when they suddenly began this pun. The grandmother was of the old school, and not quite in line with her son's research, or views on gender roles. Suddenly, the Grandmother, presumably with an address to her own son, asks: "What is the opposite of a boy Zakarias?" "A man," the boy replied promptly.

And as Michael S. Kimmel says in a commentary on that episode: "At least there's one small voice on this planet that knows we're neither from Mars nor Venus." (15)

How stuck we can get in these categories becomes almost ridiculous when one considers that embroidery and other fine motor skills, are actually among a surgeon's foremost talents, which I also pointed out to that night at the boarding-school. No one would ever think of harassing a male surgeon for having such skills? Think again!

If you are interested in checking out your own instrumental and expressive personal traits, you can do so using Sandra Ruth Lipsitz Bem's BSRI-Inventory. In the inventory, the character traits are listed continuously without being classified as masculine or feminine traits. Be honest when you do the test. The link can be found in the Appendix-part under source references. (16) Sandra Bem concluded that the most psychologically balanced people, were those whose traits were evenly spread, that is, not clustered on one or the other side of these polarized extremes. (17)

When we're out on the road with TRAX, I use to demonstrate how stuck most of us are regarding gender roles, and how "brainwashed" most of us actually are as a result of old "Just so" stories. I exemplify this by telling the following story about a dramatic day in some people's lives. Then I ask them to "connect the dots" in the story. Zakarias, who is probably in his teens now, would certainly spot the connection. Here's the story:

"A little boy and his father oversleep one dark winter morning. The situation makes the father quite stressed, as he would rather avoid the son being late for school, and himself late for work. They do away with the morning rituals in a sweep, and then throw themselves off in the car. On their way they have to pass a railway crossing without traffic lights, and this very morning it probably goes a little too fast. Just as they pass the railroad crossing, dad catches the sight of a fast approaching train.

In the stressful situation that arises, while changing to a lower gear, he suffocates the engine and is not able to start it again, before it's too late.

In the violent collision between the train and the car, the father is instantly killed. His son has visible serious head injuries, he is unconscious, but still alive. Barely. In hope of saving his life, he is transported by helicopter to the nearest university hospital. On entering the emergency room, the neurosurgeon who is to perform the brain surgery, suddenly breaks out, completely chocked and with a trembling voice: "I cannot perform surgery on him ... he's my son!"

But when we ban the raising of hands for those who already know the story, there is rarely more than one who solves it. And our audience usually consists of young boys and girls. You who read this, by the way, have received a subtle hint about the solution everywhere in this book. Either way, you will find the answer at the end of this chapter.

Most people get slightly uncomfortable when they become aware of how the different aspects of the story (the dots) are connected. People who otherwise see themselves as open minded, liberal and objective, immediately realize how "poisoned" they actually are by old "truths" and myths. It's been a few years since I first told this story, and now a days I often notice that more people are able to spot the connections. Because they've heard it before. But when I ban the raising of the hands of those who already know the story, there are rarely more than one or two in the audience who solves it. You who read this right now, have by the way got many subtle hints about the solution throughout this book. Anyway, you'll get the answer at the end of this chapter. Did you solve it?

It's probably high time that we liberate ourselves, not only from limiting categories, but also the various phobias, which are too often the results of categorization, and which ultimately affect and hinder the expression of natural human talents. And as I mentioned earlier in the book, maybe the phobia against homosexuality can be better explained and understood as biphobia.

One of the major authorities in the research field of sexual orientations, the endocrinologist and sexologist John Money, claimed early on, based on his clinical experience, that homophobia is simply "malignant-bisexuality". (18) His claim may seem almost "prophetic" to what we factually know today. His claim was, as we learned in chapter 8, also supported by Henry Adam's and other researchers' laboratory experiments on homophobia.

And talking about John Money, he is also the father of the term "gender", in addition he reintroduced and popularized the term "paraphilia". The term was originally introduced more than a century ago by Friederich Salomon Krauss, and first used by one of the great pioneers in the field of sexology, namely Wilhelm Stekel. (19)

Dr. Money initially coined heterosexuality as a normophilia, but eventually he also included homosexuality. Thus, normophilia also includes the "hybrid" bisexuality. (I'll get back to this in due course). Regarding the numerous paraphilias, they all appear across the normophile spectrum and are not regarded as basic sexual orientations. However, the normophilias do not exclude the paraphilias, but the paraphilias can exclude one or two of the normophilias. Let me give you an example: You may be a heterosexual woman (normophile), who is sexually attracted primarily to prepubescent boys, pedophile (a paraphilia). Or likewise, you may be a heterosexual man primarily attracted to prepubescent girls.

However, from 0-5 years it is called infantophilia, and from 5/6 to 11/12, or more precisely before the onset of puberty, it is called pedophilia. But these are not the only paraphilias. You might be, for example, attracted to animals (zoophilia). One cannot claim with certainty that any of the paraphilias are essential sexual orientations, whereas the normophilias probably are. Otherwise, there are very many who have paraphile sexual fantasies, but these do not necessarily have to be dominant. However, in some cases they are dominant, which means that one depends on them in order to become sexually aroused.

Let me give you some examples of the classification of paraphilia. Paraphilias and fetishes are somewhat different, but still overlapping depending on who classifies them. Initially, a fetish means having a strong sexual arousal related to objects, such as shoes, rubber, enema, etc., but also to body parts, such as breasts, navels, toes, etc.

Paraphilia, according to Robert T. Francour's "The Complete Dictionary of Sexology", refers to a sexual arousal or reaction to an unusual or socially unacceptable sexual stimulus. DSM-IV (Diagnostic Manual), describes paraphilia as a psychiatric disorder only if it causes pain to the person who is suffering from it, or if it causes harm to others. (20)

For example, until recently, SM (sadomasochism) was a paraphilia considered a psychiatric diagnosis. There's great controversy regarding what should be classified as paraphilia or not, or whether they should be classified as psychiatric diagnosis. The most comprehensive list counts 547 different paraphilias. (21) In my opinion a rather meaningless inflation. In the Appendix part of the book under source references, you will find a link (21) where you can check out which ones you might have. You are probably already aware of your own sexual tendencies, but maybe not aware of their "titles".

The idea today is that sexuality, the normophiles, is a mixture of nature and nurture (heritage and environment), and it is also believed that all sexual orientations are formed early in life. Maybe even as early as in the womb. Or perhaps before? However, no normophilic genes or paraphilic genes for that matter, have been discovered so far.

Some use the language learning metaphor as an explanatory model regarding the root cause of paraphilia. (22) In early childhood we learn language at super speed, at the same time it is impossible to unlearn a language. However, even if we're more disposed to learn languages early in life than later, it doesn't prevent us from learning new languages in addition to our "mother tongue" later in life.

When it comes to paraphilias/fetishes, there are many indications that these are formed in early childhood. Thore Langfeldt refers to two conditions that seem to be connected to the development of paraphilia. The first one is related to a person's rejection of sexuality, their own body and intimacy. The second one is related to emotional conflicts in relation to the primary caregivers, which in turn can cause sexuality to be split off from the individual and transferred to sexual objects or situations. (23) Or to put it another way: That compassion is separated from sexuality. In any case, the language learning metaphor may fit well as part of the "mechanism", or the etiology, in order to explain the development of paraphilia.

The second condition that Langfeldt refers to is partly based on research that has its origins in Mary Ainsworth's classic study on attachment styles. She observed and mapped various styles of connection between children aged 12 to 18 months and their primary caregivers. Ainsworth and her fellow researchers did this by exposing the children to a so-called "strange situation". The children were left by the caregiver alone in a room with a stranger, and then after a while reunited with their caregivers. The children's reactions were continuously observed. They were able to distinguish between three different forms of attachment: *Secure, insecure-avoidant* and *insecure-ambivalent / resistant.* (24)

In the original studies, mothers represented the caregivers. The children showed no signs of anxiety until their mother left the room. Only then did the children react. And they reacted in different ways. Children with secure attachment, about 70% of the children, show stress when the mother leaves the room. They also avoid the stranger, but may seek contact with the stranger while mother is present. They also show joy when the caregiver returns. (24)

For 15% of children, attachment to the caregiver is insecure and ambivalent. These children show greater unease and discomfort when the mother leaves the room than those characterized by secure attachment. They also show fear of the stranger. When the mother returns, the child moves towards the mother, but can also at the same time refuse contact with her. Children with this attachment behavior often have parents/caregivers who show inconsistent support. (24)

The remaining 15% of the children display an attachment style characterized by insecure avoidant behavior, and show little discomfort when the mother leaves the room. They also show little fear of the stranger, as well as little interest when the mother returns. Children with this attachment, or rather lack of attachment, often have parents who are insensitive to their needs and are absent when the child needs emotional support. (24)

The kind of attachment you've had to your caregivers as a child can have major consequences for how you ties relationships with other individuals throughout your life. The dynamics and forms of attachment that are based on Ainsworth's research have been thoroughly confirmed through numerous other studies. It is also interesting to see these studies in the light of James W. Prescott's extensive research. Especially regarding the first step in his deprivation theory. (Recap Chapter 17 for a refresher)

But let's get back to the paraphilias for a moment. A paraphilia, such as sadomasochism, appears to start developing as early as two or three years of age, based on conditions in the child's emotional environment. (25). This fits well with the language metaphor, because it is precisely at this age that we start to develop our language, and that at an exponential speed. Some call the age between 0-6 years "The Sponge Stage". The latter can fit very well as a metaphor, because within this time frame we absorb all the information from our surroundings, uncritically and without any filters. For good or worse.

However, there are also those who have claimed that paraphilias "settle" as a result of an orgasmic experience, on the grounds that an orgasm is a very powerful reinforcer. This fits well with psychological learning theory, but doesn't correspond to reality. Interesting map, but in this context the map does not describe the terrain.

Thore Langfeldt was among those who proved the latter in the early nineties. He pointed out that many of those with paraphilic arousal patterns could actually date their paraphilic attractions way before they experienced their first orgasm. He further says that paraphilia in many cases seem to be associated with the longing for, and lack of closeness in early childhood. (26) Again, one can see that Langfeldt's observations also resonate well with the findings of James W. Prescott.

In his book "Seksualitetens gleder og sorger" (The joys and sorrows of sexuality), Langfeldt gives us an example of the development of paraphilia. In this case a paraphilia called *infantilism*, or more commonly referred to as diaper fetish. It's actually quite common, more than you might think (Google it). Below I present the first part of a client's description as told to his psychotherapist and sexologist Thore Langfeldt. While reading it, keep in mind the research of Ainsworth and Prescott:

"Ole says that his mother was ill during the first years of his life. They had a maid, who according to his father was quite absent, but who washed Ole and changed his nappies. His father was travelling a lot at the time, and had little contact with his son. Nor was there anyone else who gave him closeness. When Ole was four years old, he got a sister. By then his mother had become well-functioning and able to provide care for the new child, as well as to give the newborn baby a lot of closeness."

"The patient remembers standing looking at his mother, changing his sister's nappies while cuddling, smiling to her and giving her lots of care and attention. Ole, who had long since stopped using diapers, remembers that he stole one of his little sister's diapers and brought it into his room. He put on his diaper and felt aroused, but at the same time a calm in his body. He eventually got an erection when he did this. Sometimes he wet himself too. He loved the warmth of the urine. Gradually, he used diapers every time he masturbated. Before the orgasm, he could feel a sexual arousal that he otherwise could not achieve. The orgasm was intense, but immediately after he came, the shame and guilt was like thrown at him. Then he used to go to the bathroom to shower away the shame, to "cleance" himself." (27) You can read the further course of the therapy in Thore Langfeldt's book «Seksualitetens gleder og sorger".

I could have written far more about paraphilia, but it would not fit within the physical framework of this book. The theme requires at least one separate book in itself. But let's get back to normophilia. It can be fruitful to use normophilia to indicate the basic sexual orientation, namely which gender or genders one is attracted to, and paraphilia as indications of all the various expressions the basic orientations may show, An extreme position is that there's only one basic sexuality, and that is that bisexuality is the only normophilia, the "basic tone" on which all other sexualities emerge from. That is, if man is essentially sexual and not asexual.

Part II: The liberation from the mono-sexualities

"True wisdom comes in understanding that sometimes, you are both the prison and the key."

Jonathan Jena

Oddly enough, Daryll Bem's theory "Exotic Becomes Erotic" points to either a-sexuality or bisexuality as the basic sexual orientations. However, if one is to add evolutionary thinking in this regard, then bisexuality becomes the logic answer. After all, a-sexuality doesn't support reproduction and the continuation of humanity, even if being a-sexual doesn't necessarily mean that you're not reproductive.

One can also add that there are many anthropological and ethnographic studies which also support the "The born bisexual" hypothesis. Some of these studies I will come to eventually. Against this background, one might also wonder why there are so relatively few academic voices, both in the social science and the biological science who discuss this hypothesis.

But what if we, instead of discussing sexual identity as one's preference for women or men, referred to different characteristics that attract us regarding other people? For example, "I fall for blonde, tall, intelligent individuals," or "I have a penchant for red-haired, powerful energetic people with humor." This is precisely what Daryll Bem actually claims will happen, when he, in reflections on his own "Exotic Becomes Erotic" theory, looks into his evolutionary "crystal ball".

Several of the early pioneers in the field of sexual research, such as Willhem Stekel, also claimed that humans are basicly bisexual. Just like our closest relatives among the primates, the bonobos, also called pygmy chimpanzees. I barely touched on this in Chapter 17, but you will get to know them even better in this chapter.

The endocrinologist, sexologist and researcher, John Money, states that any theory about the origin of either heterosexuality or homosexuality must first treat the origin of bisexuality. He says that monosexuals, whether heterosexual or homosexual, are evolutionarily secondary and derived from the primary bisexual or ambisexual potential. (28) (29) The term *monosexuality* will be discussed below in connection with the psychologist and sexologist Gunther Schmidt.

A little comment regarding the previous paragraphs: If you are a hetero-cultural person who perhaps are provoked or even angered by this research regarding what may, or not be the basic sexual orientation, then you also know how millions of non-heterosexuals must have been feeling for centuries. And that even without the luxury of being able or allowed to publicly share their anger. All this in fear of being rejected, ostracized, or even sentenced to death. Just pause for a minute and think about it (!)

I would like to remind you once again of some of the data I referred to in Chapter 8 regarding Daryl Bem's theory, where he and other researchers point out that "everyone" behaves as if heterosexuality is so thoroughly understood. That is not the case at all. So far, no one has found the hetero gene, or the homo gene for that matter. And there has been no lack of will, ability or funding in that regard. On the contrary, this research has probably cost billions, but yield zero results.

An internationally renowned sexual researcher who is also a professor of both psychology and sexology, Gunther Schmidt, refers to the hetero- and homo-sexualities as mono-sexualities. Stekel, once claimed that there is no such thing as an innate mono-sexuality, but that they are both a product of the environment and cultural "coercion". Gunther Schmidt further claims that these mono-sexualities, as well as any other form of "coerced sexualities", will eventually simply disappear.

The commandment of mono-sexuality is undoubtedly the overriding rule in our sexual order, Gunther Schmidt says. The basic choice of partner for the vast majority is based on gender. It is not based on character, sensuality, charisma or soul. They may be secondary reasons, but rarely the main reasons. And it applies just as much to homosexuals as to heterosexuals. (30)

Schmidt also refers to John Money, who points out that those who have a sexual orientation live obediently in accordance with this. Money believes that this also applies to bisexuals as well as hetero- and homosexuals. (31) This as a result of the essentialists discourse. (See Chapter 15)

Gunther Schmidt reminds us that homosexual behavior has occurred in all cultures at all times, and that it first became a kind of human type, a distinct identity in the 19th century. Only then was it equipped with special features. Psychiatry's description of homosexuals at the time was: "Female-like men" or "Female-degenerate men". And from then on, homosexuals became a separate "species". A kind of third gender. (32)

So with the creation of an identity, one could also create the "proper" homosexuals and the "proper" heterosexuals, and not at least the great abyssal divide between them. This was driven by both the medical professions and the law schools. They simply created coerced hetero-sexualities and coerced homo-sexualities. (33)

The latter in the form of diagnosis, which in turn meant the risk of being admitted to a psychiatric ward, or being incarcerated. This was thus the very beginning of the process of "creating" a homosexual or heterosexual identity. And for the last 150 years, these identities have been stabilized and cemented, to the point of petrification as Schmidt puts it. It's not very difficult to see when the era of mass immigration from Mars and Venus started.

This identity polarization has also paradoxically been further accentuated in our own time, partly due to the entry of the gay movement a few decades ago. This can also be observed in young people's attitudes today. When Schmidt and colleagues interviewed 16-17 year old boys in the 70s about whether they had had sex with other boys, 18 percent answered that they did. When they repeated the study in the 90s, the percentage had dropped to 2. Schmidt says: The reason is simple, because of these ubiquitous categories, adolescents have become quick to use the label "Homo" on the basis of just one same-sex experience. At the same time, they have fewer prejudices against homosexuals than before. They just don't want to be that themselves. In doing so, they actually censor their own desires and erotic notions. (34)

Gunther Schmidt believes we have the constructivists to thank for the fact that these cemented categories again are being the subjects of investigation. That it has again been questioned why psychological processes that go across anatomy, only matter after the potential partner's gender is in line with the "proper" mono-sexuality. (33) I recommend you to re-read the passage about essentialism and constructivism in chapter 14.

As a rule, both historians, archaeologists, anthropologists and brave psychologists such as Floyd Allport (See Chapter 9), are all needed to reveal not only uni-directional narrow-minded essentialisms, but also uni-directional and narrow-minded constructivisms and other narrow-minded petrified "isms" (also known as meta-theoretical assumptions or belief systems). Again, we have to apply an interdisciplinary approach. Microscopes are great, but can be very limiting without considering the view of all those other microscopes. Together they just might give us a "macroscope".

According to historian John Boswell, historically there has never been such a big difference between heterosexuals and homosexuals. (33) He is partly right about that, except that these were not categories until 1865. Perhaps it would have been more accurate to say that never since the 19'century has there been such a directly controlled process of imposing limiting identities on people on the basis of their erotic talents.

Schmidt argues that it is reasonable to assume that these mono-sexualities will be dissolved again, but not dissolved into bisexuality. Because bisexuality as a "residual category" in fact, depends on the two mono-sexualities heterosexuality and homosexuality, in order to exist as a category or a concept at all. Schmidt also says that when society "allows" a minority to be bisexual, the monosexual majority is saved. Is this the latest attempt to save the impending liberation from gender-fixation, he wonders. Certain signs of the times indicate that the petrification of the sexual forms has reached its peak. (35)

Being a clinical psychologist and sexologist, Schmidt also provides examples of otherwise completely healthy individuals who turn to the Sexological Clinic at the University Hospital in Hamburg, where he performs his clinical work. They come to him precisely because of these narrow categories, and therefore suspect that something must be wrong with them.

One of them, a bank clerk in his 20s, had come out as a proud homosexual at the age of 18. At this time, he had been living with a slightly younger man for two years. Half a year before he visited Schmidt, he had fallen in love with a woman ten years older than him. This was very confusing for him. It also created a great deal of confusion, on the verge of shock, for all his monosexual friends. Suddenly he felt like an outsider. Had he been wrong? Wasn't he gay after all? Could it be that he actually was bisexual? He also said that the sexual experiences he had with these two individuals were very different. With his female lover he felt it more soft, safe, fluid and symbiotic, while with his younger male lover he was more like a giver, more protective. With casual male partners, he described his sexual experiences more like fights or battles. (36)

There is no doubt that this young man was a hardcore essentialist. All his confusion was caused by the fact that he "saw" everything through his normosexual glasses, thinking in the categories *heterosexual, homosexual* and *bisexual.* Wouldn't it make more sense if he left out the labels, and rather asked what it was he was searching for in his various partners, and not at least what these various partners triggered in him? (36)

Women have it a little easier than men, Schmidt says, they are gradually so many who have moved from heterosexual to same-sex relationships and vice versa, that there is a concept for it. It is often called sequential heterosexuality and homosexuality. Women also make less fuss about the mono-sexual categories than their brothers. (37) In Norway today we often hear a similar term being used, namely *flexisexual*, some also use the English word *bicurious.*

In the case of young men "swinging it" slightly in both directions, they actually often feel "feminine" or "immature" in relation to their own gender. While women do not pay so much attention to the thought that sexual intercourse with another woman should have any significance for their femininity, or in other words, their gender identity. (38)

The latter is like a cold breeze from eighteenth-century's psychiatric scientific dogmas. This again makes me think that the largest "closet" of them all and perhaps also the narrowest, the male-closet. These mono-sexualities also have a lot in common with mono-theisms. As we have seen, there are several of these as well. They are also characterized by being narrow and excluding, albeit to varying degrees.

But as Gunther Schmidt points out, there are some signs that these old fossilized systems are slowly starting to disintegrate. The Swedish preschool study, as well as the British experiment at the beginning of this chapter, are two examples. There are also strong forces underway to change the clammy "pink" guidelines in marketing.

And as I have highlighted throughout this book, these petrified gender roles have had a devastating and limiting effect on most people's emotional lives. And why are there far more boys than girls who develop paraphilic tendencies? Could this be a function of narrow gender roles and lack of physical and emotional closeness in childhood? We already know that girls are treated more tenderly than boys. (I.e "Big boys don't cry). What do you think?

It could seem as if Dr. Gunther Schmidt has been somewhat "prophetic" in his observations and predictions regarding the dissolution of the mono-sexualities. What he observed just before the turn of the millennium is now starting to manifest itself. Not at least is this evident in a recent survey conducted by Yougov. This survey reveals a growing discomfort regarding the narrowness of the mono-sexualities among younger Britons. I'll come back to this survey later in this chapter.

I believe, like Schmidt, that these coercive roles will evaporate along with rigid guidelines on how to be a boy or a girl. But first we have to free ourselves just a little more from these cultural perceptions and limiting roles. Then we will most likely raise our children primarily as humans, and not as two different races from Venus and Mars respectively. And only then will we all be able to enjoy equal care and unconditional respect.

But so far, the result of this dichotomous thinking is still a force of stigmatization and suppression of various qualities, talents and emotions. Emotions that unfortunately all too often find their way out of these "prisons", in aggressive and distorted ways. And sometimes, unfortunately in violent ways, including sexual violence. This is well documented by the research of James William Prescott, Mary Ainsworth and others.

When it comes to bisexual people, many of them feel that they are squeezed into boxes, and that other categories at best offer them a "half" identity and a "half" affiliation. "Half way out of the closet" or "sexually confused", and even "identity confusion", are a relatively common views among the mainstreamers. By the way, bisexual or biracial: No one asks a mulatto if she is racially confused.

Despite the fact that Kinsey, the post-World War II "father" of sexology, in his extensive studies demonstrated a huge prevalence of bisexual behavior, this dualistic either / or thinking still stands strong, even if a growing number of studies are showing increasing reports of bisexual fantasies and experiences in the general population.

Regarding the official sizes of sexual minorities, it is important to note that they are often based on self-reporting. Respondents may not necessarily tell the truth, or remember the truth. Or even not like the truth. Such survey data often measure far more a society's current norms and values than anything else. (39) Nor is there any topic that is subjectively "bluffed" more about than sexuality. Many people are hiding and suffering in the darkness of invisibility.

The National Health and Social Life Survey (NHSLS) indicates that there are far more people reporting homosexual desire and behavior than those who self-identify as homo- or bisexuals.

One might wonder how many more people would have identified themselves as bisexuals if there would have been prestige associated with being bisexual. It is obvious that people's tendency to define themselves as either heterosexual or homosexual is influenced by the social and emotional costs associated with stepping out of this polarized standard view. (40)

But this also results in a stigmatization of everyone else, no matter what sexual lane they are driving in, who feel that their qualities and interests do not quite fit into the gender role scripts that have been forced into their heads (when it comes to boys, both their heads). Anyway, one of the worst things a human being can be exposed to is isolation. Isolation is by the way the most severe punishments allowed to use in Norwegian prisons. The same goes for most countries in the world.

I have thoroughly discussed and showed throughout this book, that governance which is influenced by religious dogmas shows little tolerance for same-sex sexual behavior. Many parents, even liberals, are nervous about their children engaging in sexual play with other children, and especially with children of the same sex. It is difficult to say how much bisexual behavior there would be in a more open society.

There are many social-science researchers who believe that in the absence of prejudice against same-sex sexuality and detailed regulation of people's love lives, we would all have been more or less bisexual. The stigma causes many people to fear their own sexuality.

In many countries, bisexuality is more tolerated and even expected than it is here in the West. In some parts of the world, boys are not allowed to get close to girls until they eventually get married. Under such circumstances, same-sex sexual behavior is often accepted. (41) Same-sex sexuality as an act (not as an identity) is as prevalent in Muslim societies as in Western societies. (42) The latter may seem surprising to many, but it becomes a little more understandable with the following as a backdrop.

It has been observed that if access to the opposite sex has been prevented, people without a history of same-sex sexual partners can develop such sexual relationships. Among the most common situations in this regard are prisons and correctional facilities. Under such conditions, men tend to take a male partner, but most often dissolve the relationship upon release. Or that they simply use other men sexually while imprisoned, and at the same time denies that the sexual acts are homosexual. They often insist that when they penetrate another man, they are acting out the heterosexual part. (43)

This same phenomenon I also mentioned in the context of religious research in Chapter 18. Dr. Fritz Klein, too, points out this phenomenon concerning same-sex sexuality among men in South American cultures, where this is very prevalent. And that despite the fact that these are very macho-oriented cultures, just like many of the Muslim cultures.

As Dr. Gunther Schmidt mentioned, as little as just one same-sex sexual experience among young men in our days, can be enough to threaten the masculine self-image and even lead to being categorized as homosexual. But field studies in Latin America, in this case Mexico, revealed a completely different "belief system" regarding masculinity and same-sex sexual behavior. The data I refer to below were collected over a 15-year period by Dr. J.M. Carrier at the University of California, Irvine. (44)

One characteristic of sociocultural aspects in Mexico is the lack of stigmatization ofbisexual behavior among men. That is, they are tolerated by society as long as they play the active part, the one who penetrates. They are rarely seen as homosexuals because their masculinity is not threatened or questioned by others. (45) On the other hand, there is a widespread belief that men and boys who display feminine traits are homosexuals. Thus, they are often targets for masculine penetrators, and are also regarded as unmanly. (46)

The following figures are based on 53 structured interviews with men in Guadalaiara and 20 unstructured interviews in the northwestern states of Mexico. In the first 53, two-thirds of men had both heterosexual and homosexual experiences. In the last 20 interviews, all had had both heterosexual and homosexual experiences. This surprisingly large proportion of bisexual behavior is often explained by low incomes, which in turn means that they cannot afford a prostitute. (47) To me the latter explanation is more of an attempt to explain why boys are not suddenly beautiful and attractive because the brothel on the corner is closed.

Another common explanation is the taboo regarding sex before marriage, which obviously only applies to women. (48) The "Whore or Madonna" thinking is very widespread in many Catholic cultures.

Dr. J.M. Carrier's data showed several different patterns of bisexual behavior in Mexico. The most common one, was that boys who had been through puberty had sexual relations with pre-pubertal boys until they got married themselves. Many of them continued to have both homo- and heterosexual relations outside their marriage. Another pattern was young men who had sexual relations with both young post-pubertal girls and feminine boys. For most of these men, this ceased upon entering their marriage, although some of them still continued their homosexual relationships. A third group, who were more romantically involved with their same-sex partners before marriage, continued to have romantic homosexual relationships even after they married. It is interesting to note that all these men also considered themselves heterosexual. (49)

Anal sex is the most preferred activity when it comes to homosexual behavior among Mexican men who consider themselves masculine and heterosexual. These men often compare the anus to the vagina when talking to other men. There is even a Mexican proverb that says, "The woman for her beauty, and the man for his narrowness" (50)

Much of the same as the study above shows, both in terms of active versus passive as the determining factors of sexual orientations, together with a high cultural macho factor, can also be found in countries such as: Brazil, Greece and Turkey. Just to name a few. (51)

We have repeatedly seen that bisexuals are often seen as sexual "outlaws" both by hetero- and homosexuals. And if they're recognized as a genuine sexual category, this is often with the assumption of being equally attracted to both sexes. This is almost never the case, no matter how this is calculated. Individual erotic attraction is not a metric measurable discipline.

A grotesque example of a scientific short circuit regarding the 50/50 myth, was committed by J. Michael Bailey et. al. Bailey is one of the most famous psychologists and researchers in the US, mostly because of his research on identical twins and sexual orientation. There are by the way several controversies surrounding Mr. Bailey's studies and his claims.

Here I will present one of them which was directed by him, Gerulf Rieger and Meredith L. Chivers. 101 men participated in the study, and his conclusion from this study was that bisexual men do not exist. His claim even made it to the first page of the New York Times, and the headline read "Gay Straight or Lying". (52) Some accused the New York Times of fake news, but I think it is more correct to call Bailey's research fake science. Why, I'll explain below.

Bailey's sample of 101 men consisted of 33 bisexuals, 30 heterosexuals and 38 homosexuals, respectively. They were shown sex videos at the same time as their physical arousal was measured with a plethysmograph, an instrument that measures the blood flow in the penis. The method is also called *fallo-metrics*. In other words, this is a physical measurement of erection. They were then shown 4 movies. First they were shown an 11 minute clip with non-erotic content for baseline measurement. Then they were shown four two-minute movie clips, the first two showing gay sex, and the last two showing lesbian sex. (53)

The conclusion was: One third of the men showed no measurable responses to the films. This was ignored by Bailey. William Burleson, for his part, says that whether such a method measures the existence or non-existence of sexual arousal, then the headline in NYT should be: "New study reveals that a third of men are asexual." (53)

The participants were also ranked according to Kinsey's Sexual Attraction Scale, which goes from 0 to 6, where 0 is 100% heterosexual and 6 is 100% homosexual. First, Bailey decided that anyone who ranked higher than 1 and lower than 5 should be considered bisexual. (54) However, the correct measurement should be higher than 0 and lower than 6.

Some other interesting findings from the study were that two of the men actually fell within the 50/50 aspect on Kinsey's scale. However, the strange thing is that one of them was 100% heterosexual and the other 100% homosexual, according to Bailey's own sample-categories. Another strange finding was that two of the twenty-five homosexual men were more aroused by lesbian porn than homosexual porn. None of this was referred to in the NY-Times article, or for that matter on CNN or other major media. William Burleson thus suggests that perhaps the headline in the New York Times should read: "12% of gay men are bisexual" (53)

By taking a closer look at the bisexual group, it turns out that the lower they were on the Kinsey scale, the more their arousal tended towards the lesbian clips. And vice versa the higher the Kinsey score the more their arousal tended in the direction of the gay clips. As Burleson says, it would be as expected.

William Burleson points out one general feature that was discussed in the study itself, but which was not included in the conclusion, namely that most of the men were to some extent aroused by all of the four sex movies. Even Bailey himself admitted that this showed that most men were to some degree excited by all four films. Even Bailey himself admitted that this showed that most men may have some potential for bisexual arousal. Burleson thus argues that the title of both the study and the New York Times' headline should read: (53)

"Study concludes that all men are, to some extent, bisexual".

Personally I'd probably go for the last one of Burleson's headline proposals, or maybe the headline should read: "A new study states that *the* normo-philia is bisexuality, with hetero- and homo-sexualities as shades of gay."

When it comes to Bailey's study, there are several things that can be criticized, one of them is that a person is considered bisexual only if he or she has equal erotic attraction to both sexes, the 50/50 myth, which is the assumption that Bailey's conclusion is based on. (55)

Another criticism is that Kinsey's scale does not measure aspects such as social or emotional attraction, or whether one turns on masculine, feminine or androgynous traits. For example, some bisexuals may only turn on androgynous traits with respect to both genders. These would most likely not have been captured by Bailey's tools of measurement. Or maybe they did indirectly, remember that 30% of the men showed no reactions. Not to forget that today, there's a wide range of paraphilic arousal patterns, which would not have been ignited by the "standard" porn-movies shown to the participants in this study. Apart from that, a selection of 101 is a rather thin basis on which to cancel the existence of bisexuality.

There is probably no topic that is subjectively misreported more than sexuality. However, the way one formulates sensitive questions can be of great importance in order to produce a truer picture. In a major survey regarding Norwegians sexual habits done by the Norwegian Sexologists 'Association (Synovate 2008), they took this into account when asking questions about sexual attraction. Instead of asking "how straight, or how gay are you?" They formulated the questions as follows:

"To what extent are you sexually aroused by people of the opposite sex?"

"To what extent are you sexually aroused by people of the same sex?"

The response options were graded as follows: 1: Very much 2: To a great extent 3: To some extent 4: Not at all 5: Can't answer.

In the age group 15-24 years, the following answers were given to the question about same sex arousal: 1: 5% - 2: 3% - 3: 23% - 4: 64% - 5: 4%. More than 30% did not identify as exclusively heterosexual.

This survey has been performed earlier in 1987 and 1997, and It's interesting to note that the same age group in 1987 answered: 1: 2% - 2: 2% - 3: 3% - 4: 90% - 5: 0%. And in 1997: 1:2% - 2: 2% - 3: 10% - 4: 82% - 5: 4%

The latter may reflect an increasing openness regarding sexual orientation over the last decades.

Back to Bailey and many others with the same meta-theoretical assumptions, there is an academic term for what they do, "Bisexual Erasure" it's called. This means, among other things, a tendency to ignore, remove or falsify the existence of bisexuality, both in academia, history writing, in the film industry and in the news media. (56) And as we've seen, "Bisexual Erasure" also occurs on an individual level.

This in turn has also given rise to the term Biphobia. The above does not necessarily imply an overtly aggressive and hostile attitude towards bisexuals, as we see regarding homophobia. Homophobia always involves a brutally expressed aggressive attitude and clear hostility.

"Bisexual erasure" is an underlying thread from Chapter 4 through Chapter 19 in this book. Because bisexuals since the 19th century have been among the greatest threats to the polarization of both sexual orientations (the mono-sexualities) and genders.

But even though more and more people have sex with both genders, the proportion of people who categorize themselves as non-heterosexuals has not increased as exponentially. That is, with the exception of a new British study which you'll learn more about below. One of the reasons for the surprising outcome of this study, may be that fewer people, especially among the young, want to be categorized. Not just because the concepts themselves can be stigmatizing, but probably also because of the limitations of social and emotional freedom that these categories represent.

We saw this clearly in connection with Sandra Bem's research. As a counterpart to these old established sexual categories, the term "Free Sexual" appeared on the US website Urban Dictionary a few years ago. Urban Dictionary is an online dictionary of new concepts. The definition reads:

"A person who is able to please the ladies and the gents, but does not like to be labeled lesbian, gay, or bi. Are you bisexual? NO! I'm a free sexual".

A more descriptive and better definition of the term can be found on Wikipedia. Here, the definition is described as one term, not as the Urban Dictionary where it's described it in two words. The term *freesexual* is spreading, and is also increasingly being used in psychology and sexology assignments and lectures. The definition reads:

"A person who is capable of fantasizing and feeling erotic attraction to others regardless of gender, and who refrains from being placed in a general category such as heterosexual, gay or bisexual. A free sexual person is free from prejudice and aversion with regard to any consenting loving sexual interaction." (57)

The term *freesexual* does not support the idea of the monosexual categories. Many also reject bisexuality as an intermediate stage, or a stage of development in a process of developing a monosexual orientation.

Psychologist M. Paz Galupo from LGBT Studies at Towson University believes that it is precisely stereotypical attitudes that have led researchers to view bisexuality as a transitional phase. Paz Galupo claims that there are also prejudices that make us believe bisexuality is just a youthful experiment. It is a problem that the sexuality of bisexuals is defined by what kind of relationship one is in, and not by how one defines one's own sexuality. (58)

Sometimes it's rather tempting to call bisexuality "The X file". In a larger postmodernist perspective, the concept of *freesexual* can probably be one of the ways to go about settling, both with the established modernist sexual "truths", including the petrified gender roles.

The psychosexual latency stage that the early psychologists were least familiar with, thus became one of the greatest false notions and myths of our time; Bisexuality as identity confusion. Hence the solid denial (and repression) on all levels in all contexts, both among scholars and eventually cultural mainstream. This myth has become a psychosocially driven stigma of sexual emotions, a punishment of feelings that don't fit into the imperative of the mono-sexualities. In short, a crash-course in denial and repression. As I've already have mentioned, this stage should therefore be defines as: "The Psychosexual Stage of Denial and Suppression".

In one of the previous chapters, psychologist Carol Tavris argued that the binary thinking regarding the cosmic abyss between women and men leads to what philosophers call "The law of the excluded middle." That is, the "law" of the excluded field that lies between the outer edges, the field where most women and men find themselves in terms of personality traits, psychological qualities, values and abilities. (59) I believe that "The Law of the excluded middle" can very well also be applied to the thinking of the homo-hetero-binary. A binary thinking that is actually getting into serious trouble. Something the following study shows.

Increasing bisexual prevalence among young people - Shades of gay and straight?

One of two young Britons reveals that they are not 100% heterosexual.

A new British study conducted by Yougov shows that the proportion of young people who consider themselves as unequivocally heterosexuals, is in free fall. At the same time, they state that the meaningless debate about the extent to which bisexuality is a reality is, to put it mildly, being challenged by these findings.

In the age group 18-24, as many as 49% of the respondents did not consider themselves exclusively heterosexual. The method Yougov used was Kinsey's scale. As I already have explained, this scale simply indicates where in the sexual landscape from 0 to 6 you consider yourself to be. Yougov briefly asked the participants to plot themselves on this scale.

The entire study as a whole showed that 72% of Britons, when all age groups were added together, placed themselves as exclusively heterosexual, ie the 0-point on the scale. At the other end, on the 6-point, 4% placed themselves as exclusively homosexual. The rest, 19%, placed somewhere from 1 to 5, indicating varying degrees of bisexuality. The majority of the latter group gravitated toward the heterosexual end of the scale. Only 2% of those surveyed considered themselves 50/50 hetero- and homosexual.

But the most interesting findings they made among the youngest respondents. With regard to the age group 18 to 24, "only" 46% considered themselves exclusively heterosexual and 6% exclusively homosexual. The rest, 43%, placed themselves between 1 and 5, the bisexual spectrum on Kinsey's scale. It's interesting to note that for each new generation, the proportion of those who consider their sexual orientation as either or, decreases. Another interesting trend that this study revealed is that all generations are increasingly accepting of sexual orientations as not two mutually exclusive monosexual variables, such as hetero- or homosexuality. Only 28% of the heterosexual respondents thought you're either hetero- or homosexual. (60) (61)

Here we see the same phenomenon as in the Norwegian study I referred to above. Namely that the way the questions are formulated is of great importance for the most precise and honest answers possible. The Norwegian study, showed an increase in the number who did not consider themselves 100% heterosexual for each time it was conducted. This doesn't mean that the number of bisexuals increases, it's rather a reflection of society's increasing acceptance of different sexualities.

In a study conducted in the US, 29% of the respondents between 18 and 29 identified themselves as non-exclusively heterosexual. And here, as in both the Norwegian and British studies, this proportion decreased the older the respondents were. (62)

The latter is again probably an echo of societal attitudes in general, and thus individual attitudes (fear) of stigma. As for the difference between the outcome of the British and the American study, this probably reflects the difference between the two cultures' acceptance of different sexualities. The United States is probably struggling more with its prejudices and attitudes towards sexuality in general, most likely due to the strong foothold of conservative Christianity in their culture.

Considering much of the twisted and biased research I have referred to in several of the previous chapters, I sometimes wonder if it is the very concept of "objectivity" that has gotten in the way of discovering scientists own bias? Not to mention prejudice, so I wonder: How can it be that so few people have conducted research on researchers (?)

Part III: How come so few have done research on scientists?

"Objectivity begins with the realization that one is subjective"

- Donovan M. Neal

Well, maybe it would be a challenge to get research funding from The Research Council, which often consists of researchers, in order to conduct research on researchers (!) However, one who incidentally has done research on researchers, albeit indirectly, is the Canadian Bruce Bagemihl. Dr. Bagemihl himself is both researcher and biologist with a doctorate in linguistics and cognitive science. Through his research on animal sexual behavior, which also included reviewing the past two hundred years of zoological research, he found evidence of scientists' own bias and prejudice, which also means their absence of objectivity.

And perhaps most importantly, Dr. Bagemihl's disclosure of scientific "blindness" as a result of "invisible" meta-theoretical "truths". This is scary, because in many of the cases it was the rule. Not the exception.

And what was it that disturbed and triggered the "blindness" of these scientists? Sex! Not instinctive sexual behavior for the purpose of biological reproduction, but steamy vigorous sex in every conceivable variants, and for some of them obviously also many unimaginable variants.

A common thread that Bagemihl found when he scrutinized this large and sometimes insurmountable research on animal sexual behavior, was the "creative" circumvention of actual sexual behavior among animals. That is, when it was not heterosexual and produced offspring, and thus fit perfectly into the "survival of the species" hypothesis. Some creative descriptions that often were repeated with regard to non-heterosexual behavior were, to mention a few: "Greeting rituals", "tension regulation", "social bonding" and "dominance". The descriptions and explanations could be almost anything other than sexual pleasure, play and God forbid, compassion or love.

To take the latter first, "dominance", also called "aggressive sexual behavior" by some, is perhaps one of the most used terms when homosexual behavior is to be explained in the animal kingdom. But also in parts of the human world, such as the human prison and military world. This meta-theoretical assumption also emerged in connection with some of the studies referred to above. It's otherwise known as explaining away.

The most common explanation for dominant (homo) sexual behavior is that the dominant mounts the subdominant to mark his rank in the herd. This hypothesis appeared in 1914 and has since then, well, dominated the field of zoological research. However, later reviews and research have shown that this hypothesis has very little explanatory power, if any at all. But it is still lives on. (63)

Moreover, it appears that this dominant practice among many mammalian species often are reciprocal. (64) "Switch" they call it in human BDSM contexts, meaning they are taking turns in being dominant or subdominant. Maybe one could call it "domination in a democratic and flat leadership structure"?

This type of mutually "dominant behavior" has been found in at least thirty of the species, and is thus a very strong candidate to reject the "dominant behavior" hypothesis all together. Homosexual mounting should be unipolar, not bipolar as in the example above, if that hypothesis were to have any relevance at all. (64)

And as a further emphasis of this: In more than thirty species, it is the so-called subdominant animal that takes the initiative to be homosexually mounted. Of course, this can also be explained as conditioned behavior in those cases where the subdominant animal constantly remains subdominant. But that's not the case in the examples mentioned above. Researchers have also completely ignored the boundary between willful and unwilling sub-dominance, in other words, the distinction between consent and rape. (64)

As for the dominance hypothesis, some went so far as to exclude same-sex mounting from the statistical calculations, just because they were engaged in role-switching. In other words, the animals neither obeyed the dominance-theory, nor to the zoological scientists. One researcher went as far as describing it as dysfunctional behavior, because they failed to conform to the dominance-hierarchy, or to display other "useful qualities", as he put it. (65)

In other words, the animals did not behave in relation to the theory, or the researchers' maps. In this connection, it may be worth recalling the introduction to Part III of the book, where I point out that if the map and the terrain do not match, it is not the terrain that's wrong. It's the map (the theory) that needs to be revised. Not the terrain.

As a final comment regarding the, well, dominant observation-skills of these zoological scientists, I will mention the giraffes. In fact they "observed" that when a male giraffe sniffs a female giraffe's rear end, and this even without mounting, penetration, erection or ejaculation is taking place, it's described as a sexual act. But if a male giraffe is sniffing on another male giraffe's genitals, and then penetrates him with an erected penis and subsequently ejaculates, then this is described as aggressive or dominant behavior. (66)

Masturbation (by partner), oral sex, anal stimulation without mounting and sexual flirting are some variants of same-sex behavior occurring among more than seventy animal species. The human species not included. Some of this I will discuss below.

Aha, so it's nutritional behavior they engage in. Off course. It cannot be sexual. Or?

"Two males, regularly mouthed the penis of the other on a reciprocal basis. This behavior, however, may be nutritious rather than sexual behavior."

TL Maple. Orangutan Behavior. (67)

When I'm on the road with the show TRAX, I often emphasize the healthy and good aspects of sex including sexual intercourse and fellatio to the audience. Because when it comes to semen, it's actually quite rich in protein. But not rich enough, it takes a hundred doses of semen to cover a person's daily need for protein. That's why I recommend extra supplements in order to not get totally exhausted. So, maybe Dr. Maple's in on to something?

Most of the research literature that Bruce Bagemihl has reviewed reveals that the very use of the words "homosexual behavior" has been so dangerous that they for the most part are absent. Instead, a battery of alternative explanations has been created to circumvent or avoid this "dangerous" topic. Instead of writing homosexual activities, they have used terms such as: *Male-male, female-female, unisexual, ambisexual,* or *intrasexual* social activities, just to mention a few. (69) The term ambisexual is probably a way to omit the mentioning of bisexuality.

Another example that shows how ridiculous some of their explanations could be, are female chimpanzees rubbing their genitals against each other until they scream out in orgasmic delight. This was described as greeting rituals. (69)

Issues like this has not only been circumvented or avoided, but also suppressed and denied. In some cases scientific evidence has even been excluded. In other words censorsing of research data that we don't like. An example of the latter was committed at a governmental level in 1979. The Moclips Cetological Society, a non-profit scientific organization, provided a report on Killer whale behavior to the US Marine Mammal Commission. (70)

In the conclusion of their report, they mentioned that homosexual behavior had been observed in many species, including killer whales, cetacean whales, wild dogs and primates. And that in some cases this behavior played a significant role regarding social order. One year later, when the study was published by the US Marine Mammal Commission as an official government document, all of the above mentioning of homosexual behavior had been wiped out. However the rest of the report remained intact. (70)

Other ways in which homosexual behavior among animals has been explained, is as a kind of pseudo-heterosexual behavior. Meaning there is a "male" and a "female" role" played out when members of the same gender are having sex. It's like an echo of a widespread view that heterosexuality must be the model for human homosexual behavior, like: "Which one of you plays the role of the man (or the woman)?" (71) Some researchers have even claimed that sex between females is caused by male animals' lack of interest, or being disabled to sexually satisfy them. (72)

Well, maybe, or could it be that the above mentioned males were more sexually interested in each other? None of these researchers have proposed the latter hypothesis. In any case, these attempts are suspiciously similar to the prejudiced explanations of human non-heterosexual behavior. Explanations which, without exceptions, have been falsified. Nevertheless, they still live in on in some environments, and as we have seen in both this and other chapters, also in "objective" scientific environments.

Then there's the supply and demand theory. Or the deficiency-theory as I like to call it. Aha, so they perform same-sex activities because there is a deficit the other gender. Well actually, in a surprising number of the species, the frequency of heterosexual and homosexual behavior is correlated. More hetero-sex leads to more homo-sex. In fact, the frequency of homosexual behavior also increases with increased access to the other sex, and ditto decreases with less access to the other sex. This totally contradicts the theory which claims that a limited access to the opposite sex leads to homosexual behavior. (73)

This latter theory is still widespread among members of the human species. This is still how many people explain the great prevalence of homosexual behavior in prisons, boarding schools and armies. We saw examples of that in Chapter 3. Among other things, this is really just another variant of the "pseudo-sexuality" theory. Few dare to use the actual name for this type of behavior. It is neither heterosexual nor homosexual. In most cases it's both. But as we have seen many examples of in this book, it becomes very disturbing when something rocks with our either-or, black or white, blue or pink thinking. The polarization syndrome. It's in such cases that it becomes so incredibly tempting to cling to those ancient and long-outdated maps, and rather shout out that there must be something wrong with the terrain. A few years ago I was on a trip to Switzerland to attend a wedding. I was quite familiar with driving through Europe, having lived in Switzerland for a two years period. But on this occasion it had been a while since I last drove from Hirtshals to La Chaux De Fonds. In the meantime, most of the stretch through Jutland had been upgraded to top standard highways. I managed the incredible, I got lost in little Denmark. Because I used old outdated maps. Well, they always worked before, so it had to be Denmark there was something wrong with, not the maps, my glasses or my head.

Speaking of glasses, another funny and widespread hypothesis among these researchers is that the reason for the prevalent homo- and bisexual behavior, is simply because they are unable to see the difference between the sexes (74) Yea, right, that must be hard without any clothes on. Well, there has been a lot of research trying to support this hypothesis as well, but with rather disappointing results, at least for the supporters of the hypothesis.

I am not going to reproduce the above mentioned research here, but simply refer to male-gorillas alternately sucking each other. Perhaps another variant of "switch", or mutual nutrition? (75) And just for the sake of balance, female-gorillas do also perform oral sex on each other. (76) And once again apropos glasses, visual disturbances and confusion: Could it possibly be that the scientists in these cases are the ones who suffer from the problem of discernment? As the saying goes: "It's all in the eyes of the beholder", or to paraphrase it: "It's all in the beholder's container behind the eyes".

And speaking of mutual hormonal nutrition and other hormone-centered hypotheses, there is no research that shows any hormonal differences between hetero- and not so hetero animals either. (77) How outrageous this prejudiced "research" can be in their quest to find evidence to support their own predetermined beliefs, is shown in the following story. It also shows how tainted many people have become as a result of the Mars-Venus, blue-pink perspective, or the extraterrestrial theory of men and women, as Kimmel would call it. Nature offers all sorts of sexes, sexualities and behaviors. Transsexual animals are no exception.

In Texas, some researchers were so disturbed by the male Velvet Horns Deer's sex role-mixing that they went through the following extent of tests in order to find the cause of this "abnormality": Dissection of the genitals to look for anomalies and possible infections. Blood tests for toxins, as well as diet profiles. Hormone injections and chromosome studies. All to no avail. They were unable to find the cause of these animals' unheard of sex role behaviors. They concluded that it was probably caused by toxins in the soil. Although they could not find any. (78)

Transgender-animals has generally been seen as abnormal, both because of "inappropriate" gender-role behavior, but also because they often cannot or will not reproduce, although some of them do. As we've seen throughout this book, the Abrahamic religions have influenced much of the early medical scientific paradigm, which in turn has been transmitted to other disciplines and eventually into mainstream thinking. Then it's easy to become "blind" to other explanations or unusual talents.

For example, among gender-mixing (trans) baboons we find that not only are they fully integrated into their herds, but they also perform leadership functions. (79) In other words, they are important, thus also important for the continuation of the herd. In this regard, it's also interesting to note that in the human tribal cultures, homo-, bisexuals and transgender individuals often had (and still have) the most important social positions, such as shamans, teachers and caregivers. (80)

Our closest relatives among the primates are all bisexual. Or are maybe freesexual?

In some species, the majority of the animals are heterosexual. In others, the vast majority are bisexual where few, if any, are exclusively heterosexual or homosexual. Some example: Dolphins, mountain sheep and bonobos, just to name a few. (81) It is the latter that I will mainly devote the last part of this section to. The bonobos are probably also the ones that have caused the most trouble for prejudiced biologists, zoologists and others who have devoted their careers to animal research.

It has obviously been difficult to swallow that many of the primates engages in widespread non-procreative sexual behavior. The bonobos also use sex in order to create harmonious relationships and cohesion in their groups. And practically everyone is bisexual. (82)

Moreover, they are not significantly influenced by the Abrahamic religions, nor are they affected by Freud's latency period. They cannot deny or suppress either. Their sexual repertoire is so varied that if one isn't aware of the fact that it is animal behavior being described, one would probably assume that the descriptions are referring to human sexual behavior.

Let me mention some of them: Oral sex, masturbation (also mutual), vaginal penetration with fingers, anal stimulation including the use of fingers, heterosexual anal sex, and believe it or not, auto-fellatio which to most people is known as self- sucking. (83) By the way, the latter exercise is something that most human boys have tried out.

I often ask the boys in my audiences how many of them that have tried to suck themselves, usually there are always some few brave souls who raise their hand, actually, everyone should do it, because you have to look long for a boy who hasn't tried it out. And by the way, how "gay" is it to suck yourself (?) However, a clear gender difference appears regarding this exercise, girls are challenged by an extra distance of at least 10 cm in order to succeed. Thus, they rarely succeed. Indeed, some things in life are biological unfair. Perhaps it's comforting to know that only a tiny minority of the boys succeed in this gymnastic exercise.

When it comes to bonobos, they are interesting in more than one way. They have even developed a relatively advanced sign language. And some researchers believe that it is precisely the wide repertoire of sexual activity that has contributed to the development of this advanced communication among some of the primates. (84) And the bonobos, or pygmy-chimpanzees as they also are called, are probably the most advanced of them all. For example, they have a wide variety of intercourse positions, regarding both hetero- and homosexual activities, with matching iconic signs to communicate their wishes.

One of the pioneers in this regard is Susan Savage-Rumbaugh with her groundbreaking research on communication among primates in the 70's. She believes that this research is also of great relevance to the understanding of language development in the human species. (85) So my comments on the Sumerian culture in Chapter 1 are perhaps not so far from the truth, when I claimed that sexual freedom and gender equality lead to high creativity, ingenuity, communication and development. Contrary to what Freud and the psychoanalytic theory claimed, namely that it is the suppression of sexuality that leads to development. *Sublimation* they call it in those circles

Savage-Rumbaugh and her colleagues discovered twelve different hand- and arm movements used by the bonobos to initiate, communicate, and negotiate intercourse positions and various other body positions with their partners, for both hetero- and homosexual activities. Most of the hand-gestures are iconic, that is, they have a physical resemblance to the meaning of what they want. In addition, they found that subtle signals were also used in connection with sexual activities, this was often signaled with their eyes, among other things. (86)

It is interesting to think that it was the chimpanzees themselves who developed this "language", as well as passing it on to the uninitiated, and that they negotiated among themselves. A brilliant example of non-aggressive sexuality. They also share other similarities with the human species, such as development of tools.

More than twenty different tools have been registered among the primates so far. However, since this part of the chapter mostly concerns the sexual life among the bonobos, I will only mention one of them, namely dildos. Or perhaps one should call them ecological dildos, since they're in most cases are made from organic materials, such as liana. In captivity, however, they also use pieces of wire in the manufacturing process. Yes, you read that right. (87)

Another interesting habit among some of the primates, like for instance the baboons, is to put their testicles in the hands of another. This as a gesture to show trust and willingness to cooperate, a kind of oath. It's also used by some indigenous people, among others the Eipa and Bendamini people in New Guinea. It is even mentioned in the Bible, Genesis 24: 9. The English words: *Testify, testimony* and *testicle* are claimed to have the same linguistic origin as *testis*, which originally meant "witness". (88)

In other words, "testament" as in "The New Testament" must have the same original origin. Interesting to think about. By the way, I don't believe the above-mentioned custom is particularly prevalent in the judicial system, or in today's evangelical congregations (at least not openly).

On the basis of all this natural variation among animals that has now been uncovered by science and which was previously not expected, it will have to have far-reaching, perhaps even revolutionary implications, according to biologist Bruce Bagemihl. (89)

Yes, perhaps it is high time we also accept the vast variations of human nature. A rapidly growing amount of biological studies and research concludes that it is natural variation that is the most sustainable and thus a prerequisite for further development. Which I think it also can be concluded in connection with the comprehensive political-psychological study I referred to in Chapter 15.

As we have seen in this and in several of the other chapters of this book, scientists are often influenced by both religious and cultural prejudices. This despite the fact that a key requirement for these professions is objectivity. Important traits and features have been misunderstood, misinterpreted and in some cases downright neglected.

It wasn't until the nineties that some biologists began to point out and expose these errors as a result of the ignorance and prejudice in this field of science. Two scientists who deserve great honor and credit for this, are the zoologists Paul Vasey and Linda Wolfe. Wolfe was also the first to say that the real name of the problem is homophobia. This is what I call "Schindler courage". The above shows clearly that "objectivity" has been totally overridden by meta-theoretical assumptions. We do not see with our eyes, we look through our eyes with our programmed minds.

Another consequence of this widespread homo- and bisexual behavior among animals has been underestimated and thus unknown for two hundred years for large parts of the science, is that the general public has also adopted these wrong attitudes and prejudice regarding natural sexual behaviors. An example of this was a preacher who on TV-2 (Norwegian national TV-channel) a few years ago snarled out to the viewers, that not even pigs engage in such filthy sexual behavior like the homosexuals. Well, actually they do too.

In any case, this should have consequences, and in that regard the general educations have a great responsibility, precisely because attitudes are formed early in life, just like languages, all kinds of languages. Moreover, it is the young ones who have to pay the highest price for all the sins and lies of the past. Children and young people are still the group most at risk of harassment and suicide. And as we've seen, "fucking faggot/homo" and "fucking bitch" are the most used methods bullying and harassment in schoolyards all over the world. And it affects absolutely everyone, completely independent of sexual orientations and genders.

To the best of our knowledge, none of the animal species referred to above have been seduced by homosexual (or heterosexual) propaganda. Nor have they been influenced by the porn industry, not even by the animal-porn industry. And how they managed to sneak on board Noah's ark is still an unsolved mystery. Anyone?

Bisexuality, which has been consistently invisible in recent centuries, is an interesting topic in many ways. Bisexuality is the "enfant terrible" regarding human categories. It's "disobedient", it is very prevalent. Perhaps, as indicated above, it may even prove to be the basis of all hetero- and homosexualities. The extensive British Yougov-survey, referred to earlier in this chapter, didn't exactly weaken that theory.

In some, one may be weak, or non-prominent, in others vice versa. (90) In other words, not entirely unlike Sandra Bem's understanding of so-called feminine and masculine traits as two independent monopolar dimensions.

Many sexologists today operate with hetero- and homosexuality as two independent monopolar dimensions, where both of these dimensions are embodied in all individuals to varying degrees. In some, one of them may be weak, or non-prominent, in others vice versa. (90) In other words, not unlike Sandra Bem's explanation of the so-called feminine and masculine features as two independent monopolar dimensions.

It's possible that this view that both a hetero- and a homo-dimension are embodied in all individuals, is inspired by what is known as epigenetics. In this perspective, bisexuality probably means that both "switches" are turned on, that all lights are on, so to speak. But what is epigenetics?

Epigenetics is very briefly explained, the science of reversible changes in inherited genetic traits. The genes contain information about the potential properties of an organism, but epigenetic mechanisms determine whether the properties are expressed or not. Epigenetics is also considered the link between heredity and the environment. (91)

A common explanation is that the genes turn on and off. It is perhaps more correct to say that they are turned on and off by external influences from the environment. It's worth noting that the concept of environment encompasses everything from cultural, social, psychosocial and intra-psychological factors, to air, water, nutrition, etc. So the factors that can activate or deactivate genes are very many and very complex. The term epigenetics itself means "control above the genes". Some also call it the third factor (where the other two are the genes and the environment). The flow of information that affects the expression of biology is no longer a one-way street.

Some while ago I heard a very musical description of the epigenetic processes, it sounded something like this: Try to see your genome as a grand piano, where each string represents a specific trait, and that all the strings together are you. The epigenetic processes are then what determines how, when, and which keys are turned on. In other words, which "melody" to play. Thus, it is of utter importance to "choose" the right note sheets (or maps) before you embark on the "soundtrack of your life", your life journey. I like the piano metaphor.

Until just a few years ago, genetic research was very deterministic, with the resulting view that genes were seen as destiny. The fact is that the genes control biology, is another hypothesis that has never been proven. Yet this deterministic thinking still prevails among many scientists. But researchers such as Reik, Walter, Surani, Watters, Cloud and others have proven that genetics is not deterministic. They have documented that environmental impact can modify the genes, and that this modification also can be passed on to future generations. (92)

Waterland and Jirtle at Duke University in North Carolina performed an exciting epigenetic experiment with pregnant genetically identical mice. All were carriers of a gene called agouti which produces a yellowish coat and can lead to extreme obesity, diabetes and cancer. They divided the mice into two groups, where one group was given a dietary supplement consisting of vitamin B12, betaine, choline and folic acid. This supplement was chosen because several other studies had shown that these substances were involved in epigenetic modifications. (93)

A second group functioned as a control group and did not receive any supplement of the mentioned dietary supplement. The mice that received these supplements gave birth to healthy slender brown-haired baby-mice, although they were also carriers of the same agouti gene as their mothers. The control group gave birth to offspring as themselves, and ended up being twice the weight compared to the other group of baby-mice. (93) Given that epigenetic research is still in its "infancy," we certainly have a lot of future revelations to look forward to.

As we have seen, sexuality is about much more than just reproduction, both for humans and animals. It has many other equally important functions, such as socialization. Sex can (and should) also be one of several "musical" expressions of love, as well as an affirmation of being wanted, loved and good enough. That one belongs.

The meta-theoretic assumption that heterosexuality is the only right and natural way to have sex, because it produces children, is originally an Abrahamic invention, which later on was "adopted" by the early medical science, and eventually embraced by the first evolutionary biologists and the social-Darwinian view. However, same-sex behavior doesn't preclude the continuation of the human race. There are still many bonobos around. Moreover, depopulation doesn't appear to be the most pressing challenge we face on planet earth. We are more than 7 billion inhabitants living here at the beginning of the postmodern era.

Anthropological research - An important corrective to sociology and psychology

Anthropology is an interesting research discipline, primarily because it can, with its approach, tell us some other and parallel stories, than the stories we're used to hear. And by comparing these parallel stories, one can demonstrate differences in, among other things, sexual behavior in cultures with a greater or lesser (or absent) degree of shame, compared to cultures colored by the Abrahamic heritage (shame and guilt).

The absence of shame also gives researchers the opportunity for a more direct observation of sexual behavior, and thus possibly also a more true description of human's natural sexual potential. At the same time, such studies can indirectly give us valuable knowledge regarding the effect of shame and guilt in general, as well as teach us something about the processes, mechanisms and dynamics involved in producing shame and guilt.

There are many interesting anthropological research studies from our own time that support bisexuality as the norm. One of them is William Davenport's famous Eastbay study, I'll get to that in a moment.

Several of the cultures that have been studied by social anthropologists show a remarkable respect for and inclusion of same-sex sexual behavior. In three of these, all men are "homosexual" in behavior throughout puberty, and bisexual after marriage, heterosexual marriages. These three cultures are as follows: Aranda in Australia, Siwans in Africa and Keraki in New Guinea. (94).

There are also cultures that prefer same-sex sexuality to heterosexuality. Two of these are found in New Guinea, the Etero and Marind Amin cultures. One of these, the Eteros, may even be accused of being hetero-phobic. For them, it is taboo to have hetero-sex most of the year, except at full moon, when all women ovulate. On the other hand, same-sex sexual acts between men are strictly forbidden during the full moon. (94)

Heterophobia is, if possible, even more pronounced among the Marind-Amin people. Having as much heterosexual intercourse as the Eteros is not preferable for them. As a result, the birth rate of these warriors is so low that they go on raids every year to kidnap babies from other tribes. (94)

But one of the most interesting of all social anthropological studies, is the study I mentioned above conducted by William Davenport. Davenport's ethnographic study, called the East Bay-Study, showed that all men in this culture practiced bisexuality. Virtually all the men in this culture practiced same-sex sexuality throughout their lives, while also being heterosexual and married to women. None of them are exclusively homosexual, but some few of them are exclusively heterosexual. Both men and women in this culture are seen as equal in terms of sexual behavior. (94)

When it is claimed that homosexuality is culturally conditioned, it may be a bit like shooting oneself in the foot, not to say, shooting it off. Because, if there is one sexual direction that has really been culturally conditioned and psychosocially reinforced, it is heterosexuality. In that regard it must be considered a miracle that homosexual behavior exists at all.

"Either the culture promotes natural diversity, or it inhibits the development of the same colorful diversity."

Espen Esther Pirelli Benestad

But no matter what minorities we are talking about, the smallest entity in any group is still the individual. And the vast majority of us, regardless of biological and social classification, probably believe that we have a kind of innate right to be respected for who we are and what feelings we have. Or at least that we dream of being respected for our individual uniqueness.

Yet, despite the many individual differences, there are many similarities between us humans. For example, who among us hasn't asked the questions "Who am I, and why am I as I am?" So simple, yet so hard to answer. Anyway, we're here. And it should ideally be a universal right for all of us to be and exist here as we are, on an equal basis. Regardless of which box others are trying to push us in to, or in between.

As we saw in Chapter 15, the political-psychological study, and in Chapter 17 in connection with Prescott's research, it is more than evident that violent societies and cultures are building up where equality is absent, and where one inhibits natural human expression, variety and unfoldment.

So why not just accept your own and everyone else's love skills and talents, as well as managing them with compassion. If there is one thing that has been thoroughly proven through more than a hundred years of research, it is that your basic sexual preferences cannot be reversed. But they can be developed and they can certainly be expressed more musically.

The solution to the story about the Father, the Son and the Neurosurgeon: The neurosurgeon was the boy's mother.

CHAPTER 20

NDE – A New Spiritual Paradigm

"Show me the key that the builders rejected: That's the keystone"

Logos 66. The Gospel of Thomas

"Juno was on the verge of giving up. How many brick walls does a person have to run into before throwing up his hands in despair? There was so much prejudice wherever he turned. Why was it so damned difficult for some people to accept others for being the way they were born into this world? Juno took a deep breath and summoned every ounce of his strength...he couldn't give up now! He had once promised himself that he would never ever stop fighting for the most important of all human-rights, your Birth-right, the right to be who you are...the right to be.... You! He couldn't give up now, it was his purpose, the very reason why he was here! Besides, he had long since passed velocity one, point of no return… There will be no surrender"

Excerpt from TRAX

Part I: Juno's journey to freedom

October 1998: I'm sitting here looking at my "new car" outside in the driveway, a shiny blue-metallic Peugeot. It is freshly polished, and the raindrops bead on the glossy surface. I have just closed a book on religious research. One of several books in what that to me seems like an endless journey into the origins of religions. It all started with the decision to read the Bible. It continued with the Qur'an and Jewish scriptures. To end up with scriptures and books that had been banned by the early Christian leaders, and the research around it all. And here I sit with an ambivalent sense of loss, but also win. I have "lost" my religion and childhood beliefs. But still regained the spiritual mysticism and magic. Especially through the Gospel of Thomas's presentation of the Man from Nazareth. I have another glance at the car, and decide to call it Thomas.

There have been several car "baptisms" since October 1998, and they have all been given names that reflects both my view of reality and my journey onward since this dark rainy October evening in 1998. That experience was a so-called "Life defining moment", one in a series that began all the way back with the six-year-old's wonder under the stars, and continued with the thirteen-year-old's thoughts and experiences up there by the dam. There have been several "Life-defining experiences" further along the way.

Another "life-defining moment" which has been of great importance to me and my view on reality was when I discovered the research on the phenomenon/ topic of NDE (Near Death Experiences). It was psychiatrist Raymond Avery Moody who showed me the way into this universe. You will become better acquainted with this research later in this chapter. I will also argue why this research can have a moderating effect on all dogmatic belief systems. How, I'll come back to.

Throughout this process, in fact ever since 2001 when we first appeared on stage with the performance TRAX, I have been looking forward to writing this chapter. I just didn't know it back then in 2001, at least not consciously. At the time, I even had no idea that I was going to write a book. However, I first realized what the last chapter of this book was about as I began to write the first words of the introduction. Or, let me rather call it the foundation of this book. It is the case that you actually have to start with the foundation before you build anything at all. And prior to that, you even have to dig out a lot of "dirt" before you hit the bedrock on which you want to put the foundation. I like that word "Bedrock".

And once the foundation is in place, only then can you begin with the very architecture and construction itself. The visualized building that for my part may have been lying there unconsciously ever since the time up there by the dam at 13, and not least as a 14-year-old when I threw my "mysterious" time capsule into the pond in the hope that someone in a distant future would read it.

In the meantime, I have learned a lot and not least unlearned a lot. I have had many wonderful mentors and teachers. Both directly and indirectly. Another one who has meant a lot to me is the biologist Bruce Bagemihl. He too believes that the time is more than ripe for an expanded view of reality, a new paradigm. A new architecture.

But such thinking doesn't go without resistance. This resistance may be best understood as "religiously" entrenched notions. Scientific theories and paradigms become almost "religious" over time. A phenomenon that I have clearly shown throughout this book. They become belief systems which in turn produce dogmatic attitudes. "Science becomes scientism".

And as we have seen, neither religious nor academic deep-rooted attitudes change very easily. Especially not where the academic attitudes in addition also consist of religious heritage. The latter is something we have seen more or less as a black thread through all three parts of the book. Especially in Part II.

A failing foundation - Or is it the bedrock that's unstable?

Changes are forcing themselves anyway. We have seen it in physics, we see it today in psychology and in the consciousness research. The latter still clings to an assumption that the mind is a function of the brain.

This is an assumption, a meta-theory which has never been proven. On the contrary, there is a rapidly growing body of data that weakens this hypothesis. Both from physics, parapsychology and the NDE research. Determinism itself, as we know, was put to rest by quantum physics ninety years ago. (1)

So here we are, right at the beginning of a new millennium. The third in our time, based on the Christian era. This new millennium lies here before us like a giant unwritten blank sheet, just waiting to be filled with new understandings, new values and new meaning. A new architecture. Do we want values that respect all members of the planet's largest congregation, the humanity, or will we continue as before, applying the policy of outdated "value-apartheid" systems based on old assumptions?

When it comes to sciences that are based on statistical probabilities as a method of creating knowledge about man, they say very little about the individual. By the way, they say a lot about many people's habits, about groups- and mainstream behavior. But they say virtually nothing about the individual's subjective experience of being human. Subjective views of life, human emotions, dignity and beliefs disappear between the numbers of the statistics.

Psychology is also getting problems by sticking to the old conceptions of the senses, this is due to an ever-increasing amount of evidence for the existence of ESP (extra sensory perception). The good old five limiting senses are no longer suffice to explain phenomena such as telepathy, intuition or NDE experiences.

Also genetics is challenged, it is no longer sufficient to explain everything "between heaven and earth" to identical twins by genetics alone. Some identical twins even have the nerve to develop different genetic diseases and different sexual orientations, even though they have completely identical genomes. Nor can genetics explain the mystical unconscious connection between identical twins who have never been in physical contact with each other since the day they were born. Most of them weren't even aware that they had an identical twin.

Psychologist Thomas Bouchard is among some of the most famous researchers on genetic influence. What probably made him famous was his research on identical twins who had been separated at birth. They are not very numerous, moreover they are also very difficult to trace. Today it is not allowed to separate twins, adoption agencies around the world prohibit this practice, luckily. This line of research, all started with Bouchard reading an article about two reunited monozygotic twins who had been separated shortly after birth. Their first encounter as adults revealed an astonishing and extra-ordinary series of "coincidences".

Both of them, James Lewis and James Springer, had been married to and divorced from women with the same name (Linda). They both remarried with each his own Betty. Both were educated police-officers. As children, they both had pets named Toy. They shared identical smoking and drinking habits. Both bit nails and had sons named James Alan and James Allan respectively. Eventually, Bouchard managed to track down 81 identical twins that had been separated at birth. And similar stories were repeated time and time again. Psychologist Susan Farber, who has carried out a number of case studies on twins, confirms that such startling similarities, sometimes annoying similarities as she puts it, are not uncommon in this field. (2)

It's difficult to explain these findings within the old paradigm, without claiming the existence of genes for specific names and divorces, just to name a few. And by the way, so far no one has been able to identify the genes for choosing pink scooters, or dark blue ties for that matter.

Regarding biology, which as we have seen, can prove to be as mysterious as both quantum mechanics and the psychology of consciousness, I think the philosopher and theologian James B. Carse describes it well when he claims that it's our vision which is limited. Not what we see.

(3) Hence, the old paradigm is too narrow to see twins' behaviors and other "mystical" phenomena existing outside the old "truths".

A rethinking of some of the most fundamental concepts in biology is needed according to Bruce Bagemihl. He further argues that indigenous peoples' observations and views regarding, for example, sexual behavior, including non-procreative heterosexual and homosexual behavior, as well as gender-crossing behavior, require an extended paradigm.

Indigenous peoples see and interpret this diversity as different expressions of a far greater picture (or paradigm) regarding reality. Their observations and views of reality also have remarkable similarities with recent scientific discoveries regarding the behavior of different species.

Not only that, these observations of the indigenous people (in some places called First Nations) also coincide with "new" philosophical and scientific observations within branches such as chaos science, post-Darwinian evolution, Gaia theory and biodiversity studies. (4)

While modern science has observed nature for just a few centuries, indigenous peoples have accumulated a vast amount of observations spanning thousands of years. Regarding the observations and the valuation of non-heterosexual behavior and gender-crossing behavior, these are almost identical among indigenous peoples in North America, New Guinea/ Melanesia and among Siberian and Arctic peoples. Bagemihl mentions these in particular, because there have been carried out very many and thorough anthropological studies, with a wealth of documentation, precisely among these above mentioned indigenous people. (5)

It is also interesting that people in these cultures have consistently designated bisexual and transgender individuals to be shamans and healers. (6) Both animals and humans that combine aspects of the sexes, or show sexual variation are consistently and ceremonially honored in these cultures. (7)

Many anthropologists also portray the shamans as the intellectuals of these cultures. They have served as healers, lyricists, dancers, musicians and hypnotists. It was they who contributed to unity and strength. With their rituals, they also contributed to increased sexual desire and child production. It is interesting to note that these shamanistic functions are universally identical, even in societies without any connection or historical contact with each other. (8) The latter simply cannot be explained by the classical paradigm and its scientific theories.

Esben Esther Pirelli Benestad and Elsa Almås come up with some interesting considerations with regard to expressions of shaman-like traits in our modern cultures, where such talents really have no cultural place. They claim that individuals with such talents and potentials therefore develop in different ways such as artists, or mediators in other fields, such as therapists. Or, that as a result of a lack of belonging, some unfortunately also develop drug addiction or mentally illness. It is also a tragic fact that many of the latter see no other way out but to end their lives. (9)

It is thus a cruel price some of these people have to pay due to narrow paradigms with resulting cultural narrow-mindedness and ignorance. Instead of celebrating the diversity and all the different talents they contribute, they are simply culturally crucified. Instead of biological, cultural and psychological diagnosis, it would serve both them and society as a whole if we show just a little more biological excitement and cultural inclusion.

Bruce Bagemihl emphasizes that the concept of "Biological Exuberance", which is also the title of his monumental work, should not be seen as a theory. But that it rather represents a radical shift in perspective: A new and alternative view of something that we thought we understood so well. More than a desire to add new facts, it is rather an intention to see existing knowledge through new lenses. (10)

A bit like the map and terrain metaphor in other words. As I previously mentioned, it is not new terrain we need, but new and better maps.

And perhaps most of all, new lenses. In any case, there is some light on the postmodern horizon, as many biologists are asking new and critical questions about the old maps. Not least with regard to the "sacred" evolutionary maps.

Survival of the fittest, natural selection, competition for resources, random genetic mutations, are all well-known concepts from evolutionary theory. But, according to Bagemihl, there has been a quiet revolution in biology over the past decades, where some of the most fundamental principles and concepts of evolutionary theory are questioned, challenged, re-examined and, in some cases even rejected. (11)

A new paradigm seems to be emerging in this field. It's called post-Darwinian evolution. It is about concepts such as *self-organization* of life and that the environment can beneficially alter the genetic code. (11) This latter sounds familiar, it resembles the epigenetic science which I described in the previous chapter.

Post-Darwinian evolutionary biologists synthesize the development of many different disciplines, such as physics, mathematics, chemistry, molecular biology, and developmental biology. (11) There are also parallels between post-Darwinian theory and chaos theory. The latter rests on a basic recognition of unpredictability and non-linear phenomena, both in nature and in humans. Chaos researcher Joseph Ford describes evolution as chaos with feedback. (12)

This research may seem quite inaccessible to most of us, but it will probably become more accessible and understood when this new perspective eventually makes it way to the mainstream media. Both social and not so social media. For those of you who want to know more about this silent revolution as Bagemihl calls it, just google the disciplines, concepts and scientists mentioned above, and you'll find a lot of interesting information.

I myself think it is just as interesting to note that the methods and thoughts these researchers use, are very similar to the sexological approach. As mentioned in a previous chapter, sexology has recognized the necessity of interdisciplinary research, knowledge and methods. Synthesis. In other words, an interdisciplinary constructive collaboration within an expanded perspective, instead of interdisciplinary warriors with inflated and vulnerable academic egos.

Pirelli Benestad expressed this in his own picturesque and poetic way during one of his lectures at UiA (University in Agder) as follows: Everywhere on this planet there are scientists who grind and polish their own tiny little pieces of the mirror. But only when these scientists meet, in order to puzzle all these little jewels into a bigger coherent mirror, only then will we be able to understand a little more of this big wonderful picture. Again, this reminds me of Niels Bohr and his complementarity. Bohr argued that as the picture gets bigger, seemingly contradictory facts will complement each other.

As mentioned earlier, Bohr also believed that this thinking should be taken seriously within the social sciences. He used anthropology as an example. Anthropology has two modes of behavior, one based on instinct and the other on logical reasoning. Instinct, he thought, can be seen as a discontinuity without any history. On the other hand, he argued that reasoning is a process based on logic and continuity. (13) I think Bagemihl, Pirelli Benestad and Bohr are onto something.

Stubborn Classical Building Blocks

"It has largely benefited the humanity to upgrade its worldview according to "new" discoveries." (The world is no longer flat)."

Esben Esther Pirelli Benestad

As mentioned earlier, the difference between what falls within the classical hard sciences such as mathematics and physics and the soft sciences is that the "hard" sciences can be falsified, and that they can be tested and repeated experimentally, everywhere and anytime. And that they mostly will produce the same results as the theory predicts. That is if the theory is able to hold water. Regarding soft sciences such as psychology and psychiatry, one must be far more cautious with one's inclination to claim truths. These latter sciences change in relation to cultures, societies, times in history and individual uniqueness.

Charles Tart was probably right when he warned against "The scientism in today's sciences". Many of the so called hard science can be life-threatening when its methods are "religiously" applied to other and softer "subjects" such as humans. It is not everything one can or should force into measurable metric absolutes.

At a fundamental level, nature also behaves so strange that our metric conceptual apparatus is not sufficient. Then we are forced to use, among other things, philosophy to try to understand. In this way, it also becomes a slightly more humble and respectful approach.

Speaking of scientific theories, it is worth noting that Karl Popper as early as 1934 showed that nothing can be proven, only verified or falsified! Some decades later, the physicist and philosopher of science Thomas Kuhn published his revolutionary book, "The Structure of Scientific Revolutions". In short, the reality of science is a phenomenon, which periodically breaks down when it can no longer explain and predict phenomena. Or when the old paradigm is unable to absorb anomalies. When this happens, it is replaced by a new picture of reality. Kuhn called this a paradigm shift. (14) (15)

These dynamics also have their parallels in the description of some of the childhood stages in developmental psychology, such as *assimilation* and *accommodation,* as Piaget called them. Or *cognitive dissonance* as it's explained by cognitive psychology, the "adult" version. (See Chapter 12)

The term «Anomaly» otherwise means deviation from the theoretically expected (16)

In my view, that's where scientists and the rest of us, stands today. At the transition to a new paradigm shift. A new worldview. Science is no longer able, with its old classical paradigm, to explain an ever growing number of anomalies. Anomalies which are nevertheless detected time and time again to an increasing degree.

In fact, there has already been a paradigm shift in physics. Physics, which is also said to be the mother of all sciences, has long since abolished, among other things, objectivity and determinism. (17) In this connection, it may be worth recalling that our classical scientific "hard-science" methods are not carved in stone either. Although they certainly have generated great material success and better lives for the vast majority of us. And smart phones too.

Max Planck, along with John Von Neumann, Heisenberg and indirectly Albert Einstein, were among several other scientists who destroyed some of the cornerstones of the classical scientific paradigm. There wasn't much left of the old classical foundation after they had finished their demolition. (18) In addition, Alain Aspect went further on with his famous laboratory experiment, and with that abolished time and space as the real limit of the universe. (19) The latter is since referred to as the Aspect experiment. This research shakes up the entire classical foundation. It's simply scientific rock'n roll.

Taking classical cornerstones from Newtonians or Darwinians is probably a bit like taking the Mosaic Laws from a Pentecostal and offering him Darwin's collected works instead. They behave pretty much the same as I see it. Again, "Science becomes scientism". Many of them have invested so much of themselves in their theories, that they've simply glued their own identity to a theory which in the process has become a dogmatic belief system. Therefore they react with anxiety when they feel that someone is trying to "take" it away from them. *Assimilation.*

The ghosts in the machinery

Max Planck, Nobel Prize winner and one of the founders of quantum physics, stated the following as a conclusion of his research on atoms: "As a physicist who has devoted his whole life to rational science, to the study of matter, I think I can safely claim to be above any suspicion of irrational exuberance. Having said that, I would like to observe that my research on the atom has shown me that there is no such thing as matter in itself. What we perceive as matter is merely the manifestation of a force that causes the subatomic particles to oscillate and holds them together in the tiniest solar system of the universe. Since there is in the whole universe neither an intelligent force nor an eternal force (mankind, for all its yearnings, has yet to succeed in inventing a perpetual motion machine), we must assume that this force that is active within the atom comes from a conscious and intelligent mind. That mind is the ultimate source of matter." (20)

One of the foremost theorists of quantum physics, John Wheeler said at the 1974 Relativity Conference at Oxford that we would probably not find any central mechanism or "machinery" in the universe. He thought magic was a better description of what awaited us. (21) Schrödinger (you know, the one with the cat) called this "magic" probability waves without any material existence. (22)

As for Planck's quote above, some have rejected his description on the ground that he was a religious person, and thus must have been colored by it. Well, the "God" of the classics (Isaac Newton) was far more religious. One of the missing links of the classical "Newtonian machine" was precisely that it should have collapsed as a result of the force of gravity. But according to Newton, it was God who prevented it from happening. (23)

"The Ghost in Newton's Machinery" some call it. However, when Newton talked about God in a religious understanding, Planck talked about consciousness in a quantum physical understanding.

THE NDE VISIONS

Part II: The NDE Visions – A new and liberating worldview

"I don't mind saying that after talking with over a thousand people who have had these experiences, and having experienced many times some of the truly baffling and unusual features of these experiences, it has given me great confidence that there is a life after death. As a matter of fact, I must confess to you in all honesty, I have absolutely no doubt, on the basis of what my patients have told me, that they did get and a glimpse of the beyond."

Raymond Avery Moody

NDE, Near Death Experience.

In the introduction to this chapter, I mentioned that one of the people who would mean a lot to me and my view of reality is the philosopher, physician, and psychiatrist Raymond A. Moody. Moody was the first to start systematically documenting patients' experiences while being declared clinically dead. Patients he had managed to bring back to life in the emergency room.

One of Moody's probably most shocking cases was a woman in her 70s, who, after having been clinically dead, could literally retell the conversations between the doctors and the nurses in the emergency room. She also described advanced instruments in detail, including measurements the devices showed during surgery. In addition, she could describe the colors of the inventory in the emergency room. It was just one thing, she wasn't only clinically dead, she was also one hundred percent blind! (24)

Before I continue I would like to emphasize that Dr. Moody wasn't the first who produced near-death information in the literature, but he was the first to name and systematize this phenomenon. He established the pattern and laid the foundation for the growing amount of NDE research that has since then taken place, and still continues with increasing interest.

Dr. Moody eventually discovered that there were several things that recurred during the NDE experiences his patients went through. One of them was described as a light experience. Most of the patients realized during this light experience that the only lessons which matters are love and knowledge, and that these are the only lessons you can bring with you to a future existence or the afterlife. (25)

Psychologist Kenneth Ring, who was the first to further refine and legitimize Dr. Moody's pioneering work, demonstrated in one of his studies (108 participants) that religion played as little a role as age or race in those who experienced an NDE. Ring was also the first researcher to perform statistical analyzes on NDE. (26)

Before proceeding, I will briefly summarize the characteristics or stages Moody identified in an NDE. Not everyone goes through all of stages, but every one completely change their personalities after an NDE experience. I shall return to the latter.

The first thing they experience is the sense of being dead. At this stage, they both perceive and understand what doctors and nurses communicate with each other. Even if they have no medical background. Many of them try to communicate with the surgeons, but quickly discover that they are not being heard. In this phase, many of them also gain a stronger sense of identity. They are no longer their parents' children, or their husband's wife, etc. They experience themselves as a whole and complete self. (27)

The next stage is the experience of a total peace and absence of pain, and that the pain is transformed into an intense pleasure. Then an out-of-body experience (OBE) occurs. In this situation, they can observe their body from an external perspective while the doctors are trying to bring this body to life. In this phase, they experience themselves as energy bodies, this is followed by what most of them describe as a tunnel experience. It's also at this stage that most of them really understand that this has to do with death. (28)

When they have passed through the tunnel, they all encounter something most of them call luminary people who permeate them with love. At this stage they often meet deceased friends and relatives. Some also tell about beautiful landscapes and luminary cities. At this stage, they describe all communication as telepathic. (28)

The following stage is perhaps the most fascinating one, and in my opinion also the most important regarding my decision to include the NDE research as an important part of this book, and the message I want to convey.

This stage is what most of the NDEs describe as the encounter with the Supreme Luminary being. On this stage something very interesting is happening. If you're a Jew, the supreme luminary being is often called Yahweh, if Christian, it's often called Jesus Christ, the virgin Mary or God, while Muslims call it Allah and Buddhists call it Buddha. Still others just call it the Luminary Entity (agnostics and atheists for example). However, they all describe this being as total love and comprehension. It's also at this stage that they are told to return. But prior to that they are being guided through a life review, a looking back at what they have been through so far in their earthly incarnation. (29)

In this retrospective phase, you experience absolutely everything you have done in life in a sort of three-dimensional panoramic vision where everything is present at once. Actually, it is more accurate to say that you are part of this panorama. You are a participant in the "movie", you are experiencing it! All sense of time is erased. During this process, you not only see (experience) your own actions through life, but you also experience and feel all that you have inflicted on other people, their reactions of both joy and pain as a result of your actions, and you experience it entirely from the other person's perspective. Through this process you are being guided by this Supreme Luminary Being. (29) (30)

When they experience scenes from their earthly lives where they've learned something, the luminary being points out that the only thing you can bring with you from this life, is love, compassion and knowledge. (30) It's common for people who have had an NDE to become very eager for new knowledge after they've return back to life. They often start to study completely different subjects than they did prior to the NDE. But it's not just for the sake of knowledge itself, most of them believe that knowledge is only important if it's about becoming more complete and whole humans. Knowledge is only good if it contributes to create wholeness and coherence. (31)

The following is an example of how powerful this retrospective "life review stage" actually can be. This story was reported to psychologist Kenneth Ring by a truck driver after having experienced a very emotional NDO. During the life-review stage, this truck driver experienced (relived) a traffic incident where he in a rage had beaten up a pedestrian. In his life-review he both experienced and felt the humiliation, the fear and the frustration he had inflicted upon this unsuspecting pedestrian, but from the pedestrian's perspective. Not only that: "I also felt the pain when his teeth were crushed and drilled through his lower lip", he added. Cases where NDEs report experiences like this are far from uncommon in the NDE research field. (32) (33)

Let's all reflect for a moment on all of the above. The knowledge regarding the universal message conveyed by this diverse group of people who have experienced an NDE, should have a huge potential to become a moderating effect on aggressive and hostile human behavior. Both on an ideological and a religious level, but also regarding human interactions on an individual level. Just to think that the NDE-messages are literally universal, regardless of their religious, cultural or ideological backgrounds and beliefs. With this knowledge, perhaps we might reflect a little more before letting our "righteous" aggression, condemnation and prejudice towards others escalate to the breaking point (!)

There are also other common features regarding people who have been through an NDE. Virtually all of them undergo a comprehensive change as individuals. They become much more enjoyable to be with for other people, and they often engage actively in the real world. This despite the fact that an NDE is the result of a traumatic experience. Unlike others who experience life-threatening crises, these people do not suffer from adverse effects such as PTSD (Post Traumatic Stress Syndrome). In other words, they do not become emotionally trapped or "frozen" in a dramatic past event. (34)

On the contrary, they feel that they have to do something constructive with their lives, and they also become very preoccupied with the well-being of other people. The fear of dying is also blown away. Because, as most of them put it, they know that death does not mean the annihilation of their individual consciousness. (34)

Furthermore, an NDE almost always leads to some form of spiritual curiosity. This doesn't mean that they become preoccupied with traditional religions and their various laws and dogmas, very often they throw religious doctrines overboard. Regardless of their previous faith (or lack of faith) or what religion they might profess, all of them say that religion is a matter of your ability to love, not about confessions or doctrines. Belief-systems simply don't matter. (35)

One of Moody's patients who was a theology student stated after his NDE, that many people will probably be surprised when they find out that God is not interested in theology. And that God is not at all concerned with which denomination you belong to. God just wanted to know what was in my heart, not what was in my head, he told Moody. (35)

"Have you learned to love?" This question is posed by the Luminary Entity to everyone who undergoes an NDE. Virtually everyone says that love is the most important thing of all, and that this is precisely the reason why we're all here. In other words, most of them change their perceptions of values. Love and friendship become far more important than material wealth. They also experience the notion of everything in the universe as connected and that you don't stop learning when you "die". One of them told Moody that if you think you can harm others without harming yourself, you are sadly mistaken. We are all bound together, she concluded. (36)

Interestingly, even children who undergo an NDE also report exactly the same as adults. In fact, children all the way down to the toddler age. And this occurs in all cultures. (37) This is important to bear in mind, as some of the criticism of this phenomenon concerns things such as people experiencing an NDE have been influenced by their religions. However, the same critics avoid mentioning that the NDE-experiences are identical across religious upbringing. In addition, atheists also report identical experiences. Nor do they mention the fact that those who actually were followers of dogmatic religious beliefs prior to their NDE, are very rarely governed by religious doctrine and dogma in the aftermath of their NDE. (38)

By the way, most of the criticism regarding the NDE-research has been solidly put to rest. For example, endorphins as the cause of NDE "hallucinations" are a widespread and popular claim, but there exist no known research that can prove either that, or NDE as "psychotic" visualizations. (39)

However, I would like to briefly mention that some researchers claim that an NDE experience is a neurological defense mechanism against the fear of dying. But apropos the youngest NDE experiencers, they simply don't have any psychological concept of death. They experience death as something temporary (!) Like a holiday or similar. Yet, they experience exactly the same as anyone else undergoing an NDE. Another thing is that the very youngest among us, simply haven't had the time to become religiously influenced prior to their NDE. And interestingly enough, those same children do not develop dogmatic religious beliefs as adults either. (40)

But what exactly is the definition of being dead? Classically, it has meant that one doesn't return after having passed this border. Therefore, there are several who question whether these people actually have been dead.

Nevertheless, they (the NDEs) have met death criteria such as cardiac arrest, respiratory arrest, some of them also hypothermia (a dramatic drop in body temperature) and possibly the most important criteria of them all, no signs of brain activity. Many of them have also complied with the six-minute rule, which means that after six minutes it is not very expedient to continue the resuscitation attempts. After six minutes, the brain will have such a large deficit of oxygen that in most cases it will be dead. (41) However, Cardiologist Pim Van Lommel expands this limit to be between five and eleven minutes. (42)

Some clinicians have also claimed that an NDE simply is a psychotic condition. In a psychosis, one loses contact with the real world, one hallucinates. However, this claim is easy to refute. While a psychosis is incoherent and often consists of voices and terrifying paranoid experiences, an NDE is both coherent and fairly identical to anyone who experiences it. In addition, they experience it as a very constructive and positively life-changing transformation. (43) Exactly the same criteria we use to describe a successful therapeutic transformation.

But perhaps the strongest argument against the psychosis-hypothesis is that hallucinations have a strong effect on an EEG. During an NDE experience, there is no measurable effect on the EEG. Let me also remind you that a flat EEG is often used as the legal definition of a patient's death. (44) (45) Moreover, this is also the most important criterion that must be met with regard to organ donation.

It has also been claimed that an NDE is caused by an increased level of carbon dioxide in the blood during, for example a cardiac arrest. Inhalation of carbon dioxide was used in the fifties as a psychotherapeutic method, and one of the effects was the experience of moving through a tunnel, or a kind of light experience. (Let me add that this "therapy" method is no longer used). However, there is no information that these patients experienced Luminary beings or went through «Life-review» experiences. (46) (47) Or for that matter, constructive personality changes. If the latter would have been the case, this "therapy" method would most certainly be celebrated worldwide by now.

Yet another criticism claims that drugs and heavy medication are the causes of these NDE experiences. But on the contrary, it turns out that strong medication rather prevents such experiences, at least the memories of them. Moody's research clearly showed that those who were least medicated also had the strongest NDE experiences. (48)

Another interesting and surprising effect of an NDE was discovered by psychiatrist Bruce Greyson. He is clinically trained in crisis psychiatry, a field where he also holds a professorship. Dr. Greyson is dealing with suicide issues on a daily basis. In his work, he discovered that among those who had experienced an NDE during their suicide attempts, virtually no one of them tried to end their life again. Among those in this same group who didn't experience an NDE, a large percentage tried to commit suicide again. (49)

Attempts have also been made to use the knowledge from the NDE research as part of the therapy for suicidal people. In an experiment were they did use this knowledge, suicide as a solution simply evaporated. This experiment was repeated many times, and with the same result each time. (49) This should attract the interest of many people who deals with this issue. Hopelessness is by the way, one of the main reasons why some people choose to commit suicide.

Since NDOs occur, and are subjectively far more constructively transformative than any of conventional therapies (cf. the statistical effects of the latter), the empirical sciences can no longer demand to have a monopoly on human insight. And certainly not the sciences that fall under "hard-sciences".

NDE and non-heterosexuals

"If this world was to ever find out just a small amount of what sexually diverse (...) people are here to do on this planet, there would never be one single wisecrack or hurtful remark made ever again. Instead there would be great respect! People who speak disrespectful things about people of this orientation enact judgment, and do so from a place of un-enlightenment, insecurity, ego and socially induced

prejudice. Some may use mistranslated scriptures taught to them, not by the Holy Spirit ... but by fear-filled human beings. Many will choose to sustain a Divinely un-supported satanic hate-based rage against these children of God, rather than using Love to bring understanding and healing between both peoples (..) When people sling condemnation, judgment and bitterness at others, they are not practicing the great commandment. They are allowing their Souls to fall into darkness" (50)

Christian Andreason

The quote above stems from an NDE experience the American singer & songwriter artist Christian Andreason had in 1995. Christian identifies himself as bisexual and also says that this had bothered him throughout his life. He goes on to say that during the NDE, his Luminary guide showed him a large "screen" upon where two luminous figures were shown in an act of love. He was then asked to tell which of them was male and who was female. When he couldn't answer that, his guide told him that it doesn't matter. This is how God sees people, as beings of light. Not as gender. (50)

His Luminary guide further added that gender role identities are not something that will persist, they are temporary. Furthermore, he learned that God is at the same time both a mother and a father essence. Thus, God also have an understanding for the attraction between individuals of the same sex. Christian was also reminded that there is nothing wrong in acting from his heart. (50)

Then he was shown another couple on this "screen", this time two figures who had a more egocentric focus on sexual desire in a compulsive way, rather than a compassionate sexual act of love. They will face many challenges, he was told. Then the two luminous figures faded into a dark gray-like energy cloud. The Luminary guide told him that there will come a time when these two individuals must learn to come to terms with their sexual selves, so that they can be helped to apply their sexuality in a more loving and compassionate way. At the end of the experience, Christian learned that the two luminary figures on the "screen" were a woman and a man who had previously been married. (50)

A few years ago, when my first interest in NDE was awakened, I began to explore this large and ever-growing material myself, including all the individual case-stories that never cease to amaze me. Soon I became a member of IANDS (International Association for Near-Death Studies), back then they had the largest archive of NDE research located at Cornell University in New York. Since then, NDERF (Near Death Experience Research Foundation) has also entered the scene with an impressive archive consisting of NDE related research and literature. NDERF was founded by Oncologist and researcher Jeffrey Long.

Eventually I began to explore the numerous cases of all the different types of people who had experienced an NDE, including the cases involving non-heterosexual individuals. According to this literature, there exists no difference between the NDE experiences, whether we talk about gender, race, religion or sexual orientation. In that sense, Christian Andreason may serve as one of an endless number of examples regarding the universalities of the messages received during an NDE. This is important knowledge for all people who struggle with who they are, for example in relation to shame, cultural and religious condemnation, and not least fear of eternal damnation and torment in "hell".

One of those who has particularly addressed the non-heterosexual NDE experiences is clinical psychologist Liz Dale. She's the author and pioneer of the first study that explores and addresses non-heterosexual NDE experiences, "Crossing Over and Coming Home" is the title of the book she wrote based on her research. The foreword is written by Dr. Melvin Morse. Dr. Morse is a specialist in pediatrics (pediatrician) and has been appointed the USA's best pediatrician no less than six times. He is probably best known for his research on children who've experienced an NDE. (51) (52)

"The law of God is written in each of our hearts, so we need only to be true to ourselves and who we are!" Excerpts from some of what Steven, a gay boy, experienced during an NDE. He, like most others, was also told that love is the key, no matter who you are and what you believe in. Similar stories run like a red thread throughout Dr. Dale's book. (53)

So when I began my own deep dive into this material, I quickly discovered that I was not the first to explore NDE in terms of sexual orientation. To me, it was very reassuring to discover that this Supreme Luminary being, which some call God, Allah, Yahweh, or simply the Light, is obviously as uninterested in dogmatic religion as in race, gender, or sexual orientations. Only love, knowledge, and how you communicate this to your surroundings is the only thing that matters. And again, the only thing you can bring with you from this life

It should also be mentioned that there are a few people, one to two percent, that go through a distressing "hell"-like NDE, filled with fear and anxiety. By all accounts, these frightening experiences have nothing to do with who you are as a human being. For example, none of the contributors to Liz Dale's material had had such experiences. Some in the field claim that such "hellish" experiences rather have to do with evil deeds. John Price is one of those who claims this. But there is still nothing in the increasingly extensive NDE literature that points to the existence of a "hell". (54)

However, consider the truck driver's NDE that I mentioned above, his experience was very painful, though not destructive. It was probably some sort of an awakening for our truck driver. He also confirms what Kenneth Ring points out, that this process should be described as a "life-reliving" rather than a "life-review".

Some years ago I watched an interview with Psychologist Kenneth Ring, where he talked in-depth about the "Life-review/Life-reliving" part of an NDE. In this interview he claimed that the "Life-review" part of an NDE carries the most important message to us humans living on this planet. Namely, that any action you perform in this life, good or bad, will eventually hit back at you. At the same time, he wondered whether Hitler ever would finish his "Life review" on the other side (55). On my part, I like to call the "Boomerang effect". Some also refer to it as "What goes around comes around".

I have long since lost count of how many NDE cases I have studied, and all the fascinating and picturesque descriptions some of these people give. Some of them are almost poetic. And some of them use metaphors most of us can relate to. One of them was young man who was interviewed by Kenneth Ring. When Ring asked him to describe the emotional aspect of his Luminary-stage experience as thoroughly as possible, he answered: "It cannot be compared to the love you feel in relation to your wife, children or even love in form of very intense sexual experiences ... It is not comparable at all" (56) (57). There are countless similar descriptions of these elevated ecstatic feelings that many experience during an NDE, but maybe not quite as straight to the point as the one above.

This story reminds me of my first day as a sexology student at UiA. The lecturer this first day was Christian Graugaard from Denmark. Graugaard is an MD and holds a professorate in sexology. He is definitely one of my favorite lecturers, he simply has to be experienced. Out of the blue in the middle of the lecture he wrote the word "sex" on the whiteboard. Then he asked us to come up with some immediate associations to this word, and he would then add them to the whiteboard. The response from the auditorium wasn't long in coming. Most of them suggestions were rather obvious and somewhat "academically correct", such as "procreation", "recreation", "bonding", etc.

I so wanted to come up with my own suggestion, but hesitated a bit. Christian perceived my hesitation, probably given away by my body language. He stared at me, pointed at me and asked with a slightly rude grin: "You, yes you up there, what's your association with the word "sex"?". "Spiritual yearning", I replied. "Wow, none of my students have ever come up with anything even close to this one," he said, while writing "Spiritual yearning" in bold letters covering the entire whiteboard. And all the other associations.

I guess my fellow students were just as shocked as I was, but I must also confess that I felt a little childishly pride (I guess that must have been my inner child). I was aware that Christian Graugaard is an internationally known authority in the field of sexology, and that he gives lectures all over the world. However, this incident happened before I started my own deep questing into the NDE research-field.

Sometimes I wonder whether it would have been easier for "Maria", the girl I told you about in chapter 11 who wanted to end her own life, if I'd had the knowledge about NDE back then at the café in Oslo. I guess that I probably could have made the road even easier for her with the knowledge I now possess. However, fortunately things turned out well for her anyway.

It still happens that I get inquiries from desperate young people who struggle with their sexuality in relation to religion. Often in the aftermath of TRAX performances. NDE has given me a powerful tool that enables me to help these people see themselves in a far better, and not least enhanced light. To put it that way. To help them understand that their own unique color of love is an important talent, no matter what lane they drive in on life's emotional highway. And if there's something that should be diagnosed as sick, well then it must be the inability to love, the lack of compassion. Ego-philia is probably the most aggressive and destructive "orientation" of them all.

If Humanity would relate to the messages conveyed by the NDE's, what could happen?

Would we ever consider war as a means of conflict "solutions", if these universal messages conveyed by a dimension this numerous NDEs obviously have "visited", were taught in schools and elsewhere worldwide? Just as we do regarding religious belief-systems, or philosophical and ideological belief-systems for that matter. A dimension that communicates love, compassion and knowledge as the only values. A dimension where everyone is being asked: "Have you learned to love?"

So far, none has been posed the question: "Have you learned to hate?" (!) Not to mention the Life-review stage where we are obviously "doomed" to relive everything we've done onto others, good or bad. Don't you think that all this would make us rethink any aggressive action when conflicts are looming? I strongly agree with Kenneth Ring when he claims that the messages conveyed during the Life-review stage (or more precisely "Life-relive" stage), isn't just for those who experience an NDE, it's for all of us.

I think we would relate to each other in a completely different and far less destructive way if we were more familiar with The NDE-research and I think that eventually, this is going to happen. Gradually. An ever more growing number of witnesses, returning with the same universal "Testament" every day, makes me hopeful.

This is not least thanks to the exponential development of emergency medicine during the recent decades. With today's medical technology and knowledge, people are resuscitated back to life to an extent that would have been unthinkable just fifty years ago. Prior to this medical revolution, we only had scattered anecdotal and historical narratives to relate to regarding NDE. Just as we had regarding historical religious narratives.

In fact, I believe that this research and these "Testaments" can have a moderating effect on all religions and ideologies. I do not believe that the NDE is a "religion-killer", because most religions have some core messages which are important to all of us. The "Golden Rule" is one of them. In addition, they represent rituals at important crossroads end life events. Moreover, symbolic rituals are very important to us humans. However, it's a shame that good religious messages too often are drowned out or overruled by dogmas and domination based on human distortions and interpretations.

However, people make mistakes, we have always made mistakes. Therefore, I believe that these NDE "Testaments" may act as sources of inspiration and moderation, and even become an incentive for a more constructive development of all dogmatic belief systems and political ideologies. And off course for all of us on an individual level.

To sweep away the NDE research by saying that it is "only" a new form of spiritual faith, is all too easy. Moreover, all science is grounded in faith. For example, today's natural sciences are products of the struggle between the church and the emerging field of science during the enlightenment. Descartes dualism. In this struggle, the church agreed that science could do research on all matter, in exchange for the church being allowed to keep the soul. Thus man, in the "spirit" of science, had also become part of matter. Man had become a "machine."

Based on this, the assumption (belief) has arisen that all aspects of human consciousness can be explained through the interaction between the cells in the human brain. And consequently, consciousness dies when the human-machine brain dies. This assumption is, as I mentioned above, a belief. Just like the Pope's.

In my opinion, the preliminary "last nail in the coffin" of the view that NDE is just another spiritual belief-system, is nailed by the Dutch cardiologist Pim Van Lommel. He conducted the first prospective longitudinal study on NDE at 7 hospitals in the Netherlands. The study was also reproduced in its entirety in the prestigious international medical journal "The Lancet". Of the 344 patients who participated, 18 percent reported an NDE. These were followed up after 2 and 8 years, together with a control group consisting of patients who had also been treated for cardiac arrest, but who did not report (remembered) a NDE. Age, gender, ethnicity, religion or degree of religiosity had no bearing on whether or not a NDE occurred. (58)

Dr. Van Lommel's study confirmed what retrospective studies have previously established, namely that NDEs undergo a psychological transformation afterwards. Among other things, that they become more empathetic, more intuitive and sensitive, less concerned with status and competition, the fear of dying disappears, etc. They also become more spiritually concerned, regardless of previous religious upbringing, or lack thereof. Showing love and care as well as acceptance and inclusion of others is becoming far more important. The control group did not show this degree of transformation, although many of these also had become more reverent for life in general. (59)

Quantum physics and parapsychology - And the anomalies of the Newtonian paradigm

"I believe that once and for all, we must abandon the attempt to place or explain parapsychological phenomena within the three-dimensional framework of reality, as we specifically imagine it on the basis of our physical research. I think we need to acquire a totally different attitude towards such phenomena."

Pascual Jordan. Pioneer in quantum physics, nominated for the Nobel Prize by Albert Einstein among others. (60)

It's also the new physics, that with its expanded foundation offers the best "architecture" in order to explain ESP (Extra sensory perception), OBE (Out of Body Experiences) and NDE as genuine individual experiences. The "old" Newtonian physics cannot contain any anomalies that manifest themselves outside the "five corners" (senses) of the physical body.

OBE (Out of Body Experiences) is one of the phenomena that does not fit within these five Newtonian boundaries. OBE is by the way one of the phenomena that always occurs during an NDE. Psychologist Charles Tart conducted a sensational experiment on OBE, in which the subject was told to memorize a 5-digit number (25132), which had been placed on a shelf high up beneath the ceiling. Thus, this number was only visible from a bird's eye-view. The experiment was conducted in the sleep laboratory at the University of California. (61)

The experiment went on for several nights, with a girl who had had such experiences every night as far back as she could remember. She thought it was normal, that everyone else was also able to leave the body too. Only on the fourth night was she able to see the numbers, which by the way were changed every night. For the first few nights, she had only hovered around as she stated, including being outside the room, without noticing the paper with the 5 digit number. (61)

Shortly thereafter, psychologist Stanley Krippner, then head of the sleep laboratory at Maimonides Medical Center in New York, heard about Tart's experiment in California. He repeated this experiment with a medical student who claimed that he often had OBE experiences. In Krippner's experiment, images were used instead of numbers. Also in this case, the object was identified, only this time as a picture of a sunset. The picture also had "sunset" in the title. (62) (63)

Perhaps it is the same with OBE as with dreams, maybe we all have them, but not everyone remembers them. However, both Tart and Krippner's experiments were monitored. The EEG measurements showed high alpha-wave activity at the time the observations were made.

A fairly comprehensive project that involves several hospitals, including countries like the UK and Switzerland, (several others are considering joining), has been launched by Dr. Sam Parnia. In this experiment, hidden objects are placed in the emergency rooms, only visible from a bird's eye view.(probably inspired by Tart and Krippner). It's going to be exciting to follow this process as the reports are being published. So far, NDE and OBE experiences have been confirmed. However, as relatively few of the patients with cardiac arrest remember an NDE, more material is needed. Let's just hope that these researchers will receive sufficient financial funding to continue their research. (64)

As for the hypothesis of consciousness as a function of the brain, parapsychological research has long shown that the mind does not operate only in a closed circuit within the brain. This has been proven especially by the existence of ESP (Extra Sensory Perception), which means perception beyond the five physical senses. This is rocking the foundation of the traditional scientific paradigm to the degree that it should now be reassessed, or rather expanded.

If you wish to immerse yourself in scientific literature referring to ESP and parapsychological research in general, there are quite a few sources. One of them is: Atkinson, R.L, Atkinson, R.C, Smith, E.E. & BEM, D.J (1990). "Introduction to Psychology." This is an introductory book which is also part of the curriculum at several universities around the world. And for the first time in history (1990), they included a separate chapter on parapsychological research.

They simply couldn't ignore these results anymore. If so, they would have to omit all other scientific research on human consciousness, as well as a large part of other psychological research literature that doesn't yield any better results than the ESP research. If you want to dive in even deeper, Daryl Bem and the late Charles Honorton's famous study, which also was published in the renowned psychological journal "Psychological Bulletin", is absolutely recommended. (65) The article can be ordered from most university libraries.

However, there are still many critics who claim that this is a pseudoscience. Perhaps the most famous of these critics is James Randi. He has promised a prize of one million dollars to anyone who can prove the existence of ESP. No one has so far claimed the price. And there are good reasons for that.

This competition he has announced has some lugubrious conditions, such as that it is Mr. Randi himself who is to decide whether the evidence is strong enough or not. An independent scientific committee or court is not allowed, and those who want to claim the prize, must sign this contract. (66) To me, this seems as convincing as a North Korean court. Most serious researchers do not want to have anything at all to do with him. Perhaps not so strange.

One of the more serious criticisms of experimental parapsychological research, in my opinion, is also the greatest confirmation of ESP as a function of human factors, such as emotions. And emotions should be taken seriously in all human research. Humans are not biological cognitive robots, even if we "became" so the moment science gave away the soul to the church in exchange for matter. However, it turns out that both emotions, beliefs, intention and interest are strong factors that play a major role in ESP laboratory experiments.

"ESP is not about physical distance, but emotional closeness" - Unknown

But as we are about to see, this also applies to other research disciplines, not just ESP. The phenomenon is often called "The Decline Effect", which means that the effect of the experiments decreases over time. Parapsychological researchers were the first to identify this effect. They found that with repeated and prolonged laboratory experiments, the results became weaker towards the end of an experimental series. This is due to exhaustion, fatigue or boredom of the subjects. This phenomenon has also been demonstrated at another level in other sciences, for example in medical research.

An example of the above comes from psychiatry, and a new antipsychotic medicine that turned out to give remarkably good results to begin with. However, the effect diminished over time, only to end up being completely ineffective. And then ultimately being rejected as treatment. (67)

This phenomenon is actually quite widespread, but very few talk about this mysterious aspect of this phenomenon. Perhaps because it simply cannot be explained within the boundaries of the traditional scientific paradigm. There is also a related phenomenon called the experimental leader effect: A new method or new medicine works best in the "hands" of the person who discovered it. The Pygmalion effect?

Phenomena like placebo, nocebo and pygmalion are often dismissed as "Just so stories". They appear too mysterious to most people, because they simply won't fit into the Newton's clockwork-narrative. Nevertheless, placebo is always present as control, whenever new drugs are being tested. You may even have participated in such a trial yourself, where neither you nor your doctor know whether you are getting the genuine drug or the placebo.

When religions claim: "God works in mysterious ways", whenever they're unable to explain, or justify something, Newtonian scientists often call the same "unexplainable coincidences."

"Be careful what you wish for, you might get it" - N.N

One of the most startling findings in ESP research that confirms the effect of faith, was made by psychologist Gertrude Schmeidler. And as we all know, faith is always associated with strong emotions, so is resistance. This was confirmed when Schmeidler prior to an ESP experiment, asked the participants whether they believed in the phenomenon or not. Those who believed scored significantly above statistical probability. But just as interesting was the fact that those who did not believe, scored significantly below statistical probability. In other words, both groups confirmed the existence of ESP. The latter group probably reluctantly so. This phenomenon has since been confirmed by a number of other researchers, and has later been referred to as "The sheep-goat effect". (68)

The observant reader may have discovered the two close relatives of the "Sheep-goat effect", namely the placebo and nocebo effect (!) (69)

Let's get back to belief, disbelief and James Randi for a moment. Randi has himself been caught cheating and deceiving in several contexts. Even the US Department of Defense went on one occasion public with a criticism of him. (70) If you are interested in delving deeper into the controversies regarding James Randi, I can recommend the philosopher Terje G. Simonsen's book "Våre skjulte evner" (Our hidden abilities). This book also highlights the many different forms of ESP in an excellent way. Terje G. Simonsen also communicates in an entertaining, enlightening and very captivating way.

Finally, let me add that one of the most prominent researchers in the field of parapsychology, Dean Radin, has spent twenty years reviewing virtually all of the parapsychological research litterature that exist, and Dr. Dean Radin concludes that ESP must be considered proven. (71)

As for the blind woman's NDE Experience, which I described at the beginning of this chapter, it seems to me ridiculous if a blind clinical dead person's precise description of an emergency room, including colors, exact readings of gauging instruments and retelling of the dialogue between the emergency room staff, including the surgeon's thoughts (down to the smallest detail) should be written off as subjective illusions or hallucinations. If that is the case, I guess we have to declare absolutely all human observation as subjective illusions or hallucinations. Including yours and mine (!) Think again.

As most of us know, scientific experiments in the classical sense must follow a rigid methodology. The method must be transparent and the entire material must be published and made available, so that other researchers are enabled to perform and replicate the same experiments in order to possibly confirm, or weaken the findings. Even within this rigid imperative, cheating often occurs, academically this is often referred to as "The File-drawer problem". (See Central Concepts).

Nevertheless, this rigid system has given us an enormous technological and materialistic development and progress. Without this, we wouldn't have had Alfa Romeos, washing machines, internet porn or smart phones. It is understandable that in the light of such a resounding scientific success, it may be tempting to also think of humans as machines with the potential of scientific modifications and technical improvements.

However, this requirement of replication, is obviously a problem for those researching near-death experiences. They are (fortunately) not allowed to kill a random sample of people in a laboratory-setting, and then try to revive them again. But, as we have seen, all the alternative hypotheses trying to dismiss NDE as a genuine non-medical or non-physical phenomenon, have all been proven wrong. Or declared dead (so to speak). Still, the requirement of replication, in the rigid sense, has yet to be met.

It may be worth considering the following words by Rollo May, existential psychologist and one of the pioneers of the third force of psychology:

"People who claim that they are absolutely convinced that their views are the only correct ones, are dangerous."

One such "dangerous" view as Rollo May refers to above, is the quintessence, not only of dogmatism, but also of it's far more destructive and prejudiced relative, namely fanaticism. Again, it may be worth recalling the integrative perspective, and not least George Engels' model. An integrative perspective does not preclude, it is dynamic and is able to absorb new knowledge and new methods. Both dogmatism and fanaticism are "dangerous" enemies of expanded thinking. New criteria are needed for a new research paradigm. The philosopher Ken Wilber, and others, have argued for just that. They have also come up with specific suggestions as to what and how. (To recap George Engels'model, see Chapter 15)

Since the Enlightenment and the scientific revolution in the 18th century, a scientific view has prevailed, where this view of reality itself has been developed with an anchoring in narrow methods. Thus reality itself has in turn been reduced to the limitations of the methods. Huston Smith points out that dimensions such as values, qualities, meaning and purpose of life slip through the science, as water leaks through the fisherman's net. (72)

Classical scientific methods do no longer serve us as complete "eyes of cognition" in order to understand the whole mystery of the human being. The old paradigm has become too narrow, the shoes have simply become too small. It would be more than arrogant to believe that our current knowledge, generated from our current classical paradigm, is perfect, and that the answers to an ever-increasing number of anomalies could be resolved within this same paradigm's theories and methods.

I would also like to point out that there are already several sciences that have never been able to satisfy the scientific requirement of conducting and replicating laboratory experiments, anywhere and anytime. Astronomy and geology are two of these sciences. To take the latter, it is not possible to induce an earthquake in the laboratory. Yet most of us rely on the knowledge generated by these sciences.

There's a lot of talk about the cornerstones of classical physics. Just as the classic Abrahamic worldview and their four corners of this flat earth. But the new physics, quantum physics or quantum mechanics, has neither corners nor cornerstones. To the extent that it has anything at all, it is original waves. Some call them waves of knowledge (Planck & Schrødinger). (73)

Throughout this book, we've seen that the Abrahamic "fingerprints" have left their marks all the way up to our present time, often in the forms of sinfulness, shame and limitation of individual talents, freedom and emotions. The sciences are no exception as we've also seen throughout this book. Indirectly, this shows which research- questions, disciplines and methods that have been left out by this limiting paradigm. Methods, which in turn may shed a new and far more fruitful light on the diversity of human emotions and expressions.

The "objective" classical sciences doesn't approve of subjective emotions. They are "ghosts" in their mechanical theories. Especially sexual emotions, which are probably the most powerful of them all, are treated like "sand in their well-oiled classical machinery."

Social Darwinism also clings to a classical corner, not unlike the classical Abrahamic view on human beings and the abysmal difference regarding traits and values between the genders. We've also seen some historical examples of this throughout this book. The "toxic" way of social Darwinian thinking has crept into the subconscious of many people. The rape hypothesis is just one horrible example of how psychologically brainwashed "objective" scientist can become.

Some classical scientists cling to their own corners by claiming that science is currently limited, but that tomorrow will bring better measuring instruments which will show that the old paradigm still holds true, especially regarding extra sensory perceptions. Yes, the classical paradigm is limited, but new data are pointing out into a larger and more incomprehensible room, a room beyond the classical three-dimensional one. Quantum physics, parapsychology and the NDE research give, in my opinion, some very interesting pointers. If one is willing to take the time needed to familiarize oneself with the research literature. It's not dangerous. It is at best consciousness-expanding. (Accommodation)

Many people, including scientists, suffer from "contempt before the investigation". Those who suffer from this have rarely provided people with any new knowledge. And when it comes to objectivity, there are at best only degrees of subjectivity. I'm not talking about objective predictable machines like cars or i-phones, but the "objective" sciences that deal with human beings, and human consciousness.

The psychological impact of NDE experiences, and the emotional factors in ESP

The criticism of ESP also reveals science's ignoring of human's most important traits, namely feelings and emotions. Yes, we know that mechanisms such as clockworks, planetary systems, micro-processors, astronomical and geological systems, smartphones and statistics have no emotions. But humans do. Emotions are the driving force and the basic organizing principle for us humans! And again, as a comment to the latter: Sexual emotions are not an insignificant part of this (!)

In the case of NDE ("The Six Minutes Therapy"), no clinical-therapeutic disciplines are even close to produce such astonishing effects and life-transforming changes in a constructive sense compared to the NDE-transformation. And personal changes are always rooted in strong emotions. What NDE experiencers tell us about their emotional journey on "the other side" is not quite unlike Plato's cave parable.

Many of them say that language alone is not enough to describe what they experienced in that dimension, like the ecstatic feelings, the bright light, and the colors "outside the cave".

And not least for the billions of people who actively believe in our world religions and ideologies, as well as their dogmas about what is right and wrong. And as we have seen, these religions and ideologies very often focus on what is "wrong" with you, me and everyone else.

The reason I pay so much attention to NDE and ESP research in this last chapter of the book is first and foremost the impact this important research, with its surprising findings, can have on very many people living in this reality, in this room, now. And then not least for the billions of people who passively rely on our world's dogmatic religions and ideologies, as well as their theologies of right and wrong, and who suffer under these regimes. And as we have seen, many religions and ideologies too often focus on what's "wrong" with you, me and everyone else, instead of celebrating us, with all our glorious traits, talents and possibilities.

However, if you happen to be one of those who are provoked by the NDE research, then I ask you: "Why is it provoking to you?" Is it because the results of this research do not support any kind of "value-apartheid" systems, where individuals are classified as either superior or inferior, or polarized as good or bad according to their personal traits?

When it comes to most sung word on this planet, *love*, which "everyone" speaks of and know the meaning of, of course. However, this 4-letter word is probably the most widely used and abused word in most languages. Love in itself is a universal language and does not really need any interpretation or instruction manual. And not least: Love is not rational. Love is *always* emotional. Love is always about the most distinctive feature of being human: *Emotions*! In other words: Human's most central organizing principle (!) Yours and mine central basic organizing principle: *Emotions*!

Part III: No Fingerprints are "Normal" – They're All Natural

"We have lived for a hundred years characterized by normality thinking. Instead of accepting the unusual as a minority expression, it has been defined as deviation, as sick, as criminal or as sinful, depending on which position of power one has expressed oneself from"

(Esben Esther Pirelli Benestad & Elsa Almås)

The reason why I have included so much of the failed research in this book is to show how tragic the consequences can be when research is being "mated" with dogmatic ideologies and their underlying assumptions about reality.

Dogmatic ideologies and some scientific theories (scientism) are often built on a hierarchical value system, where there is consensus on who is good enough to be included in the upper part of their value hierarchy. And consequently, who they categorize as inferior. In other words "Value-apartheid". Otherwise, consensus simply means agreement. But you will rarely hear an academic use the word "agreement". Consensus sounds, well, more academic than agreement. Maybe even slightly objective.

Speaking of consensus, it is hardly surprising that people who are brought up in the same culture with associated values and methods easily agree. However, it's far more startling that people from all religions, ideologies, sciences, political discourses and genders, who have experienced an NDE, completely agree without arranging international conferences to form consensus (!)

And when it comes to the concept of "normalcy", this concept seems to confuse most of us. "Normal" is derived from norm, which means "guideline". It is often based on an average, and rarely has anything at all to do with naturalness. In the United States, they circumcise about 60% of all boys, which is "normal" in their culture. At the same time, it is totally unnatural. The reason is to be found more than 100 years back in time, when England and the United States began to circumcise boys to prevent the "sinful masturbation". Since then, it has just become a "habit" that most people don't reflect on. In other words, the cause has become "invisible". And the effect is considered normal.

The good news is that we can all switch to slightly more "progressive glasses", precisely because we are more than instinct-driven animals. What sets us apart from other species, is the ability to reflect, which gives us the opportunities of critical observation and conscious planning including: Choosing, asking questions, acquiring more knowledge, which together can give us a better and extended perspective. Victor Frankl called this human talent the "Reflection Pause.", you know, that tiny little "space" between "fight or flight".

Our "normalcy", as I have shown, very often has its "hidden" origins in dogmatic religions and ideologies, just as in the example I mentioned above. This in turn affects cultures and subcultures. And at the end of the day it affects you and me, and by then it often has turned into "glasses" that we see ourselves and others through. Unfortunately, all too often "aggressive glasses".

But as we have seen, we are not at the mercy of gods, genes, cultures, or other "deterministic" authorities, even though we are all more or less colored by them. Or to use the term that none of us like: "Brainwashed". But still, we are not mindless biological, cultural or subcultural "brainwashed" (or programmed) robots. We are all agents equipped with a will, as well as the ability to investigate, explore, change, rethink, shout out and thus be able to defend both ourselves, but more important, to speak out for those who are exposed to violent authorities and not just cultural indoctrination.

But yes, it takes courage! Perhaps the greatest enemy of mankind is "the silent majority". And when it comes to "normality", the whole term should have been sent off to where it belongs, to the historical graveyard for failed projects. Then we would be left with naturalness and diversity. Besides, there are no "normal" fingerprints, just natural ones. Just like DNA. And none of them are alike. By the way, no one talks about the average of fingerprints (!) As a matter of fact, it is variety that is the natural thing.

And when it comes to love, it can never be "normal." But, love is always natural! Love is not measurable either. Love cannot be measured, neither in weight, nor strength. Love can only be felt. And if you don't feel it, well, then it isn't Love.

With his research, James W. Prescott emphasizes the importance of early emotional and natural physical contact with children, regardless of gender. As well as the importance of teaching them that their bodies are not inferior, but a wonderful source of beauty and sensuality, and that our bodies at the same time also are part of the way we emotionally relate and communicate with each other. Not as something inferior or shameful, like many have been taught to believe.

Furthermore, shame never leads to anything good, guilt however, can be a powerful behavior-moderator. But shame is always destructive! We must strive to educate those who succeed us to become more emotionally competent, compassionate and loving, instead of teaching them to exploit each other for their own gain. As we ourselves all too often do, and remember, our actions are their teachers. It must also be accepted that expressing sexuality during puberty is not only natural but also desirable in a perspective that emphasizes interaction and respect, rather than competition, aggressiveness and ego-philia. (Read Chapter 17 again) (74)

This ubiquitous competition ethic (zap through your TV channels) also teaches children that advancement, getting ahead in this world, is something that should happen at the expense of others, and that in that perspective there is no guilt. Only "losers and winners". Ego-philia and conquest thus become "proud" emotions. If that is what we fill their backpacks with, then sexuality is not going to be expressed in a compassionate, lovingly and naturally way. Neither in adolescence nor in adulthood. The tyranny of competition (like the tyranny of normalcy), also provides fertile ground for aggressive behavior. Remember: Injured people injure people.

"From Plato through Augustin, Christianity and the enlightenment, they all have brainwashed us to believe that we are rational beings, but we are not, we are emotional beings (...) Especially boys are victims of this rationality, they are raised to be "train-wrecks" further down the track." - Douglas Noll

Regarding "normalcy," it should also be clear by now that it's far more than the non-heterosexuals who are suffering from this tyranny of normalcy. As we have seen, there are many heterosexuals who also suffer and feel inhibited by these stereotypical role-norms. Today, it's probably the boys who experience the heaviest pressure in terms of living up to gender expectations. "Be a man!", "Grow some balls", "Don't be a sissy" etc. Many young ones do not recognize themselves in these petrified perceptions of what it means to be a "man". We no longer live in the Stone Age. Or do we (?)

And remember: How enlightened we are always depends on who's in control of the spotlight, and thus also the "invisible" information left in the shadows. We are all more or less involved in continuing the ignorance of the previous generations and their "Just so stories". So, we're all co-responsible for where the spotlight is directed, and thus what to make visible.

The fact that so many people have to fight every day to justify and defend their existence and their natural talents, prevents the same people from living out their own potential to the fullest, and thus also the opportunity to make their contribution to humanity. To us. But at the same time, it also prevents all those who spend their time and energy to oppose human rights and equality. Energy that they too could use to live out their own unique innovative potentials, both for the benefit of themselves, and the rest of us.

So why not just acknowledge the differences, and even celebrate that we're all individually, unique emotion-based creatures, regardless of the so-called causes of these differences. And let's be honest now, what do you really think is the worst that could happen if we set the gender roles, sex roles and the people, including you, free?

The perspective, or "map" this book represents, right or wrong, highlights no one as better or worse than others. It does not indicate degeneracy or exclusion of any human beings, regardless of their inner or external "colors". The side effect of this perspective can only be constructive, inclusive and life-affirming for all temporary residents on planet Tellus. You *are* good enough. After all, maybe the only reason why we are here, is as "banal" as learning to accept and respect each other, ourselves and the diversity of human expressions in general. As simple as that. Who you genuinely are, may by the end of the day turn out to be who you originally were meant to be. Your birthright, your script, your map.

Anita Moorjani emphasizes this very clearly in her book "Dying to Be Me". Anita is one of the countless people who have been through a powerful and transformative NDE experience. Today she travels the world to tell about her experiences. Just like other NDEs, she is also concerned with contributing love, compassion and knowledge to her fellow human beings. Hers, and all the other NDE messages, also reminds me of an Australian palliative nurse named Bronnie Ware, who began exploring "BDE" ("Before Death Experiences") as I call it.

Bronnie Ware spent the last time in the lives of many people who were on the threshold of death. Some messages were repeated by most of these dying patients. Their stories made such an impression on her that she decided to write a book about it. The book is called "Regrets of The Dying". She discovered several common regrets of these individuals, including: "I wish I'd had the courage to live a life true to myself, not the life others expected of me" and "I wish I'd had the courage to express my *feelings*" "I wish I had spent more time with my friends." In other words, they expressed regrets for what they had *not* done (!) (75) (My italics)

Anita Moorjani also emphasizes the importance of living a life true to your own self and that this is exactly what is both your mission and your contribution to yourself, and everyone else in life. She goes on to say that gender roles are cultural roles which do not exist on the "other side". Another consideration she makes with regard to communication (in this realm), is that it seems like most people use language to hide their emotions, rather than the actual origin of all languages: Namely to be able to communicate *emotions.* (76) (My italics)

"*There is no gender in the other realm*" - Anita Moorjani

TRAX: Excerpts from the concluding part of Juno's journey

"There is only one sin. Theft. All other sins are aspects of it: If you take the life of a human being, you steal someone's friend, mother, father, brother, sister, child, lover or dream. If you lie, you steal someone's opportunity for truth"

From the book "The Kite Runner" by Khaled Hosseini

"Juno was upset by all these endless fights between and within these «congregations». Mankind should develop congregational guidelines beneficial for everyone" he thought, "and therefore Humanity should be the only congregation. And if he should ever be in need of a catechism, it would be the South African constitutional paragraph on Human Rights, which states": "The State or no Person may unfairly discriminate against anyone on grounds including; Race, Gender, Sex, Ethnic or Social origin, Color, Sexual-orientation and Belief"

"And if he should ever need any commandments, it would have to be the following ones. The first one that appears in both the Quran and the Jewish Talmud says: "Whosoever saves the life of one, it shall be as if he had saved the life of all mankind" (Quran, 5:32 & Sanhedrin 4:5). Then he would add Jesus' powerful commandment from the Gospel of John (15:17) stating: "This is my commandment to you, Love each other sayeth the Lord". And the third commandment would be the Universal statement communicated by the vast majority of the people who have experienced an NDE (Near Death Experience), quote: "There are only two things of real importance, both here and in the after-life: Love and Knowledge"

"Well, then the foundation should be in place, he thought. Just a few and easy guidelines to remember, yet so challenging to live by, he reluctantly admitted to himself"

"Juno now knew what he wanted with his life:" I now want to go out in the world, and tell everyone what I've seen, I want to tell the stories of these people, I will sing out about all these "invisible" people's suffering, yearning, grief and tears. And to you Matthew, Seth, and all of you who have no more tears to shed: Where ever you are, you will never be forgotten. I promise to be your voice on this reality, on this side of "the veil"!

"Juno never had to search for the meaning of life anymore, because now he was able to accept who he is, be who he is. And that this was exactly what had always been the meaning of his life, anyone's life, namely to become who you are, and that his individual colors of love also was part of his individual identity, and thus also the story he was meant to live".

"Orientations of love, whether between equal or different genders, was to Juno now only different, unique and individual expressions for one and the same thing. Love! And Love is not a disease. It is hatred that makes sick! And it is hatred that is the original sin!"

"Juno was grateful that God hadn't listened to his prayers, up there by the dam on the mountainside, ages and ages ago."

TRAX

"This is my commandment to you, Love each other sayeth the Lord"

The Gospel of John 15:17

Some years ago I was a guest in a talk show on Norwegian TV (NRK) called "Styrk Live". The subtitle of the TV-show was "Do religions control our sex lives?" The short answer to that is off course: Yes! However, in an interview prior to the show, I said, among other things, that in my opinion we only need one biblical quote, and that is John 15:17 (which I have quoted several times in this book). I also suggested to add the Gospel of Thomas, which was banned ca 1700 years ago.

Regarding John 15:17, I have discovered at least 4 different translations of this quote, during my research, which in itself is an interesting observation (!) The shortest one was simply "Love each other". Personally I'm more fan of the ones that are starting with: "These things I command you...", indicating that there's just *one* commandment. The message in 15:17 also has a mysterious resemblance to the NDE messages. Could it even be that the Superstar from Nazareth experienced an NDE while he was absent during the years between the age of 11 and his comeback at 30?

Somehow, that commandment also captures the core message of this book. Anyway, if you have understood this message, not rationally, but emotionally, then I suggest you pass this book on to someone you think might be strengthened by it. (Paying it forward).

After having read the first parts of this book, you may have gotten the notion that I am an atheist. Well, as you've probably understood after reading this chapter, I am not. I do not even like the term. I'm not an agnostic either. I do however, believe in something greater than us. Feel free to call it a Luminary entity, to which all NDEs refer. So, if you should be in need of categorizing me, you may call me spiritual. I myself am not a very big fan of categories in general, I rather refer to myself as a curious human being with a meta-physical view. Neither am I a feminist nor a masculinist, I'm a humanist.

And speaking of this light, which virtually everyone who has experienced an NDE describes, and who always asks the challenging question: "Have you learned to love?" I have also seen glimpses of that "light" in all of the three Abrahamic religions. But perhaps most of all in the eyes of the many people I have met on my way. Strange enough, this light is equally visible in the eyes of joy, as it is in the eyes of mourning.

And as I mentioned in a previous chapter, I do not think that one neither can nor should "take" away religion from a human being. However, one can and sometimes one should add new knowledge. The NDE research is a good example of the latter, because it shows that Jews, Christians, Muslims, Hindus, atheists, Buddhists, Taoists, communists, capitalists, surgeons, plumbers, doctors, psychologists and truck drivers, all experience the same during this mystical NDE-Stage. They all communicate the same messages from the Light.

If you profess to any of the Abrahamic religions, while at the same time feel that they have taken away from you a lot of the mysticism and the magic, I recommend you to explore the directions within both Judaism, Christianity and Islam, which go in depth regarding mystery and magic. They are also far more consistent than polarized. Moreover, you don't even have to be religious in order to learn something from these "hidden" Abrahamic treasures.

Judaism has its Kabbalistic scriptures, Christianity its Gnostic scriptures and Islam has its Sufi scriptures. (78) (79) (80). Regarding the latter, Sufi, most people have probably heard of Rumi. Quotes by Rumi often appear in the feed on social media. However, in many ways, all these scriptures are pointers to part of what these NDEs experience. There is more that unites us than polarizes us.

Moreover, division, polarization and competition are not the way to the future. And speaking of faith, three of the greatest influencers of humanity: Socrates, Jesus, and Mohammed, never wrote down a single word of their visions. In any case, written texts from these "Big Three" have never been discovered, so far. They are only quoted in the writings of others.

And speaking of texts, if there is to be a headline for what I care most about and am most passionate about, it must be the birthright of all individuals. Everyone. Thus, what provokes me the most and makes me both sad and angry is: Harassment, bullying and rejection of individual human beings. Because there is nothing wrong with the individual. There are however many flaws with the systems, but the individual should always rank above the systems. The systems should be there to serve and to help us develop our individual talents and potentials. Not the other way around.

As for Green's "sissy kids" (Chapter 8) and everyone else who does not fit into the culturally polarizing norm systems, including the transgender kids who feel they're born into an alien body: I consider them as mentors for the rest of us. As guides, who in their various ways are saying: "What are you doing? Why on earth do you think that *you* are the chosen tailors to design and decide which "straitjacket" I should wear?" Who these children are, can not be unlearned, it should be understood by now! Neither is it possible to unlearn taste or language. But one can be scared from both eating and communicating. Think Again!

To me, these "kids" appear as an unconscious collective wave of protest. A protest against those narrow, limiting and polarizing gender-roles. Most of them probably don't see themselves as that. But I do. Anyway, they are for sure empaths who subconsciously are trying to awaken the apaths among us. And this we need more than ever. Furthermore, these non-heterosexual and non-gender role-conforming individuals are the "litmus" test on human rights. Whether we like it or not. They are the very test of the individual's birthright, the test of whether we manage to live up to "The Golden Rule": To love our neighbors as ourselves! What they really *are* asking us is this:

"Have you learned to love?"

EPILOGUE

In the prologue to this book, I wrote about my thoughts, and the heavy and difficult feelings I went through, but also the philosophical reflections I made, as a thirteen- fourteen-year old boy up there by the dam, in the previous millennium. Hadn't it been for those experiences, I would probably never have chosen the track that eventually formed my life. Neither would I have chosen the educational and occupational path that I'm on now. And certainly not written a book. At least not this book. I am therefore eternally grateful to my creators, two of them I know, that I was born. Born as the one I initially was meant to be, and that after many years, and some crash landings along the way, finally dared to be.

Amor Fati

The Eagle's Nest, Hovden-Norway, Passover 2018. I've just arrived at the top of the southern mountains, and it's starting to snow again. It settles like a thin white veil covering the valley below. And the tracks of my car in the last hairpin bend, just before the parking space here at the top of the Mountain Park, are also covered in white now. But the tracks are still there, just beneath this silky veil-like surface. They are invisible, but they *are* there. They will always *be* there …

"A Child will be born tomorrow…"

APPENDIX I

EXCERPT FROM THE PILOT STUDY

Arne Utne and Richard Bruvoll jr

The quantitative part of the pilot study

Especially the questions: 8/9/10/11/12 / gave some interesting answers. We have combined “Strongly Agree” and “Somewhat Agree” as well as “Somewhat Disagree” and “Strongly Disagree” to agree or disagree, respectively:

No. 8 I am not open about my bisexuality because I am afraid that others will distance themselves.

Men: agree 20 / disagree 3
Women: agree 15 / disagree 7

Comment: In itself not a surprising answer, but confirms the general fear of rejection.

No. 9 I am not open about my bisexuality because it breaks with my perception of my own gender role identity

Men: agree 11 / disagree 10 (of these 11, 8 completely agreed)
Women: agree 7 / disagree 7

Comment: These answers possibly reflect the differences between men and women's perceptions of their gender role identity. In the last 40 years, as a result of women's fight for equality, the girls have been allowed to open up a little more, and thus have been "allowed" to play on more strings than the boys.

No. 10 I am not open about my bisexuality because it breaks with others' perception of gender role identity

Men: agree 19 / disagree 3 (of these 19, 13 completely agreed)
Women: agree 13 / disagree 7 (of these 13 were 12 somewhat agree)

Comment: This reflects the culture's strict norms and guidelines on what a gender role identity can be allowed to accommodate, and again results are reflected in the "extended" female role. The gender role identity requirements are made clear here as the absolute biggest obstacle to climb out of the closet.

No. 11 I think the gay / lesbian communities include the bisexuals in a good way

Men: agree 11 / disagree 6
Women: agree 12 / disagree 7

Comment: These answers possibly reflect the ambivalence of gays and lesbians regarding their bisexual «brothers and sisters». However, perhaps not as bad as we had previously thought from "hearsay". In any case, several of the respondents felt exposed to both homophobia and hetero-phobia. This is also reflected in the Nova report (1999), which states that bisexuals struggle more with their mental health than lesbians and gays.

No. 12 I believe that bisexuality is a transitional phase to becoming gay, lesbian or heterosexual

Men: agree 4 / disagree 16 (of these 16, 15 completely disagreed).
Women: agree 0 / disagree 20 (of these 20, 15 completely disagreed).

Comment: These answers are in very strong contrast to general perceptions about this, namely the myth that bi- homosexuality as a phase towards adult heterosexuality. These answers do not support psychodynamic theoretical "truths" such as "identity confusion" (development-arrest), trial / transition phases, etc. Not least, these answers are interesting in the light of the respondents' average age, especially men's average age which in this study was 32.5 years.

The "Coming of Age" regarding sexual awakening

As mentioned, the average age for the men in the survey was 32.5 years, for the women 21.4 years. The age range was 16 to 63 years for males, and 14 to 39 for females, respectively. In terms of age for the "discovery" of their bisexuality, the average for men was 17.2 years, and for women 14.3 years. However, it is interesting to note that some of them were quite old when they "discovered" it. One of the males was actually 55 years old, and one of the women 28 years old. Could it be that this latter reflects a process of denial that has resulted in suppression?

It may also be interesting to see these numbers in the light of Dr Henry Adams et al's laboratory experiment on homophobia plus the more recent study which I described in Chapter 8.

Could it be that it was underlying bisexuality these experiments revealed? (Denied or suppressed bisexuality). As mentioned, almost all the men who were aroused by the homo-sex video, also showed equal penile reactions to both the hetero-sex video and the lesbian video in Dr. Adam's experiment.

EXCERPT FROM THE NOVA REPORT 1999

Sexual orientation and living conditions

First, I will refer to some key findings in the Nova report, which is one of the most comprehensive Norwegian studies in this field. The report is based on two sources as a basis for the empirical data. One is 23 qualitative interviews with homosexuals of both sexes. The other, which is quantitative, consists of a questionnaire-based data set with approximately 3000 homosexuals of both sexes. (Nova, 1999, p. 109)

One of the weaknesses of the quantitative part of the Nova study is that it is not based on a random sample, which the researchers themselves also point out. The interview objects were obtained via established channels for homosexuals in Norway, including a questionnaire that was attached to the magazine Blikk. They did the same via the Norwegian GBLHT-organization called FREE. They point out that one of the main purposes of the quantitative part was to compare the data with the knowledge that already exists about living conditions for the general population, which *is* based on random samples. The 23 in-depth interviews were primarily used to exemplify trends in the quantitative part of the survey. (Nova, 1999, p.113, 114, 116, 118)

The report is thus based on more or less self-reported openly gay and lesbian. It therefore don't captures the hidden segment of the population, then not least those who are bisexual. The report also refers to relevant foreign quantitative studies based on random samples, which can be a useful basis for comparison.

The first Norwegian comprehensive attitude survey, which included general views on homosexuality, was conducted by Scanfact in 1967. It revealed among other things that 72% of the men and 81% of the women claimed that homosexuals had to do what they could to combat their inclinations. (Nova, 1999, p.33)

This probably reflected both society, culture and the scientific attitudes of the time. Societal: The survey was conducted 5 years before homosexuality was decriminalized. Scientific: Homosexuality was still a clinical diagnosis. The culture: A probable reflection of the first two. However, the situation has changed, and is far better today than when this survey was conducted.

Although conditions have improved considerably in our day, many are still struggling to accept their non-heterosexual feelings. Some of the central things that the Nova report reveals are the problems that the very youngest are struggling with. And this is of great importance.

Much psychological research has been done on how people experience the revolutionary changes, both physical and mental, that occur during puberty. In a relatively short and intense period, we become women and men. We begin to ask the big questions about our identity and our place in the world. One of the big questions we are trying to find answers to is; "who am I?" Non-heterosexuals face challenges on top of the general challenges during this phase of life, and an additional question for those often is: "Why am I not like the others?"

It's easy to imagine what this might mean when "the others" also distance themselves from these individuals, and even show contempt for the nascent answer to this question. Psychologist Annbjørg Ohnstad has given a pretty good picture of this additional burden these young people go through, a double-edged sword. She says:

"The burden of hiding one's stigma, being invisible, is the fear of revelation, the burden of showing one's stigma, of being visible, is contempt." (Nova, 1999)

First, the research referred to in the Nova report confirms the invisibility. Not least when it comes to the youngest ones that I focus on in this book. For example, to the question "How old were you when you first talked to someone about your sexual orientation?" The group "Young adult" (25-34 years, N-1082, women and men included) answered that they were on average 20.5 years old. (Nova, 1999, p.156)

That is, the average for the time of the first intimate trust in a close person was more than 20 years old. Again, it is appropriate to remind that the data is retrospective, so here one must take into account that they refer to an event that took place about 5 to 15 years earlier in their lives. On the other hand, one may assume that such a central experience (and for most probably a risky act), is probably not subject memory loss.

At the same time, one must take into account that the average age for the first intimate revelation about their sexual preference has probably decreased during the last two decades. This is due to the ever-increasing openness regarding this topic, as well as the general population's increasing knowledge and acceptance.

However, it's primarily among the youngest ones that we see the greatest and most obvious contempt for non-heterosexuals. Also in our time. The latter is clearly reflected in two comprehensive Norwegian surveys conducted by Ungforsk in 1994 and 1995, where the samples consisted of 5,400 and 4,000 young people, respectively. Both of these surveys showed that the young ones themselves ranked gay people the least popular. (Eva Friis, med.uio.no)

Once again, we have to take into account that the general perception expressed by these young people has probably changed since these surveys were conducted. Nevertheless, based on other and more recent studies, one can assume that these attitudes have not changed in a dramatic sense for the very youngest among us. I would like to remind you again that "you're fucking gay" is the most used "tool" of harassment among boys in our schools.

If we compare Ohnstad's description of the dilemma which many young non-heterosexuals experience during their early teens, and the picture that is drawn regarding the general attitude towards them, one can also see the contours of what traumatic effects this may mean for many of these young ones, who in many ways can be described as an invisible minority.

What could this mean for their mental health? Is the research literature able to tell us anything something? And what, if anything, are the indicators?

In the quantitative part of the Nova report, a number of questions were asked regarding mental health. The answers to these were compared with answers given by the general population. I will address here three of these questions, and the answers that were given by the age group

16 - 24. The answers represent those who had been quite / very much bothered by mental difficulties during the last 14 days. The Health Survey-1995. (Nova, 1999, p.267)

18% of the females and 17% of the males had been plagued by feelings of hopelessness regarding the future. The corresponding figures for the same age group in the general population were 10 and 5%, respectively. 16% of the females and 20% of the males experienced feelings of loneliness, versus 6 and 2% in the general population, respectively.

22% of the females and 16% of the males were depressed. The corresponding figures in the general population were 5 and 2%, respectively. It was also clear that the youngest were those who struggled the most (Nova 1999, p.268, 269)

There are thus clear differences between the non-heterosexuals and the heterosexuals when it comes to mental illness.

Upon closer examination of various underlying variables, they also found that being bisexual seems to cause more psychological distress than those who defined themselves as exclusively homosexual. In addition, they found that those who integrated their hetero- and gay friends in their circle of friends had the fewest mental ailments (Nova, 1999, p.272)

Speaking of bisexual and psychological distress, the former finding is interesting as there is a relatively widespread perception that bisexuals have it easier than homosexuals because they have "greater choices". At the same time, there is also a widespread perception that bisexuals are confused about their sexual identity. Furthermore, bisexuals in homosexual environments have also often been perceived as "halfway out of the closet". The latter is probably a consequence of the fact that some homosexuals actually take this gradual path out of the closet. In addition, there have been few organizations (virtually none) that represent bisexuals.

Those who came out best with regard to mental illness in Nova's survey were precisely those who had integrated their heterosexual and homosexual friends into their circle of friends. This also confirms the importance of how crucial the recognition from others is. One can cautiously conclude from this that integration is very important.

One of the most disturbing findings of Nova's research was the high proportion who had tried to end their own lives. There has been a lot of research on suicide in recent decades, but the general suicide research says relatively little regarding problems associated with having a non-heterosexual orientation. This is literally a "black hole" in the general research literature.

As many as 27% of the males and 25% of the females in the age group 16-24 reported that they had tried to take their own lives one or more times. This is almost seven times as high as in the general population (Nova, 1999, p.283, 284)

Among the stated motives for the suicide attempts, the most prominent were: "I felt lonely and isolated", "I wanted to get away from an unbearable situation", "I could not bear the thought of the future", "It was too difficult to accept myself." Other motives that also were prominent among the young ones, were that they hated themselves, that they felt unworthy and that they could not bear their own thoughts (Nova, 1999, p.287)

EXCERPT FROM THE 2013 STUDY

Sexual orientation and living conditions - Norman Anderssen and Kirsti Malterud

"It seems that the burden for mental illness among LGBT people in our sample is highest in the age group under 30 and among bisexual women. In all the groups, some had thought that they could not live any longer (30-65%), highest among bisexual women and men. However, the question does not directly include suicidal thoughts, but may be about an experience of despair. In NOVA 1/99, 20% of lesbian women and 16% of gay men reported that they had tried to take their own lives (Hegna, Kristiansen et al. 1999), and the incidence of suicide attempts was particularly high among those under 25 years of age."

For the record, let me add that the percentages they refer to in the latter part of the section above apply to all age groups as a whole, and not just the youngest ones that I cited from the NOVA -1999 study.

"In our sample, the proportion who reported suicide attempts was higher among lesbians (12%) and bisexual women (19%) than among heterosexual women (5%). Among men, the proportion of homosexuals (10%) and bisexual men (11%) was higher than among heterosexual men (4%)."

"In the age group under 25, the proportion was highest among bisexuals (19%) and lesbian women (14%). Previous studies have shown a higher incidence of suicide attempts among LGBT people compared to heterosexuals, especially among bisexuals and young people.

(Garofalo, Wolf et al. 1999; Wichstrom and Hegna 2003; Gransell and Hansen 2009; Institute of Medicine 2011; Mathy, Cochran et al. 2011). Our analyses indicate that the incidence of suicide attempts among lesbian, gay and bisexual women and men in Norway is probably somewhat lower than that found in the sample of NOVA 1/99 (Hegna, Kristiansen et al. 1999)". (K1 S8 / 9)"

"More women and men were negative about two women or two men holding hands or kissing each other than if two people of different genders are doing it. We only asked these questions in 2013. (Not in previous surveys). Among men, there was the greatest opposition to two men kissing each other in a public place (62%) (K1S16 / 17)"

This latest finding suggests that cultural homophobia has not changed much since the NOVA survey in 1999.

"A small survey on attitudes towards lesbians and gays among 523 19-year-olds in Hordaland, a county in Norway (Anderssen 2002), showed that 63% of the boys had negative attitudes towards gay boys / men, and 39% were negative towards lesbian girls / women. Among the girls, 43% had negative attitudes towards gay boys / men, and 43% were negative towards lesbian girls / women. Two years later, the same participants answered the same questions. As 21-year-olds, more participants had become more benevolent. For the boys, the corresponding incidences of negative attitudes were reduced to 59% and 33%, respectively, and to 33% and 32% among the girls ". (S-128)

Bullying and harassment of LGBT teens.

"We would like to point out a larger survey among upper secondary school students. In 2009, Roland and Auestad conducted a nationwide survey on bullying and sexual orientation among 3046 students who went to 10th grade (Roland and Auestad 2009). Students answered while at school an anonymous web-based questionnaire. The definition of bullying that they used was: "We call it bullying when one or more (together) are unfriendly and unpleasant towards another who cannot easily defend themselves, and when this behavior is repeated. This can be in the form being kicked, beaten or pushed. It's also bullying when he / she is overly teased or banned from the others." (S-128)

"They map three situations of bullying: face-to-face, by mobile phone and over the internet. The proportion of LGBT girls and boys who had been subjected to one or more of these forms of bullying 2-3 times a month or more often, was large: among gay boys 48% (n = 24), among bisexual boys 24% (n = 10), among heterosexual boys 7% (n = 109 boys). Corresponding figures for girls were: among lesbians 18% (n = 7), bisexual girls 12% (n = 11), and among heterosexual girls 6% (n = 76 girls). Although the figures are statistically uncertain due to the small samples, they give us a well-founded concern that a good number of young LGBT people are exposed to harassment and bullying." (S-128)

My comments:

This 2013 study and the NOVA report, are both thorough and comprehensive studies. Yet they say almost nothing about the most vulnerable of the groups, children and young teenagers. Most studies on sexuality include only people from the aged 18. The Nova study however, did include 16-year-olds, and one of the studies which Anderssen and Malterud referred to included 15-year-olds. The tenth-grade study mentioned above is thus an exception to the rule, and it also confirms that acceptance of non-heterosexuals lessens along with the younger the age of the respondents are.

This should be a warning to all of us, not least as we now know that bullying all the way down to primary school-levels utilize sexual harassment as the most used bullying "tool": "Fucking gay" and "bitch / whore".

We know today that children already at the age of ten search for porn on the internet. This is more than "just" curiosity. It's sexual curiosity. They are sexual individuals, and not all of them are heterosexual. We must therefore take this seriously. In my view, further research should therefor also address those who do not fit into the hetero-normativity. They are often the most vulnerable of them all, however, all of them, whether hetero- or non-heterosexual, pay a high price for the homophobic terror.

Richard Bruvoll Jr

Therapeutic approaches

I see human individual development as a ladder taken down from the wall and placed in a horizontally position on the ground, with individuals both in front of me, and behind me. All equal, but at different steps (stages) in our development. Surely no one accuses a child in the third grade of not being a tenth grader?

Teachers are perhaps the most important therapists in a society. They are important because they are the ones who both cement old and sometimes outdated "truths", however, at the same time they have the key to further development and new learning, based on new truths in their pockets. In that sense, teachers are potentially both the worst and the best. Regardless, they are the most important key holders.

By "teachers" I mean teachers in the broadest sense: Scientists, Doctors (which is actually Latin for "Teacher"), psychologists, health workers in general, preschool teachers, teachers, lecturers, mentors, sports leaders, youth leaders in general, trendsetters, fashion designers, TV and movie authorities, journalists, bloggers, game developers, the popular industry in general and not least you and me through the way we relate to other people of different internal and external colors. We're all potential therapists.

Here are some tips to guide those of you who work as a therapist in the health-sector, when you meet your young clients, perhaps for the first time. Since internal colors necessarily aren't visible to the observer, you may want to decorate your office with posters, encyclopedias, books or the like, which signal that non-heterosexual orientations are as natural as heterosexual orientations. This can be very reassuring to people who are struggling with their orientations, at the same time it signals that it is safe to talk to you about this. Also remember that many non-heterosexuals, have internalized anti-gay attitudes towards themselves. Excessive external homophobic attitudes can also be a signal that it's their own orientation that they are struggling with. The vulnerability here can be skyhigh, so it's about making you think carefully.

To teachers, sports and youth leaders, miljeu therapists and other first-line workers: Psychiatrist Reidar Kjær has put his finger on a very important but alas so neglected topic, namely the attitude to homophobic statements. As he points out, people in these professions are very good at cracking down on racism, but too often look through the fingers regarding homophobia (if they "see" it at all).

This last piece of advice has become even more important now than before, due to the large number of young people from other cultures, where such attitudes are prevalent in all walks of life, and even institutionalized in some of these cultures. I myself have pointed this out time and time again in the youth arenas where I have worked, often to no avail. Sometimes the sound of silence can be devastating to both the visible and the invisible among us.

Richard Bruvoll Jr

APPENDIX II

RISK AND RESILIENCE: A NEW EXTENDED INTERACTIONAL PERSPECTIVE ON PERSONALITY, DEVELOPMENT AND ENVIRONMENT

By Richard Bruvoll Jr - Bachelor student at UiA

In this essay, I will consider a relatively new direction within developmental psychology, which is often referred to as the risk and resilience perspective.

During the short history of psychology, the risk perspective has always been the main focus, and this has in turn probably led to an over-preoccupation with the "pathological human being". The fact that a large number of people seem to be doing rather well despite great psychosocial strains during their childhood years, has led to an expanded focus which now also asks: Why did they manage so well?

Three key individual resilience factors: *mastery, creativity* and *meaning*. The first two I will here give a brief description of, and then precede with a little more in depth description with regard to the latter.

Regarding risk factors, I will focus on the harmfulness of chronic versus acute risk, because chronic risk can prove to be among the most devastating risks for the individual. In this connection, I will shed light on an issue that is not necessarily captured by the risk and resilience research. Which I think is important because it points to the need for a more in-depth examination of the first level of analysis (the individual), as well as cultural and psychosocial alienation (analysis level two) and on an (Extended-Analysis level three). With regard to the latter, I will use Cooley's "Looking Glass-self" to illustrate the complexity.

The term *resilience* is taken from physics, and means an object's ability to return to its "baseline" after being stretched or bent. (Waaktaar & Johnsen, 2000. p-17). In this sense, this term fits well as a term for people who have been exposed to great strain and stress, but who still manage well and live their lives without signs of having been harmed by the stresses they have been exposed to.

An introduction to the risk and resilience perspective.

More than half of all children who are exposed to risk do not suffer injuries in the form of mental disorders. Even in cases where the upbringing conditions are described as extremely difficult, it seems that every other child actually does well. These children have not received any significant attention from researchers until recently. The focus has mainly been on those who did not do so well. This in turn has led researchers to miss out on valuable information regarding factors (both personal and in the environment) that may have contributed to the development of resilience. (Borge, 2003).

Aaron Antonovsky believes that such a one-sided pathogenetic perspective within the health care system (= what creates disease), is contributing to this deficient knowledge of resilience. Antonovsky advocates an expanded perspective, where one sees health as a dimension where pathogenesis and salutogenesis constitute the polarity. (Salutogenesis = the origin of health.) He says that any human being can be placed somewhere on this health dimension, and that no one is one hundred % healthy or sick. He therefore believes that the important question then should be "What is it that can bring the person more in the direction of health in this health dimension?" In other words, a salutogenetic perspective. (Waaktaar & Johnsen, 2000. p-29).

One of the first resilience studies is Werner and Ruth Smith's prospective longitudinal study from Kauai, Hawaii, where they followed up an entire birth cohort from 1955. These were the subject of data collection at two, ten, eighteen, thirty-two and forty years of age. Werner and Smith's ingenious idea was to study the interaction between children's upbringing and the environmental risk through childhood, adolescence and adulthood. Their focus was not to give a description of the misery of these conditions, but to examine what characterized the children and their families, who, despite great burdens and high risk, still did well.

The actual collection of data consisted of both intelligence tests, interviews and psychological tests, they wanted to map individual differences in the form of temperament (Borge, 2003. p-22). To be categorized as children at risk, they must have been exposed to at least four of nine risk factors. These consisted of:

Perinatal stress (eg birth defects)
Chronic poverty
Parents with low education
Disorganized family environment
Little stability in the family
Alcoholic parents
Violence
Teenage mother
Care failure

One third of the children who were defined in the category of at-risk children who developed into becoming both good, caring and well-functioning people at the age of eighteen.

The most common resilience factors were:

Good self-esteem
Normal intelligence
Charming behavior (which attracted positive response from other family members),

Androgyny
Mastery
Autonomy
Meaning
Internal locus of control
Experience of context
Creativity

Factors in the environment outside the family, such as support staff in connection with school, church and youth groups, were also important.

In other words, it seemed that innate qualities in the form of intelligence and personality were also strong contributing factors when it came to triggering resilience factors in the family and in the external environment. (Borge, 2003. p-24).

The three levels of analysis that should be the focus of the risk and resilience research should therefore be the individual, the family and the external environment as well as the interaction between these.

There have been a number of other studies in this field research and they show that some of the risk and resilience factors are recurring. Waaktaar and Johnsen have examined studies of Anthony and Cohler (1987), Antonovsky (1988), Garmezy and Rutter (1983) and Rutter and Rutter (1997) and categorized the most important resilience factors that appear in this research, and then divided them into the three respective analysis levels (as mentioned above).

Regarding innate individual resilience factors, there were some recurring factors; including normal intelligence, good (light) temperament and the absence of hereditary strains and birth defects. (Waaktaar & Johnsen, 2000). This also confirms Werner and Smith's findings.

Other individual resilience factors that recurred in the above studies were mastery, meaning and creativity. I will return to these under the next heading.

Resilience factors that recurred at the second analysis level (family) were among others; good parent-child interaction in infancy; fixed structures in terms of rules, rituals and boundaries; and that at least one of the parents functioned well.

At the third level of analysis (the external environment), there was one factor in particular that stood out as almost universal, namely that there was at least one significant person outside the family who had followed the child through the upbringing and shown it care, support and been a solid "anchoring-point". This significant person hasn't necessarily been able to implement concrete measures in relation to the strains the child was exposed to, but still knew the conditions and been there as a safe and stable person for the child (Waaktaar & Johnsen, 2000). Societal and social structures that support the person's coping strategies are also important.

In the past, the term "dandelion child" (at least in Norway) was often used to refer to these children's miraculous ability to cope despite very stressful family situations. Many have later argued that it may be precisely this external caregiver who is the "hidden" explanation for these children's ability to master their lives.

Mastery, meaning and creativity.

I mentioned above that I would expand on the three individual resilience factors *mastery, meaning* and *creativity*, these three have proven to be consistent and important factors in order to develop resilience. I will first briefly describe *mastery* and *creativity*, and then go a little more in depth when it comes to meaning and context in life.

First *mastery,* in the sense of mastering a skill or social situations has proven to be of great importance in being able to develop resilience. Here one can also talk about the difference between an inner versus an outer «Locus of Control». Secondly, *creativity*, a "high frequency" of this has been registered in resilient people.

One often distinguishes between two subgroups, or two forms of creativity. One is referred to as artistic creativity, and refers to people who engage in symbolic activities such as music. The second sub-group is often called system-creating creativity. The latter is often found among researchers, and it is claimed that these people, through their stressful upbringing, have developed the ability to see order and system in what is otherwise perceived as chaos. (Waaktaar & Johnsen, 2000).

Based on the latter, system-creating creativity, one can thus claim that the resilience of these people has not only been important for their own survival and mastery, but perhaps in many cases also has great significance for the development of culture and society in general.

The third of these individual resilience factors *meaning*, is particularly interesting because it goes deeper into a person's perception of situations and life as such. But *meaning* is also one of several factors that may appear as both resilience or risk (stressful) factors. An example of the latter is that meaning in a larger perspective such as religion, can be stressful if this condemns or excludes people with different identities or sexual orientations.

Resilience research has shown at the individual level that the meaning one attributes to different experiences is of great importance for the development of resilience. For example, growing up with an alcoholic mother may be perceived by the child as she's either drinking because she has problems, or she's drinking because the child is the problem. Here we see that the very meaning the child attributes to its mother's behavior, may also be based on internal or external assumption of attribution ("Locus of Control")

Meaning, as I mentioned above, is also a key factor in the meaning of being based on different views of life or reality. For example, one person may believe that the evil that happens is "God's judgment," while another sees himself as a casual victim of the circumstances. (Waaktaar & Johnsen, 2000). When it comes to people who are exposed to serious traumatic experiences, integrating the events into a context that makes sense is a central and important part of the trauma processing. This also brings me to the next topic, which I mentioned in the introduction, the chronic risk factors, which also can be among the most devastating.

Chronic risk factors

In DSM-IV 1995, trauma is explained as "a wound", and is defined as an event beyond of what we can call ordinary experiences. Something that will be a strain for most people and that leads to an experience of powerlessness and deep helplessness. But trauma is also about confusion, difficulties in understanding contexts and an uncertainty that for many leads to a deep distrust to the world around them. Man-made disasters such as war, mistreatment and abuse also go beyond the experience of self-worth. (Waaktaar & Johnsen, 2000)

Recent research has shown that acute crises do not necessarily lead to lasting problems, it's more often being exposed to chronic risks that lead to trauma. Richard Lazarus (1998), who is one of the most famous theorists in risk research, stated that: "It's not the big things that send a man to the madhouse". Even small doses of chronic risk can be far more threatening to children's functioning than large doses of acute risk. Some examples: Persistent illness, long-term refugee status or growing up in a poor environment. (Borge, 2003. p-54) In addition, I would like to mention racism, sexism and persistent harassment (which some also refer to as bullying).

An example, which has not been much researched in this connection, is cultural and/or individual contempt for non-heterosexuals. I think this can be a good picture due to the invisibility of the damage. It's also arguable that cultural contempt is relatively chronic. Very few children and teens appear as non-heterosexual until their late teens. They are therefore usually invisible, and thus often carry an additional burden as a result of being completely alone with their suffering. That the problem is real is shown by a study on homosexuality and suicide attempts, which concluded that as many as one in four among young bisexuals and homosexuals had tried to end their own lives. (Nova-99).

In addition, research shows that man-made disasters and traumas versus natural ones have a far more severe traumatic effect. Acts of the will (as opposed to natural disasters or accidents) affect the experience of self-worth. The experience of disrespectful treatment and degradation merges with the experience of being worthless!

I would argue that the example of traumatization as a result of homophobia clarifies the need for a deeper examination of the first level of analysis, the individual. It can help to reveal the causes of risk behavior of some individuals that may otherwise be misinterpreted and therefore even misattributed to other factors. In other words, if not being thoroughly investigated, they might go «under the radar».

I have chosen the example above because it makes it clear that a collectively accepted negative behavior can also be very traumatic for some people, and that raising awareness about this should therefore be a topic for this field of research. I think Professor C.H Cooley gives a very good description of how easy it can be to ignore how important the experience of being valued by your fellow human beings is:

"Many people of balanced mind and congenial activity scarcely know that they care what others think of them, and will deny, perhaps with indignation, that such care is an important factor in what they are and do. But this is illusion. If failure or disgrace arrives, if one suddenly finds that the faces of men show coldness or contempt instead of the kindliness and deference that he is used to, he will perceive from the shock, the fear, the sense of being outcast and helpless, that he was living in the minds of others without knowing it, just as we daily walk the solid ground without thinking how it bears us up". (Scheff,1994. s-10)

Cooley claimed with his theory of "The Looking-glass Self", that pride and shame are the primary social emotions, and that they are highly connected to the nature of our relationships. He described them as the social self-feelings and included in this any feeling that the self directs towards itself. An example: "I am ashamed"

We do not think about this much as long as we are fairly accepted by other people and are confirmed by our surroundings. Cooley argued that self-monitoring consisted of three basic elements: our notion of our appearance in other people's minds, our notion of these other people's judgment of that appearance, and our self-esteem as a result.

He also claimed that this self-monitoring is a constantly ongoing process, even when we are alone, and that social self-monitoring implicitly involves an evaluation of ourselves. This self-evaluation will in turn either lead to either pride or shame. (Scheff, 1994)

I believe that this focus on cultural stigma can be a wake-up call and lead to an awareness that some factors can also be found on an *extended* third level of analysis as risk-factors, "hidden" among assumed resilience factors. And that these factors can propagate as poison through the other levels, to ultimately result in the traumatization of individuals, who are not necessarily visible to observers and therapists.

In any case, Waaktaar and Johnsen claim that the very change of perspective that this research entails, will eventually lead to the view of the human being as a survivor and not just as an injured person.

Litterature

Borge, Anne Inger Helmen: Resiliens-risiko og sunn utvikling, 2003. Oslo: Gyldendal Akademisk.

Norsk levekårsundersøkelse for homofile og lesbiske. Nova-rapporten, 1999. Oslo.

Scheff, Thomas J.: Microsociology. Discourse, Emotion, and Social Structure, 1994. Chicago: The University of Chicago Press.

Waaktaar, Trine. & Johnsen Christie, Helen: Styrk sterke sider. Håndbok i resiliensgrupper for barn med psykososiale belastninger, 2000. Oslo: Kommuneforlaget.

THE INTEGRATION OF TRANSPERSONAL EXPERIENCES IN A RESILIENCE - PSYCHOLOGICAL PERSPECTIVE

This is based on an article I published in Parapsychological Notes no. 2 - 2004. In this article I go even wider and deeper into some of the resilience and risk factors. Especially the ones regarding meaning and context. (Richard Bruvoll Jr, Easter 2018)

This article is not so much about parapsychological research per se, but it is rather a spotlight on some phenomena that have been identified through research in this field, and which in my opinion should have consequences for a more holistic psychology. The phenomena I am referring to are: NDE, ESP and OBE.

Before I continue, let me give you a brief explanation of these three acronyms. NDE (Near Death Experiences) are sensory experiences that are relatively frequently reported by people who have been declared clinically dead, but who have nevertheless been managed to revive.

ESP (Extra Sensory Perception) simply means all communication that takes place beyond the five physical senses. Telepathy, clairvoyance and precognition are three examples of ESP. All three can be elements of an NDE experience.

OBE (Out of Body Experience) is the experience of movement in time and space, independent of one's physical body. OBE has been reported throughout history in various mystical traditions such as shamanism. In our time, this is a frequently reported phenomenon in connection with NDE, and is considered one of the special features of such an experience. OBE has many similarities with clairvoyance and it can therefore in some cases be difficult to distinguish between these two.

The NDE has often been reported and described throughout human history, but it is only in recent decades that this has been the subject of systematic research. This simply as a result of the enormous progress in emergency medicine, with consequent improved abilities to "bring back" people who per. definition has been declared clinically dead.

NDE should have attracted massive interest from everyone who researches awareness and personality. Personality changes after such an experience is not just an ESP phenomenon. People who have been through an NDE, for example, are not emotionally locked in, despite the traumatic experiences that often cause an NDE.

Many people who experience life-threatening situations may for example develop PTSD (Post Traumatic Stress Disorder), but the NDEs on the other hand are emotionally released and opened up. They change personality (in six minutes!) In some cases to the unrecognizable, and always in a positive, constructive direction. Not only that, the changes persist. In these cases we are talking about zero decline effect. Something the fewest clinical therapies can produce.

As for the light experience itself, which is a central part of most NDE experiences, there was one individual who described his intense feelings in this way: "Like all the orgasms you have experienced multiplied by 1000, and yet it is not a sufficiently good enough description" (!)

Regarding NDE, as I mentioned, both OBE and elements of ESP are more often than not, present in such experiences. These phenomena should be included in a broader psychological understanding of how we look at ourselves, each other and reality and life as such. Today we have an academic psychology that is rooted in the Newtonian paradigm, and thus not able to embrace the whole person and all his experiences and behavior in a serious way. From a clinical perspective, this can in some cases even be directly anti-human. This may in the worst case scenario result in the diagnosis of an individual's valuable experiences, because it cannot be understood within existing academic psychological theories.

In today's academic psychology, it may seem that the psychological "off-spring" of the theory of evolution is one of the most trend-setting perspectives. In this perspective, the individual is considered a biological robot in interaction with a mechanical environment, where the genuine "I" is absent and arrogantly dismissed.

Psychologist Astrid Bastiansen, a researcher and teacher at the Department of Psychology at The University of Oslo, has extensive experience in the research field of personality- and social psychology. I myself have had the pleasure of having her as a teacher during my studies at UiO. Bastiansen has also written a textbook in psychology with a courageous and critical look at research in academic psychology. Courageous, because she also addresses unconventional topics such as ESP research.

She points out that the absence of the ESP research, and the significance it may have on inter-personal relationships, but also for our understanding of reality and our worldview, results in a limited understanding of the human mind. Unfortunately, this is still so controversial in academic circles, that her book hardly can be seen as an application for research funding.

Psychology as an academic discipline is otherwise very young, barely 150 years old. Maybe it's in a kind of "academic puberty" (a world champion in everything). However, there are exceptions. One of the directions that can show the way forward in a more integrated and unifying perspective is developmental psychology. It does not use a one-sided mechanistic approach in the study of the human being.

Within developmental psychology, there is a relatively new and interesting direction that should be able to accommodate a more expanded perspective, at least allow for the integration of the effects of, for example NDE. I'm referring to what is called the Resilience Perspective. In addition, there is also a new direction in mainstream psychology called Positive Psychology.

Let me first give a brief description of the resilience perspective of developmental psychology, and what the very concept of resilience means. The term resilience comes from physics, and refers to an object's ability to return to its "baseline" after being stretched or bent.

It is not my intention to frighten you, but the next time you're in an airplane, set off an imaginary point of the tip of the wing against the window from your seat position. Do this before the plane takes off, and then repeat it after take-off, and finally when you are safely back on the ground. You may become a little sweaty from the observed difference.

On an Airbus, the difference level of the wingtips is more than seven meters from being on the ground to being in an airborne condition. You should be happy about that difference, the alternative is that the wings break like matches due to the great physical strain they are subjected to during the flight.

The concept of resilience has proven to be useful in identifying and describing factors that can be effective in a positive sense, in and around people who seem to withstand trauma and great stress. Stresses that just as often may cause other people to break down.

Psychological resilience research operates with three concentric levels of analysis: the individual, the family and the external network, and the interaction between them. Resilience factors can be identified at all these levels, ie there is no longer a narrowly limited search at only one level. This is in itself a step towards a more integrated psychology.

Traditionally, psychology has been over focused on pathogenesis (pathogenesis = what creates disease), and then usually attributed to only one of the above levels of analysis, often the individual itself, or only the environment.

This traditional focus thus led to the loss of a wealth of factors that may be both supportive, empowering as well as developing for a human being. Dr. Aaron Antonowsky claimed that a one-sided focus on pathogenesis results in one-sided risk research and treatment. He therefore believed that health should be seen as a dimension with pathogenesis and salutogenesis (= what creates health) as polarities. In other words, a far more positive, integrated and dynamic vantage point.

I will not elaborate on the various levels and the associated and numerous risk and resilience factors, but will rather limit myself to one resilience factor, briefly described as "meaning" in the sense; "An experience of meaning and coherence in life."

Within the clinical resilience research, it quickly became apparent that some of the positively effective factors were recurring and were almost universal. On an individual level, "meaning" was one of the most prominent.

An example is Mashego's study of young South Africans during the racial conflicts that ravaged before the fall of the apartheid regime, of which almost 90% in a local community had experienced physical political violence. This apparently without having had any particular psychological damaging effects for most of them. The young people themselves explained the experiences as meaningful, although they also perceived them as negative. The desire for freedom in a cultural context where dreams were interpreted as a supernatural contact with ancestors, and where this was perceived as supportive and protective, gave meaning to their struggle and their suffering.

Recent non-clinical research, which in developmental psychology deals more with human development throughout the course of life, has also identified a factor that is highly related to the above-mentioned resilience factor "meaning". Researchers identified a factor that they described as a religious or spiritual experience factor.

This branch of development psychological research is also a consequence of the expanded and positive focus which includes salutogenesis and resilience. Previously, developmental psychology mostly dealt with human development from conception to the completion of puberty, the rest of the life course was (brutally said) more or less described as a decline into "crapitude" with death as the final and inevitable outcome, ie not exactly a cheerful perspective.

Fortunately, both resilience and life course researchers have contributed to an incipient change in this negative, limited and limiting view of the human being. When it comes to the researchers' identification of religious or spiritual experience as an important factor for quality of life, this factor is mostly described as an elevated sense of well-being and an inner emotional calm, as well as a general satisfaction with life (Marcoen, 1994). In other words, the opposite of depression, hopelessness and meaninglessness, which are prominent elements of what is often referred to as the great the epidemic of our time, namely depression.

However, there is a big difference in how the various researchers define and measure religious or spiritual experiences. McFadden is a researcher who advocates a differentiation between a functional and a substantial definition of religion, whereas the functional is more directional with elements of external social control, and whereas the substantial mainly consists of a perceived link between a higher power and the individual.

Others believe that Spirituality as an individually experienced connection with a higher power, is both the most motivating and emotional reason for people's quest for meaning in life. However, although some of the research has focused on the individual experience, most studies have focused on the most easily measurable criteria, namely the behavioral markers that indicate religiosity, ie more in line with McFadden's functional description. The latter probably because it's less expensive, as well as much easier to conduct compared to time-consuming in-depth interviews.

However, the functional description of religiosity can have debilitating side effects that are anything but resilience-building for some, depending on the dogmas on which social control is based. It should be sufficient to mention religious oppression and stigmatization of certain races, women and non-heterosexuals.

The functional perspective as a starting point for research on religion as a resilience factor, becomes almost meaningless if one doesn't examine the same perspective also as potential harming, ie as a risk factor. Therefore, the substantial definition should be the main-subject of further research, as it is the only one that focuses on the individual' perceived experience. It goes without saying that the enormous amount of data from the NDE research should be included here.

Richard Bruvoll Jr.

APPENDIX III

ARSENOKOITÉS AND MALAKOS: MEANINGS AND CONSEQUENCES

(To be added In a later edition)

NOTES

I wish to thank Elizabeth A. Clark and Anthony Neil Whitley for assistance in the research for this chapter.

1. For a similar ideological analysis of modern interpretations of Romans 1 and homosexuality, see my "Heterosexism and the Interpretation of Romans 1:18- 32," Biblical Interpretation 3 (1995), forthcoming.
2. So most of the commentaries. See also Else Kähler, "Exegese zweier neutestamentlicher Stellen (Römer 1.18-32; 1 Korinther 6.9-11). Problem der Homophilie in medizinischer, theologischer, und juristischer Sicht, ed. Th. Bovet (Bern and T,bingen: Paul Haupt, 1965), 33; Jiirgen Becker, "Zum Problem der Homosexualität in der Bibel," ZEE 31 (1987):51.
3. William F. Orr and James Arthur Walker, I Corinthians (Garden City, N.Y.: Doubleday, 1976), 199. While not tying *arsenokoités* to *malakos* directly, Wolfgang Schrage says that the former should not be taken to refer to pederasty alone but to all homosexual relations, this on the basis of Romans 1 (Der erste Briefandie Korinther [Zurich: Benziger, 1991], 1.432). Of course, unless we can be certain that *arsenokoités* refers simply to homosexual relations in general, an appeal to Romans 1 is irrelevant.
4. "Practicing homosexuals" was suggested several years ago for a Catholic lectionary translation. I do not know if the suggestion was finally adopted or published. The arguments by John Boswell (Christianity, Social Tolerance, and Homosexuality [Chicago: University Press, 1980]), while useful

as a corrective to many overly confident claims that *arsenokoités* "of course" means a "male homosexual," are I believe flawed by overstatement and occasional interpretive errors. On the other hand, some of those arguing against Boswell seem not completely to understand his arguments, make textual mistakes of their own, and operate from uncritical linguistic assumptions (e.g., David F. Wright, "Homosexuals or Prostitutes? The Meaning of ARSENOKOITAI [1 Cor. 6:9, 1 Tim. 1:10]," VC 38 [1984]:125-53; see my comments on Wright in following notes). To enter into a detailed tit-for-tat with Boswell, Wright, or other individual treatments of the issue would result in a quagmire. I will, instead, offer my reading with an occasional note on those of others.

5. The history of the invention of "homosexuality" as a psychological, indeed medical, category is now well known. See e.g., Michel Foucault, The History of Sexuality I: An Introduction (New York: Random, 1978); and David M. Halperin, One Hundred Years of Homosexuality (New York: Routledge, 1990); for a comparison with ancient concepts see Martha Nussbaum, "Therapeutic Arguments and Structures of Desire," Differences 2 (1990):46-66, esp. 49.
6. See note 2 and William. L Petersen "Can ARSENOKOITAI Be Translated by 'Homosexuals'?" VC40 (1986):187-91.
7. David Wright, "Homosexuals or Prostitutes?" VC 38 (1984):129; Robin Scroggs, The New Testament and Homosexuality (Philadelphia: Fortress, 1983), 85-86.
8. See James Barr, The Semantics of Biblical Language (London: Oxford, 1961), 107-10.
9. Anton Vögtle, Die Tugend- und Lasterkataloge im Neuen Testament (Miinster: Aschendorffschen Buckdrockerei, 1936), 13-18; for comparative texts, see Ehrhard Kamlah, Die Form der katalogischen Parades imp Neon Testament (Tübingen: Mohr/Siebeck, 1964).
10. The dates for the document and its different sections are uncertain. This section of the oracle quotes Pseudo-Phocylides (excepting those verses in parentheses). See comments by John

J. Collins in The Old Testament Pseudepigrapha, ed. James H. Charlesworth (~rden City, N.Y.: Doubleday, 1983), 1.330.

11. Dio Chrysostom 46.8; Philostratus, Life of Apollonius 1.15.
12. Wright argues (136-38) that since Pseudo-Phocylides elsewhere shows his disapprobation of homosexual conduct, the term must here be a reference to homosexual conduct. Of course the second point does not proceed from the first.
13. I use the edition by Robert M. Grant: Ad Autolycum (Oxford: Clarendon, 1970). Wright's quotation of this passage (134-35) has a different order for the vices because he is relying on the Greek text of Gustave Bardy, Théophile d' Antioche, Trois Livres a Autolycus; Sources chrétiennes 20 (Paris: du Cerf, 1948). There seems to be no textual evidence for Bardy's version-at least he gives none in the apparatus, and no edition I have examined suggests any textual variation here among the manuscripts. Bardy admits he is mainly following the edition by J. C. T. Otto: Theophili Episcopi Antiocheni, Ad Autolycum, libri tres. Co7pus Apologetarum Christianorum Saeculi Secundi 8 (Wiesbaden: Martin Sändig, 1969; reprint of 1861). It is not clear, therefore, why he gives a different order for the vice list than do Otto and the other modem editions. Perhaps Bardy altered the order to conform more nearly to that of 1 Cor. 6:9, or he carelessly placed *arsenokoitės* after pornos because he assumed it belonged with the "sexual sins." If the latter is the case, it provides interesting evidence that the order of vices in the lists is important.
14. The term pornos would have been understood most often to refer to a male prostitute. See Jeffrey Henderson, The Maculate Muse: Obscene Language in At- tic Comedy (New Haven: Yale, 1975); Scroggs, The New Testament and Homo- sexuality, 40. Eva Cantarella takes it as such even in its occurrence in 1 Tim. 1: 1 0 (Bisexuality in the Ancient World [New Haven: Yale, 1992], 192-94). Pornos also seems to have become, at least in Jewish and Christian circles, a more general term for all sorts of persons considered "sexually immoral."

15. This reading may find support even from the position of the term in 1 Tim. 1:10, if pornoi there is taken to be a reference to male prostitutes rather than "fornicators" or sexually immoral persons in general (see Scroggs, The New Testament and Homosexuality, 118-21). Since Cantarella does read pornoi in 1 Tim. 1:10 as referring to male prostitutes and the term following *arsenokoités* as a reference to people who enslave other people in order to prostitute them (andrapodistai), I am puzzled by her insistence that *arsenokoités* in the same pas- sage cannot refer to prostitutes but must instead be a reference to male-male sex in general (see Bisexuality, 192-94). If, on the other hand, we read pornoi as referring to prostitutes, the list supports my reading of *arsenokoités*, occurring as it does between two other terms that refer to sex and economic injustice.:
16. Preparation for the Gospel 6.1 0.2 5; Die Fragmenta der griechischen Historiker, ed. .I Felix Jacoby (Leiden: Brill, 1969), vol. 3C fr. 719.
17. Ibid.; see also Die Pseudoklementinen II Rekognitionen in Rufius Übersetzung, rev. 1 ed. Bernard Rehm, earlier ed. Georg Strecker (Berlin: Akademie, 1994), 284-87.
18. I do not discuss other occurrences of the term mentioned by Boswell and Wright because I see no possibility that they shed light on the first-century meaning of *arsenokoités*. Its meaning in a ninth-century inscription, for example, is unclear, in spite of Wright's overconfident interpretation; besides, the usage is very late (Greek Anthology 9.686; see Boswell, 344, n. 22; Wright, 130). The meaning in the sixth-century "Penetential" of (perhaps) John the Faster (see Boswell, 363-65) is equally unclear. Though Wright accuses Boswell of .j "irrepressible resourcefulness" and "desperate reasoning" in this case (139-40), I find Wright's exegesis no less fanciful or strained. Such late and opaque 1 uses of the term should be set aside until we have clearer evidence about their j meaning and relation to first-century usage.'.
19. This is certainly true of the later translations of the Greek into other languages. But later translations provide little reliable

evidence for the meaning of the term in a first-century Greek contest.

20. See my The Corinthian Body (New Haven: Yale, 1995), 32-34,222,230-31, 241-42.
21. Some scholars define *malakos* as simply a synonym for kinaedos, citing texts where the two terms occur together. See, for example, Gaston Vorberg, Glossarium Eroticum (Rome: "L 'Erma," 1965), s. v. Vorberg's citations do not sup- port his definition; in every such case, kinaedos is better interpreted as constituting a subcategory within the larger category of malakoi (Diogenes Laertius, Lives 7.173) or simply another vice in a list of vices (plutarch, Moralia 88C; Vettius Valens, Anthologiae 2.37.54 [ed. David Pingree, p. 108, 1. 3]; Appendix 1.173 [p. 384, 1. 11]). I take arrLtopoios in Vettius Valens to be a reference not to homosexual sex but to oral sex-which could, of course, be performed on a man or a woman (see Artemidorus, Dream Handbook 1.79). No text I have found equates *malakos* with kinaedos or defines one term by the other. Note the list of terms for "fucked men" from Attic comedy: Henderson, Maculate Muse 209-15,222; *malakos* is not among them.
22. Plutarch, Gaius Gracchus 4.4; Cicero 7.5; Athenaeus 565E. Scroggs (The New Testament and Homosexuality, 42, n. 45) misuses such references to argue that dressing like a *malakos* would signal that someone was a kinaedos, and therefore *malakos* meant an "effeminate call boy." This ignores the fact that *malakos* more often occurs where neither homosexual sex nor prostitution per se is involved.
23. Hellenica 3.4.19; 6. 1.6; Apology 19; Memorabilia 1.2.2. Note that in this last case, the reference to *malakos* relates to work, and it follows a reference to sex (aphrodisiac akrateis); *malakos* here has nothing to do with sex.
24. Epictetus 3.6.9; 4.1.25; "Epistle of Crates" 19 (Malherbe, p. 68); "Epistle of Diogenes" 29 (Malherbe, p. 126): in both cases, sleeping and eating too much are important.
25. Dio Cassius 58.4.6; Plutarch, Pericles 27.4; Josephus, War 6.211, Antiquities 19.197.

26. Xenophon, Hiero 1.23; Plutarch, Moralia 831B; 136B; Pericles 27.4; Athenaeus, Deipnosophistae 12.536C; 543B.1n one of Philo's condemnations of decadence, he includes remarks about penetrated men as being thus made effeminate (On Abraham, 133-36). The term *malakos*, however, is used of this entire process of degenerating decadence and effeminacy due to luxurious living-including the effeminacy of heterosexual sex; the aspects of homosexual sex play only one part.
27. In Dionysius Halicamassus, Roman Antiquities 7.2.4, people cannot tell whether a ruler earned the sobriquet "*malakos*" because he had allowed himself to be penetrated as a young man or because he possessed an exceptionally mild nature.
28. The "softness of the Lydians" (ta Lydon malaka) is reflected in their luxurious living, gourmet food, use of too many female prostitutes, and lots of indiscriminate sex with men and women (Athenaeus, Deipnosophistae 12.540F). Plutarch relates the "Lydian mode" in music to softness and general decadence: Moralia 83F.
29. Note a similar assumption mentioned by Athenaeus; the Syracusans are re- ported as forbidding women to wear gold or colorful clothing unless they confess to being prostitutes; similarly, men were not allowed to "dress up" unless they admitted to being either adulterers or kinaedoi (Deipnosophistae 12.521b).

    Dressing up was considered effeminate, but that could mean an attempt to attract either men or women.
30. The suitors of a young girl arrive at her door adorned with long hair styled prettily (Athenaeus, Deipnosophistae 528d, citing Agathon, Thyestes). This entire section of Athenaeus is instructive for the ancient concept of effeminacy; it usually is related to luxurious and decadent living in general and is expressed far more often here by heterosexual activities than homosexual. For example, the Lydians, according to Clearchus, expressed their effeminacy by laying out parks with lots of shade, gathering the wives and virgins of other men and raping them, and then finally adopting "the manner of life of women,"

whatever that means (Deipnosophistae 12.515e-516a). There is no mention here of homosexual sex.

31. This point was made by John Boswell (Christianity, Social Tolerance, and Homo- sexuality, 340) but generally ignored by biblical scholars, who continue naively to assume that any concern about effeminacy would involve at least an unconscious anxiety about homosexuality. Thus, Paul's concerns about long hair on men in 1 Corinthians 11 must harbor a concern about homosexuality. See Scroggs, "Paul and the Eschatological Woman," The Text and the Times (Minneapolis: Fortress, 1993), 88, n. 38; originally in JAAR 40 (1972): 283-303; The New Testament and Homosexuality (Philadelphia: Fortress, 1983), 53-55, 62-65; Jerome Murphy-O'Connor, "Sex and Logic in I Corinthians 11:2-16," CBQ 42 (1980): 482-500.
32. For a character in Achilles Tatius's novel Clitophon and Leucippe, male love is natural, frank, real, and lacking in any softness or effeminacy (2.38; ou malthassei). Even Dio Chrysostom, no advocate of male-male love, knows that love of a woman is liable to be thought excessively feminine (7.151-52).
33. Noted also by Scroggs, The New Testament and Homosexuality, 46-48.
34. The degradation of the female comes to be linked with asceticism in general, especially but not exclusively in Jewish and Christian writers. Philo praises women who give up sex entirely, thereby becoming "manly," and Thecla, through celibacy, becomes masculinized and saved (On the Contemplative Life, 40-64; see Richard A. Baer, Jr., Philo's Use of the Categories Male and Female [Leiden: Brill, 1970],99-100; Acts of Paul and Thecla).
35. A common practice among New Testament scholars has been to define *malakos* as the "passive partner" due to its proximity to *arsenokoités*, which is taken to be the "active partner" (see, e.g., Gordon Fee, First Epistle to the Corinthians [Grand Rapids: Eerdmans, 1987],243-44). But this is circular reasoning. The meaning of *arsenokoités* is famously problematic, and there is no evidence that it was a special term for the "active" partner in homosexual sex (even if one concedes, which I do not, that

it is a reference to "men who sleep with men"). Furthermore, while there is no evidence that *malakos* was considered a special ("technical") term for the "passive" partner (as Fee admits), its general meaning as "effeminate" independent of sexual position or object is easily demonstrated. To define *malakos* by *arsenokoités* is to define something already clear by something that is obscure.

36. Every text cited by Scroggs in support of this reading, in his terminology "effeminate call boy" (The New Testament and Homosexuality), is better read as I have-by being penetrated, a boy shows his effeminacy, but *malakos* refers to the effeminacy, not the penetration; there were many other signs, many heterosexual, that could also reveal "effeminacy."
37. The list, of course, could be expanded. This is taken mainly from H. Herter, "Effeminatus," Reallexikon für Antike und Christentum (Stuttgart: Hiersemann, 1959),4.620-650; for the associations of hair with effeminacy and decadence, see also Pseudo-Phocylides, Sentences 210-12, and the commentary by P. W. van der Horst, The Sentences of Pseudo-Phocylides (Leaden: Brill, 1978),250; Hubert Cancel, Untersuchungen zur lyrischen Kunst des P. Papianus Statius, Spudasmota 13 (Hildesheim: Olms, 1965), 58. For masturbation as evidence of malakia, see Vorberg, Glossarium Eroticum s.v.
38. I say this to forestall one possible objection to my method. One might argue that although *malakos* and *arsenokoités* did not mean, in the common linguistic currency, the "passive" and "active" partners in homosexual sex, that was surely what Paul intended by his use of the terms. The goal of translation, however, is to translate the text, not some guessed-at authorial intention. See Ferdinand Deist, "Presuppositions and Contextual Bible Translation,"]NSL 19 (1993): 13-23, esp. 19-20. Furthermore, contrary to some assumptions of modernist historiography, the scripture for the church is traditionally the text, not a historically reconstructed authorial intention. Thus we translate and interpret not what Paul meant to say but what he said.

"SEX, LIES & PHONECALLS"

(To be adden In a later edition)

THE INTERNET: INTERNATIONAL RESOURCES AND ORGANIZATIONS

https://no.wikipedia.org/wiki/Friseksualitet

www.freesexual.org

https://www.facebook.com/TRAX-395406827265552/

https://www.kinseyinstitute.org/

https://www.iands.org/

http://www.nderf.org/

The Gospel of Thomas: http://gnosis.org/naghamm/gosthom.html

BIBLIOGRAPHY

The numbering of the sources starts from 1 in each new chapter

Chapter 1

(1) http://www.dramandaforeman.com/documentaries/
(2) https://en.wikipedia.org/wiki/%C3%87atalh%C3%B6y%C3%BCk
(3) https://alumni.stanford.edu/get/page/magazine/article/?article_id=68851
(4) https://www.dhushara.com/paradoxhtm/fall.htm
(5) Langfeldt, Thore. (2005). «Erotikk og fundamentalisme, fra Mesopotamia til kvinnefronten». Oslo: Universitetsforlaget. S-13, 14
(6) Langfeldt, Thore. (2005). «Erotikk og fundamentalisme, fra Mesopotamia til kvinnefronten». Oslo: Universitetsforlaget. S-15
(7) http://www.thefreelibrary.com/How+gay+was+Gilgamesh%3F-a0133947653
(8) http://www.britishmuseum.org/explore/themes/same-sex_desire_and_gender/same-sex_desire.aspx#1
(9) http://www.dramandaforeman.com/documentaries/
(10) https://no.wikipedia.org/wiki/hjul
(11) https://snl.no/Sumer
(12) Langfeldt, Thore. (2005). «Erotikk og fundamentalisme, fra Mesopotamia til kvinnefronten». Oslo: Universitetsforlaget. S-15
(13) http://www.dramandaforeman.com/documentaries/
(14) https://no.wikipedia.org/wiki/Akhnaton
(15) Langfeldt, Thore. (2005). «Erotikk og fundamentalisme, fra Mesopotamia til kvinnefronten». Oslo: Universitetsforlaget. S-21
(16) Langfeldt, Thore. (2005). «Erotikk og fundamentalisme, fra Mesopotamia til kvinnefronten». Oslo: Universitetsforlaget. S-20, 21
(17) Gregg Braden. (2012). "Deep Truth". Hay House; 1 edition
(18) Platon. (1988). "Drikkegildet i Athen". Oslo: Dreyers Forlag A/S. Pausanias tale. S-39

(19) Platon. (1988). "Drikkegildet i Athen". Oslo: Dreyers Forlag A/S
(20) Endsjø, Dag Øistein. (2009). «Sex og religion». Oslo: Universitetsforlaget. S-98, 99
(21) «Greek Homosexuality» http://www.livius.org/ho-hz/homosexuality/homosexuality.html
(22) http://www.androphile.org/preview/Library/Biographies/Alexander/Alexander.htm
(23) http://www.androphile.org/preview/Library/Biographies/Alexander/Alexander.htm
(24) Dr Karl Evang. (1951). «Seksuell opplysning». Oslo: Tiden Norsk Forlag. S-331
(25) Endsjø, Dag Øistein. (2009). «Sex og religion». Oslo: Universitetsforlaget. S-99
(26) http://listverse.com/2013/08/06/10-fascinating-facts-about-the-samurai/
(27) Finn Jor. (2002). «Vær sterk, historien om Sokrates og Xantippe». Oslo: Pantagruel. S-66, 207

Chapter 2

(1) Caplex-2007
(2) Langfeldt, Thore. (2005). «Erotikk og fundamentalisme, fra Mesopotamia til kvinnefronten». Oslo: Universitetsforlaget. S-24
(3) Langfeldt, Thore. (2005). «Erotikk og fundamentalisme, fra Mesopotamia til kvinnefronten». Oslo: Universitetsforlaget. S-24
(4) Langfeldt, Thore. (2005). «Erotikk og fundamentalisme, fra Mesopotamia til kvinnefronten». Oslo: Universitetsforlaget. S-24, 25
(5) Caplex-2007
(6) http://www.psychologistanywhereanytime.com/disorders_psychologist_and_psychologists/psychologist_multiple_personaility_disorder.htm
(7) Langfeldt, Thore. (2005). «Erotikk og fundamentalisme, fra Mesopotamia til kvinnefronten». Oslo: Universitetsforlaget. S-25
(8) Langfeldt, Thore. (2005). «Erotikk og fundamentalisme, fra Mesopotamia til kvinnefronten». Oslo: Universitetsforlaget. S-27
(9) Kolbein Falkeid. (1969). Etymologisk kart over byheiene i Haugesund.
(10) http://ansatte.uit.no/rune.hagen/nnhekser.htm
(11) Langfeldt, Thore. (2005). «Erotikk og fundamentalisme, fra Mesopotamia til kvinnefronten». Oslo: Universitetsforlaget. S-28
(12) Endsjø, Dag Øistein. (2009). «Sex og religion». Oslo: Universitetsforlaget. S-21
(13) Raymond A. Moody Jr. (1988). «Lyset bortenfor». Oslo: Aventure Forlag. S-110

(14) Endsjø, Dag Øistein. (2009). «Sex og religion». Oslo: Universitetsforlaget S-143, 144
(15) Endsjø, Dag Øistein. (2009). «Sex og religion». Oslo: Universitetsforlaget S-150

Chapter 3

(1) Endsjø, Dag Øistein. (2009). «Sex og religion». Oslo: Universitetsforlaget. S-13
(2) https://www.britannica.com/topic/Ten-Commandments
(3) The Council of Hippo - 393 e.Kr (Nikea Konsilet)
(4) "The Nag Hammadi Scriptures: The Revised and Updated Translation of Sacred Gnostic Texts" Complete in One Volume Paperback – May 26, 2009 by Marvin W. Meyer (Editor), Elaine H. Pagels (Introduction) "The Gospel of Thomas With The Greek Gospel of Thomas" S-133
(5) The Nag Hammadi Scriptures. (2009). S-137
(6) Endsjø, Dag Øistein. (2009). «Sex og religion». Oslo: Universitetsforlaget. S-128
(7) http://www.tv2.no/a/5748491/
(8) Dr Karl Evang. (1951). «Seksuell opplysning». Oslo: Tiden Norsk Forlag. S-333
(9) Tom Ovlien. Homofili og psykisk helse. 2001. Oslo: Rådet for psykisk helse.
(10) Endsjø, Dag Øistein. (2009). «Sex og religion». Oslo: Universitetsforlaget. S-113
(11) http://www.psykologtidsskriftet.no/index.php?seks_id=120649&a=3

Chapter 4

(1) https://en.wikipedia.org/wiki/Modern_history
(2) Langfeldt, Thore. (2005). «Erotikk og fundamentalisme, fra Mesopotamia til kvinne-fronten». Oslo: Universitetsforlaget. S-33
(3) http://www.telegraph.co.uk/culture/books/3591661/On-the-one-hand-.-.-.-and-on-the-other.html
(4) Notat fra forelesning av Thore Langfeldt. (2008). Sexologi-utdannelsen ved Uia.
(5) Langfeldt, Thore. (2005). «Erotikk og fundamentalisme, fra Mesopotamia til kvinne-fronten». Oslo: Universitetsforlaget. S-35, 36
(6) Langfeldt, Thore. (2005). «Erotikk og fundamentalisme, fra Mesopotamia til kvinne-fronten». Oslo: Universitetsforlaget. S-35, 36

(7) Langfeldt, Thore. (2005). «Erotikk og fundamentalisme, fra Mesopotamia til kvinne-fronten». Oslo: Universitetsforlaget. S-27
(8) Langfeldt, Thore. (2005). «Erotikk og fundamentalisme, fra Mesopotamia til kvinne-fronten». Oslo: Universitetsforlaget. S-37
(9) Alan P. Bell, Sue Kiefer Hammersmith, Martin S. Weinberg. (1982). «Heterofili – Homofili» Kinsey-rapporten om seksuell orientering og partnervalg. Oslo: Universitetsforlaget. S-117
(10) Engler, Barbara. (2014). «Personality Theories. An Introduction». USA: Wadsworth. S-188
(11) https://www.dagbladet.no/magasinet/onaniens-historie/66007905
(12) Langfeldt, Thore. (2005). «Erotikk og fundamentalisme, fra Mesopotamia til kvinne-fronten». Oslo: Universitetsforlaget. S-40, 41
(13) Kimmel, Michael S. (2004). «The Gendered Society». New York: Oxford University Press. S-61, 62
(14) Langfeldt, Thore. (2005). «Erotikk og fundamentalisme, fra Mesopotamia til kvinne-fronten». Oslo: Universitetsforlaget. S-35
(15) https://www.dagbladet.no/magasinet/onaniens-historie/66007905
(16) http://edition.cnn.com/2005/US/07/18/cnn25.tan.elders/index.html

Chapter 5

(1) Dr Karl Evang. (1951). «Seksuell opplysning». Oslo: Tiden Norsk Forlag. Etterskrift S- 661
(2) https://no.wikipedia.org/wiki/Friseksualitet
(3) https://en.wikipedia.org/wiki/Homophobia
(4) www.freesexual.org
(5) http://people.ucalgary.ca/~ptrembla/homosexuality-suicide/04-kurt-cobain-god-gay.htm
(6) Langfeldt, Thore. (2005). «Erotikk og fundamentalisme, fra Mesopotamia til kvinne-fronten». Oslo: Universitetsforlaget. S-58, 59
(7) Langfeldt, Thore. (2005). «Erotikk og fundamentalisme, fra Mesopotamia til kvinne-fronten». Oslo: Universitetsforlaget. S-58, 59
(8) Langfeldt, Thore. (2005). «Erotikk og fundamentalisme, fra Mesopotamia til kvinne-fronten». Oslo: Universitetsforlaget. S-58, 59
(9) Langfeldt, Thore. (2005). «Erotikk og fundamentalisme, fra Mesopotamia til kvinne-fronten». Oslo: Universitetsforlaget. S-64, 65
(10) Langfeldt, Thore. (2005). «Erotikk og fundamentalisme, fra Mesopotamia til kvinne-fronten». Oslo: Universitetsforlaget. S-64, 65
(11) Langfeldt, Thore. (2005). «Erotikk og fundamentalisme, fra Mesopotamia til kvinne-fronten». Oslo: Universitetsforlaget. S-64, 65

(12) Langfeldt, Thore. (2005). «Erotikk og fundamentalisme, fra Mesopotamia til kvinne-fronten». Oslo: Universitetsforlaget. S-64, 65
(13) Caplex-2007
(14) Langfeldt, Thore. (2005). «Erotikk og fundamentalisme, fra Mesopotamia til kvinne-fronten». Oslo: Universitetsforlaget. S-67
(15) Langfeldt, Thore. (2005). «Erotikk og fundamentalisme, fra Mesopotamia til kvinne-fronten». Oslo: Universitetsforlaget. S-67

Chapter 6

(1) Langfeldt, Thore. (2005). «Erotikk og fundamentalisme, fra Mesopotamia til kvinne-fronten». Oslo: Universitetsforlaget. S-65
(2) Langfeldt, Thore. (2005). «Erotikk og fundamentalisme, fra Mesopotamia til kvinne-fronten». Oslo: Universitetsforlaget. S-62
(3) Engler, Barbara. (2014). «Personality Theories. An Introduction». USA: Wadsworth. S 41
(4) Langfeldt, Thore. (2005). «Erotikk og fundamentalisme, fra Mesopotamia til kvinne-fronten». Oslo: Universitetsforlaget. S-75, 81
(5) http://www.theguardian.com/world/2001/oct/07/books.booksnews
(6) https://en.wikipedia.org/wiki/Lothar_Machtan
(7) Bastiansen, Astid. (2003). «Den tusende dråpe. På sporet av en humanistisk sosial-psykologi». Oslo: Pax Forlag. S-214, 215
(8) Langfeldt, Thore. (2005). «Erotikk og fundamentalisme, fra Mesopotamia til kvinne-fronten». Oslo: Universitetsforlaget. S-80, 81

Chapter 7

(1) Ernulf, Innala.(1992).Psykologotidningen.Nr18,s.14
(2) Engler, Barbara. (2014). «Personality Theories. An Introduction». UK: Cengage. S-6, 8, 9
(3) http://www.intropsych.com/ch12_abnormal/defining_abnormal_behavior.html
(4) http://arkivverket.no/manedens/mai2003/hovedside.html
(5) http://universitas.no/magasin/56422/hol-i-huet-pa-gaustad
(6) http://www.dagbladet.no/2010/03/19/kultur/debatt/debattinnlegg/hjernevask/homofili/10907423/
(7) http://www.aftenposten.no/meninger/debatt/Overgrepet-mot-taterne-6360190.html
(8) https://en.wikipedia.org/wiki/Ant%C3%B3nio_Egas_Moniz

Chapter 8

(1) https://www.gaysir.no/artikkel.cfm?CID=13271
(2) http://www.dalchowsverden.no/be.html
(3) Egidius: Psykologisk leksikon. S.218, 456
(4) Money, John. (1988). "Gay Straight and Inbetween. The Sexology of Erotic Orientation". New York: Oxford University Press. S-123
(5) Hamer/Copeland, psych. cornell. edu/dbem,nett
(6) Kimmel, Michael S. (2004). «The Gendered Society». New York: Oxford University Press. S-35, 37, 38
(7) Kimmel, Michael S. (2004). «The Gendered Society». New York: Oxford University Press. S-35, 37, 38
(8) Kimmel, Michael S. (2004). «The Gendered Society». New York: Oxford University Press. S-35, 37, 38
(9) Kimmel, Michael S. (2004). «The Gendered Society». New York: Oxford University Press. S-43
(10) Kimmel, Michael S. (2004). «The Gendered Society». New York: Oxford University Press. S-50)
(11) Bastiansen, Astid. (2003). «Den tusende dråpe. På sporet av en humanistisk sosial-psykologi». Oslo: Pax Forlag. S-13
(12) Bukatko, Danuta. Daehler, Marwin W. (1998). "Child Development" Boston: Hougthon Mifflin. S-93
(13) Bukatko, Danuta. Daehler, Marwin W. (1998). "Child Development" Boston: Hougthon Mifflin. S-86
(14) Bukatko, Danuta. Daehler, Marwin W. (Scarr & McCartney) (1998). "Child Development" Boston: Hougthon Mifflin. S-88
(15) Alan P. Bell, Sue Kiefer Hammersmith, Martin S. Weinberg. (1982). «Heterofili – Homofili» Kinsey-rapporten om seksuell orientering og partnervalg. Oslo: Universitetsforlaget. S-6, 59, 117
(16) http://dbem.ws/Exotic%20Becomes%20Erotic.pdf
(17) http://dbem.ws/APA%20Address.pdf
(18) http://dbem.ws/Exotic%20Becomes%20Erotic.pdf
(19) http://dbem.ws/APA%20Address.pdf
(20) Impuls nr. 3 1999. (Tidskrift for psykologi-studenter ved UiO)
(21) Kimmel, Michael S. (2004). «The Gendered Society». New York: Oxford University Press. S-254
(22) https://www.enotes.com/research-starters/cooley-looking-glass-self
(23) https://en.wikipedia.org/wiki/Looking_glass_self
(24) Scheff, Thomas W. (1994). "Microsociology. Discourse, Emotion and Social Structure". Chicago Press. S-122

(25) Adams, H. E., Wright, L. W., & Lohr, B. A, (1996). Is homophobia associated with homosexual arousal? Journal of Abnormal Psychology, 105, 440-445.
(26) https://www.psychologytoday.com/files/u47/Henry_et_al.pdf
(27) Journal of Abnormal Psychology 1983. Vol. 92, No. 1, 49-54
(28) http://psycnet.apa.org/journals/psp/102/4/815/
(29) Money, John. (1988). "Gay Straight and Inbetween The Sexology of Erotic Orientation". New York: Oxford University Press. S-110
(30) http://www.ranker.com/list/top-10-anti-gay-activists-caught-being-gay/joanne
(31) Bastiansen, Astid. (2003). «Den tusende dråpe. På sporet av en humanistisk sosial-psykologi». Oslo: Pax Forlag. S-123
(32) Gardiner, Harry W. Kosmitzki, Corinne. (2002). "Lives Across Cultures". Boston: Allyn and Bacon. S-11
(33) Gardiner, Harry W. Kosmitzki, Corinne. (2002). "Lives Across Cultures". Boston: Allyn and Bacon. S-20
(34) https://www.simplypsychology.org/asch-conformity.html
(35) Gardiner, Harry W. Kosmitzki, Corinne. (2002). "Lives Across Cultures". Boston: Allyn and Bacon. S-22, 25
(36) Bastiansen, Astid. (2003). «Den tusende dråpe. På sporet av en humanistisk sosial-psykologi». Oslo: Pax Forlag. S-33, 71, 73
(37) Nova-rapporten. (1999). S-33
(38) http://nova.no/asset/6857/1/6857_1.pdf

Chapter 9

(1) http://www.explainthatstuff.com/suicideinyoungpeople.html
(2) https://www.thetrevorproject.org/resources/preventing-suicide/facts-about-suicide/#sm.00000btjs9556fec6rnuozyi4hqmi
(3) Duckitt Psy 2100 Kopisamling. UiO
(4) Duckitt, Psy 2100 kopisamling. UiO. S-80
(5) Bukatko, Danuta. Daehler, Marwin W. (1998). "Child Development" Boston: Hougthon Mifflin. S-344
(6) psychology.ucdavis.edu
(7) Hellquist, Gens "It's a Strange, Strange World." Perceptions Vol. 15 Jan. 29, 1997, pp6-7
(8) http://www.dagbladet.no/magasinet/2006/07/27/472414.html
(9) AAUW. American Association University Women
(10) http://.no.wikipedia.org/wiki/J. Edgar Hoover
(11) http://www.bbc.com/news/magazine-25142557

(12) http://www.dagbladet.no/2014/11/24/nyheter/utenriks/homofili/36390087/
(13) http://www.christianitytoday.com/gleanings/2013/june/alan-chambers-apologizes-to-gay-community-exodus.html
(14) http://www.huffingtonpost.com/2013/04/25/john-paulk-ex-gay-therapy-apology_n_3155536.html
(15) http://edition.cnn.com/2009/US/01/29/lkl.ted.haggard/
(16) https://www.youtube.com/watch?v=qkWcT9CVOrs
(17) Endsjø, Dag Øistein. (2009). «Sex og religion». Oslo: Universitetsforlaget. S-166
(18) https://en.wikipedia.org/wiki/Hell_house
(19) https://en.wikipedia.org/wiki/Rosa_Parks
(20) https://en.wikipedia.org/wiki/Claudette_Colvin

Part III The Postmodern Era - A New Order – The Way Forward

(1) https://www.nrk.no/hordaland/xl/platesjappen-som-svommer-mot-strommen-1.12955501
(2) Diamendis, Peter H. Kotler, Steven. (2012). "Abundance" New York: Free Press. S-53
(3) https://no.wikipedia.org/wiki/Verdens_befolkning

Chapter 10

(1) Bolsø.2006. Forskning.no
(2) Skårderud, Finn. (2008). «Uro». Oslo: H. Aschehoug & Co. S-133, 135, 137, 139
(3) http://www.telegraph.co.uk/news/2016/06/14/orlando-gunman-was-a-regular-at-lgbt-nightclub-pulse-before-atta/
(4) http://www.dagbladet.no/kultur/panikk-for-egne-homofile-folelser/60238435
(5) Dagblader Fredag 12'August 2011 S- 6, 7, 8
(6) http://www.aftenposten.no/kultur/Knausgard---At-han-er-homoseksuell-er-Breiviks-hemmelighet-149432b.html
(7) «Vi trenger en kjønnsfrigjøring» Hanna Helseth Dagbladet 21.06 2006

Chapter 11

(1) Dawes, Robyn M. (1996). "House of Cards. Psychology and Psychoterapy Built on Myth". New York: The Free Press. S-135, 136
(2) https://en.wikipedia.org/wiki/Rosenhan_experiment

Chapter 12

(1) http://www.barnebokkritikk.no/disse-trange-kjonnsrollene/#.WKN-64WcHIU
(2) Bjerrum Nielsen, Harriet. Rudberg, Monica. (1989). «Historien om jenter og gutter. Kjønnsosialisering i et utviklingspsykologisk perspektiv». Oslo: Universitetsforlaget. S-9, 12, 13,14
(3) Bjerrum Nielsen, Harriet. Rudberg, Monica. (1989). «Historien om jenter og gutter. Kjønnsosialisering i et utviklingspsykologisk perspektiv». Oslo: Universitetsforlaget. S-12, 16
(4) Bjerrum Nielsen, Harriet. Rudberg, Monica. (1989). «Historien om jenter og gutter. Kjønnsosialisering i et utviklingspsykologisk perspektiv». Oslo: Universitetsforlaget. S-13
(5) Bjerrum Nielsen, Harriet. Rudberg, Monica. (1989). «Historien om jenter og gutter. Kjønnsosialisering i et utviklingspsykologisk perspektiv». Oslo: Universitetsforlaget. S-14
(6) Engler, Barbara. (1995/2014). «Personality Theories. An Introduction». UK: Cengage. S-183
(7) Geels, Anton. Wikstrøm, Owe. (1999). "Den religiøsa Menneskan: En introduktion till religions psykologin". Natur & Kultur Akademisk. S-403
(8) Geels, Anton. Wikstrøm, Owe. (1999). "Den religiøsa Menneskan: En introduktion till religions psykologin". Natur & Kultur Akademisk. S-414
(9) Geels, Anton. Wikstrøm, Owe. (1999). "Den religiøsa Menneskan: En introduktion till religions psykologin". Natur & Kultur Akademisk. S-404
(10) https://www.britannica.com/topic/defense-mechanism#ref195659
(11) Bjerrum Nielsen, Harriet. Rudberg, Monica. (1989). «Historien om jenter og gutter. Kjønnsosialisering i et utviklingspsykologisk perspektiv». Oslo: Universitetsforlaget. S-16
(12) Bjerrum Nielsen, Harriet. Rudberg, Monica. (1989). «Historien om jenter og gutter. Kjønnsosialisering i et utviklingspsykologisk perspektiv». Oslo: Universitetsforlaget. S-31
(13) «Nå skal gutta på kjønnsrollekurs» Dagbladet Tirsdag 5. Oktober 2004
(14) https://www.regjeringen.no/contentassets/838b18a31b0e4b31bbfa61336560f269/ungdomshelsestrategi_2016.pdf

(15) http://www.vg.no/forbruker/helse/sex-og-samliv/halvparten-av-unge-jenter-har-hatt-uoensket-sex/a/532021/
(16) «Sex uten grenser» VG 20.08.2016. Journalister: Maria Knoph Vigsnes, Kari Spets og Christina Quist.
(17) Leder i Haugesunds Avis 19.08. 2009
(18) Kimmel, Michael S. (2004). «The Gendered Society». New York: Oxford University Press. S-179

Chapter 13

(1) https://www.brainpickings.org/2009/12/11/pink-and-blue-project/
(2) Kimmel, Michael S. (2004). «The Gendered Society». New York: Oxford University Press. S-2
(3) Kimmel, Michael S. (2004). «The Gendered Society». New York: Oxford University Press. S-24
(4) Kimmel, Michael S. (2004). «The Gendered Society». New York: Oxford University Press. S-160)
(5) Kimmel, Michael S. (2004). «The Gendered Society». New York: Oxford University Press. S-11
(6) Kimmel, Michael S. (2004). «The Gendered Society». New York: Oxford University Press. S-11
(7) http://forskning.no/hjernen-kjonn-og-samfunn-psykologi/2012/09/hjerneforskning-beviser-ikke-kjonnsforskjeller
(8) https://faculty.washington.edu/eloftus/Articles/sciam.htm
(9) Schwartz, Pepper & Rutter, Virginia. (1998). «The Gender of Sexuality» London: Fine Forge Press. S-26
(10) Schwartz, Pepper & Rutter, Virginia. (1998). «The Gender of Sexuality» London: Fine Forge Press. S-28
(11) Schwartz, Pepper & Rutter, Virginia. (1998). «The Gender of Sexuality» London: Fine Forge Press. S-28
(12) Schwartz, Pepper & Rutter, Virginia. (1998). «The Gender of Sexuality» London: Fine Forge Press. S-28
(13) Schwartz, Pepper & Rutter, Virginia. (1998). «The Gender of Sexuality» London: Fine Forge Press. S-30
(14) https://no.wikipedia.org/wiki/Kinsey-skalaen
(15) Schwartz, Pepper & Rutter, Virginia. (1998). «The Gender of Sexuality» London: Fine Forge Press. S-194
(16) http://www.arthaus.no/kommer/article949561.ece
(17) Bjørk Matheasdatter, Dagbladet Magasinet, 30.08. 2014

Chapter 14

(1) Bjerrum Nielsen, Harriet. Rudberg, Monica. (1989). «Historien om jenter og gutter. Kjønnsosialisering i et utviklingspsykologisk perspektiv». Oslo: Universitetsforlaget. S-11

(2) Schwartz, Pepper & Rutter, Virginia. (1998). «The Gender of Sexuality» London: Fine Forge Press. S-2, 4, 5

(3) Schwartz, Pepper & Rutter, Virginia. (1998). «The Gender of Sexuality» London: Fine Forge Press. S-2, 4, 5

(4) Schwartz, Pepper & Rutter, Virginia. (1998). «The Gender of Sexuality» London: Fine Forge Press. S-2, 4, 5

(5) Kimmel, Michael S. (2004). «The Gendered Society». New York: Oxford University Press. S-53, 54

(6) Kimmel, Michael S. (2004). «The Gendered Society». New York: Oxford University Press. S-53, 54

(7) Kimmel, Michael S. (2004). «The Gendered Society». New York: Oxford University Press. S-231

(8) Kimmel, Michael S. (2004). «The Gendered Society». New York: Oxford University Press.S-69

(9) Kimmel, Michael S. (2004). «The Gendered Society». New York: Oxford University Press. S-25

(10) Kimmel, Michael S. (2004). «The Gendered Society». New York: Oxford University Press. S-12

(11) Kimmel, Michael S. (2004). «The Gendered Society». New York: Oxford University Press. S-25

(12) Kimmel, Michael S. (2004). «The Gendered Society». New York: Oxford University Press. S-27

(13) Engler, Barbara. (1995/2014). «Personality Theories. An Introduction». UK: Cengage. S-9

(14) Kimmel, Michael S. (2004). «The Gendered Society». New York: Oxford University Press. S-29

(15) Kimmel, Michael S. (2004). «The Gendered Society». New York: Oxford University Press. S-280

(16) Dagbladet. 2003, 22. juni. Kjønnsforskning og biologi. Inger Nordal

(17) Schwartz, Pepper & Rutter, Virginia. (1998). «The Gender of Sexuality» London: Fine Forge Press. S-14

(18) Schwartz, Pepper & Rutter, Virginia. (1998). «The Gender of Sexuality» London: Fine Forge Press. S-21, 22, 23

(19) Schwartz, Pepper & Rutter, Virginia. (1998). «The Gender of Sexuality» London: Fine Forge Press. S-21, 22, 23

(20) Schwartz, Pepper & Rutter, Virginia. (1998). «The Gender of Sexuality» London: Fine Forge Press. S-21, 22, 23
(21) Schwartz, Pepper & Rutter, Virginia. (1998). «The Gender of Sexuality» London: Fine Forge Press. S-25
(22) Kimmel, Michael S. (2004). «The Gendered Society». New York: Oxford University Press. S-266
(23) Schwartz, Pepper & Rutter, Virginia. (1998). «The Gender of Sexuality» London: Fine Forge Press. S-26
(24) Allgeier, Elisabeth Rice. Allgeier, Albert Richard. (2000). "Sexual Interactions". Boston: Hougthon Mifflin Company. S-135
(25) https://www.tu.no/artikler/einstine-er-hun-mulig/264405
(26) Kimmel, Michael S. (2004). «The Gendered Society». New York: Oxford University Press. S-257
(27) Kimmel, Michael S. (2004). «The Gendered Society». New York: Oxford University Press. S-215

Chapter 15

(1) Almås, Elsa. (2004). «Sex og Sexologi». Oslo: Universitetsforlaget. Innledningen
(2) Forelesninga-ElsaAlmås-UiA2007
(3) Wolf, Fred Alan.(1989). "Taking The Quantumleap". New York: Harper & Row Publishers. S-123,124
(4) Pirelli Benestad, Esben Esther & Almås, Elsa. (2001). "Kjønn i bevegelse". Oslo: Universitetsforlaget.S-111,112
(5) Pirelli Benestad, Esben Esther & Almås, Elsa. (2001). "Kjønn i bevegelse". Oslo: Universitetsforlaget.S-111,112
(6) https://facultystaff.richmond.edu/~bmayes/pdf/dsmiii.pdf
(7) Renshon, S., Duckitt, J. (2000). "Political Psychology, Cultural and Crosscultural Foundations". Palgrave Macmillan. "The political culture of state authoritarianism": Jos D. Meloen-S-112,113
(8) https://spssi.onlinelibrary.wiley.com/doi/abs/10.1111/j.1540-4560.1981.tb01068.x
(9) Langfeldt, Thore. (2005). «Erotikk og fundamentalisme, fra Mesopotamia til kvinne-fronten».Oslo:Universitetsforlaget.S-112
(10) Artikkelen: "Fordeler for et ikke-homofobisk samfunn i et antropolgisk perspektiv".1992: S-257,272
(11) Endsjø, Dag Øistein. (2009). «Sex og religion». Oslo: Universitetsforlaget. S-118

Chapter 16

(1) http://kjonnsforskning.no/nb/2011/11/gir-trange-rammer-menn
(2) Redd Barna Magasinet - Nr 1 2016. S-48, 49
(3) Langfeldt, Thore. (2005). «Erotikk og fundamentalisme, fra Mesopotamia til kvinne-fronten».Oslo:Universitetsforlaget, S-130
(4) Langfeldt, Thore. (2005). «Erotikk og fundamentalisme, fra Mesopotamia til kvinne-fronten».Oslo:Universitetsforlaget.S-112
(5) http://www.dagbladet.no/kultur/folk-over-hele-verden-klikker-pa-denne-norske-katta-fra-1987/68528411?userhash=b6975c2601fccc73b682a4e250a93df1&utm_source=Communicator&utm_medium=Email&utm_content=Tittel2&utm_campaign=DagbladetPluss_AutoNB
(6) Langfeldt, Thore. (2005). «Erotikk og fundamentalisme, fra Mesopotamia til kvinne-fronten».Oslo:Universitetsforlaget.S-133
(7) http://www.bbc.com/news/health-40410459?SThisFB
(8) Agnes, Ravatne.Dagbladet13.Desember.2014.S-53
(9) https://www.ssb.no/utdanning/statistikker/barnehager/aar-endelige/2016-04-20
(10) http://www.bbc.com/news/magazine-21151350
(11) Mari, Grinde, Arntzen.Kronikk, Dagbladet.Tors,28,mai
(12) Skårderud, Finn. (2008). «Uro». Oslo: H. Aschehoug & Co. S-330, 331

Chapter 17

(1) Kahlisto, Frida & Mohn, Eva. (2005). «Venus. Norske kvinner sett nedenfra» Oslo: Gyldendal Norsk Forlag AS. S-86, 102, 103, 108
(2) http://www.side3.no/dittsexliv/dette-er-pornoen-kvinner-sker-pa/8505856.html
(3) https://www.gaystarnews.com/article/country-world-watches-gay-porn/#gs.cxjzGHQ
(4) https://www.huffingtonpost.com/2013/06/14/gay-porn-pakistan_n_3437529.html
(5) https://www.nrk.no/sorlandet/_-transpersoner-er-overrepresentert-i-sexindustrien-1.13651143
(6) https://www.salon.com/2016/05/21/the_red_state_gay_porn_habit_why_conservative_states_like_mississippi_and_north_carolina_lead_the_nation_in_same_sex_porn_consumption/
(7) https://www.rawstory.com/2016/06/states-suing-obama-over-transgender-bathroom-order-love-watching-transgender/

(8) http://www.bbc.co.uk/programmes/p030qpfb
(9) http://journals.sagepub.com/doi/abs/10.1177/1077801210382866
(10) https://www.psychologytoday.com/blog/all-about-sex/201601/evidence-mounts-more-porn-less-sexual-assault
(11) http://www.violence.de/prescott/bulletin/article.html
(12) Allgeier & Allgeier. (2000) «Sexual Interactions». Boston New York: Houghton Mifflin Companay. S-151, 152
(13) http://www.violence.de/prescott/bulletin/article.html
(14) http://www.violence.de/prescott/appp/ald.pdf
(15) http://www.violence.de/etff/etff.html

Chapter 18

(1) http://www.wouldjesusdiscriminate.org/biblical_evidence/leviticus.html
(2) https://web.archive.org/web/20110720085024/http://www.clgs.org/category/resource-author/dale-b-martin
(3) Endsjø, Dag Øistein. (2009). «Sex og religion». Oslo: Universitetsforlaget. S-108
(4) Endsjø, Dag Øistein. (2009). «Sex og religion». Oslo: Universitetsforlaget. S-74, 75, 83
(5) http://www.violence.de/prescott/bulletin/article.html
(6) Bibelen. Første Mosebok 19:1-11
(7) http://www.violence.de/prescott/bulletin/article.html
(8) Endsjø, Dag Øistein. (2009). «Sex og religion». Oslo: Universitetsforlaget. S-107
(9) Endsjø, Dag Øistein. (2009). «Sex og religion». Oslo: Universitetsforlaget. S-117
(10) Endsjø, Dag Øistein. (2009). «Sex og religion». Oslo: Universitetsforlaget. S- 80
(11) Endsjø, Dag Øistein. (2009). «Sex og religion». Oslo: Universitetsforlaget.S-26, 169
(12) Endsjø, Dag Øistein. (2009). «Sex og religion». Oslo: Universitetsforlaget. S-122
(13) Endsjø, Dag Øistein. (2009). «Sex og religion». Oslo: Universitetsforlaget. S-205

Chapter 19

(1) https://www.youtube.com/watch?v=C1G1K7-kJxY
(2) Journal of Experimental Child Psychology. Volume 162. October 2017, Pages 1-17
(3) https://link.springer.com/article/10.1007/BF00289251
(4) https://theconversation.com/stereotypes-can-hold-boys-back-in-school-too-72035
(5) http://www.bbc.co.uk/bbcthree/item/991ea351-1e67-46dc-824d-a13033526ca6
(6) https://www.ft.com/content/729db638-6ae4-11e7-bfeb-33fe0c5b7eaa
(7) Endsjø, Dag Øistein. (2009). «Sex og religion». Oslo: Universitetsforlaget. S-134, 135
(8) https://www.dagbladet.no/kultur/kroppslos-identitet/67484208
(9) Journal of Consulting and Clinical Psychology. Vol 4, s-155
(10) Allgeier & Allgeier. (2000) «Sexual Interactions». Boston New York: Houghton Mifflin Company. S-29
(11) http://faculty.webster.edu/woolflm/sandrabem2.htm
(12) Kimmel, Michael S. (2004). «The Gendered Society». New York: Oxford University Press. S-291
(13) http://citeseerx.ist.psu.edu/viewdoc/download?doi=10.1.1.472.525&rep=rep1&type=pdf
(14) Kimmel, Michael S. (2004). «The Gendered Society». New York: Oxford University Press. S-89
(15) Kimmel, Michael S. (2004). «The Gendered Society». New York: Oxford University Press. S-293, 294
(16) http://garote.bdmonkeys.net/bsri.html
(17) Kimmel, Michael S. (2004). «The Gendered Society». New York: Oxford University Press. S-89
(18) Money, John. (1988). "Gay Straight and Inbetween. The Sexology of Erotic Orientation". New York: Oxford University Press. S-108, 109
(19) https://en.wikipedia.org/wiki/Paraphilia
(20) http://kinseyconfidential.org/sexual-fetish-blog-post/
(21) https://en.wikipedia.org/wiki/List_of_paraphilias
(22) Esben Esther Pirelli Benestad. Forelesning UiA-2008
(23) Langfeldt, Thore. (2003). «Sexologi». Oslo: Gyldendal Norsk Forlag. S-189
(24) https://psykologisk.no/2015/05/en-studie-av-tilknytning/
(25) Langfeldt, Thore. (2003). «Sexologi». Oslo: Gyldendal Norsk Forlag. S-98
(26) Langfeldt, Thore. (2013). «Seksualitetens gleder og sorger: Identiteter og uttrykksformer». Oslo: Fagbokforlaget Vigmostad & Bjørke. S-73, 74

(27) Langfeldt, Thore. (2013). «Seksualitetens gleder og sorger: Identiteter og uttrykksformer». Oslo: Fagbokforlaget Vigmostad & Bjørke. S-73, 74
(28) Money, John. (1988). "Gay Straight and Inbetween". The Sexology of Erotic Orientation". New York: Oxford University Press. S-13
(29) Klein, Fritz & Wolf, Timothy J. (1985). "Bisexualities: Theory and Research".. New York, London: The Haworth Press. S-72
(30) Schmidt, Gunter. (1996). "Hvad skete der med seksualiteten". København: Hans Reitzels Forlag a/s. S-102, 103, 104, 105, 105
(31) Schmidt, Gunter. (1996). "Hvad skete der med seksualiteten". København: Hans Reitzels Forlag a/s. S-102, 103, 104, 105, 105
(32) Schmidt, Gunter. (1996). "Hvad skete der med seksualiteten". København: Hans Reitzels Forlag a/s. S-102, 103, 104, 105, 105
(33) Schmidt, Gunter. (1996). "Hvad skete der med seksualiteten". København: Hans Reitzels Forlag a/s. S-106, 107, 108
(34) Schmidt, Gunter. (1996). "Hvad skete der med seksualiteten". København: Hans Reitzels Forlag a/s. S-106, 107, 108
(35) Schmidt, Gunter. (1996). "Hvad skete der med seksualiteten". København: Hans Reitzels Forlag a/s. S-106, 107, 108
(36) Schmidt, Gunter. (1996). "Hvad skete der med seksualiteten". København: Hans Reitzels Forlag a/s. S-108, 109, 110, 111
(37) Schmidt, Gunter. (1996). "Hvad skete der med seksualiteten". København: Hans Reitzels Forlag a/s. S-108, 109, 110, 111
(38) Schmidt, Gunter. (1996). "Hvad skete der med seksualiteten". København: Hans Reitzels Forlag a/s. S-108, 109, 110, 111
(39) Schwartz, Pepper & Rutter, Virginia. (1998). «The Gender of Sexuality» London: Fine Forge Press. S-36
(40) Schwartz, Pepper & Rutter, Virginia. (1998). «The Gender of Sexuality» London: Fine Forge Press. S-30
(41) Schwartz, Pepper & Rutter, Virginia. (1998). «The Gender of Sexuality» London: Fine Forge Press. S-196
(42) Murray& Roscoe. (1997). https://nyupress.org/books/9780814774687/
(43) Schwartz, Pepper & Rutter, Virginia. (1998). «The Gender of Sexuality» London: Fine Forge Press. S-197
(44) Klein, Fritz & Wolf, Timothy J. (1985). "Bisexualities: Theory and Research". New York, London: The Haworth Press. S-75
(45) Klein, Fritz & Wolf, Timothy J. (1985). "Bisexualities: Theory and Research". New York, London: The Haworth Press. S-77, 78
(46) Klein, Fritz & Wolf, Timothy J. (1985). "Bisexualities: Theory and Research". New York, London: The Haworth Press. S-77, 78
(47) Klein, Fritz & Wolf, Timothy J. (1985). "Bisexualities: Theory and Research". New York, London: The Haworth Press. S-80, 81, 82

(48) Klein, Fritz & Wolf, Timothy J. (1985). "Bisexualities: Theory and Research". New York, London: The Haworth Press. S-80, 81, 82

(49) Klein, Fritz & Wolf, Timothy J. (1985). "Bisexualities: Theory and Research". New York, London: The Haworth Press. S-80, 81, 82

(50) Klein, Fritz & Wolf, Timothy J. (1985). "Bisexualities: Theory and Research". New York, London: The Haworth Press. S-84

(51) Allgeier & Allgeier. (2000) «Sexual Interactions». Boston New York: Houghton Mifflin Companay. S-324

(52) http://www.nytimes.com/2005/07/05/health/straight-gay-or-lying-bisexuality-revisited.html

(53) http://www.bisexual.com/forum/showthread.php?3799-quot-Gay-Straight-or-Lying-Bisexuality-Revisited-quot-Revisited-Part-1

(54) https://en.wikipedia.org/wiki/Kinsey_scale

(55) https://en.wikipedia.org/wiki/Bisexuality

(56) https://en.wikipedia.org/wiki/Bisexual_erasure

(57) https://no.wikipedia.org/wiki/Friseksualitet

(58) https://forskning.no/samliv-seksualitet/2008/04/bifili-varer-hele-livet

(59) Kimmel, Michael S. (2004). «The Gendered Society». New York: Oxford University Press. S-11

(60) https://yougov.co.uk/news/2015/08/16/half-young-not-heterosexual/

(61) https://en.wikipedia.org/wiki/Kinsey_scale

(62) http://www.hrc.org/blog/more-young-adults-are-identifying-as-bisexual?utm_content=buffer1e920&utm_medium=social&utm_source=plus.google.com&utm_campaign=hrcsocialteam

(63) Bagemihl, Bruce. (1999). «Biological Exuberance: Animal Homosexuality and Natural Diversity". New York: Martin's Press. S-106, 107, 108, 110

(64) Bagemihl, Bruce. (1999). «Biological Exuberance: Animal Homosexuality and Natural Diversity". New York: Martin's Press. S-106, 107, 108, 110

(65) Bagemihl, Bruce. (1999). «Biological Exuberance: Animal Homosexuality and Natural Diversity". New York: Martin's Press. S-114

(66) Bagemihl, Bruce. (1999). «Biological Exuberance: Animal Homosexuality and Natural Diversity". New York: Martin's Press. S-117

(67) Bagemihl, Bruce. (1999). «Biological Exuberance: Animal Homosexuality and Natural Diversity". New York: Martin's Press. S-115

(68) Bagemihl, Bruce. (1999). «Biological Exuberance: Animal Homosexuality and Natural Diversity". New York: Martin's Press. S-97

(69) Bagemihl, Bruce. (1999). «Biological Exuberance: Animal Homosexuality and Natural Diversity". New York: Martin's Press. S-106

(70) Bagemihl, Bruce. (1999). «Biological Exuberance: Animal Homosexuality and Natural Diversity". New York: Martin's Press. S-104

(71) Bagemihl, Bruce. (1999). «Biological Exuberance: Animal Homosexuality and Natural Diversity". New York: Martin's Press. S-133, 134, 135
(72) Bagemihl, Bruce. (1999). «Biological Exuberance: Animal Homosexuality and Natural Diversity". New York: Martin's Press. S-133, 134, 135
(73) Bagemihl, Bruce. (1999). «Biological Exuberance: Animal Homosexuality and Natural Diversity". New York: Martin's Press. S-133, 134, 135
(74) Bagemihl, Bruce. (1999). «Biological Exuberance: Animal Homosexuality and Natural Diversity". New York: Martin's Press. S-148
(75) Bagemihl, Bruce. (1999). «Biological Exuberance: Animal Homosexuality and Natural Diversity". New York: Martin's Press. S-115
(76) Bagemihl, Bruce. (1999). «Biological Exuberance: Animal Homosexuality and Natural Diversity". New York: Martin's Press. S-60
(77) Bagemihl, Bruce. (1999). «Biological Exuberance: Animal Homosexuality and Natural Diversity". New York: Martin's Press. S-164
(78) Bagemihl, Bruce. (1999). «Biological Exuberance: Animal Homosexuality and Natural Diversity". New York: Martin's Press. S-166
(79) Bagemihl, Bruce. (1999). «Biological Exuberance: Animal Homosexuality and Natural Diversity". New York: Martin's Press. S-166
(80) Bagemihl, Bruce. (1999). «Biological Exuberance: Animal Homosexuality and Natural Diversity". New York: Martin's Press. S-169
(81) Bagemihl, Bruce. (1999). «Biological Exuberance: Animal Homosexuality and Natural Diversity". New York: Martin's Press. S-53, 174, 178
(82) Bagemihl, Bruce. (1999). «Biological Exuberance: Animal Homosexuality and Natural Diversity". New York: Martin's Press. S-53, 174, 178
(83) Bagemihl, Bruce. (1999). «Biological Exuberance: Animal Homosexuality and Natural Diversity". New York: Martin's Press. S-209
(84) Bagemihl, Bruce. (1999). «Biological Exuberance: Animal Homosexuality and Natural Diversity". New York: Martin's Press. S-65, 66, 67
(85) Bagemihl, Bruce. (1999). «Biological Exuberance: Animal Homosexuality and Natural Diversity". New York: Martin's Press. S-65, 66, 67
(86) Bagemihl, Bruce. (1999). «Biological Exuberance: Animal Homosexuality and Natural Diversity". New York: Martin's Press. S-65, 66, 67
(87) Bagemihl, Bruce. (1999). «Biological Exuberance: Animal Homosexuality and Natural Diversity". New York: Martin's Press. S-69
(88) Bagemihl, Bruce. (1999). «Biological Exuberance: Animal Homosexuality and Natural Diversity". New York: Martin's Press. S-75
(89) Bagemihl, Bruce. (1999). «Biological Exuberance: Animal Homosexuality and Natural Diversity". New York: Martin's Press. S-79
(90) Langfeldt, Thore. (2003). «Sexologi». Oslo: Gyldendal Norsk Forlag. S-107
(91) https://sml.snl.no/epigenetikk
(92) Lipton, Bruce H. (2015). "The Biology of Belief". New York: Hayhouse. S-44

(93) Lipton, Bruce H. (2015). "The Biology of Belief". New York: Hayhouse. S-47, 48

(94) Kimmel, Michael S. (2004). «The Gendered Society». New York: Oxford University Press. S-67

Chapter 20

(1) Sheldrake, Rupert. (2012). «Vitenskapens vrangforestillinger». Oslo: Flux forlag. S-24, 25

(2) https://www.livescience.com/47288-twin-study-importance-of-genetics.html

(3) Bagemihl, Bruce. (1999). «Biological Exuberance: Animal Homosexuality and Natural Diversity". New York: Martin's Press. S-214, 215, 216

(4) Bagemihl, Bruce. (1999). «Biological Exuberance: Animal Homosexuality and Natural Diversity". New York: Martin's Press. S-214, 215, 216

(5) Bagemihl, Bruce. (1999). «Biological Exuberance: Animal Homosexuality and Natural Diversity". New York: Martin's Press. S-214, 215, 216

(6) Bagemihl, Bruce. (1999). «Biological Exuberance: Animal Homosexuality and Natural Diversity". New York: Martin's Press. S-214, 215, 216

(7) (Bagemihl, Bruce. (1999). «Biological Exuberance: Animal Homosexuality and Natural Diversity". New York: Martin's Press. S-230

(8) Pirelli Benestad, Esben Esther & Almås Elsa. (2001). "Kjønn i bevegelse". Oslo: Universitetsforlaget. S-152

(9) Pirelli Benestad, Esben Esther & Almås Elsa. (2001). "Kjønn i bevegelse". Oslo: Universitetsforlaget. S-152, 157

(10) Bagemihl, Bruce. (1999). «Biological Exuberance: Animal Homosexuality and Natural Diversity". New York: Martin's Press. S-245, 245, 247

(11) Bagemihl, Bruce. (1999). «Biological Exuberance: Animal Homosexuality and Natural Diversity". New York: Martin's Press. S-245, 245, 247

(12) Bagemihl, Bruce. (1999). «Biological Exuberance: Animal Homosexuality and Natural Diversity". New York: Martin's Press. S-245, 245, 247

(13) Wolf, Fred Alan. (1989). "Taking The Quantumleap". New York: Harper & Row Publishers. S-123, 124

(14) https://no.wikipedia.org/wiki/Thomas_Kuhn

(15) Falao, Jack. (1997). «Det store eventyret om virkeligheten: En fantastisk fortelling om den nye fysikken.» Oslo: Spatacus Forlag AS. S-282, 283

(16) https://no.wikipedia.org/wiki/Anomali

(17) Falao, Jack. (1997). «Det store eventyret om virkeligheten: En fantastisk fortelling om den nye fysikken.» Oslo: Spatacus Forlag AS. S-65, 69, 138

(18) Falao, Jack. (1997). «Det store eventyret om virkeligheten: En fantastisk fortelling om den nye fysikken.» Oslo: Spatacus Forlag AS. S-156, 157, 158, 235
(19) Dammann, Erik. (1987). «Bak tid og rom». Oslo: Dreyer Forlag AS. S-56, 57, 58
(20) en.wikiquote.org/wiki/Max_Planck
(21) Hurley, Finley J. (1985). «Sorcery». London: Routledge & Kegan Paul plc. S-26, 30
(22) Hurley, Finley J. (1985). «Sorcery». London: Routledge & Kegan Paul plc. S-26, 27
(23) Hurley, Finley J. (1985). «Sorcery». London: Routledge & Kegan Paul plc. S-26, 27
(24) Moody, Raymond A Jr. (1988). «Lyset bortenfor». Oslo: Aventura Forlag. S-124
(25) Moody, Raymond A Jr. (1988). «Lyset bortenfor». Oslo: Aventura Forlag. S-11
(26) Moody, Raymond A Jr. (1988). «Lyset bortenfor». Oslo: Aventura Forlag. S-114
(27) Moody, Raymond A Jr. (1988). «Lyset bortenfor». Oslo: Aventura Forlag. S-16
(28) Moody, Raymond A Jr. (1988). «Lyset bortenfor». Oslo: Aventura Forlag. S-17, 18, 19
(29) Moody, Raymond A Jr. (1988). «Lyset bortenfor». Oslo: Aventura Forlag. S-19, 20
(30) Ring, Kenneth. (2006). «Lessons From The Light». Moment Point Press. S-296
(31) Moody, Raymond A Jr. (1988). «Lyset bortenfor». Oslo: Aventura Forlag. S-20, 40
(32) https://www.youtube.com/watch?v=DJIfxwrDs40
(33) Randi, James. (2010). «Randi's Prize». UK: Troubador Publishing Ltd. S-265
(34) Moody, Raymond A Jr. (1988). «Lyset bortenfor». Oslo: Aventura Forlag. S-33, 43
(35) Moody, Raymond A Jr. (1988). «Lyset bortenfor». Oslo: Aventura Forlag. S-44, 69
(36) Moody, Raymond A Jr. (1988). «Lyset bortenfor». Oslo: Aventura Forlag. S-37, 38
(37) Moody, Raymond A Jr. (1988). «Lyset bortenfor». Oslo: Aventura Forlag. S49
(38) Moody, Raymond A Jr. (1988). «Lyset bortenfor». Oslo: Aventura Forlag. S-132
(39) Moody, Raymond A Jr. (1988). «Lyset bortenfor». Oslo: Aventura Forlag. S-136
(40) Moody, Raymond A Jr. (1988). «Lyset bortenfor». Oslo: Aventura Forlag. S-51
(41) Moody, Raymond A Jr. (1988). «Lyset bortenfor». Oslo: Aventura Forlag. S-66

(42) https://www.ncbi.nlm.nih.gov/pmc/articles/PMC5570697/
(43) Moody, Raymond A Jr. (1988). «Lyset bortenfor». Oslo: Aventura Forlag. S-87
(44) Moody, Raymond A Jr. (1988). «Lyset bortenfor». Oslo: Aventura Forlag. S-130
(45) Randi, James. (2010). «Randi's Prize». UK: Matador. Troubador Publishing Ltd. S-249
(46) Moody, Raymond A Jr. (1988). «Lyset bortenfor». Oslo: Aventura Forlag. S-129
(47) Randi, James. (2010). «Randi's Prize». UK: Troubador Publishing Ltd. S-248, 249
(48) Moody, Raymond A Jr. (1988). «Lyset bortenfor». Oslo: Aventura Forlag. S-102
(49) Moody, Raymond A Jr. (1988). «Lyset bortenfor». Oslo: Aventura Forlag. S-77
(50) http://www.near-death.com/experiences/notable/christian-andreason.html
(51) http://lizdale.com/index.html
(52) https://en.wikipedia.org/wiki/Melvin_L._Morse
(53) Dale, Liz. (2017). «Crossing Over and Coming Home». Crossing Over Publications, Inc. Locale-1517 (Kindle page-reference)
(54) http://www.nderf.org/NDERF/Articles/gay_fundamentalism_jpc.htm
(55) https://www.youtube.com/watch?v=DJIfxwrDs40
(56) Ring, Kenneth. (1987). «På rett vei mot Omega». Oslo: Dreyers Forlag A/S. Side-66
(57) Ring, Kenneth. (2006). «Lessons From The Light». Cambridge: Moment Point Press. S-28, 46
(58) Van Lommel, Pim. «Near-death Experience in Survivors of Cardiac Arrest: A Prospective Study in The Netherlands". The Lancet. Volum 358, 2001. S-2039, 2040, 2042
(59) Van Lommel, Pim. «Near-death Experience in Survivors of Cardiac Arrest: A Prospective Study in The Netherlands". The Lancet. Volum 358, 2001. S-2039, 2040, 2042
(60) Simonsen, Terje G. (2013). «Våre skjulte evner». Oslo: Pax forlag. S-163
(61) https://www.near-death.com/experiences/out-of-body/charles-tart.html
(62) https://www.youtube.com/watch?v=UwmZ1JohClc
(63) https://iands.org/research/nde-research/research-news35/807-veridical-obe-perceptions-in-a qstandstillqoperation.html?highlight=WyJvYmUiLCJvYmVzIiwib2IiLCJvYmUncyIsInJlc2VhcmNoIiwicmVzZWFyY2hlcnMiLCJyZXNlYXJjaGVyIiwicmVzZWFyY2hlZCIsInJlc2VhcmNoZXJzJyIsInJlc2VhcmNoaW5nIiwicmVzZWFyY2hlcidzIiwicmVzZWFyY2hlcyIsIm9iZSByZXNlYXJjaCJd
(64) https://iands.org/news/news/front-page-news/1060-aware-study-initial-results-are-published.html

(65) BEM, D.J & Honorton, C. (1994). Does PSI exist? Replicable evidence for an anomalous process of information transfer. Psychological bulletin, 115, 4-18

(66) Simonsen, Terje G. (2013). «Våre skjulte evner». Oslo: Pax forlag. S-190

(67) https://en.wikipedia.org/wiki/Decline_effect

(68) http://archived.parapsych.org/sheep_goat_effect.htm

(69) http://www.webpsykologen.no/artikler/noceboeffekten/

(70) Simonsen, Terje G. (2013). «Våre skjulte evner». Oslo: Pax forlag. S-189, 190

(71) Simonsen, Terje G. (2013). «Våre skjulte evner». Oslo: Pax forlag. S-196

(72) http://www.williamjames.com/transcripts/smith.htm

(73) Hurley, Finley J. (1985). «Sorcery». London: Routledge & Kegan Paul plc. S-27, 28

(74) http://www.violence.de/prescott/bulletin/article.html

(75) https://bronnieware.com/blog/regrets-of-the-dying/

(76) https://londonreal.tv/e/anita-moorjani-life-after-death-surviving-cancer/

(77) Mishnah Sanhedrin 4:9; Yerushalmi Talmud,

(78) Koranen, kapitel 5

(79) https://en.wikipedia.org/wiki/Cabala

(80) https://en.wikipedia.org/wiki/Gnosticism

(81) https://en.wikipedia.org/wiki/Sufism

Printed in the United States
by Baker & Taylor Publisher Services